Enslaved Women in America

Enslaved Women in America

AN ENCYCLOPEDIA

Daina Ramey Berry, Editor in Chief,
with Deleso A. Alford, Senior Editor

AN IMPRINT OF ABC-CLIO, LLC
Santa Barbara, California • Denver, Colorado • Oxford, England

Copyright 2012 by Daina Ramey Berry and Deleso A. Alford

All rights reserved. No part of this publication may be reproduced, stored in a retrieval system, or transmitted, in any form or by any means, electronic, mechanical, photocopying, recording, or otherwise, except for the inclusion of brief quotations in a review, without prior permission in writing from the publisher.

Library of Congress Cataloging-in-Publication Data

Enslaved women in America : an encyclopedia / Daina Ramey Berry, editor in chief, with Deleso A. Alford, senior editor.
    p. cm.
  Includes bibliographical references and index.
  ISBN 978–0–313–34908–9 (hard copy : alk. paper) — ISBN 978–0–313–34909–6 (ebook)
1. Women slaves—United States—History—Encyclopedias. 2. Slavery—United States—History—Encyclopedias. I. Berry, Daina Ramey. II. Alford, Deleso A.
E443.E57   2012
306.3'620820973—dc23   2011053291

ISBN: 978–0–313–34908–9
EISBN: 978–0–313–34909–6

16 15 14 13 12   1 2 3 4 5

This book is also available on the World Wide Web as an eBook.
Visit www.abc-clio.com for details.

Greenwood
An Imprint of ABC-CLIO, LLC

ABC-CLIO, LLC
130 Cremona Drive, P.O. Box 1911
Santa Barbara, California 93116-1911

This book is printed on acid-free paper ∞

Manufactured in the United States of America

Contents

Alphabetical List of Entries

Topical List of Entries

Africa and the Diaspora

African Women and African-born
   Women

Burial Customs

Creoles

Gullah Culture

Islam

Voodoo

Biographical

Celia

Craft, Ellen

Delaney, Lucy A.

Dickson, Amanda America

Freeman, Elizabeth

Garner, Margaret

Hemings, Sally

Jacobs, Harriet

Keckley, Elizabeth

Key, Elizabeth

Laney, Lucy Craft

Prince, Lucy Terry

Scott, Harriet Robinson

Taylor, Susie King

Thomas, Sally

Tituba

Truth, Sojourner

Tubman, Harriet

Wheatley, Phillis

Commodification

Domestic Slave Trade

Fancy Girls

Prices

Daily Life

Community

Courtship

Elderly Women

Family

Girlhood

Life Cycle

Mobility

Slave Quarters, Life in

Gender and Sexuality

Gender Conventions

Jezebel Stereotype

Mammy Stereotype

Miscegenation

Representations

Sexuality

Preface

The institution of racial slavery looms large in the history of the United States and, for centuries, defined the black experience in mainland North America as one of captivity, exploitation, abuse, and suffering as well as one of resistance, fortitude, strength, and perseverance in the face of oppression and deep injustice. For free blacks in the South—and even in the North where the institution was largely forbidden by the nineteenth century—the presence of an entire culture of slavery made clear the social, political, and economic limitations of black life in America and the tenuousness of freedom. For women, the practices associated with slavery were doubly oppressive because they combined demeaning beliefs about racial and gender inferiority to produce not only particular forms of sexual and reproductive exploitation in addition to forced labor, but also a wide range of stereotypes about black women that persisted for decades after the demise of slavery in 1865 with very real, lasting consequences. In the past 25 to 30 years, scholars have focused their attention on these and many other distinctive concerns that women faced under slavery within their families, communities, and everyday lives to better understand the "peculiar institution" and its legacy from a gendered perspective. Synthesizing this vast but ever-expanding body of dynamic scholarship and the knowledge of many of the field's top and upcoming scholars, *Enslaved Women in America: An Encyclopedia* is the first reference volume of its kind to compile this information in 101 rich entries devoted exclusively to bondwomen's experiences in the United States, in the period beginning with the first slave ships in the sixteenth and seventeenth centuries until the end of slavery in 1865.

Enslaved Women in America is designed to be an invaluable resource for a broad readership including secondary students at the high school level, postsecondary students at the undergraduate and graduate levels, and even interested readers outside of academia who seek to gain a broader understanding of women's lives. Arranged alphabetically, the volume contains 101 thematic, chronological, and geographical entries of varying length that address numerous facets of enslaved life for women across time and space. Seventy-eight scholars of various ranks—from endowed professors to junior faculty and independent scholars to graduate students immersed in study who hail from a range of institutions across the United States and from around the globe—contributed to this collection. These scholars draw on both classic and cutting-edge disciplinary methods and theories of their respective fields in history, sociology, economics, archeology, and others as well as interdisciplinary fields like African American studies to illuminate the problems and hardships bondwomen faced, their agency and strength in responding to the circumstances forced upon them, and the everyday banalities of plantation life that were shaped by gender.

As the title suggests, *Enslaved Women in America* deals with slavery in mainland North America but, given the significant influence of scholars focused on West Africa and the African Diaspora, it includes some important material on the Transatlantic Slave Trade and Middle Passage, African-born women, and African influences on American bondwomen. The changing circumstances and contexts of enslaved life during major epochs of the nation's past are also examined—such as colonial America, the Civil War era, and emancipation—while entries on regions like the North, South, and West provide important geographic specificity. Finally, the volume provides important discussion of the state of the field, historiographic trends, and current as well as forthcoming scholarship so that readers might also grapple with the politics of history and, particularly, with politics of enslaved women's history in the United States. With its specific focus, breadth of scope and innovative features, *Enslaved Women in America* makes a considerable contribution to furthering knowledge about the experience of captivity in the United States.

Special Features

A number of useful features are found throughout the encyclopedia such as convenient cross-referencing for each entry to facilitate quick access to interrelated information as well as suggested reading of the most pivotal scholarship on specific topics so that readers can easily locate additional resources produced by reliable and reputable experts. The volume also includes numerous sidebars so that readers may experience firsthand a sampling of the many types of primary sources that scholars of American slavery rely on as they amass evidence to build their historical arguments. These include images, poetry, court documents, ship manifests, slave lists, letters, excerpts of narratives, interviews, and other visual and textual sources, many of which come directly from enslaved women themselves. A timeline of slavery detailing major events relevant to the history of enslaved women in the United States provides additional information for readers. In the appendix, readers will find useful population tables of enslaved people in the United States at various time periods, and a comprehensive bibliography of helpful print and Internet sources that range from personal histories and novels to scholarly studies and published primary documents, enabling all readers to find more information about enslaved women. A list of entries arranged by broad topic at the beginning of the volume, as well as a comprehensive index at the end, make the volume more accessible to readers.

Acknowledgments

When asked to serve as editor of this encyclopedia, I had no idea that this journey would take so many interesting turns. Yet, nearly six years later, I've been in conversation with hundreds of scholars across the globe at different institutions and in different states in their professional development. More importantly, I met enslaved women whose lives and testimonies have been incorporated in this volume. A significant portion of this work was completed while I was a fellow at the National Humanities Center. I am grateful to the staff for their continued support with special appreciation for Marianne D. Wason who is the inspiration behind the cover image. I would also like to thank my wonderful team of research assistants from two institutions who have literally kept this project alive: Jenifer L. Barclay, Terry P. Brock, Nedra K. Lee, Nicole "Nik" Ribianszky, Kate Shelton, and Jermaine Thibodeaux. Words cannot express my deep appreciation for the late nights, office conversations, and archival research that each of these scholars completed in support of this project. I am also deeply grateful to my advisory board, Sharla Fett, Jessica Millward, and Wilma King, for their profound and often timely advice as well as editorial suggestions. Finally, this project would not have been complete if an unnamed bondwoman did not *insist* that these stories were told; I dedicate this volume to her and all of the other nameless women who wish to be recognized.

Daina Ramey Berry
Austin, Texas
October 2011

Introduction

Daina Ramey Berry

"I look upon slavery as the worst evil that ever was. My life has been taken from me in a measure by it," claimed a fugitive bondwoman. After successfully escaping slavery in the United States and surviving the journey to Canada, this woman, referred to only as "Mrs.," made the following remark: "If any are disposed to apologize for slavery, it would be well for them to try it awhile" (*A North-Side View of Slavery* 1856, p. 21). These chilling words, from the mouth of a former bondwoman, offer a fresh perspective on the thoughts and feelings of those held in bondage against their will. Were these words a prophetic challenge to contemporary apologists for slavery and/or calls for reparations? Or, were these remarks simply a commentary on one woman's experience with newfound freedom in Canada? How universal were her feelings about enslavement? And perhaps more important, what did the experience of enslavement look, feel, taste, smell, or even sound like for "Mrs." and the millions of bondwomen who found themselves victims of a similar fate? This encyclopedia attempts to answer these very questions and to do so explicitly from the gendered perspective of enslaved women.

Scholars of the twenty-first century conclude that slavery was deplorable. But in order to understand the complexities and nuances of daily life for enslaved women, one must delve into the diversity of their experiences. These varied, depending on where bondwomen lived, the type of crop they cultivated or the kind of labor they undertook, the attitude of their enslavers and others in positions of authority, the strength or contentiousness of their family and community ties, and a host of other demographic, economic, and historical factors. Exploring these diverse facets of enslavement through the female lens is the primary objective of this volume.

The aforementioned woman's story also raises another interesting methodological twist: the anonymity of slavery, whether self-imposed or not. This woman wished to be referred to as "Mrs.," an unidentifiable prefix that was not followed by a formal surname. We do not know the full identity of this bondwoman and can assume that her anonymity represents a deliberate choice to protect herself from being captured and sold back into slavery. Likewise, we can conclude that the intentional act of erasure in which this woman removed the most obvious trace of her identity, her *own* name, can also symbolize the historical obliteration, or perhaps the long-term marginalization, of enslaved women from the most penetrating slavery studies until the mid-1980s. It is also clear from her statement that apologies for slavery in the nineteenth century, like today, meant little to the enslaved who experienced the day-to-day challenges, deprivations, and degradations of life in bondage.

Terminology

When I sat down to write this introduction, I knew that a considerable part of the work I needed to accomplish in it would involve my explanation of how and why certain terms were used in the volume and the editorial decisions behind them. Present-day scholars do a great service to the profession when they provide detailed discussions defining, very specifically, the key terms they use in their work. In fact, until recently, historians' assumptions about the terms they used to describe the enslaved were hardly discussed or, equally unfortunate, were left buried and hidden within their footnotes (mine included). This changed, however, with the influx of web-based discussion groups such as Humanities Net (H-net) and the expansive, democratizing nature of the Internet in general. Now more than ever, scholars and interested readers can share in the enterprise of writing and interpreting the past and, together, both groups can also aim for common ground on the use of important terms in these collaborative efforts. For matters of clarity, precision, or even to acknowledge the evolution of thought on a particular topic, it is best to make the case for the terms used in historical conversations at the outset and with utter transparency.

From my own professional experience, I have come to realize that the business of doing history is indeed a communal effort, one in which scholars and the larger public forge a symbiotic relationship to advance sound knowledge. As I began to edit the entries that comprise this volume, I noticed a number of inconsistencies in the ways in which different scholars referred to bondwomen and other key aspects of slavery. I quickly saw the need to first develop a standardized language rubric and then justify it, especially after participating in series of public debates on this very issue. The field is evolving and so is the way in which scholars are grappling with how to describe the millions who toiled as America's slaves with accuracy and nuance. With this in mind, I came up with the following: this volume employs the terms *human chattel, enslaved, bondwomen, bondmen,* or *bondpeople* to discuss people of African descent held against their will. Likewise, the terms *enslaver(s)* and *slaveholder(s)* are interchangeable for those who used human chattel as laborers. These phrases replace terms such as *master* which automatically implies that a "superior" individual held absolute control and power over an "inferior" other and represents an oversimplified and inherently biased interpretation that obscures the wide range of resistance tactics that enslaved people undertook.

With the importance of language in mind, I (along with the editorial board and staff) also made a very deliberate and calculated decision about another, perhaps less obvious, aspect of the terminology used in this volume. This revolves around the use of the terms "slave" versus "enslaved." Referring to bondpeople as "enslaved" emphasizes the reality that enslavement was an *action*—a verb enacted on individual(s) rather than a noun, "slave," that describes a social position these individuals presumably accepted. This marked our first joint decision and set in motion the clear and cautious attention to language that can be seen throughout this volume. This simple rephrasing—which some may dismiss as unnecessary, overly sensitive, or just plain finicky—indeed serves an important purpose. It allows us to recast slavery as an institution that was both oppressive *and* a space within which people could and did make a number of decisions about their own actions instead of them being either one or the other, victims or agents. In the early stages of this project, for example, the proposed title was simply *The Female Slave* which ultimately suggested a singular, monolithic, and timeless experience for all black women in bondage that overshadowed the point of this encyclopedia: to emphasize the diversity of slavery in the United States through an examination of many different women's lives.

The stories offered here indeed show that enslaved women found numerous ways to survive the institution of slavery. For some, this meant the dramatic and almost unfathomably difficult decision to take the lives of their children; for others it meant running away; and for others yet it meant forming relationships with partners who lived in close proximity or great distances from them and creating as much stability for themselves and their loved ones as was possible. Black women made distinct decisions about childbirth and childcare as well as resistance strategies and health. Sometimes these were spontaneous decisions and on other occasions they involved careful planning. Viewing the history of *Enslaved Women in America* and even thinking about the seemingly innocuous language through which we now discuss their lives, provides a rich understanding of a not-so-familiar part of the American past. It also highlights the complicated reality that even in spite of ever-present constraints on bondwomen's free will they nevertheless were actors in their own lives even as they simultaneously experienced a range of victimization, abuse and oppression.

By focusing on these actions and the *process* of enslavement, readers have the ability to understand the "subjects" of this volume as human beings who had lives beyond their enslavement and possessed their own subjectivity. In some cases, contributors to this volume grappled with how to fully center women and often capitulated to old methodologies that frame enslaved women as peripheral and passive victims rather than central actors in this story. However, since the objective of this work is to make women central, the dedicated authors who contributed to this work struggled with and did their best to re-conceptualize their thinking, writing, and analysis in an effort to accomplish this goal. Considering bondwomen as enslaved people challenges one to think about them beyond the sum total of the work that they did as "slaves." In other words, they were more than "human hoeing machines" and we now have broader access to the records that document their humanity.

The Women in This Encyclopedia

The voices of several dozen nameless enslaved women fill the pages of this volume. Their stories are as important as more well-known figures such as Harriet Tubman, Sojourner Truth, and Margaret Garner. For decades, scholars overlooked the female experience during bondage and assumed that enslavement in the United States was a universal experience viewed primarily through the lives of bondmen. Therefore, when scholars published their work in the early to mid-twentieth century, the term "slave" was virtually synonymous with "male," and much of the iconography surrounding the institution of slavery had a particular male bias as well. Historians described the plight of enslaved Africans through an uncomplicated, myopic male lens that ignored the significance of gender. But a gendered analysis is not the only aspect of enslaved life that historians overlooked, as the variations between locations and crops were equally blurred so that the "typical slave" lived on a large plantation in the Deep South. Publications in the second half of the twentieth century expanded our interpretations of "the peculiar institution" as John C. Calhoun—former vice-president and secretary of state of the United States and a staunch defender of slavery—once described it and gave way to more nuanced studies about enslaved life and labor in the United States. From fine studies on urban and industrial slavery to detailed inquiries into the nature of the institution in the less frequently considered Northern states and even to analyses of Native American slaveholding, all of this new work has built on decades of scholarship to further complicate much of what we thought we already knew about chattel slavery. Likewise, this volume adds to our prior knowledge of slavery, but unapologetically foregrounds the gendered experiences of bondwomen of all ages.

The topic of racial slavery in the United States and, particularly, the black family under slavery has long been a deeply contentious and politicized topic in American society. Politicians, intellectuals, pundits, and social commentators across the political spectrum have used various interpretations of this topic to either denounce or justify the continuation of racial inequality in the United States long after the end of slavery. In doing so, they have reified and perpetuated a series of stereotypes about black women in their roles as wives and mothers both under slavery and in contemporary times. The cast of stereotypes is clear to all of us and they include domineering matriarchs, promiscuous and unstable figures, "welfare queens," or helpless victims. W.E.B. Du Bois and E. Franklin Frazier, two intellectual giants of African American thought, carried out an impassioned academic debate about the black family during slavery and freedom in the early twentieth century that continues to echo in contemporary scholarship. In the 1960s, then-Assistant Secretary of Labor Daniel Patrick Moynihan thrust a discussion about the impact of slavery on black families into popular consciousness with his now infamous government report. He characterized black families as "a tangle of pathology" that spiraled into poverty and crime because black women had forged a necessary independence during the era of slavery that they passed on to their female descendants which led to the devaluation and disrespect of black men and destabilization of the family unit. Moynihan ultimately produced a certain image of enslaved women that had a direct, negative bearing on American society's views of twentieth century black women even as he was attempting to advance the social justice aims of President Lyndon B. Johnson's vision for a "Great Society."

This same tendency—to promote a specific narrative about racial slavery and its impact on black families for a specific political agenda—continues even at the present time. Two Republican candidates seeking their party's nomination for president of the United States in 2012—Michele Bachmann and Rick Santorum —signed a "Marriage Vow" to protect and strengthen marriage as an institution reserved for "one man and one woman," as the controversial Defense of Marriage act defines it. In this 14-point pledge, a conservative organization, The Family Leader, initially included the argument that "a child born into slavery in the 1860s was more likely to be raised by his mother and father in a two-parent household than was an African-American baby born after the election of the USA's first African-American President [Barack Obama]." This inflammatory language was later removed by The Family Leader and despite the problematic suggestion that African Americans were "better off" under slavery, this interpretation appropriates and misrepresents an argument made by historian Herbert Gutman in response to Moynihan and mobilizes it behind a particular political position that opposes gay marriage, single-parent households, and a host of other interrelated hot-button social and political issues of the day. Embedded within these pliable and politically expedient representations of "the black family" are various notions about enslaved women and, by extension, all African American women that connect them to damning views of single motherhood and broken families which, in turn, encourages assumptions about poverty, unemployment, public welfare, crime, and a host of other contemporary issues.

The continued politicization of the topic of slavery and slave families illuminates the importance of this volume for presenting a clear but complex picture of the many multifaceted realities of enslavement for women. These women cannot be reduced to simplistic caricatures to be bandied about in contemporary culture wars and mobilized behind present-day political agendas; the goal of this volume is, indeed, to encourage a more thoughtful, careful, and multivalent understanding of these diverse experiences and, as much as possible, to do so by listening to the very voices of women who were once enslaved in the United States.

Chronology of Enslaved Women in America

Nedra K. Lee

1526   Following the era of European exploration, black women of African descent are documented in Spanish settlements throughout the present-day states of Florida, New Mexico, and California. African men and women had long accompanied European travelers to the Americas on Spanish, Portuguese, and English expeditions. However, in the early to mid-fifteenth century small numbers of enslaved women were brought to New World plantations as part of the Transatlantic Slave Trade.

1565   Africans help found St. Augustine in Florida, the first permanent European settlement in North America.

1600   Isabel de Olvera, living in present-day New Mexico, is the earliest known free woman of African descent.

1619   Nearly 20 Africans are documented as indentured servants in Jamestown —the first English colony in the region. Although scholars debate the exact number, it is estimated that 17 were men and 3 were women.

1641   The colony of Massachusetts legalizes slavery and stipulates that a child's enslaved status derives from his or her mother. This reversed English common law, which stated that a child inherited their social status from their father.

1650   Following Massachusetts, Connecticut gives statutory recognition to slavery; Virginia does the same in 1661; Maryland, 1663; New York and New Jersey, 1664; South Carolina, 1682; Rhode Island and Pennsylvania, 1700; North Carolina, 1715; Georgia, 1750.

1656   Elizabeth Key Grinstead, the daughter of an English settler and an enslaved black woman, successfully sues for her freedom in a Northumberland County, Virginia court, challenging the transferable status of slavery from the mother to the child.

1662   Following Elizabeth Key Grinstead's suit, Virginia follows Massachusetts and similarly decrees that black children's social condition is derived from their mothers.

1692   The Salem Witch Trials begin with the arrest of Tituba, an enslaved woman of African or Native American ancestry, and eight other women.

1708   A slave revolt occurs in Newton, Long Island, New York. Seven whites are killed, a black woman is burned alive, and one Indian man and two black men are hanged.

1712   A slave revolt in New York City leaves nine white men dead. While the captured conspirators were sentenced to death, one pregnant woman is pardoned.

1746   Lucy Terry Prince writes the poem, "Bars Fight, August 28, 1746." This poem recounts the Abenaki attack against a group of white settlers in Deerfield, Massachusetts. It was published nearly 100 years after it was written.

1765   Jenny Slew successfully sues the Massachusetts Superior Court for her freedom. She becomes the first enslaved person to win her freedom via jury trial.

1773   Phillis Wheatley becomes the first enslaved person to publish a book of poems with the printing of her *Poems on Various Subjects, Religious and Moral.*

1775   The Revolutionary War begins with fighting between the Continental Army and British troops in Lexington, Massachusetts.

1781   Elizabeth Freeman, commonly referred to as Mum Bett, successfully sues the Massachusetts court for her freedom. Her case set the precedent for the legal abolition of slavery in the state in 1783.

1783   The Revolutionary War ends with the signing of the Treaty of Paris.

1792   A British slave ship captain is tried for the death of a 15-year-old girl who refused to dance while in transport on the Middle Passage.

1793   Eli Whitney invents the cotton gin (patented in 1794), which aids in the expansion of slavery to the Deep South.

U.S. Congress passes the Fugitive Slave Law, which guarantees slaveholders the right to arrest, capture, and repossess runaways.

1796   Poet Lucy Terry Prince is the first woman to appear before the U.S. Supreme Court because of a property dispute. Prince argues her case before the court and is praised for her oratory skills.

1800   Nancy Prosser joins her husband Gabriel in the planning of a slave insur-rection in Richmond. The plan is unsuccessful, resulting in the mass exe-cution of Gabriel Prosser and many of his co-conspirators.

1802   During Thomas Jefferson's second presidential term, journalist James T. Callender discloses Jefferson's intimate relationship with the mixed-race enslaved domestic, Sally Hemings. The two had a relationship that spanned 38 years and yielded six children.

1808   U.S. Congress abolishes the Transatlantic Slave Trade. Despite the prohibition, an estimated 1.2 million Africans are imported into the United States illegally according to statistics at the National Archives.

1811   Authorities uncover the maroon community of Cabarrus County, North Carolina in 1811. However, a militia attacked the maroons and destroyed the community. Two of the four fugitives captured during the battle were women.

1820   The Missouri Compromise admits Missouri as a slave state but prohibits slavery in future states north of the 36°30' lines longitude and latitude.

1825   Juana, a 14-year-old girl, is believed to be the first enslaved person in the western territory of California. She arrived in San Francisco from Lima, Peru.

1829   David Walker's *Appeal* is published. This radical anti-slavery pamphlet decries American slavery and warns the enslaved to "kill or be killed." Once the *Appeal* travels South, authorities in various slave states place a bounty on Walker's life, and he dies mysteriously in Boston in August 1830.

1830   Benjamin Lundy's *The Genius of Universal Emancipation* first publishes the image of the kneeling bondwoman under the words, "Am I Not a Woman and a Sister?"

1837   Madame Couvent, an 80-year-old enslaved woman, builds a school for poor black Catholic orphans in New Orleans.

1843   Sojourner Truth changes her name from Isabella Baumfree and begins publicly advocating for emancipation and women's rights.

1844   Upon her marriage to free man, John Tubman, an enslaved woman, Ara-minta Ross, born on the Eastern Shore of Maryland, changes her name to Harriet Tubman.

Lucy Delaney, an enslaved woman in Missouri, successfully sues slave-holder, David Mitchell for her freedom. She recounts her life before and after slavery in the book, *From the Darkness Cometh the Light; or Struggles for Freedom.*

1848   William and Ellen Craft escape from slavery in Georgia. Ellen Craft, who was fair-skinned, disguised herself as a physically ill white male who was traveling North with her enslaved body servant.

1849   Harriet Tubman escapes to freedom in Philadelphia. She is said to have returned to the South numerous times and emancipated hundreds of enslaved blacks.

Amanda America Dickson is born. Upon the death of her white, large planter father, she became one of the wealthiest black women in the country with nearly 15,000 acres of land and $500,000 in cash and bonds.

1850   The U.S. Congress passes the Compromise of 1850. This legislation dealt with the acquisition of new lands after the Mexican War; California's petition to enter the Union as a free state; and slave trading in Washington, D.C. The Fugitive Slave Law was the most controversial part of this act; it denied fugitive slaves a right to a jury trial. Blacks also could not provide evidence in official assessments of their enslaved or free status. The law required all citizens and the U.S. government to assist in the recovery of fugitives. Most importantly, slaveholders could reclaim slaves who escaped to free states.

1851   The abolitionist, Sojourner Truth, reportedly gives her famous "Ain't I A Woman" speech at a Women's Rights Convention in Akron, Ohio. Frances Gage first publishes the speech in the *Anti-Slavery Standard* (1863). To this date, scholars disagree about the occurrence and authenticity of the speech.

1854   Lucy Laney Craft is born into slavery in Macon, Georgia. She becomes a renowned educator, who established the city of Augusta's first kindergarten, a nurse's training program, and a coed school that would send graduates to prestigious schools like Fisk and Howard University.

1855   Celia, an enslaved woman in Missouri, murders her enslaver, Robert Newsom after he enters her cabin to rape her. She was later tried, found guilty, and sentenced to death via a public hanging.

Elizabeth Keckley buys her and her son's freedom for $1,200. She later becomes a modiste (dressmaker) in Washington, D.C., for elite clients which included Mary Todd Lincoln.

1856   Margaret Garner and her family attempt to escape from slavery with fifteen others. Upon capture, Margaret kills one of her four children; another drowns during a subsequent escape attempt. Abolitionists praise her for choosing death for her children rather than slavery.

1857   In the Supreme Court case, Dred *Scott vs. Sanford*, Chief Justice Roger B. Taney rules that blacks are not U.S. citizens, are not entitled to sue in federal court, and that Congress has no power to exclude slavery from the territories. Prior to this ruling, enslaved persons Dred and Harriet Robinson Scott separately and unsuccessfully petitioned the Missouri courts for their freedom, arguing that their enslavers had taken them into free territory, hence making them free.

1859   John Brown raids the Federal Arsenal at Harper's Ferry, West Virginia, with the hopes of ending slavery.

1860   Madame Cyprien Ricard and her son are found to be the largest black slaveholders. They own a sugarcane plantation in Louisiana with 152 enslaved people.

1861   The Civil War begins with the first shots fired by Confederate soldiers at Fort Sumter, South Carolina.

        Harriet Jacobs publishes her autobiography *Incidents in the Life of a Slave Girl* under the pseudonym Linda Brent and recounts the sexual exploitation she faced from her enslaver in this text.

1863   On January 1, Abraham Lincoln issues the Emancipation Proclamation, which frees all bondpeople in the states of rebellion (the Confederate territory). This does not include enslaved blacks in parts of Louisiana, West Virginia, Missouri, Kentucky, and Delaware.

        Upon Union soldiers' capture of Port Royal off the coast of South Carolina, Susie King Taylor begins writing about her encampment with the 33rd United States Colored Troops. Married to an officer in the regiment, Taylor works as a nurse, laundress, and teacher.

1865   The Civil War ends with the surrender of Confederate General Robert E. Lee and the Army of Virginia at Appomattox.

        On January 31, the U.S. Congress passes the Thirteenth Amendment to the Constitution, which abolishes slavery in the country. The amendment reads that, "Neither slavery nor involuntary servitude, except as a punishment for crime whereof the party shall have been duly convicted, shall exist within the United States, or any place subject to their jurisdiction."

A

Abolitionism

From the mid-1600s until the Civil War, white and black Americans sought to end slavery in the United States. Enslaved women found numerous ways to resist their enslavement and to lessen slavery's impact on themselves and their loved ones. Their role in abolitionism, however, was necessarily limited by their situation, yet bondwomen managed to support those seeking freedom, and occasionally won freedom for themselves. In the latter case, fugitives who reached the North worked with white and free black abolitionists to campaign against slavery's immorality and harshness, including its violation of enslaved women. As a result, the negative image of black people, particularly women, needed attention in order to further the abolitionist movement.

Opponents of slavery first took public form in the late 1600s. Quakers initiated this movement by producing the first American abolitionist writings. As the Enlightenment and the American Revolution inspired growing opposition to the enslavement of Africans, white male antislavery advocates formed organizations opposing the slave trade and slavery, with the first antislavery society forming in 1775. Antislavery proponents achieved the end of slavery in northern states in the late 1700s and early 1800s just as the newly formed United States prohibited the international slave trade in 1808. This date also marked an important moment for enslaved women because their reproductive capabilities were of paramount importance after the closing of the trade. At the same time, free blacks in the North formed benevolent societies, many of which soon shifted to reform efforts, including antislavery. Likewise, several southern states increased their free black populations through relaxed restrictions on manumission. By the 1810s, in answer to antislavery and antiblack feelings, a small number of blacks joined a growing number of whites in supporting colonization, the removal of enslaved people (and African Americans in general) from the United States.

By the 1830s, however, white, black, male, female, and mixed "antislavery" groups in the North increasingly rejected colonization to advocate the "immediate," uncompensated, and total elimination of slavery and the end of racial discrimination. These abolitionists—seen by most Americans of the antebellum period as fanatics—relied on "moral suasion" through lectures, publications, and societies against the sin of slavery and promoted the fugitive slave, male and female, as symbols and spokespeople for abolition. Because slavery subjected bondwomen to sale, coercion, and sexual violence, male abolitionists often used "ladies" to present them as the particular victims of slavery. Recent scholarship suggests that enslaved men had an equally difficult time during slavery and their stories often became postwar autobiographies.

In the South

While the abolitionist societies struggled to convince the nation that slavery's end would benefit, not harm, the United States, bondpeople struggled on a day-to-day basis to resist their enslavement. In doing so, they inspired abolitionists to oppose slavery regardless of fears of race war, economic dislocations, and national disunion. Bondwomen had many reasons to support this effort through seeking their own freedom and, more generally, through the abolition of an institution that denied their children liberty. However, they had limited resources to do so. Even though these women faced forced separation from their husbands and children, as well as sexual abuse at the hands of slaveholders and other whites, enslaved men absconded more frequently than women. Women were guided and restricted by various gender- and cultural-defined obligations. Often playing the central role in the lives of their children, they were expected not to reject their primary responsibility, which was childcare of both black and white children. Enslaved women were not expected to abandon their offspring in a quest for personal freedom. In addition, unlike enslaved men, bondwomen had few legitimate reasons to travel away from plantations and thus had little knowledge of regions beyond their plantations; as a result, escape—with or without children—was that much more difficult and dangerous.

Nevertheless, they could help others—both those seeking freedom in the North and those engaged in short-term escape (also known as truancy)—to avoid the harshness of slavery or to visit family and friends. In one case, despite her master's suspicions, a South Carolina house servant helped several relatives escape in 1864; another bondwoman provisioned her sister while avoiding detection by the plantation owner. Such efforts to support "self-emancipation" inspired the organizational efforts of northern white abolitionists. Despite bondpeople's enforced illiteracy, at least some of the abolitionists' publications included graphic images to reach literate and illiterate audiences. Some of these periodicals found their way into the slave South and, to an unknown degree, into the hands of enslaved women. As a result, those bondpeople—and the children they taught—became part of the abolitionist movement in a region where whites greatly outnumbered enslaved and free blacks, where bondpeople were geographically isolated from each other, and where whites, who held all political power, were quick to use the law to authorize restrictions on bondpeople's mobility, education, and opportunities for escape.

In the North

Enslaved women participated in other antislavery platforms beyond the South. From the early 1700s, they initiated freedom suits—often building their legal cases on wills, state laws, and constitutions—and purchased their own freedom and that of others. By the antebellum period, such legal roads to freedom were limited; however, enslaved women who escaped to the North had the opportunity to contribute to the efforts of various abolitionist groups, ranging from the national American Anti-Slavery Society, which came to include both black and white men and women, to the predominately black and female Manhattan Anti-Slavery Society. Even though Frederick Douglass, an escaped slave from Maryland became a leading abolitionist, he argued that only free blacks had the right to be called abolitionists because they sought the freedom of others, not themselves. However, fugitive bondpeople played a critical, if limited, role in abolitionism. Through narratives and lectures, they shared their experiences with slavery in order to generate support for abolition. White abolitionists acknowledged time and time again that northern audiences were particularly receptive to African American speakers and, even more so, to former bondpeople. Fugitives' speeches not only revealed their personal stories, but also demonstrated the impact of illiteracy, physical, and mental abuse during slavery. Their accounts presented the horrors of the institution in ways that white abolitionists believed could generate sympathy and provoke white actions and monetary contributions.

Among those who told their stories were fugitive bondwomen. As described in the 1860 narrative *Running a Thousand Miles for Freedom*, the light-skinned Ellen Craft escaped the South in late 1848 dressed as a sickly white man; she became an abolitionist speaker and fund-raiser in the United States and in England. Harriet Jacobs, Sojourner Truth, and Harriet Tubman represent additional enslaved women who escaped to freedom and then worked for the abolition of slavery. As the Civil War began, Harriet Jacobs's *Incidents in the Life of a Slave Girl* (1861) explained through the character of Linda Brent the particular horrors of slavery for one woman. Jacobs described the sexual intimidation and pressures that she faced—even as a 15-year-old—in North Carolina at the hands of her obsessive master. Sojourner Truth fled slavery in 1826, one year prior to New York abolishing slavery in 1827. Upon freedom, Truth began lecturing on abolitionism and women's rights across the North, once noting that "I go round a'testifyin', an' showin' their sins agin my people" (Sterling 1984, 151). Through her own example, she argued that enslaved women did taxing physical labor, lost their families to the slave trade, and suffered from violence and deprivation. Harriet Tubman, born a slave in Maryland sometime between 1819 and 1825, took a different approach, making nearly two dozen trips to the South to guide hundreds of slaves to freedom through the network of the Underground Railroad. The lives of other enslaved women were recounted by escaped bondmen, including Frederick Douglass, as part of the abolitionist campaign. In *Twelve Years a Slave* (1853), Solomon Northup told the story of Eliza whose life as a privileged concubine ended when her lover/master failed to manumit her; both she and her children were sold.

Abolitionism's View of Slavery and Women

In 1830, Benjamin Lundy's *The Genius of Universal Emancipation* first published the image of the kneeling bondwoman under the words, "Am I Not a Woman and a Sister?" Paralleling the 1787 image of a bondman ("Am I Not a Man and a Brother?"), the pleading woman emphasized the sexual aspect of slavery on which Harriet Jacobs would later focus. William Lloyd Garrison's *The Liberator* used it to introduce contributions from various female abolitionists, including Maria W. Stewart of Boston, a free black woman generally known for being the first American-born woman to lecture publicly, and Sarah Forten, the daughter of black Philadelphia sail maker and abolitionist James Forten. George Bourne's *Slavery Illustrated in Its Effects Upon Woman and Domestic Society* (1837) not only began with the kneeling bondwoman, but was dedicated to female abolitionist societies working for the freedom of enslaved women. Calling attention to slavery's conflict with marriage and its desecration of the home, Bourne and other abolitionists emphasized that slaveholders, not husbands, defined both the power of enslaved men and the status of bondwomen.

While "genteel" white readers would not read explicit accounts of rape, slave narratives and abolitionist lectures clearly suggested the violation of enslaved women's bodies and southern white men's general sexual access to bondwomen. Detailed accounts of white slaveholders maliciously whipping bondwomen, stripped of their clothing, gave abolitionist propaganda an eroticism that conflicted with white society's sexual and literary standards. Drawings and stories revealed that enslaved women, stripped partially or completely naked, were whipped and kicked for such offenses as not working hard enough; they also detailed how slave traders examined the bodies of unclothed enslaved women before making their purchases. The images of enslaved women historically characterized as immoral, promiscuous, and animalistic were inconsistent with white American values of womanhood.

Even with this inconsistency, abolitionists had to counter their own and others' thinking about women and race to allow female abolitionists both to actively oppose slavery and to use the repression of enslaved women in their arguments. Nineteenth-century attitudes included only whites as exemplars of "true womanhood": blacks did not share experiences of white womanhood (for example, bondpeople could not legally marry) or conform to white standards sexually. Unlike white women, black women—slave and free—were not presumed to be "virtuous," but rather "degraded." Beyond that, abolitionists had to counter increasingly entrenched stereotypes of blacks as a lazy and ignorant race and as morally incapable of handling freedom. To do so, they had to define the debate over slavery in passionate, uncompromising terms at a time when most white northerners cited a wide range of reasons—from constitutional to economic—for tolerating and even supporting slavery. Many abolitionists argued for a peaceful, gradual, natural, and eventual end to slavery. Those who focused on the treatment of enslaved women did not fit this category as they also questioned the moral status of a degenerate white southern society when they recounted how it degraded and exploited black people in general and women in particular.

Female Abolitionists

Supporting Frederick Douglass's pronouncement that slavery was particularly a woman's issue, female abolitionists were concerned about enslaved women because of shared gender roles and, especially, the experience of motherhood. Antislavery women in Canton, Ohio, explained that "they could not be 'deaf to the cry of the sable mother' . . ." (Jeffrey 1998, 65). Unlike most male abolitionists, these women and others sought to defend their "oppressed sisters" whose "innocence" and "purity of loveliness" became dismantled by slavery (Jeffrey 1998, 41). Although white abolitionists' general paternalistic attitudes toward bondpeople (as well as "colored Americans") complicated their efforts in waging a unified attack on slavery, Jacobs' editor, Lydia Maria Child, was one of the northern white female abolitionists who risked their reputations as submissive, modest women in order to give significant attention to the plight of bondwomen. To do so, they publicly spoke of sex, the female body, and sexual violations.

In Child's book-length *An Appeal in Favor of That Class of Americans Called Africans* (1833), the well-known author detailed the life of enslaved women: "They are allowed to have no conscientious scruples, no sense of shame, no regard for the feelings of husband, or parents; they must be entirely subservient to the will of their owner, on pain of being whipped as near unto death if it suit his pleasure" (Child 1833, 22). She saw blacks' alleged inferiority as being the result of slavery, not nature, and in her writings she focused on enslaved women's inherent morality, faithfulness, and fitness for marriage and childrearing. In "The Quadroons" (1842), she skillfully tackled the sensitive issue of enslaved women's sexual victimization in order to convince skeptical northern readers of slavery's cruelty. The next year, in "Slavery's Pleasant Homes, A Faithful Sketch," she used interviews with fugitive bondpeople to create a compelling look at enslaved women's sexual oppression—from rape to violence-induced miscarriage and death. Also calling attention to slavery's devastating impact on women were Abby Kelley, a

Quaker from Massachusetts, and Angelina and Sarah Grimké, expatriates from South Carolina. By giving this attention to enslaved women—to motherhood and to the capabilities of the female body and mind—these and other white women were inspired to advocate for the rights of women in general. As a result, bond-women contributed both to the antebellum period's abolition movement and to its women's movement.

Claudine L. Ferrell

See also Celia; Civil War; Craft, Ellen; Domestic Slave Trade; Emancipation; Free Women; Gender Conventions; Jacobs, Harriet; Manumission; Motherhood; Narratives; North, The; Resistance; Truancy; Truth, Sojourner; Tubman, Harriet; Underground Railroad; Violence, Sexual.

Suggested Reading

"Abolition." The African American Mosaic. http://www.loc.gov/exhibits/africa/afam005.html; "Abolitionism." Africans in America, Part 4: 1831–1865. http://www.pbs.org/wgbh/aia/part4/narr2.html; Stephanie M. H. Camp, *Closer to Freedom: Enslaved Women & Everyday Resistance in the Plantation South* (Chapel Hill: University of North Carolina Press, 2004); Lydia Maria Child, *An Appeal in Favor of That Class of Americans Called Africans* (1833; reprint, New York: Arno Press, 1968); Julie Roy Jeffrey, *The Great Silent Army of Abolitionism: Ordinary Women in the Antislavery Movement* (Chapel Hill: University of North Carolina Press, 1998); Dorothy Salerno, ed., *We Are Your Sisters: Black Women in the Nineteenth Century* (New York: W.W. Norton, 1984); Shirley J. Yee, *Black Women Abolitionists: A Study in Activism, 1828–1860* (Knoxville: University of Tennessee Press, 1992); Jean Fagan Yellin, *Women and Sisters: The Antislavery Feminists in American Culture* (New Haven: Yale University Press, 1989); Jean Fagin Yellin and John C. Van Horne, eds., *The Abolitionist Sisterhood: Women's Political Culture in Antebellum America* (Ithaca: Cornell University Press, 1994).

Abortion

Enslaved women engaged in practices that allowed them to have some measure of control over their fertility. Though poorly understood due to the secrecy that often surrounded such practices, enslaved women utilized both contraception methodologies and deliberate abortion.

Enslaved women's access to knowledge about methods of pregnancy control undoubtedly had roots in their African heritage. Extant records documenting the reproductive strategies of women in early West African cultures, the origins of so many enslaved persons transported to the Americas, are lacking. Still, there are compelling reasons to believe that West African women, like indigenous women in North America and women in North Africa, may have had access to a variety of abortifacients and contraceptives derived from local plants and herbs. White observers of Amerindian and African peoples in the New World described efforts by women in both cultures to prevent or terminate unwanted pregnancies.

Some of the same substances used to regulate fertility, including the management of menses and contraception, may have also been used to facilitate abortion. African plants with abortifacient properties that were transported to the New World include okra and aloe. Women's knowledge about the ability of cotton root and snake-root to induce deliberate abortion, also seem to have survived the transatlantic passage. In the Americas, women circulated information about reproductive strategies among themselves. Within the enslaved community, women had greater access to knowledge about regulating fertility only after they bore one child and accordingly, younger women were generally restricted from the community of women and circulation of reproductive knowledge. Women's ability to use common substances to bring on menses and terminate a pregnancy made it difficult for others to know whether abortion was intended. Enslaved men and slaveholders knew about the usage of cotton root and other abortifacients among women, but women could also use them privately and without detection. Southern doctors recommended the cotton plant's root as a way to regulate menstruation among white clients. And, it is plausible that doctors first learned of the cotton plant root *from* enslaved women. While cotton root was accessible to many enslaved women, ergot, rue, and other substances used by white women to facilitate abortion were less widely available to black women.

For most antebellum southern whites, abortion was appropriate only in instances where the life of the mother was at risk. Many slaveholders valued black women's reproductive capacity, as evidenced by discussions of enslaved women's fertility and overall health in medical texts and other publications. This was also evident in the many suits brought before southern courts in which slaveholders sought recompense for the apparent inability of a woman to bear children. The distribution and storage of rags used to absorb monthly menstrual fluid informed slaveholders about menstrual regularity and irregularity. Slaveholders' concerns about the financial potential of unborn children contributed to exaggerated fears about bondwomen's intentional termination of pregnancies. Foremost, slaveholders recognized that enslaved women's bodies, including the bodies of pregnant women, could simultaneously be the sites of both domination and resistance.

Over time, especially with the official end of the Transatlantic Slave Trade in 1808, greater focus centered on ways to prevent spontaneous miscarriage and deliberate abortion among enslaved women. Slaveholders' suspicions regarding black women's intentional manipulation of their fertility and pregnancies gained momentum from doctors. Increasingly, any efforts by black women to regulate fertility—including child spacing—might be dubbed abortion or deliberate avoidance of pregnancy. Slaveholders worried that enslaved women, in consultation with midwives, pursued deliberate abortions and even infanticide. Occasionally doctors might point to the harsh labor conditions under which pregnant bond-women worked as a rationale for stillbirth and infant mortality. Doctors were summoned when the miscarriage of black women seemed imminent. However, women undoubtedly hid their pregnancies, due to a desire to avoid interference from doctors or invasive medical procedures. Secrecy and internal communication were core elements within slave community life, as enslaved women relied on midwives and others in the community for advice on reproduction and tried as best they could to manage their fertility and pregnancies beyond the direct oversight of enslavers and other whites.

Kimberly Sambol-Tosco

See also Breeding; Contraception; Female Slave Network; Folk Medicine and Healing; Life Cycle; Midwives; Mortality and Life Expectancy; Motherhood.

Suggested Reading

Stephanie M. H. Camp, *Closer to Freedom: Enslaved Women and Everyday Resistance in the Plantation South* (Chapel Hill and London: University of North Carolina Press, 2004); Sharla M. Fett, *Working Cures: Healing, Health, and Power on Southern Plantations* (Chapel Hill: University of North Carolina Press, 2002); Stephanie Li, "Resistance through the Body: Power, Representation, and the Enslaved Woman" (PhD dissertation, Cornell University, 2005); Jennifer L. Morgan, *Laboring Women: Reproduction and Gender in New World Slavery* (Philadelphia: University of Pennsylvania Press, 2004); Marie Jenkins Schwartz, *Birthing a Slave: Motherhood and Medicine in the Antebellum South* (Cambridge, MA and London: Harvard University Press, 2006).

Abroad Marriage

See Marriage, Abroad

African Women and African-born Women

Enslaved African women in the early American colonies lived during a time when the economic, agricultural, ideological, and cultural development of the United States depended on their productive and reproductive labor. Their everyday lives developed as much by bondage as well as their knowledge and memories of Africa. It is the unique experience of the Middle Passage coupled with skills in agricultural and domestic labor that added dimensionality to African women's abilities of biological and cultural reproduction. African females adjusted to racialized slavery in the United States in ways that involved both continuities from their African past and the creation of new practices. African-born bondwomen brought with them systems of knowledge and cultural heritage upon which they built, adjusted, and sometimes even abandoned, to fit their experience of U.S. slavery.

But uncovering the details of enslaved African women in North America is difficult due to the paucity of sources; colonial primary sources were rarely concerned with the lives of African-born slave women. However, recent developments in databases such as *The Transatlantic Slave Trade, 1527–1867* (1999), a massive CD-ROM project now available via the internet at slavevoyages.org (2008), has

My ma was a black African an' she sho' was wild an' mean . . . Dey couldn' whup her widout tyin' her up firs'. Sometimes my marster would wait 'til de nex' day to git somebody to he'p tie her up, den he'd forgit to whup 'er . . . She tol' me how dey brought her from Africa. You know, like we say "President" in this country, well dey call him "Chief" in Africa. Seem like de chief made "rangements wid some men an" dey had a big goober grabbin' for de young folk. Dey stole my ma an' some more an' brung 'em to dis country.

—Susan Snow, former bondwoman
(*Born in Slavery: Slave Narratives from the Federal Writers' Project, 1936–1938 Mississippi Narratives, Volume IX,* 136)

brought together documents in attempts to record slaving voyages from Africa to the New World, and Gwendolyn Midlo Hall's *Afro-Louisiana History and Genealogy, 1719–1820* (2000), are shedding new light on African-born women's presence in the Americas. These detailed databases allow scholars to ascertain the general demography of the enslaved in the Transatlantic Slave Trade. Generally, the ratio of females to males varied according to region and time, and when considering the number of children transported, women and men arrived in near-balanced numbers (Eltis 2000). This balance was unique to slavery in North America and critical to considering the effect of African women's presence among the enslaved on the rate at which slaveholders needed African imports to maintain the enslaved population. The databases also enable scholars to trace the ethnicity of enslaved African women along the slave route from Africa to destination. While Europeans did not always record the origins of the captured correctly, or use uniform terminology for ethnicity, the ability to trace enslaved women to regions in Africa is critical to understanding which, when, how, and why knowledge of Africa was transferred to the next generations of American-born slaves.

Scholarly work building upon these databases shows that early colonial enslavers depended on African-born bondwomen not only for physical labor to reap economic profits from the fields, but also for their reproductive capabilities and ideological functions. Enslaved African women initially constituted the majority of available females for procreation and were often subjected to sexual exploitation and violence. Their reproductive identities served in the cost-benefit calculations of slaveholders who valued their ability to bear additional sources of labor. European ideas about African female sexuality and their "monstrous bodies" contributed to the development of a racialized slavery (Morgan 2004).

In addition to reproductive capabilities, African-born bondwomen brought agricultural productive systems of knowledge to the New World. For example, in South Carolina in the early eighteenth century, they used their expertise in rice farming to experiment with rice growing in the Carolina wetlands. Throughout West Africa, rice was primarily a woman's crop in cultivation, processing, and cooking. This specialized knowledge system, including the use of the hoe and winnowing baskets as preeminent tools, sowing the seed with the feet or encased in mud, tidal cultivation, and the milling of rice with a mortar and pestle, was transferred and adjusted according to the enslaved African women's experience under slavery in South Carolina (Carney 2001).

Similarly, the medical-botanical knowledge of African slave women contributed heavily to the development of medicine in the South. African slave women used their plant expertise to make medicine, sharing the knowledge of how to prevent, cure, abort, or even poison using plants traditionally employed in Africa, in the Caribbean, and the Americas. In the early Virginia colony, an enslaved Igbo woman named Dido was among three Igbos who used their knowledge of herbs and plants as a weapon of resistance in the murder of their master Ambrose Madison (Chambers 2005).

As transmitters of culture, enslaved African women came from diverse African backgrounds and thus, no single cultural heritage could define that which was passed down. But enslaved women did share important beliefs about kinship and were particularly critical to the preservation and spread of African culture in Louisiana. The presence of African parents and grandparents living with American-born children played a vital role in the Africanization of Louisiana creole culture. African mothers and grandmothers transmitted an African grammar structure to the creole language, and Senegambian idioms, folklore, and music (Midlo Hall 1992). This was consistent throughout the South, such as in Georgia where the Gullah song, "Amelia's Song" was traced to a Sierra Leonean village. Ethnomusicologists and linguists found the song to be preserved by women in both cultures who had learned it from their grandmothers (*The Language You Cry In*, 1998).

Enslaved African women were also the protectors of African religious traditions, which they practiced and passed on to succeeding generations. African women combined their knowledge of West African spirituality with Roman Catholic traditions in the development of American Voodoo. These women served as conjurers and priestesses for their families and communities, aiding in healing, prevention, and protection.

While studies of women in slave communities have surged since the 1980s, much remains to be done, particularly on African-born females in the Americas. African women were exploited for their economic, reproductive, and ideological functions and yet survived to preserve and adapt their African systems of knowledge and culture under the experience of enslavement.

Jill E. Kelly

See also Burial Customs; Creoles; Folklore and Folktales; Middle Passage; Violence, Sexual; Voodoo.

Suggested Reading

Afro-Louisiana History and Genealogy, 1719–1820. http://www.ibiblio.org/laslave/; Judith A. Carney, *Black Rice: The African Origins of Rice Cultivation in the Americas* (Cambridge: Harvard University Press, 2001); Douglas B. Chambers, *Murder at Montpelier: Igbo Africans in Virginia* (Jackson: University Press of Mississippi, 2005); David Eltis, *The Rise of African Slavery in the Americas* (Cambridge: Cambridge University Press, 2000); David Eltis et al., *The Trans-Atlantic Slave Trade: A Database on CD-ROM* (Cambridge: Cambridge University Press, 1999); Michael A. Gomez, *Exchanging Our Country Marks: The Transformation of African Identities in the Colonial and Antebellum South* (Chapel Hill: University of North Carolina Press, 1998); Gwendolyn Midlo Hall, *Africans in Colonial Louisiana: The Development of Afro-Creole Culture in the Eighteenth Century* (Baton Rouge: Louisiana State University Press, 1992); Jennifer L. Morgan, *Laboring Women: Reproduction and Gender in New World Slavery* (Philadelphia: University of Pennsylvania Press, 2004); *The Language You Cry In*, produced and directed by Alvaro Toepke and Angel Serrano, 52 min., California Newsreel, 1998, videocassette.

American Revolution

Event Date: 1776–1783

The American Revolution was and remains a watershed event in American history. Following the French-Indian War (1763), the imperial relationship between Britain and her American colonies grew strained. Questions regarding the payment of newly accrued war debts, the frequency and reach of British imposed taxes, and the colonists' increasing desire to understand their place within the larger imperial framework altogether set the stage for war. Moreover, for many colonists, the lack of elected representation in the British Parliament especially signaled the appropriate moment to sever ties with the mother country. By 1776, a year after the start of actual fighting, Thomas Jefferson, a young Virginia statesman, penned the Declaration of Independence, which enumerated the colonists' grievances with the Crown, affirmed the notion of universal equality among men, and famously maintained that all men were entitled to the pursuit of life, liberty, and happiness. These revolutionary principles, however, would be co-opted by enslaved blacks to make their case for personal liberty during and after the Revolution. After nearly seven years of intense fighting, the War for Independence concluded with both sides signing of the Treaty of Paris in 1783, which officially ended fighting and declared the rebellious 13 American colonies as sovereign and independent states.

As with most wars, the American Revolution affected most severely those populations already on the lower rungs of society, and particularly enslaved and free black families. Historians estimate that there were more than 500,000 blacks living in the colonies at the time of the war. Comprising one-fifth of the total population, at least 95 percent of those blacks were held in bondage. Slavery existed in every colony, though more than half of all bondpeople lived in Virginia and Maryland. And as blacks made up 50 to 60 percent of the Chesapeake population during the Revolutionary era, one year before the signing of the Declaration of Independence, South Carolina boasted a two-thirds slave majority. Thus, the 13 American colonies contained a considerable slave presence on the eve of the Revolution.

Since the Stamp Acts or Townshend Duties figured minimally in their everyday lives, enslaved blacks worried most about their own survival in the midst of the ensuing political and military chaos. However, bondwomen found themselves drafted into the colonists' boycott of British goods. In South Carolina and other major port cities, many enslaved women served as the backbone of the homespun campaign. Refusing to import or purchase British textiles for patriotic reasons, white colonists relied on slave labor to keep up with the insatiable demand for spun goods. Therefore, in their roles as spinners and seamstresses during this patriotic campaign, enslaved women also involuntarily entered the tense political debate between Britain and the American colonies, and it is likely that their efforts informed their decisions to employ the revolutionary fervor of the day for their own means, namely freedom.

In Massachusetts, the epicenter of revolutionary activities, enslaved women like Jenny Slew and Mum Bett pressed white patriots for their freedom, thus capitalizing on the rhetoric of revolution to make and ultimately, win their historic cases. Jenny Slew, a woman with a white mother and black father, lived in freedom in the Bay colony until 1762. While in her early forties, Slew was kidnapped from her home and enslaved by John Whipple, Jr. In 1765, Slew filed a civil suit against Whipple, maintaining that since a child's legal status follows that of the mother, she, too, like her mother, deserved her freedom. Though Massachusetts was one of the few colonies to allow enslaved persons to bring civil suits in court, Slew still faced obstacles to getting her case serious consideration from the empanelled justices. Dismissing the case on a technicality, the justices chastised Slew for filing her complaint in the wrong jurisdiction and misrepresenting herself as a spinster since she was once married. In the end, the court ruled in favor of Whipple and ordered Slew to pay court costs. Still determined, however, Slew later appealed to the Superior Court, and this time, she stood trial by jury. During the trial, Whipple argued that he possessed a bill of sale for Slew, and thus challenged her kidnapping charges. He also maintained that her status as a married woman nullified her legal right to sue; her husband, he argued, would have to sue on her behalf since married women's legal rights were subsumed by those of her husband under the doctrine of couverture. The court did not agree, and this time, Slew won her case and became the first enslaved person to win her freedom by jury trial. For her troubles, the jury awarded Slew court costs and four pounds.

Another enslaved woman in Massachusetts later followed Slew's lead during the Revolutionary period and fought for her freedom. Mum Bett, or Elizabeth Freeman, lived in Sheffield, Massachusetts with her owner Colonel John Ashley. She was illiterate and worked primarily as a nurse. Shortly after the appearance of the Declaration of Independence, Massachusetts enacted a new state constitution. A key provision in that constitution borrowed language from the Declaration and stated that all men are "born free and equal." For Freeman, the state's explicit claim of freedom for all was enough to push her to challenge the legality of slavery in Massachusetts. She reasoned that if both the Declaration of Independence and the state's constitution underscored notions of personal liberty, especially during the age of revolution, then there was no logical or legal reason for slavery to exist in the state. In 1781, she and a co-petitioner filed suit in court with money raised by other enslaved persons in the area. Freeman and her co-plaintiff eventually won their freedom suit and the case became the first challenge to slavery using language lifted directly from a state constitution. Though Freeman won her freedom, Massachusetts was slow to outright abolish slavery, but it ultimately ended the institution in 1783 and set an example for other northern states to follow.

Besides petitioning for their freedom in the courts, enslaved women also sacrificed their husbands and sons during the Revolutionary conflict. For blacks, what mattered most before, during, *and* after the Revolution was freedom, so it was not uncommon to witness blacks siding with either the British or the Americans since both made enticing promises of freedom to those blacks that would join their cause. Black soldiers fought in George Washington's army and were instrumental to the eventual American victory. Nonetheless, in 1775, Lord Dunmore, the last royal governor of Virginia, promised freedom to enslaved men who vowed to fight on the British side. In response to Dunmore's Proclamation, hundreds of bondsmen fled from their masters and took up arms against the patriot cause. Historian Benjamin Quarles has termed Dunmore a paradoxical figure, one who could easily be characterized as either a tyrant or liberator. However, one thing remains clear: Lord Dunmore both directly and indirectly encouraged the enslaved to seek freedom by openly rebelling against their masters, even if it meant disorganizing and displacing black families throughout the colonies. Though Dunmore's actions provided an avenue to freedom for many bondsmen, his calculated military strategy left enslaved women with broken families or on a perilous run toward freedom near the end of the war.

Perhaps the most famous enslaved woman in America and Europe at the time of the Revolution was Phillis Wheatley. Born in West Africa and sold into American slavery in 1761, Wheatley spent most of her life in Boston and died in 1784.

Ironically, Wheatley carried the same name as the slave ship that brought her to America—the *Phillis*. While enslaved in Boston, Wheatley worked for a wealthy merchant and tailor named John Wheatley and his wife, Susanna. The couple immediately converted the young Phillis Wheatley to Christianity and often introduced her to their evangelical friends. John Wheatley's daughter, Mary, also took special interest in the young slave girl, teaching her to read and write in English and Latin. Within four years of her arrival to the Wheatley household, Phillis Wheatley began to write and publish numerous religious poems and reflections. Buoyed by her owners' patronage and elite connections, Wheatley became the first black published poet in America. Yet when the Revolution ensued, Wheatley lost most of her financial support and publishing connections. Though members of the Wheatley family were loyalists during the conflict, Phillis Wheatley found herself writing on behalf of the patriot cause and for the freedom of all enslaved peoples. She penned several poems memorializing the heroics of men like Crispus Attucks and later George Washington. In fact, before 1776, she met both Benjamin Franklin and George Washington, which signaled how many whites at the time respected both her and her work. Moreover, some of her poetry also questioned the morality of the institution of slavery. As Wheatley began to interrogate the contradictions in the Patriot cause and their support of slavery, her popularity in America waned. The same nation fighting for its independence from the British "slavery" was too dependent on black slavery at home to also fight for its total abolition. Consequently, she struggled for the remainder of her life to publish more of her work. However, despite living in poverty on the outskirts of Boston and enduring a lifetime of skeptics who questioned whether an enslaved woman could master the English language and write such provocative poetry, Phillis Wheatley died as both a free and celebrated woman.

Ultimately, the American Revolution provided enslaved women with the language and audience to express their desire for freedom. As the Revolutionary War brought tremendous devastation and change to many throughout the colonies, enslaved women and their families often experienced the war on many fronts. They battled the British, the Americans, and most importantly, the institution of slavery.

Jermaine Thibodeaux

See also Freeman, Elizabeth; Wheatley, Phillis.

Suggested Reading

Henry Louis Gates, Jr., *The Trials of Phillis Wheatley: America's First Black Poet and Her Encounter with the Founding Fathers* (New York: Basic Civitas, 2003); Darlene Clark Hine and Kathleen Thompson, *A Shining Thread of Hope: The History of Black Women in America* (New York: Broadway, 1998); Jacqueline Jones, "Race, Sex, and Self-Evident

Truths: The Status of Slave Women During the Era of the American Revolution," in *Half Sisters of History: Southern Women and the American Past*, ed. Catherine Clinton (Durham: Duke University Press, 1994), 18–35; Sidney Kaplan, *The Black Presence in the Era of the American Revolution, 1770–1800* (Greenwich, CT: New York Graphic Society, 1973); Benjamin Quarles, *The Negro in the American Revolution* (Chapel Hill: University of North Carolina Press, 1961); George W. Williams, *History of the Negro Race in America, 1619–1900* (New York: G.P. Putnam's, 1882).

B

Bondwoman (Bondwomen, Bondman, Bondmen, Bondpeople)

Throughout this book, the terms "bondwoman" ("bondwomen"), "bondman" ("bondmen"), and "bondpeople" have been used to mean people who have been enslaved, or who have been historically called *slaves*. The name comes from the fact that the people lived under bondage, against their will. Many scholars have chosen to discuss people of African descent held against their will with these terms, which better emphasizes their humanity.

Suggested Reading

Henry Louis Gates, Jr., *The Bondwoman's Narrative: A Novel by Hannah Crafts* (New York: Warner Books, 2002); Walter Johnson, "On Agency," *Journal of Social History* 37, No. 1 (2003): pp. 113–124; National Park Service, "Underground Railroad Terminology: The Language of Slavery," www.nps.gov/subjects/ugrr/discover_history/terminology.htm (accessed February 11, 2012) and H-Slavery Discussion, "Use of Enslaved" (February 2010).

Branding

Branding was a means of social control and torture as well as an identifying marker that relegated enslaved Africans as "human property." Historian Marcus Rediker refers to branding as "the hardware of bondage" (Rediker 2007, 72). These tools included branding irons, manacles and shackles, feet and neck irons, chains, handcuffs, and thumbscrews. Most branding irons had a distinguishable symbol or letter. In addition to branding as a means of control, bondpeople also received brands to hold slave ship captains accountable for loss due to mortality or other extenuating circumstances during the Middle Passage. Rediker argues that branding usually occurred for merchants of large charter companies such as the Royal African Company or the South Sea Company and it was essential to avoid confusion of ownership between Dutch, English, Danish, French, and Portuguese slaves. Branding therefore prevented traders from "craftily substituting bad slaves for good ones" (Pope-Hennessy 2004, 78).

Enslaved people of all ages prior to being branded. *Anti-Slavery Almanac*, 1840. (Library of Congress.)

Slave traders assured their investors in human chattel that they would not harm African captives during branding. However, after receiving complaints about the deep burns that captives received under his custody, slave trader Willem Bosman wrote the following to his merchants: "we will take all possible care that they are not burned too hard, especially the women who are more tender than the men" (Pope-Hennessy 2004, 76). Europeans placed hot branding irons into the flesh of enslaved African women, men, and children's backs, shoulders, upper chests, or thighs, imprinting permanently their symbol or letter of ownership. Once enslaved, branded, and transported to the New World they were redefined as valuable commodities—free labor and chattel property purchased for the primary purpose of building and sustaining New World plantations. For some, branding marked the beginning of a series of emotional, physical, and sexual violations that African captives, especially women, experienced in the New World.

Renee K. Harrison

See also Middle Passage; Violence, Sexual.

Suggested Reading

John S. Mbiti, *African Religions and Philosophy* (New York: Praeger, 1969); James Pope-Hennessy, *Sins of the Fathers: The Atlantic Slave Trade 1441–1807* (Edison, New Jersey: Castle Books, 2004); Marcus Rediker, *The Slave Ship: A Human History* (New York: Viking, 2007).

Breeding

Breeding represented a form of sexual reproduction wherein enslaved people were involuntarily forced to have nonconsensual sexual intercourse. The goal of this exploitative process involved producing additional sources of labor-making bondwomen particularly vulnerable. Given that black women had no legal protection against rape, they experienced sexual exploitation from both black and white men. Although scholars have yet to determine the frequency of such acts, enslaved narratives are rich with descriptions of sexual coercion. Such evidence confirms the rampart nature of sexual violence in North America.

Master would sometimes go and get a large hale hearty Negro man from some other plantation to go to his Negro woman. He would ask the other master to let this man come over to his place to go to his slave girls. A slave girl was expected to have children as soon as she became a woman. Some of them had children at the age of twelve and thirteen years old. Negro men six feet tall went to some of these children.

—Hilliard Yellerday, former bondman
(*Born in Slavery: Slave Narratives from the Federal Writers' Project, 1936–1938 North Carolina Narratives, Volume XI, Part 2,* 434)

On the auction block, bondwomen's bodies were exposed and often slave buyers kneaded their stomachs to determine how many children they could bear or if they were done breeding. Enslaved women recalled having their clothes stripped off so that potential buyers could examine them as merchandise. There was a high premium for women who were considered "good breeders." Former bondpeople testified that they were forced to mate like animals and that slaveholders selected specific men and women for that purpose. Proslavery newspapers and flyers printed detailed accounts of enslaved people's capacity for breeding. Historian Deborah Gray White notes that the "merits of a particular 'breeder' were often the topic of parlor or dinner table conversations" (White 1985, 31).

Women and men who resisted breeding were considered a detriment to the slave economy. They were severely beaten in public to incite fear in the slave community. Enslaved women beaten beyond the capacity of childbearing were sometimes sold, demonized, and considered "ruined for breeding." Mary Reynolds, a former enslaved woman from Louisiana was left barren following a traumatic beating. She recalled: "Old man Kidd . . . tied my wrists together and stripped me. He hanged me by the wrists from a limb on a tree and spraddled my legs round the trunk and tied my feet together. Then he beat me. He beat me worser than I ever been beat before. . . . Massa looks me over good and says I'll git well, but I'm ruin' for breedin' chillum" (Reynolds, WPA Slave Narratives, Library of Congress).

Renee K. Harrison

See also Pregnancy; Violence, Sexual.

Suggested Reading

Pamela Bridgewater, *Breeding a Nation: Reproductive Slavery, the Thirteenth Amendment, and the Pursuit of Freedom* (Cambridge: SouthEnd Press, 2008); Edward Donoghue, *Black Breeding Machines: The Breeding of Negro Slaves in the Diaspora* (Bloomington: AuthorHouse, 2008); Richard Sutch, "The Breeding of Slaves for Sale and the Westward Expansion of Slavery, 1850–1860," in *Race and Slavery in the Western Hemisphere*, eds. Stanley Engerman and Eugene D. Geonvese (Princeton: Princeton University Press, 1975); Deborah Gray White, *Ar'n't I a Woman?: Female Slaves in the Plantation South* (New York: W.W. Norton & Company, 1985).

Burial Customs

Burial customs were an integral aspect of enslaved life. The burial practices of bondpeople represented a variety of different African and American cultural traditions, all dependent on who the enslaved were and where they were buried. Some practices such as decorating graves with broken glass, personal items of the deceased, shells, and other objects appear to be traditions that are unique to African burial communities. Aspects of folk culture and Christianity also influenced enslaved burial practices. For example, some enslaved individuals sang songs influenced by biblical references such as "Lay Dis Body Down" or "Hark from de Tomb."

Slave burial customs were a communal affair that sometimes occurred at night. This was typically due to the demanding physical labor that occupied enslaved persons' days; nighttime burials also provided a shroud of secrecy from the slaveholders and overseers. Enslaved women played an important role in both the preparing of the body and the grave for the transition of the deceased into the afterlife. Women were responsible for cleaning and dressing the body of the deceased, occasionally tying up the mouth in order to keep the body's spirit from escaping. At night, on some plantations, the enslaved congregated at the cabin of the deceased and from there, started a procession leading all the way to the burial site. Upon arrival, mourners formed a circle, where the African-influenced ring shout occurred. In this ritual, the enslaved danced counterclockwise, being careful to not lift their feet off the ground. The circle represented the complete cycle of birth, death, and rebirth.

After the ceremony, the men began to cover the homemade wooden casket, often made of pine, with dirt. Women decorated the grave with flowers and broken household objects such as plates, glass, mirrors, shells, beads, and clocks. Such decoration allowed the grave to glimmer in the light. These objects were broken in order to break the chain of death within the community. Burial customs represented a space for bondpeople to express African and African American cultural traditions.

Terry P. Brock

See also Mortality and Life Expectancy.

Suggested Reading

Michael A. Gomez, *Exchanging Our Country Marks: The Transformation of African Identities in the Colonial and Antebellum South* (Chapel Hill: University of North Carolina Press, 1998); David R. Roediger, "And Die in Dixie: Funerals in the Slave Community," *Massachusetts Review* 22 (1981); Sterling Stuckey, *Slave Culture: Nationalist Theory and the Foundations of Black America* (New York: Oxford University Press, 1987); "The African Burial Ground: Return to the Past to Build the Future," http://www.african burialground.gov/ABG_Main.htm; Robert Farris Thompson, *Flash of the Spirit: Afro-American Art and Philosophy* (New York: Vintage Books, 1983).

C

Celia

Birth Date: ~1836
Death Date: December 21, 1855

Celia was an enslaved woman who became known for the retaliatory murder of her abusive owner, Robert Newsom. Her subsequent indictment, trial, and death sentence were influenced by the political debates and volatile confrontations between proslavery advocates and abolitionists in Missouri and Kansas. Celia's life story received renewed scholarly attention with the 1991 publication of Melton A. McLaurin's well-documented biography, *Celia, A Slave*.

In 1850, Celia was sold to Robert Newsom when she was about 14 years old. On the way to his home in Callaway County, Missouri, Newsom raped Celia, thus beginning four years of sexual abuse. Celia gave birth to two children who probably had been fathered by Newsom. Eventually, Celia became drawn to George, an enslaved man who also was owned by Newsom. Upon her third pregnancy, George, who was uncertain about the child's paternity, informed Celia that he would leave her unless she somehow ended her relationship with Newsom. In response, Celia appealed to Newsom's daughters, Virginia and Mary, indicating that she wanted the forced sexual relationship to stop and that her pregnancy and sickness made his advances particularly unbearable. The records do not show whether or not the sisters, both of whom were financially dependent on Newsome, were able or willing to intervene on Celia's behalf. It is known that although Celia threatened to hurt Newsom, the sexual abuse continued.

Celia confronted Newsom directly sometime on or shortly before June 23, 1855. Newsom dismissed her request with a threatening promise that "he was coming to her cabin that night" (McLaurin 1993, 33). Pushed to her limits, Celia secured a large stick, determined to physically defend herself if necessary. Newsom entered her cabin that night and demanded that she have sex with him. Upon his approach, Celia brought the stick down on his head. A second blow to his skull killed him. In an attempt to get rid of the evidence of the murder, Celia built a roaring fire in which she put the large stick and Newsom's body, stoking the fire all night, and carrying out most of the ashes before dawn.

Presiding over the trial, Circuit Court Judge William Hall held Unionist sympathies. In an effort to ensure that Celia would receive a trial that would not be easily dismissed, he assigned the well-respected John Jameson to defend Celia.

Using witness testimony, Jameson emphasized the fact that Newsom had continually raped Celia since she was 14 years old. Celia, he argued, had acted out of desperation to stop the abuse, but had not intended to kill Newsom. In spite of his attempts to argue that Celia had the legal right to refuse Newsom's sexual advances, Judge Hall supported the prosecutions' contention that jurors could not acquit Celia on grounds of self-defense or based on the idea that she had the right to repel with force Newsom's sexual advances.

The jury found Celia guilty and sentenced her to hang. Celia delivered a stillborn infant in October. On December 21, 1855 she was executed. Celia's tragic story not only illuminates the vulnerability of enslaved women, but also recovers the experiences of enslaved women who were willing to resist sexual exploitation at all costs.

Alexandra Cornelius-Diallo

See also Conflict, Intraracial; Miscegenation; Resistance; Violence, Sexual.

Suggested Reading

Diane Mutti Burke, *On Slavery's Border: Missouri's Small-Slaveholding Households, 1815–1865* (Athens: University of Georgia Press, 2010); Harriet C. Frazier, *Slavery and Crime in Missouri, 1773–1865* (Jefferson, NC: McFarland & Company, Inc., Publishers, 2001); Melton A. McLaurin, *Celia, A Slave: A True Story* (New York: Avon Books, 1993).

Childbirth

Mothers didn't stay in after their chillun was born then like they do now. Whenever a child was born the mother came out in three days afterward if she was healthy, but nobody stayed in over a week. They never stayed in bed but one day.

—Unknown woman, former bondwoman
(*Born in Slavery: Slave Narratives from the Federal Writers' Project, 1936–1938 Georgia Narratives, Volume IV, Part 4*, 362)

Childbirth in pre-Civil War United States was frequently a difficult and dangerous experience, particularly for enslaved women. While slaveholders often aimed to control as much of the birthing process for enslaved females, midwives and other members of the slave community provided invaluable assistance to women during pregnancy, childbirth, and the postpartum period. Most enslaved women did not give birth in isolation or free from intervention.

For most enslaved women in the United States, a free black or enslaved female midwife typically provided most of the care associated with childbirth, including the management of pain. Mothers, female friends, and other members of the slave community lent support to the expecting mother and presented gifts of food and other offerings. Sometimes plantation mistresses, who controlled blankets, clothes, and other supplies needed for childbirth, were present during slave births. Slaveholders might check in from time to time during the birth, but more typically, they exerted their influence prior to the commencement of labor by making their views known on the way the birth process should proceed, including the participation of a physician, if deemed appropriate. They also considered contacting a doctor if complications arose, but many seemed content to allow midwives to handle most slave births. White doctors were more likely to provide gynecological services to enslaved females rather than attend uncomplicated slave births. Even when a physician's services were requested, enslaved healers and midwives often continued to provide care to the woman in labor.

Although the overwhelming majority of slave births were handled by black midwives, slaveholders increasingly relied on doctors to attend the births of enslaved women during the antebellum period. Hemorrhaging, prolonged labor, and the cessation of labor pains were some of the reasons a doctor's presence might be requested. Southern physicians and the slaveholding clients they served were concerned about the slave infant mortality rate and the future health of enslaved women who experienced childbirth, including their ability to continue to reproduce. When a doctor provided care to an enslaved woman, he might dictate the position a woman used for labor, use forceps to facilitate delivery, or administer ergot, a fungus that grows on rye plants, to restart or increase contractions. In addition, doctors prescribed medications, manually manipulated babies as women entered active labor, and used bloodletting with the belief that doing so could relax the reproductive organs, speed labor, ease pain, and reduce inflammation.

In contrast with the practices of physicians, midwives regularly used roots and herbs and might have also placed an axe or other sharp object under the bed in an effort to reduce the pain of childbirth or the afterbirth process. Midwives upheld cultural beliefs among slaves dictating that very specific steps be taken when certain things occurred during the childbirth process such as a child being born with a caul or the remnants of the amniotic sac intact and covering the body. There was also a strong belief that the placenta in any birth be handled in a specific way. Enslaved women sought to control childbirth as much as possible and to describe it in terms that were meaningful to them. Sometimes women were working in the fields when labor began and a small number gave birth in the plantation house. The majority, however, gave birth in their cabins, where they could control the position they used to deliver the baby. Despite efforts by planters, overseers, and other whites to control the birthing process, due in part to the presence of African American midwives, slave births might be at least partially understood within the context of extended African American kinship networks and protection, rather than in accordance with the chattel principle.

Due to concerns about a woman's recovery and ability to return to productive labor, slaveholders closely watched bondwomen who had just given birth for days following childbirth. Midwives too were concerned with the vulnerability of women in the postnatal period. They administered roots and herbal cures to facilitate recovery and offered advice on resuming daily activities. In addition, midwives typically remained in close proximity to a postpartum woman for several days, providing both assistance and advice to the new mother who remained in bed for nine days following birth. Midwives, for their part, were concerned about both the woman's and the child's survival and thus sought out assistance from other women in the postpartum period. One month after birth, the slave cabin was ritualistically cleansed under the attending midwife's supervision and further efforts were taken to protect the new baby from illness and bad luck.

Kimberly Sambol-Tosco

See also Breeding; Female Slave Network; Folk Medicine and Healing; Midwives; Mortality and Life Expectancy; Motherhood; Pregnancy.

Suggested Reading

Sharla Fett, *Working Cures: Healing, Health, and Power on Southern Plantations* (Chapel Hill: University of North Carolina Press, 2002); Wilma King, *Stolen Childhood: Slave Youth in Nineteenth-Century America* (Bloomington: Indiana University Press, 1996); Jennifer L. Morgan, *Laboring Women: Reproduction and Gender in New World Slavery* (Philadelphia: University of Pennsylvania Press, 2004); Marie Jenkins Schwartz, *Birthing a Slave: Motherhood and Medicine in the Antebellum South* (Cambridge: Harvard University Press, 2006); Marie Jenkins Schwartz, *Born in Bondage: Growing Up Enslaved in the Antebellum South* (Cambridge: Harvard University Press, 2000).

Childcare

I reckerlecks my mammy was a plow han' an' she'd go to work soon an' put me under de shade of a big ol' post-oak tree. Dere I sat all day, an' dat tree was my nurse. It still standin' dere yit, an' I won't let nobody cut it down.

—Oliver Bell, former bondman
(*Born in Slavery: Slave Narratives from the Federal Writers' Project, 1936–1938 Alabama Narratives, Volume I, 28–29*)

Enslaved women struggled to balance the demands of taking care of their children with the productive labor requirements they performed in service to slaveholders. While enslaved mothers tended to most of the needs of their own children due to imbalanced sex ratios, gender conventions, and the separation of families, other members of the enslaved community might assist in the care of children in the living quarters.

Like other children, enslaved youth required care from the very moment they were born. Initially, mothers cared for their new babies during a period of

Enslaved women and children on a Mississippi plantation in the 1860s. (Miller, Francis Trevelyan and Robert Sampson Lanier, *The Photographic History of the Civil War*, vol. 9, 1911.)

lightened work requirements that often, though not always, followed childbirth. As a mother transitioned back to her full-time work responsibilities, she might take the child to the fields with her and strategically position him or her as best she could in a shady spot under a tree or near a fence. Though such an arrangement might expose children to the hot sun or other potential harm, it also helped facilitate more regular nursing and allowed mothers to keep a watchful eye on their babies. Other options included leaving children in the cabin to fend for themselves or placing them in the care of older children. Alternatively, on large plantations that began to use common nurseries during the antebellum period, a mother might leave the child in the care of elderly women or others deemed unfit for regular labor. While mothers still nursing their children visited the plantation nursery a few times a day, children in nurseries often received inadequate attention from overburdened elderly or partially debilitated caregivers who sometimes looked after dozens of children.

Though southern slaveholders were generally supportive of the birth itself due to the prospect of the infants maturing into productive laborers in their own right, they were reluctant to give mothers full responsibility or even adequate time and resources to properly care for their children. The development of nurseries was an attempt by slaveholders to ensure the health and safety of enslaved children while also allowing adult women with children to fulfill productive labor without inter-ruption. Women did what they could to exert control over their children and to improve their chances of survival despite alarmingly high infant and child mortal-ity rates throughout the institution of slavery in the United States. Parents kept child-rearing tasks such as food preparation and other household duties as simple as possible. In addition, they often welcomed any supplemental assistance slave-holders provided, but recognized that such help encroached further on their autonomy in raising their children according to their own ideas and values.

Children were sent to work for slaveholders at an early age, with most beginning to work as early as age 7 but by age 11 many youth served as part of "children's squads" or "trash gangs." Their duties included weeding, cleaning, hoeing, or picking cotton. Children might be whipped by their slaveholders with no parent able to defend them. As a result of this interference and oversight, children were often torn between their loyalty and sense of duty to their parents on the one hand, and their recognition of the power of enslavers over all those deemed his dependents. The typical six-day work week that kept parents away from their children other than at night and on Sundays further undermined the parenting abilities of enslaved mothers and fathers. Despite formidable obstacles, mothers endeavored to raise their children on their own terms, including teaching critical lessons of obedience and domination while shielding them as best as possible from the excesses of racial slavery.

Kimberly Sambol-Tosco

See also Breeding; Childbirth; Elderly Women; Family; Female Slave Network; Gender Conventions; Motherhood; Wet Nursing.

Suggested Reading

Wilma King, *Stolen Childhood: Slave Youth in Nineteenth-Century America* (Blooming-ton and Indianapolis: Indiana University Press, 1995; 2011); Wilma King, " 'Suffer With Them Till Death': Slave Women and Their Children in Nineteenth-Century America," in *More Than Chattel: Black Women and Slavery in the America*, eds., David Barry Gaspar and Darlene Clark Hine (Bloomington and Indianapolis: Indiana University Press, 1996), 147–68; Marie Jenkins Schwartz, *Born in Bondage: Growing Up Enslaved in the Antebel-lum South* (Cambridge, MA and London: Harvard University Press, 2000).

Civil War

Event Date: 1861–1865

Tensions among northern and southern politicians over the institution of slavery mounted during the first half of the nineteenth century and came to a head with the presidential election of Illinois Republican Abraham Lincoln in November of 1860. Many white Southerners feared that the "black Republican" president would threaten their ability to be slaveholders. The South consequently seceded from the Union. Confederate forces' bombardment of Fort Sumter in Charleston Harbor, South Carolina on April 12, 1861 started the Civil War and consequently gave enslaved people hope that their lives of servitude would end soon.

W'en de Civil Wah wuz startin' dere wuz soldiers en tents eve'ywhar. I had ter 'nit socks en he'ps mak soldiers' coats en durin' de wah, de marster sent 100 ob us down in Georgia ter keep de Yankees fum gittin' us en we camped out durin' de whole three years."

—Precilla Gray, former bondwoman (*Born in Slavery: Slave Narratives from the Federal Writers' Project, 1936–1938 Tennessee Narratives, Volume XV*, 25)

As Union forces occupied the South, especially after the Emancipation Proclamation went into effect on January 1, 1863, scores of southern bondpeople flocked to Union contraband camps in search of safety, work, and shelter. They also desired to relocate loved ones and begin their lives as families in freedom. Freedom, however, did not guarantee a life of ease for enslaved women as they faced discrimination from both the Union Army and white southerners. Enslaved women assumed the workload of bondmen who left plantations to join the northern forces, withstood the possibility that whites could force them back into slavery after they achieved liberation, and received little protection from the federal government both during and after the war.

Transition from Slavery to Freedom

As chattel, people of African descent had no rights. For enslaved women, this translated to little autonomy over their bodies, their children, or the maintenance of family ties. The two prevailing views that threatened to undermine slavery as an institution were geographically defined at best. The northern abolitionists called for the termination of slavery on moral grounds, whereas southerners insisted that slavery provided for the well-being of enslaved people by offering them food, clothing, work, and shelter. White southerners strove to depict slavery as a benevolent institution in part by creating the

There are many people who do not know what some of the colored women did during the war. There were hundreds of them who assisted the Union soldiers by hiding them and helping them to escape. Many were punished for taking food to the prison stockades for the prisoners... others assisted in various ways the Union army. These things should be kept in history before the people. There has never been a greater war in the United States than the one of 1861, where so many lives were lost, not men alone but noble women as well.

—Susie King Taylor, former bondwoman and Civil War nurse (*Reminiscences of My Life in Camp with the 33rd US Colored Troops, Late 1st South Carolina Volunteers*, 68)

image and stereotype of the black Mammy, who happily looked after white children and cared for the mistress's household. To them, the image of Mammy helped camouflage the harsh reality of sexual exploitation, spontaneous sale of family members, onerous physical labor, and harsh punishment that were significant parts of enslaved women's lives. Black women withstood these hardships by forming female kin networks through ties of blood or friendship. These networks included aunts, grandmothers, cousins, and sisters who provided moral support, helped raise children, and sometimes enabled escapes. While these networks helped enslaved females withstand and sometimes resist the confines of bondage, they eagerly anticipated the prospect of freedom during the Civil War.

At the beginning of the war when Union troops started to occupy the South, numerous enslaved people supported the war by participating in acts of resistance as part of a continuum of resistance they began in Africa at the point of capture. Enslaved people equated the presence of Union troops with freedom and defiantly refused to complete tasks that they usually performed for slaveholders or, in more extreme cases, left the plantation to follow the Union Army. In the war's early years, enslaved men primarily followed the army since they were expected to provide physical labor and were not expected to take their own children with them. Enslaved women, meanwhile, also refused to perform undesirable tasks and felt that freedom entitled them to the rights to protect their own bodies, their children, and their family ties. As enslaved women watched their husbands go to war, they found that freedom would not initially guarantee a markedly better life.

Family Separation and Work

When young enslaved men decided to follow the Union Army in search of freedom, or as the Confederacy impressed them into service as a continuation of their servitude, they often left behind wives, children, and elderly kin who were unable to flee either because of either physical constraints or parental responsibility. Men's decision to flee, or their undesirable abandonment of families, forced young, healthy enslaved women to assume many of the responsibilities and workloads of absent males in order to provide for dependents, maintain personal farms, or avoid punishment from slaveholders. Although enslaved women were accustomed to completing hard physical labor in the fields, the absence of males intensified their workload and presented an emotional toll as they endured the pain of separation while hoping for reunification. Elderly women also played an important role in maintaining a stable community during the war. As the war progressed, enslaved women began to follow the Union Army in order to be with their husbands, to find work, or even to support the cause. Their decision to follow the Union Army consequently presented a new set of hardships.

Enslaved Women and the Union Army

Multiple political measures directly impacted enslaved women's decision to leave plantations and take up residence with the Union Army. On August 6, 1861, Congress passed the First Confiscation Act, which negated slaveholders' claims to fugitive slaves if they had been used to support either the Confederate war effort, in general, or Confederate military purposes, in particular. Enslaved people understood these ambiguous terms as direct justification for and sanctioning of their freedom. They consequently began to follow the army in droves. Congress soon clarified the First Confiscation Act by passing the Second Confiscation Act on July 17, 1862. This measure permitted the seizure of Confederate property, forbade Union soldiers from returning fugitive slaves, and permitted the president to employ blacks in order to fight the Confederacy. The passage of each of these measures provided enslaved people with hope for the complete abolition of slavery.

As 1862 progressed, enslaved women were more inclined to follow the Union Army, therefore many men and women deserted plantations. White southerners were shocked that their seemingly contented "Mammies" eagerly fled from bondage; however, this decision did not ease enslaved women's hardships as they faced discrimination from Union soldiers and withstood continued separation from family members. Formal emancipation came on January 1, 1863, when Lincoln's Emancipation Proclamation went into effect, liberating all bondpeople held in states participating in open rebellion against the United States.

While Union soldiers and officers were eager to liberate bondpeople in order to strip the Confederacy of the majority of its labor force, they did not necessarily support emancipation on moral grounds or provide for recently freed bondpeople's well-being. As the Union Army passed through the South, enslaved women who waited for their chance to follow the army in hopes of acquiring freedom were sometimes raped by soldiers whose sentiments towards bondpeople were difficult to gauge. On the one hand, gender did not deter acts of violence against enslaved women and many instances of rape occurred on plantations, causing bondwomen to wonder if the Union Army intended to protect them. On the other hand, many bondwomen took refuge with the Union Army and provided manual labor to aid the troops. Enslaved women in the South who remained on plantations also often decided to help Union prisoners of war who were fleeing from southern prisons such as Andersonville.

Enslaved Women and Work in the Union Army

When women deserted plantations in order to follow the Union Army, they performed valuable labor either voluntarily or by order of Union commanders. Bondwomen fled plantations not only to escape the confines of slavery, but also in search of sustenance. The Civil War took a toll on the South's food supply, often leaving farmlands barren as crops were sent to feed soldiers or as Union and Confederate soldiers lived off of the land through which they passed. Following the Union Army, then, would not only liberate enslaved women, but would also, they hoped, provide them with food, clothing, and shelter.

When bondwomen followed the Union Army, many labored as cooks and laundresses. They also sometimes nursed sick or wounded soldiers. The services that they provided for the Union Army were demonstrated most commonly in two ways. Bondwomen sometimes provided these services for voluntary or practical reasons, desiring to aid enlisted husbands, show gratitude for their freedom, or prove to the Union officers that they could be of use in the hopes of discouraging Union officers from sending them away from camp. As bondwomen began following the Union Army in droves, Union officials made few preparations for providing food, clothing, and shelter for the "contrabands" and so Union officers often put women to work so that the army could benefit from their efforts.

Oftentimes, there was no work for the wives of black Union soldiers to perform. Fearing separation from their loved ones, bondwomen—often accompanied by children and elderly bondpeople—followed the army closely and camped nearby. The droves of freed people posed a challenge for Union authorities. Federal soldiers received priority when it came to food, clothing, and medical attention. Because of this, many formerly enslaved women, children, and elderly followers became ill, went hungry, or lacked proper clothing.

Many Union soldiers and officers often welcomed the sight of former bondpeople following their army since this phenomenon significantly damaged the southern labor force. However, many members of the Union Army also became wary of the presence of thousands of former bondpeople following their forces since they could become a distraction to enlisted men. Not only did such contrabands create an added expense for the army, but many Union soldiers and officers deemed black women to be a sexual threat to white enlisted men. Because of this as well as the logistical problems inherent in caring for thousands of freed people, Union soldiers encouraged the formation of independent contraband camps, which freedpeople also desired.

Contraband Camps

Freed people established contraband camps of various sorts throughout the North and South. Following the issuance of the Emancipation Proclamation, Sojourner Truth and Harriet Jacobs, former bondwomen and prominent abolitionists, organized a freedmen's village for newly freed people in Washington, D.C. Another northern contraband camp was located at Cairo, Illinois. While other freed people who fled to the North either sought such villages or pursued job opportunities, freed people in the South often, with the help of the Union Army, frequently drew on family and kin networks to establish contraband camps where they received protection and lived in freedom with family members. Many contraband camps came into existence in the fall and winter of 1862 and were located at Corinth, Mississippi; Holly Springs, Mississippi; Lake Providence, Louisiana; Memphis, Tennessee; Lagrange, Tennessee; Bolivar, Tennessee; Grand Junction, Tennessee; and Jackson, Tennessee. Similarly, with the invasion of the Union Army, the Sea Islands of Georgia and South Carolina, once prominent cotton-growing locales in the antebellum South, became safe havens for former bondpeople both during and after the Civil War. In addition to these examples of large-scale contraband camps, small-scale camps were formed in areas of the South that the Union Army gained control of as the war progressed. In such locations, Federal officers often took over plantations formerly owned by white southerners and enabled former bondpeople to live on these plantations and perform work for the Union Army under their direction. Oftentimes, these arrangements facilitated the reunification of bondpeople's families that had been separated under slavery. While contraband camps often proved to be positive constructs for many bondpeople, some Union commanders operating in the Confederacy refused former bondpeople admission to such camps or even expelled some from camps for military reasons.

Summary and Postwar

The coming of the Civil War raised the hopes of enslaved people that freedom was within reach. As the Union Army pushed further into the South and achieved battlefield victories over the Confederacy, bondpeople's hopes for freedom increased. While Lincoln's Emancipation Proclamation officially made liberty a reality for some enslaved people, many learned that freedom was not going to immediately afford them a better life. As enslaved people left plantations to follow the Union Army, they continued to encounter discrimination and often found it difficult to procure food, clothing, and medical attention. Emancipated bondpeople also found themselves subject to the threat of recapture. Formerly enslaved women continued to face sexual threats from both northern and southern white men. Former bondpeople were wary of recapture until the ratification of the 13th Amendment in 1865, but still faced struggles adjusting to freedom in the postwar years. Although Congress established the Freedman's Bureau in 1865 in order to help educate, feed, clothe, and provide medical attention for newly freed people in the South, they continued to face struggles for full equality throughout the remainder of the nineteenth and even twentieth centuries.

Angela M. Zombek

See also Domestic Slave Trade; Family; Female Slave Network; Jacobs, Harriet; Labor; Mammy Stereotype; Truth, Sojourner; Violence, Racial; Violence, Sexual.

Suggested Reading

Ira Berlin and Leslie S. Rowland, eds., *Families and Freedom: A Documentary History of African-American Kinship in the Civil War Era* (New York: The New Press, 1997); Jim Downs, "The Other Side of Freedom: Destitution, Disease, and Dependency among Freed-women and Their Children during and after the Civil War," in *Battle Scars: Gender and Sexuality in the American Civil War*, eds. Catherine Clinton and Nina Silber (New York: Oxford University Press, 2006); Ellen Carol DuBois and Lynn Dumenil, *Through Women's Eyes: An American History* (New York: Bedford/St. Martin's, 2005); Michael Fellman, Lesley J. Gordon, and Daniel E. Sutherland, *This Terrible War: The Civil War and Its Aftermath*, 2nd ed. (New York: Pearson Longman, 2008); Noralee Frankel, "The Southern Side of 'Glory': Mississippi African-American Women during the Civil War," in *We Specialize in the Wholly Impossible: A Reader in Black Women's History*, eds. Darlene Clark Hine, Wilma King, and Linda Reed (Brooklyn: Carlson Publishing, Inc., 1995); Jacqueline Jones, *Labor of Love, Labor of Sorrow: Black Women, Work, and the Family from Slavery to the Present* (New York: Basic Books, Inc., Publishers, 1985); Susan A. Mann, "Slavery, Sharecropping, and Sexual Inequality," in *We Specialize in the Wholly Impossible: A Reader in Black Women's History*, eds. Darlene Clark Hine, Wilma King, and Linda Reed (Brooklyn: Carlson Publishing, Inc., 1995); Susie King Taylor, *Reminiscences of My Life: A Black Woman's Civil War Memoirs*, eds. Patricia W. Romero and Willie Lee Rose (New York: Markus Wiener Publishing, 1999); Deborah Gray White, *Ar'n't I a Woman?: Female Slaves in the Plantation South* (New York: W.W. Norton & Company, 1985).

Clothing

Dere wuz a lady dey had on de place did the weavin'. I had many a striped dress woven on dat big loom and dey wuz pretty, too.

—Suzanne Wyman, former bondwoman (*Georgia Narratives, Volume IV, Part 4*, 315)

Enslaved women were often involved in the production and consumption of cloth/clothing as field laborers, house servants, and other types of workers on southern plantations. Clothing was made of a variety of fabrics. These fabrics usually offered at least minimal protection from the weather. However, it had to be durable, inexpensive, and easy to make. Bondwomen's clothing changed little over the centuries of slavery; they wore long, rather full skirts with tied or buttoned front bodices (tops or blouses). Undergarments typically included a plain, white cotton shimmy (shift or chemise) and a petticoat. Shoes, when available, were usually made of coarse leather and tied up the front. Enslaved women might also wear a straw or cloth bonnet or a large handkerchief wrapped around the head. Clothing worn by enslaved females was usually made of white or blue cotton or cotton-wool blend in striped or calico patterns. Men's trousers and shirts were also made of cotton and cotton-wool blends; jackets were generally made of wool. Enslaved children wore garments similar to those of adults, although little boys often wore long shirttails. House servants seemed to fare better than field hands by receiving hand-me-down clothing from the planter and members of his family. This practice meant some slaves wore styles of clothing more closely related to fashionable dress of the period, better made, and of more expensive types of fabric: silk and silk-wool blends.

On the production end, enslaved seamstresses cut the fabric into distinctive rectangle and square pattern pieces for slave clothing as well as sewed the fabric pieces together. Spinning the cotton or wool into yarn was a tedious task, requiring skill and experience. Making the cloth was equally difficult, requiring knowledge of warping the loom and of specific weaving techniques in the making of homespun, the plain cloth made "at home." Planters usually distributed clothing and blankets to the slaves twice a year: in the fall and again in the spring. This allotment depended on the size of the plantation, the number of enslaved, the prosperity of the enslaver, and his/her sense of responsibility. The specific clothing dispersed also varied from plantation to plantation.

Even though clothing allotments per enslaved varied from plantation to plantation, the procurement of cloth and clothing followed a general pattern. After the mid-1850s, some plantations might have had a sewing machine, but likely much of the clothing was made by hand even after sewing machines became commonplace. If cloth or clothing was not manufactured on the plantation, it was purchased from local merchants or ordered from nearby factories.

Patricia Hunt-Hurst

Suggested Reading

Helen Bradley Foster, *"New Raiments of Self": African American Clothing in the Antebellum South* (New York: Berg Publishers, 1997); Patricia Hunt-Hurst, "Round Homespun Coat and Pantaloons of the Same: Slave Clothing as Reflected in Fugitive Slave Advertisements in Antebellum Georgia," *Georgia Historical Quarterly* (Winter 1999): 727–40; Gerilyn Tandberg, "Field Hand Clothing in Louisiana and Mississippi during the Ante-Bellum Period," *Dress* (1980): 89–102.

Community

Community is a prominent, though ill-defined concept in historical writing about slavery in the United States during the nineteenth century. It first gained common currency with the publication in 1972 of John W. Blassingame's landmark book,

The Slave Community. In a vast scholarly literature, community came to stand for a universal solidarity among slaves and their autonomy from slaveholders. Attention to slave women in the work of scholars such as Deborah Gray White and Brenda E. Stevenson has vastly complicated this portrait. Sexual exploitation of enslaved women such as rape and forced concubinage are grim testimony to the slaveholders' onslaught on the most elementary bonds among slaves. Solidarities among bondwomen and their contentions with bondmen marked out gender as a pervasive fault line within slave society. Solidarity among the enslaved no longer seems so universal, and the degree of slave's control over their own affairs is now debatable. As historians probe the conditions of slave solidarity, the shifting boundaries of slaves' struggles with owners, and the terms of a new paradigm for understanding slave society, community is most useful as a general rubric for an open-ended discussion of solidarities among bondwomen and women's particular roles in the solidarities of slave society as a whole. For explanatory purposes, it is useful as well to discuss communities in terms of specific social ties among slaves, but it is important to bear in mind that families, work, sociability, and resistance were overlapping and crosscutting in everyday life.

Kinship was the strongest bond in slave communities, and women were at the nexus of making these ties. Family was necessarily a keystone in building slave communities because ownership of slaves' children was at the foundation of slaveholders' rights in human property, and buying and selling families apart was routine in practice. Between 1790 and 1860, slaveholders sent over 1 million slaves on a forced migration from states like Virginia, Maryland, Kentucky, and Tennessee in the Upper South to Georgia, Alabama, Mississippi, Louisiana, and Texas in the Deep South, most via the Domestic Slave Trade. Perhaps twice as many slaves were sold within state lines. The constant buying and selling of slaves left families with an enormous task in the making and remaking of communities. As women made new bonds of kinship, they incorporated new members into communities, engendered ties between generations, established, extended, and reconfigured families, neighborhoods, and communities of other kinds.

Women took on a large share of the tasks families performed in making communities. They entered into intimate relations with men, who incorporated them into new communities, and did the same for men new to their communities. Women took sweethearts and husbands, bore children, raised families, and encouraged their sons and daughters to do likewise. They did so amid the exactions of slave trading and the migration to the Lower South and did it all again when those exactions fell on them. Courting, marriage, and other intimate relations with men on other farms and plantations were critical to cementing and extending neighborhood ties in general. Indeed, the geography of slaves' communities may well have varied with the geography of marriage. Neighborhoods comprised adjoining plantations in parts of the Lower South, like Mississippi, in no small part because that was the terrain of slave marriage. In the Upper South, where abroad marriage brought women and men together across larger distances, the geography of neighborhoods may well have extended well beyond adjoining plantations. Women, by no means, made new family ties lightly. On the contrary, parents, siblings, children, husbands, and friends women left behind remained dear to their hearts. They honored those bonds routinely by, for example, naming children after their own parents, retaining a family surname, or returning to old neighborhoods to find family members after the Civil War.

Making family a bulwark of community was a constant struggle. Women were obliged to fend off the sexual advances from owners, overseers, and drivers; speak up for themselves, their children, their men, and other family members when owners were inclined to punish or sell kinfolk. Women's sheer hope and determination to make new bonds when slaveholders broke the old ones account in large measure for the remarkable vitality of slave families. Women's place at the center of both nuclear and single-parent families that encompassed the overwhelming majority of all slaves and slave households leads many scholars to regard slave families on the whole as matrifocal. Given the importance of families among the varied bonds between slaves, it is arguable that slave communities were matrifocal (traced through the maternal ancestry) in general.

Women made communities in work as well as kinship. Just as family was necessarily a keystone of community building because breaking up families was so routine in the practice of American slaveholding, so slaves were compelled to build their communities partly in work because slavery was a system of labor. Bondwomen not only did the lion's share of cooking, washing, cleaning, and all the other reproductive labor that went into keeping families together body and soul, but also performed much of the work slaves did for other slave families. As cooks, they prepared the meals slaves ate in common; as midwives, they brought slave children into the world; as nurses, they looked after slave children while their parents worked away in the fields. The prevalence and importance of family ties on any given farm and in every neighborhood meant that women who worked as nurses or midwives or both could cut quite a figure in their communities. Midwives and body servants, whose work obliged them to get around more than most slaves, invariably made ties to other slaves abroad. On the whole, however, women were somewhat more confined, and perhaps more deeply grounded, in their neighborhood than some men, if only because the occupations that required most mobility, such as teamsters, carriage drivers, artisans, were predominantly men's work.

Women did much of the work bondpeople performed on their own account, and this labor was critical to making slaves' communities. Not all the work that slaves performed was for owners. Bondwomen put a great deal of work into producing food, clothing, and other goods for their own use and that of their families. Bondwomen also contributed to the surpluses that slaves produced in this economy.

In every region of the South, women worked in gardens allotted to slave families, produced other goods in addition, bought and sold goods on their own account, and accumulated property in their own right. This was family labor in virtually every dimension. Slaves organized their work, and pooled tools and other resources along with their earnings as families. Family labor, in turn, contributed mightily to community building at every stage. Slave women borrowed draft animals, plows, and other means of production from other families, exchanged goods with them and looked after property for them. Slave women also had a hand in creating and reconfiguring hierarchies in their community by accumulating, displaying, and comparing their own and their family's property. The goods, services, and cash slaves exchanged were, in addition to their practical uses, tokens of friendship, respect, love, favor, and obligation. The ability to share labor, exchange goods and money, and bequeath property enabled slaves to stake claims, provide services, and impose and fulfill obligations upon one another that were essential to making slave communities.

Slave women also made communities in struggle. Slaves were bound to come into conflict with slaveholders in cultivating bonds among themselves because slavery was based on the fiction that slaves' only tie that counted was to their owners. Speaking up for slaves in their communities was only one way women contended with owners and their agents. Women protested in deeds as well as words. They gave battle on every front across the entire spectrum of slave resistance. They ran away, sabotaged production, killed owners or overseers, took part in conspiracies and rebellions. Women absconded from owners to return to their community, fed and harbored runaways. Women also used the tools of their trades to strike at owners and their agents, slowing their progress through the crop rows, hoeing carelessly, picking meagerly and to resist increases in work, violations in the norms of discipline, among other impositions. Women raised their hands to owners, overseers, and drivers from time to time, and Robert Newsom of Missouri, who was killed in 1850 by the slave Celia, was only one among many owners who died by a bondwoman's hand. Lucy, a bondwoman in her twenties in Southampton County, was hanged for capturing her mistress and turning her over to rebels in the Nat Turner revolt of 1831. In running away, sabotage, and battling slaveholders to the death, women struggled to build communities in all the ways men did.

Yet the terms of struggle differed for bondwomen in important ways that reflected their particular modes of community building. In many ways, women entered the fray of community building where that project intersected with routines of work. Advertisements for runaways indicate that women ran away less often than men, partly because the relatively few mobile occupations open to them made the terrain unfamiliar beyond a certain point. Poison seems to have been bondwomen's preferred weapon, probably because they developed the skills, obtained the resources, and had the opportunity to do away with slaveholders that way, thanks to their work as cooks. If the sexual division of labor constrained the terms of struggle for bondwomen, they also contended with owners in unique ways that promoted community. Women often absconded with their husband, children, or some other group. Thus, the burdens of reproductive labor that kept women at home also prompted them to bring people along when they did abscond.

Building communities obliged women to collaborate with owners as well as contend with other slaves from time to time. Women solicited owners' permission for husbands to visit regularly from abroad and to go visiting to see kin or friends in the neighborhood and beyond. Women advocated for others in their communities in warm tones as well as vituperative protests. Circumstances also compelled women on occasion to inform on thieves, runaways, or other bondpeople whose transgressive behavior posed risks for others in their communities. It would be a mistake to see such antagonisms with other slaves or alliances with owners simply as lapses of solidarity. No people can make communities of any kind without striking some compromises with their antagonists or brooking some conflict with other members and allies. The extreme imbalances in the power relations of slavery made such compromises and conflicts all the more necessary for slave women. The conflicting imperatives or family, work, and discipline necessarily engendered conflicts with slaves and accommodations to owners as bondpeople juggled their extraordinary obligations to slaveholders, kin, and other members of their communities. This terrain was all the more difficult for slave women to navigate, given the unique burdens they bore in reproductive labor and constraints of their terrain of struggle.

If building communities could be a struggle, it could also be a pleasure, many pleasures, in fact. Enslaved women made communities partying, visiting, and socializing of all sorts. They entertained visitors and went to visit kin and friends in other cabins in the quarters and on other farms and plantations in the neighborhood. They strutted their stuff at clandestine dances. They threw more or less formal balls and weddings with owners' approval. Women did much of the cooking, making of clothes, and other labor that went into bringing off such affairs. Women's schedule of amusements was especially full during the precious few down times in the annual routines of agricultural labor. The paths between plantations were most crowded between Saturday afternoon and Monday morning. When staple crops were "laid by" in the summer and around Christmas, before and after the harvest, respectively, were the seasons for weddings, balls, and other approved celebrations. Women also socialized at religious services, funerals, and other solemn affairs. And whenever women exchanged news, told stories, chatted, laughed, and shared conventional wisdoms along with novel lessons of experience with other slaves, they were also doing the serious and incessant work of building communities. Though women shared gossip, tales, and good cheer, they also conveyed expectations, norms, and judgments that went a long way to creating the consensus and shared experiences that forge communities and keep them together.

Women created communities among themselves as they did their part in creating communities among others. The particular burdens they confronted in their families, at work, and in struggle did much, in turn, to engender the bonds between women. Women socialized as they prepared meals day in and day out and as they washed clothes, worked the gardens in the evenings, on Saturday afternoons, and Sundays. Women contended with slaveholders on their own whenever they did work gendered female, when they hoed or plowed in separate gangs, or when they made clothing under mistress's supervision. The solidarity among women was unique to the considerable extent it was forged in struggles and joys only they experienced. Women forged singular bonds as they relied on one another for advice, help, and comfort confronting sexual exploitation, the mysteries of their bodies, of courtship, of childbearing and rearing, among other ordeals and milestones.

Enslaved women established not one but many communities. In addition to that of gender, they fashioned overlapping communities around particular activities, places, and identities. They made formidable ties in Christian worship, work gangs, and landmark struggles, on the farms or plantations where they lived, on adjoining places, in the neighborhood, and beyond. They thought of one another as family, friends, Christians, neighbors, and women. Women felt more deeply connected to some of their communities than others, felt some ties more strongly at particular moments or in particular places. They might feel their Christian fellowship with their sisters and brethren more fully on Sundays at church than another evening when they were dancing at a clandestine party with their sweetheart or friends in the woods. They might feel closer to kinfolk during evenings in the cabin than they felt to anyone in the world, yet the neighborhood could also make its presence powerfully felt visiting on nearby farms or plantations. These communities were neither universal, nor permanent, nor mutually exclusive. Rather, they were made, unmade, remade, and coexisted with other communities of women, who joined some communities and held aloof from others, finding common cause with some folks while keeping their distance from or coming into conflict with other women and men. Slavery imposed enormous obstacles in the way of creating communities, yet women demonstrated a persistence and ingenuity more than equal to the task.

Anthony E. Kaye

See also Celia; Domestic Slave Trade; Economy; Family; Runaways.

Suggested Reading

John W. Blassingame, *The Slave Community: Plantation Life in the Antebellum South*, rev. ed. (New York: Oxford University Press, 1979); Stephanie M. H. Camp, *Closer to Freedom: Enslaved Women and Everyday Resistance in the Plantation South* (Chapel Hill: University of North Carolina Press, 2004); Michael A. Gomez, *Exchanging Our Country*

Marks: The Transformation of African Identities in the Colonial and Antebellum South (Chapel Hill: University of North Carolina Press, 1998); Herbert G. Gutman, *The Black Family in Slavery and Freedom, 1750–1925* (New York: Random House, 1976); Anthony E. Kaye, *Joining Places: Slave Neighborhoods in the Old South* (Chapel Hill: University of North Carolina Press, 2007); Dylan C. Penningroth, *Claims of Kinfolk: African American Property and Community in the Nineteenth Century South* (Chapel Hill: University of North Carolina Press, 2002); Albert J. Raboteau, *Slave Religion: The "Invisible Institution" in the Antebellum South* (New York: Oxford University Press, 1978); Thomas L. Webber, *Deep Like the Rivers: Education in the Slave Quarter Community, 1831–1865* (New York: W.W. Norton, 1978); Deborah Gray White, *Ar'n't I a Woman? Female Slaves in the Plantation South*, rev. ed. (New York: W.W. Norton, 1999).

Concubinage

A concubine is a term used to describe a free or enslaved woman who was kept as a partner, usually for sexual purposes, to a man of significant social standing. The concubine relationship existed in the context of slave laws that forbade interracial marriage as a threat to hereditary racial slavery. The enslaved or free female in such an arrangement might live separated from her community in a house set up by the white male or reside in slave quarters

> *When a father can sell his own child, humiliate his own daughter by auctioning her on the auction block, what good could be expected where such practices were allowed? [. . .] That was the greatest crime ever visited on the United States.*
>
> —Amy Elizabeth Patterson, former bondwoman *(Born in Slavery: Slave Narratives from the Federal Writers' Project, 1936–1938 Indiana Narratives, Volume V, 151)*

and receive material rewards for her alleged loyalty to him. She most likely would produce children from this sexual arrangement and unless free herself, her children remained enslaved at the white male's discretion. There is evidence that where systems of slavery existed in the Americas some of these arrangements may have lasted for decades and the women involved sometimes gained significant wealth in land and property. In antebellum southern cities such as New Orleans, both enslaved and free women's sexualities were commodified in the marketplace. Enslaved and free women negotiated this market from different life circumstances.

Historians often characterize relationships between white men and women of color as mutually consenting and for enslaved women, a route to freedom for themselves and their children. Remarking on the benefits to free women of color, historians regard these relationships as providing social protection and material sustenance in communities that were inhospitable and economically limiting to free people of color. Black and mixed race women in concubine relationships sometimes built social and economic statuses that they passed onto their children resulting in complex and hierarchical relationships with other free and enslaved people. Some formerly enslaved women even became slave owners themselves. However materially beneficial these partnerships may have been for the women of color, these associations also involved unequal power relations which left many of them without choice, protection, and social or material benefit. Faced with poverty, the threat of violence, and death, free women of color and enslaved women had little choice in their sexual involvement with white men. Free women of color could never achieve the role of wife and were thus dependent on the continued favor of their white partner. The possibilities of abuse, coercion, and abandonment remained high for many of these women and the alternative to consent may have cost them their lives and the perpetual enslavement of their children. Concubine relationships afforded women of color material gains and access to freedom, but the coercive nature of these associations and the ultimate vulnerability of the women within such arrangements illuminated these women's lack of choice and control over their bodies in slave societies.

Marisa J. Fuentes

See also Breeding; Celia; Fancy Girls; Hemings, Sally; Jezebel Stereotype; Miscegenation; Sexuality.

Suggested Reading

Doris Garraway, *The Libertine Colony: Creolization in the Early French Caribbean* (Durham: Duke University Press, 2005); Saidiya Hartman, *Scenes of Subjection: Terror, Slavery, and Self-Making in Nineteenth-Century America* (New York: Oxford University Press, 1997); Jennifer Morgan, *Laboring Women: Reproduction and Gender in New World Slavery* (Philadelphia: University of Pennsylvania Press, 2004); Deborah Gray White, *Ar'n't I a Woman: Female Slaves in the Plantation South* (New York: W.W. Norton & Company, 1985).

Conflict, Intraracial

Certainly the most notable form of conflict enslaved women experienced involved members of other races ruling over them; however, they undoubtedly had altercations with members of their own race as well. The dimensions of conflict were traditionally confined to work, familial relationships, and social interactions ranging from emotional and verbal problems to physically violent encounters.

The institution of slavery placed a great deal of stress on enslaved men and women. The division of labor based on gender created a contentious atmosphere for all involved. Men's jobs generally allowed for more mobility whereas bondwomen were usually confined to the homestead, planting, performing domestic services, and caring for children. Likewise, women often received the clothing

and food allotments, which sometimes placed them at odds with their male counterparts. Large plantation records provide rich sources for interpreting the gendered division of labor and supplies. Because some slaveholders ignored the
bondman's parental connections and disrupted slave marriages, it is no surprise
that some relationships among the enslaved included domestic violence.

Marriages were difficult to maintain under the institution of slavery and men
often lived on separate plantations from their wives. Issues regarding family support and allegations of infidelity also served as a source of conflict. Some enslaved
couples did, however, marry and live together. In some marriages, verbal abuse
existed, as did physical abuse. Most commonly, men beat their wives in order to
make them work or to control their property. Women were sometimes reported
as the abusers, whether verbal or physical, but not to the extent that men were.
On occasion, extended family members had to intervene in disputes between husbands and wives.

Sexual relationships between men and women provided another area for conflict. Mothers consistently clashed with teenage daughters over their relationships
with men. Women did not want their young daughters sexually abused by men on
the plantation and their attempts to control their daughters were often met with
resentment and resistance. When young women were allowed to seek a male partner, they sometimes found themselves competing with other women for the affection of men. As a result, verbal altercations and even physical violence often
erupted over intimate relationships.

Negotiations and arguments over property were also common among the
enslaved, and women were central players in these disagreements because of their
control over the living quarters. Women spent much of their time with other
women due to the gendered distribution of work and their common household
chores. These instances of female bonding also provided women an arena for
potential disagreement. Women fought over men, argued over differences in childrearing styles, and sometimes squabbled over the access to material goods. Jealousy over clothing like hand-me-downs from a master's wife would often lead to
shouting matches and sometimes resulted in physical violence. Despite multiple
areas of conflict, it is clear that the violent nature of slavery as well as the demographics of a particular community contributed to the strain on interactions among
the enslaved.

Angela Ruth Danley

See also Gender Conventions; Marriage, Abroad.

Suggested Reading

Anthony E. Kaye, *Joining Places: Slave Neighborhoods in the Old South* (Chapel Hill:
University of North Carolina Press, 2007); Dylan C. Penningroth, *The Claims of Kinfolk:*

African American Property and Community in the Nineteenth-Century South (Chapel Hill: University of North Carolina Press, 2003); Brenda Stevenson, "Distress and Discord in Virginia Slave Families, 1830–1860," in *In Joy and in Sorrow: Women, Family and Marriage in the Victorian South*, ed. Carol Bleser (New York: Oxford University Press, 1991); Deborah Gray White, *Ar'n't I a Woman? Female Slaves in the Plantation South*, rev. ed. (New York: W.W. Norton and Company, 1999).

Conjurers

Traditional African societies like their enslaved New World descendents consulted conjurers. These practitioners were highly respected religious African women and men with "extraordinary powers" (Chireau 2003, 21). They were considered activators of *ashe*—persons possessing the power and ability to make things happen. These societies relied on the practitioner's supernatural and mental sensibilities to aid them in their revolutions; to fight the white men and protect them in their day-to-day activities. Practitioners were known to control weather, summon rain for harvest, create charms, receive and interpret communication from the spirit world, become invisible, and fly.

Various terms were appropriated to describe these women and men practitioners who "worked the spirits" (Ibid). Once the tradition migrated to North America, they came to be known as conjurers. The term "conjurer" was commonly used for identifying African supernatural practitioners in North America; persons who engage in conjuring—is an act in which "spiritual power is invoked for various purposes, such as healing, protection, and self defense" (Ibid). By the nineteenth century, enslaved and free women and men appropriated other names such as Hoodoos, root workers, Root doctors, Conjure doctors, Goopher-doctors, Two-Head doctors, or Wise men. These terms were region-specific titles for folk practitioners, as were Longheads, and Double-sighters—root workers found in Florida, South Carolina, and Georgia. Throughout Louisiana and Mississippi, conjurers were known as Voodoos, wangateurs, and horses.

Conjurers had distinguishable physical characteristics such as unusual and discernable "birthmarks or abnormalities such as harelips, red eyes, or eyes of different colors" (Ibid). The conjurer tradition was passed down from generation to generation among family members or taught to young protégés who exhibited proficiency or talent. Others were born with the gift or experienced divine commission (similar to the call to Christian ministry).

Although conjurers were considered heathens practicing evil magic, some saw conjurers as well-versed in animating the spirit world on their behalf—skilled practitioners who provided pragmatic solutions to life's challenges and problems. In North American slave communities, conjurers were "entrusted with the knowledge and responsibility for maintaining spiritual traditions"—visionaries and healers were mediators between slaves and the spirit world" (Coleman 2000, 44). They possessed the power to do harm as well as heal and the women practitioners among them "made their mark in significant numbers" (Coleman 2000; Chireau 2003, 22). Theologian Will Coleman argues that conjurers discovered effective ways to prevent attacks or to cause harm to the originator of slaves' misfortune or ill treatment. Chireau asserts black Americans utilized conjuring traditions not only because they saw them as a valuable resource for resistance, but because they believed that the supernatural realm offered alternative possibilities for empowerment.

Enslaved communities often sought conjurers' wisdom in preparation for small- and large-scale slave revolts. Conjuring arbitrated slaves' day-to-day confrontations with slaveholders' domination which was enforced through violent means and racial oppression. Although conjurers' practices and motives were often questioned, Coleman and historian Albert Raboteau note that even well-known skeptics, such as Frederick Douglass, consulted conjurers. Douglass turned to a well-known conjurer named Sandy Jenkins to help him deal with his brutal master, Edward Covey. Both female and male conjurers played a key role in the successful outcome of various individual acts of resistance and small- and large-scale slave revolts in the New World.

Renee K. Harrison

See also Religion; Resistance.

Suggested Reading

Yvonne P. Chireau, *Black Magic: Religion and the African American Conjuring Tradition* (Berkeley: University of California Press, 2003); Will Coleman, *Tribal Talk: Black Theology, Hermeneutics, and African/American Ways of "Telling the Story"* (Pennsylvania: The Pennsylvania State University Press, 2000); Albert J. Raboteau, *Slave Religion: The Invisible Institution in the Antebellum South* (New York: Oxford University Press, 1978).

Contraception

Many enslaved women were familiar with medicinal herbs and other means of delaying or preventing pregnancies. Although the claims by southern enslavers and physicians, alleging that enslaved women frequently and strategically avoided pregnancies were probably exaggerated, there is evidence that contraceptives were utilized within the slave community.

The West African societies from which so many enslaved Africans or their ancestors originated had well-established practices and rituals for regulating a woman's fertility. At the Bight of Benin, for example, pregnant women typically upheld sexual abstinence throughout the duration of the pregnancy with the belief that doing so would protect the unborn child. This policy of abstinence, which continued for at least a year and a half after birth, would have decreased a woman's chances of adverse health consequences due to stress placed on her body from back-to-back pregnancies. Birth spacing was regulated further among African women through the disruption of regular ovulation cycles due to prolonged breast-feeding. Though modified because of the constraints of slavery in the New World, abstinence, extended breastfeeding, and other practices geared toward managing the frequency of pregnancies seem to have been transported to the Americas.

In addition to the utilization of abortifacients derived from African plants such as okra and aloe, enslaved women's knowledge of emmenagogues, substances used to stimulate or regulate menstruation, could be partially traced back to Africa. Prior to the beginning of the Transatlantic Slave Trade, African women widely used the root of the cotton plant or tree as a form of birth control and in other ways. In the U.S. South, cotton roots, either chewed or brewed into a tea, was the most popular emmenagogue used by enslaved women due to its efficacy and wide availability. Because enslaved women or their counterparts in Africa did not believe that pregnancy was the only cause of suppressed menstruation, emmenagogues might be used without consciously seeking to induce a miscarriage.

Many of the medicinal plants used by enslaved women were easy to prepare and readily available. In the Americas, enslaved women in general gained familiarity with local plants used for medicinal purposes through their participation in domestic production. Slaveholding mistresses' frequently required that enslaved females gather plants for a variety of household purposes. Enslaved women also utilized their knowledge of roots and herbs for the care of their families and other members of the slave community. Equipped with a basic knowledge of local plants and their uses, an ordinary enslaved woman might use roots or herbs to regulate her fertility in secrecy and without assistance. There were, however, other substances, such as "black haw," which prevented conception and required very involved preparation and thus, were available only through knowledgeable healers. Of course, whenever a woman relied on another person for help in avoiding pregnancy, she opened up the possibility that such personal information might be shared if an enslaver or other interested party had reason to be suspicious and began to ask questions.

Other means believed to regulate fertility included the use of the lunar calendar to track menstruation regularity and techniques employed during and after sexual intercourse. Some practices that were thought to prevent pregnancy include holding a brass pin or copper coin under the tongue or being motionless during intercourse, turning on one's left side after sex, and drinking gunpowder with milk. It is unclear to what extent such practices may have been utilized. More generally, it is nearly impossible to know with any degree of certainty what factors other than conscious actions taken by an enslaved woman, may have contributed to her being described as infertile by her master. While enslavers accused female slaves of preventing pregnancy and deliberately inducing miscarriages, the conditions under which enslaved persons lived and worked also had an adverse influence on women's fertility. Southern physicians reported that enslaved women used contraceptives and abortifacients, but they also pointed to a variety of factors such as overwork and the supposed sexual indulgence of enslaved women as playing a role in the fact that they did not always reproduce as prolifically as enslavers hoped. Environmental exposures such as lead and diseases such as tetanus, whooping cough, and pneumonia undoubtedly affected the enslaved females' fertility rates. Fertility was further reduced by improper diet and nutrition and harsh labor requirements.

Enslavers looking after their long-term economic prospects preferred fertile female slaves, however enslaved women pursued ways to space their births so as to ensure their own health and the health of their children. And, though pressured by enslavers to reproduce, it is clear that enslaved women also sought to have children for reasons of their own. Because motherhood and children were valued within slave communities, enslaved women generally did not aim to prevent conception altogether. Extended breastfeeding for at least two years often provided the desired, temporary contraceptive results, though enslavers often wanted infants to be weaned as soon as possible, around 8 to 12 months. While not completely aware of how breastfeeding suppresses ovulation, enslaved women nonetheless knew that they had a decreased risk of becoming pregnant while breastfeeding.

Notwithstanding tremendous obstacles to establishing families throughout the entire period of enslavement, the fertility rate of enslaved women resembled that of white Southern women by the mid-nineteenth century. Enslaved women faced tremendous obstacles to reproduction from the time of the earliest colonial settlements through the antebellum years. Indeed, the first generation of enslaved people born in America had more children than their African mothers, who avoided pregnancy for two or more years while nursing their infants. In contrast with other places in the Americas, the North American enslaved population grew by human reproduction from the early eighteenth century. By 1825, the American enslaved population had grown to 1.75 million. By the 1850s, the natural rate of increase among the U.S. slave population was significant due to extremely high rates of birth, offsetting relatively high rates of death.

Given the impressive growth of the enslaved population over time, it would seem that female slaves' birth control strategies were insignificant. Still, it is noteworthy that many ex-slaves later recalled the widespread usage of cotton root and other contraceptive agents. Also, during the 1840s and 1850s, many enslavers focused on enslaved women's contraceptive strategies as they worked to expand and improve their management of the enslaved population and their policies for achieving greater plantation discipline and control. Enslavers' preoccupation with deception by enslaved persons centered on healers who were charged with reporting the condition of slaves, particularly with the reproductive health of enslaved women. During this time, slaveholders seemed to have fixated more than ever before on whether women deliberately brought about miscarriages and infertility through measures kept secret from whites. Though enslavers' allegations were likely exaggerated, enslaved women undoubtedly had access to a variety of contraceptive strategies to draw upon as they exerted control over their reproductive lives.

Kimberly Sambol-Tosco

See also Abortion; Breeding; Childbirth; Female Slave Network; Folk Medicine and Healing; Infanticide; Motherhood; Pregnancy.

Suggested Reading

Sharla M. Fett, *Working Cures: Healing, Health, and Power on Southern Slave Plantations* (Chapel Hill and London: University of North Carolina Press, 2002); Jennifer L. Morgan, *Laboring Women: Reproduction and Gender in New World Slavery* (Philadelphia: University of Pennsylvania Press, 2004); Liese M. Perrin, "Resisting Reproduction: Reconsidering Slave Contraception in the Old South," *Journal of American Studies* 35, 2 (2001): 255–74; Dorothy Roberts, *Killing the Black Body: Race, Reproduction, and the Meaning of Liberty* (New York: Pantheon Books, 1997); Marie Jenkins Schwartz, *Birthing a Slave: Motherhood and Medicine in the Antebellum South* (Cambridge, MA and London: Harvard University Press, 2006).

Courtship

Courtship marked an important part of the enslaved woman's life cycle. Generally, the courting process began with the onset of puberty. During this period of physiological and mental maturation, enslaved girls no longer viewed boys as playmates, but rather as objects of affection. To gain the attention of a particular enslaved boy, the girls wore makeup made from berries, adorned their hair with kerchiefs and ribbons, designed jewelry made of nuts, perfumed themselves with honeysuckles, roses, and orchids, and wore colorful, ornate dresses. This self-adornment process was not used for the daily plantation life, but rather for communal events such as weddings, funerals, harvest fests, and the like.

Enslaved adolescents engaged in the courtship process with their young mates. Work was first and foremost, thus the opportunities for courtship and leisure time were rare. The best opportunity for courtship occurred during holidays and special celebrations. Dances were also occasions to seek and establish relationships. During these events the older youth paired up with bondpeople of the opposite sex. Corn shuckings also allowed enslaved girls to mingle with boys.

Once paired off and away from the watchful eyes of enslaved adults and the curious eyes of enslaved children, enslaved girls experimented with their bodies and that of their mates. Kissing games, a part of the courtship process, catapulted enslaved girls into the adult world of minor sexual activity. These games included "Walking the Lonesome Road," "In the Well," "Fruit in the Basket," and others. In these games, the person was subjected to some type of hardship (i.e., stuck in a well) in which a kiss could only be used for his or her rescue.

Black and white adults had conflicting views concerning teen girls courting. Many enslaved parents worked diligently to delay courtship because they realized that it could propel teenage girls to an early awareness of their sexuality and the prospect of motherhood under the confines of slavery. Slaveholders, desiring that enslaved girls begin to reproduce, wholeheartedly supported courtship among the enslaved population. Some enslavers even went so far as to arrange relationships between teenage boys and girls. Despite the divergent views and interests concerning courtship among adults, it was an important part of the teen experience, though met with the realities of sexual exploitation under the institution of enslavement.

Courtship was a significant rite in the life cycle of bondwomen's experience. It introduced enslaved females to young men and made them aware of their budding sexuality. Moreover, courtship oftentimes led to pregnancy and or marriage, rites that hurled teenage girls into adulthood as well as resulting in yet more children born into slavery.

Courtney Moore Taylor

See also Gender Conventions; Hair and Headdresses; Life Cycle.

Suggested Reading

Elizabeth Fox-Genovese, *Within the Plantation Household: Black and White Women of the Old South* (Chapel Hill: University of North Carolina Press, 1988); Wilma King, *Stolen Childhood: Slave Youth in Nineteenth-Century America* (Indianapolis: Indiana University Press, 1995); Marie Schwartz, *Born in Bondage: Growing Up Enslaved in the Antebellum South* (Cambridge: Harvard University Press, 2000); Emily West, *Chains of Love: Slave Couples in Antebellum South Carolina* (Chicago: University of Illinois Press, 2004); Deborah Gray White, *Ar'n't I a Woman?: Female Slaves in the Plantation South* (New York: W.W. Norton & Company, 1985).

Craft, Ellen

Birth Date: ~1826
Death Date: 1891

In 1848, Ellen Craft and her husband William escaped slavery in Georgia. The mixed-race Craft could pass as a white person, so she disguised herself as a white

William and Ellen Craft pictured sometime after their escape and repatriation to England. (Eon Images.)

slaveholder, traveling to Philadelphia to gain treatments for rheumatism and other ailments. William pretended to be her black body servant. For several days, they traveled by rail, ship, and carriage to the free states. By 1849, they had settled in Boston, the center of the American antislavery movement.

Craft and her husband appeared at events throughout New England in order to agitate against slavery and to tell the story of their courageous, clever escape. She impressed northern audiences with her remarks and behavior that reinforced nineteenth-century notions of good women as modest, maternal, pious, and demure. Yet she also achieved celebrity in abolitionist circles for her fearlessness and outspokenness, as well as for her willingness to risk the dangers of kidnapping or recapture that she and her husband faced. The prospect of her becoming re-enslaved intensified when the U.S. Congress passed the Fugitive Slave Law of 1850, which authorized police, judges, and other officers of the law to assist enslavers in retrieving their human "property," and punished anyone who attempted to protect fugitives from discovery. Robert Collins, Craft's enslaver sent Willis Hughes and John Knight to recapture the couple and bring them back to Georgia. These efforts galvanized the Vigilance Committee, an interracial organization of black and white Bostonians created to thwart the Fugitive Slave Law. Vigilance Committee members separated Craft from William and secretly shuttled her among private homes in Brookline, Cambridge, and other suburbs. Hughes and Knight returned empty-handed to the South, and the Crafts traveled secretly to Nova Scotia, Canada, where they boarded the Cambria for Liverpool on December 11, 1850.

The Crafts continued their public activism on the other side of the Atlantic. An engraving of Craft in the masculine clothing she had worn to escape slavery appeared in the *Illustrated London News*, and the Leeds Antislavery Society sold copies of the image. In London's popular Crystal Palace, a highlight of the World's Fair, Craft accompanied William and other abolitionists to challenge and embarrass enslavers attending the American exhibit. As beneficiaries of Lady Byron's patronage, she and William spent two years getting an education at the experimental Ockham School in Surrey. They collaboratively wrote about their escapes from and experiences in American slavery in a memoir entitled *Running a Thousand Miles for Freedom*, published in London in 1860.

Ellen Craft, as depicted in a nineteenth-century illustration of her "disguised as a young planter" during her escape in 1848. (Eon Images.)

From their home in Hammersmith, outside of London, while raising their five children, Craft continued to speak out against slavery. In 1869, she and William returned to Georgia, where they used the education they had obtained overseas to educate former enslaved men and women.

Barbara McCaskill

See also Abolitionism; Gender Conventions; Narratives; North, The; Runaways; Underground Railroad.

Suggested Reading

R. J. M. Blackett, *Beating against the Barriers: Biographical Essays in Nineteenth-Century Afro-American History* (Baton Rouge: Louisiana State University Press, 1983); Georgia Women of Achievement Web site: http://www.gawomen.org/honorees/crafte. htm; Barbara McCaskill, ed., *Running 1,000 Miles for Freedom: The Narrative of William and Ellen Craft* (Athens: University of Georgia Press, 1999).

Creoles

The term "Creole" originates from the Portuguese word *crioulo*, meaning a bond-person of African descent born in the New World. Over time, however, the term acquired numerous definitions in the United States and abroad to emphasize an individual's birthplace, race, and social status within the Americas. In the United States during the eighteenth and nineteenth centuries, the word "Creole" referred predominantly to American-born individuals both slave and free, of at least partial African descent. A Creole bondwoman was an individual of African or mixed ancestry (African, European, and/or Native American) born in the United States.

In the late eighteenth century, the U.S. enslaved population was more Creole than African and by the mid-nineteenth century, it was almost entirely Creole. The rapid development of a massive Creole slave population made the United States unique in comparison to other slave societies in the Americas. Creole bond-women were the cause of this rapid population increase because they lived longer lives, were healthier, more fertile, and more willing to have children than their female African forbears (Morgan 2004, 86–87).

Creole bondwomen constituted the first generations of African American women. They were born to enslaved African or Creole women through acts of love, lust, choice, coercion, or rape. These women shaped Creole and African American culture. They played a strategic role in transmitting and transforming their ancestors' African culture into the New World. Creole bondwomen created new languages, foods, music, fashion, and cultural belief systems by retaining, adopting, blending, and abandoning different elements of African, European, and American cultures.

Two prime examples of Creole bondwomen's impact on the United States can best be found in the language and dress of Louisiana. While Creole bondpeople existed throughout the United States, Creole bondpersons and Creole slave culture is most commonly associated with the Lower South, especially in Louisiana and the city of New Orleans. The first Creole slave generation in Louisiana created Louisiana creole, a language that consists of French vocabulary and African grammatical structure, as a way to communicate with whites and other Creole bondpeople who spoke a distinctly different African language. Throughout the nineteenth century, Louisiana creole became one of the three primary languages spoken in Louisiana by both black and white, free and enslaved. Examples of Creole bondwomen's influence on Creole and African American culture include the spoken Louisiana creole language and the headcloth or wrap. Creole bondwomen adopted from their African mothers and grandmothers the tradition of wearing head-scarves. Through this transfer of culture, the headscarf, headcloth, or wrap became a key element of enslaved Creole women's dress and future African American fashion.

Lindsey Gish

See also African Women and African-born women; Folklore and Folktales; Gullah Culture; Hair and Headdresses; South, The; Violence, Sexual.

Suggested Reading

Afro-Louisiana History and Genealogy, 1719–1820. http://www.ibiblio.org/laslave/; Creoles of Color in 19th Century New Orleans. http://www.creolehistory.com/; French Creoles of America. http://www.frenchcreoles.com; Ira Berlin, *Many Thousands Gone: The First Two Centuries of Slavery in North America* (Cambridge: Harvard University Press, 1998); Gwendolyn Midlo Hall, *Africans in Colonial Louisiana: The Development of Afro-Creole Culture in the Eighteenth Century* (Baton Rouge: Louisiana State University Press, 1992): 156–200; Arnold R. Hirsch and Joseph Logsdon, eds., *Creole New Orleans: Race and Americanization* (Baton Rouge: Louisiana State University Press, 1992); Jennifer L. Morgan, *Laboring Women: Reproduction and Gender in New World Slavery* (Philadelphia: University of Pennsylvania Press, 2004).

D

Death

See Mortality and Life Expectancy

Decorative Arts

The continuation of West African cultural patterns and traditions in the production of decorative arts among enslaved women in the United States provided a meaningful basis for shared memory. It also offered bondwomen a means to address the trauma experienced by the forced separation from their homeland. This expression could be subtle, such as color preference, or more direct, such as making pottery and wearing head rags as fashion elements. Connections to a West African design heritage also appear in witch trees (or "bottle trees") and other gardening elements, in coil baskets and decorated graves, and especially in the production of textiles such as strip quilts and Harriet Powers' iconic Bible quilts.

Many of the decorative arts created by enslaved women reflect the influences of West Africa as well as of Europe and America. For example, swept yards represented African modes of landscaping and promoted family life and community identity, even though they derived from both African and European sources. Also, the enslaved women's presence in white homes accelerated some forms of acculturation by a perceived measure of power and sense of dignity through evidencing a command of the dominant culture. Many enslaved women became expert seamstresses, and innumerable masterworks of antebellum clothing and textiles are known to be by their hands. Flower cultivation, flower arrangement, food presentation and table arrangement, as well as multiple other domestic arts were practiced by enslaved women.

The adoption by enslaved women in their decorative arts of visible modes of the dominant culture allowed for an eventual claim to "American-ness," a sense that the society that had enslaved them belonged to them as well as they to it. Inherent in this sense of belonging was the demand for parity. Although this process is similar to identity transference among other immigrant groups, it is a remarkable development in terms of the power matrix of American slavery. The preservation of West African culture in the lives of American slave women, however, was central to their resistance to complete acculturation and represented empowering links to their homelands.

Perhaps most importantly, the expression of design in private space created a sense of personal order and self-empowerment over their environment that steeled these women for the burden of oppression that they faced which eventually aided them in sustaining families, creating communities, and gaining freedom. Throughout the slave interviews are references to home improvement, private quilting, and sources for dyes and even "teas" for color-staining furniture. Clearly, enslaved women were able even in restricted circumstances to carve out a unique domain in their lives for the expression of their decorative sense and to engage in a distinct measure of personal joy that such expressions provide.

Ashley Callahan and Dale Couch

See also Burial Customs; Clothing; Gardening; Hair and Headdresses; Quilting; Seamstress Work; Slave Quarters, Life in.

Suggested Reading

Daina Ramey Berry, " 'We Sho Was Dressed Up': Slave Women, Material Culture and Decorative Arts in Wilkes County, Georgia," in *The Savannah River Valley to 1865: Fine Arts, Architecture, and Decorative Arts*, ed. Ashley Callahan (Athens: Georgia Museum of Art, 2003), 73–83; John Burrison, *Roots of a Region: Southern Folk Culture* (University of Mississippi Press, 2007); Edward D. C. Campbell, *Before Freedom Came: African-American Life in the Antebellum South* (Charlottesville: University Press of Virginia, 1991); Leland Ferguson, *Uncommon Ground: Archaeology and Early African America, 1650–1800* (Washington, DC: Smithsonian Institution Press, 1992); Gladys-Marie Fry, *Stitched from the Soul: Slave Quilts from the Antebellum South* (Chapel Hill: University of North Carolina Press, 2002); Dale Rosengarten, *Row Upon Row: Sea Grass Baskets of the South Carolina Low Country* (Columbia: University of South Carolina Press, 1993); John Michael Vlach, *By the Work of Their Hands: Studies in Afro-American Folklife* (Charlottesville: University Press of Virginia, 1991); John Michael Vlach, *The Afro-American Tradition in Decorative Arts* (Athens: University of Georgia Press, 1978).

Delaney, Lucy A.

Birth Date: ~1828
Death Date: 1910

Lucy Ann Delaney was an enslaved woman who sued for her freedom in St. Louis, Missouri in 1844. She wrote a narrative in the early 1890s, entitled *From the Darkness Cometh the Light; or Struggles for Freedom*, which discusses her successful freedom suit against David Mitchell, as well as her life before and after the case. Delaney's narrative is significant because hers is the only existing firsthand description of a slave's experience in a freedom suit and it addresses a variety of aspects of the female slave experience.

Records of Delaney's parents, Polly Crockett (later referred to as Polly Berry or Polly Wash) and her father's name unknown appear in the 1820s on the plantation of Taylor Berry. The couple lived in Franklin County, Missouri, and had two children, Delaney and her sister Nancy. In their youth, they experienced the effects of separation and sale when their father was sold to the Lower South. After this heart-wrenching separation, Delaney's mother encouraged her daughters to escape slavery. They listened to their mother and Delaney describes Nancy's successful escape to freedom in Canada, as

Lucy A. Delaney. Portrait from her book, *From the Darkness Cometh the Light.* (Delaney, Lucy A., *From the Darkness Cometh the Light, or Struggles for Freedom*, St. Louis, MO: Publishing House of J.T. Smith, 189?.)

well as her mother's attempted escape to Chicago in the narrative. Even after being captured as a runaway slave, and her return to St. Louis, Delaney's mother successfully sued for freedom in 1839.

Delaney's narrative chronicles the work lives of enslaved women in St. Louis, Missouri. She took care of children and worked as a laundress, washing and ironing clothes. After arguing with her enslaver, Martha Mitchell, and defending herself against Mitchell's physical attacks, Mitchell's husband threatened to sell Delaney. Upon hearing the news, Delaney ran away to her mother's nearby home and the two of them hired a lawyer so that she could sue for freedom. The bulk of the narrative details the lawsuit, including Delaney's jail time and her constant fear of being sold to the Lower South.

Delaney's narrative provides extensive moral commentary on the evils of slavery, especially the effects of separation and sale on families. After winning her freedom, Delaney worked with her mother as a seamstress in St. Louis until she married Frederick Turner in 1845. He died shortly after their union in a steamboat explosion. She then married Zachariah Delaney, and the couple had three daughters and one son. Delaney outlived all of her children, none of whom survived beyond the age of 24. After the Civil War, Delaney's mother also died. She was not without immediate family for too long. She and her sister Nancy ultimately reunited with their father. Delaney's painful description of the reunion with her father reveals some of her tragic memories of slavery. Delaney later became an active member of the St. Louis black community. She joined the Methodist Episcopal Church in 1855, and became a leader in the black women's Masonic movement. The year and circumstances surrounding Delaney's death remain largely a mystery.

Kelly Kennington

See also Civil War; Family; Narratives; Runaways; Seamstress Work; South, The.

Suggested Reading

Lucy Delaney, *From the Darkness Cometh the Light; or Struggles for Freedom* (St. Louis: Pub. House of J.T. Smith, 1892, reprint 2001), http://docsouth.unc.edu/neh/delaney/delaney.html; Eric Gardner, " 'Face to Face': Localizing Lucy Delaney's from the Darkness Cometh the Light," *Legacy* 24,1 (2007): 50–71; Eric Gardner, " 'You Have No Business to Whip Me': The Freedom Suits of Polly Wash and Lucy Ann Delaney," *African American Review* 41,1 (2007): 33–50.

Dickson, Amanda America

Birth Date: 1849
Death Date: 1893

Amanda America Dickson was born in 1849 in Hancock County, Georgia, legally enslaved by her white grandmother, Elizabeth Dickson, and the daughter of "The Prince of Georgia Farmers," David Dickson. She was conceived when her enslaved mother, Julia Frances Lewis (Dickson), age 12, was raped by her father, David Dickson, age 40. As soon as Dickson was old enough to be weaned, Elizabeth and David took her away from her mother and black grandmother, Rose, to be raised in her white relatives' household, sleeping in a trundle bed in her white grandmother's room. In that unrealistically protected space, Dickson learned to read and write, play the piano, and to affect the manners of a young lady. Prominent white male farmers and politicians came to visit the Dickson plantation at the invitation of David, who wrote widely in the agricultural literature of the day and offered to teach others the "Dickson Method" of farming which had made him very wealthy. Guests often sat at the table with Amanda while being waited on by Julia who "managed the household," but did not sit at the table. At the age of 16, Dickson "married" her white first cousin—Civil War veteran Charles Eubanks—and moved to Rome, Georgia, where she bore two sons, Julian and Charles. While her sons were small children, Dickson moved back home to her father's domain and remained there until David died in 1885, leaving her the bulk of his huge estate—15,000 acres of land and approximately $500,000 in cash, bonds and notes. After an interesting legal battle in the Hancock County Superior Court and the Georgia Supreme Court, which Amanda

America Dickson Eubanks won based on the sanctity of private property, she moved to the nearby city of Augusta, Georgia, purchased a seven-bedroom house in the wealthiest section of the city, and settled down to begin a new life.

In Augusta, Amanda's sons married into the elite black community. Eldest son Julian married Eva Walton, the daughter of George Walton and his wife Isabella, an African American barber at the exclusive Augusta Hotel. The Walton family tradition holds that George was the descendant of the white George Walton who signed the Declaration of Independence for Georgia. Amanda's second son, Charles married Kate Holsey, the daughter of Bishop Lucius Henry Holsey and his wife Harriet, also of Hancock County.

In 1892, Amanda America Dickson Eubanks married another wealthy mulatto former bondman, Nathan Toomer, from Perry, Georgia. She died on June 11, 1893, of neurasthenia (nervous exhaustion), after trying to rescue Toomer's young daughter from the clutches of her son Charles by placing the child in an African American Convent in Baltimore, the Convent of the Oblate Sisters of Providence. Nine months later, Dickson's widower, Nathan Toomer, married Nina Pinchback, the daughter of Reconstruction Senator-elect from Louisiana P.B.S. Pinchback, and eventually became the father of Harlem Renaissance author Jean Toomer. Dickson died an oxymoronic mulatto lady. And the Deep South in which she lived was becoming more and more impersonally racist.

Kent Anderson Leslie

See also Free Women; Miscegenation; Violence, Sexual.

Suggested Reading

Kent Anderson Leslie, *Woman of Color, Daughter of Privilege, Amanda America Dickson, 1849–1893* (Athens: University of Georgia Press, 1995).

Diet and Nutrition

The slavery debates of the 1830s defined many topics of current historical research, including the care and feeding of slaves. Abolitionists documented instances of hard work and poor diets, but apologists claimed that owners had economic incentives to maintain the health and value of their property. Research in this area, like many others in American slavery, suffers from a lack of evidence because few detailed records are available that bear directly on the question. As of the late

> De food am mostly cornmeal and 'lasses [molasses] and meat that am weighed out and has to last you de week. De truth am, lots of time weuns [we] goes hungry.
>
> —Annie Row, former slave (Howell, Donna, ed., *I Was a Slave: True Life Stories Told by Former Slaves in the 1930s*, 8)

1970s, all scholars agreed that the diet was monotonous, and based on rations of corn and pork supplemented with slave-grown garden produce in season. Despite some 4,000 calories per day, their food was deficient in recommended amounts of vitamins and minerals such as vitamin C, iron, and niacin.

Over the past 30 years, researchers have developed new methodologies and new sources of evidence that shed enormous light on the nutritional status of slaves using data on age, sex, and height recorded for identification purposes on thousands of slave manifests. The law that abolished the African slave trade in 1808 allowed the coastwise shipment of slaves to continue if ship captains arriving at the port of destination presented a cargo manifest proving the slaves originated in the United States.

To help understand the value of these height records, it is useful to think of the body as a biological machine, which consumes food as fuel—a blend of calories, protein, micronutrients, and other ingredients. This machine expends fuel at rest (basal metabolism) amounting to some 1,200 to 1,400 calories per day (depending upon size of the person) to breathe, keep warm, circulate the blood and so forth, and in physical effort, fighting infection and physical growth. In the most arduous activities, such as mushing in Alaska's 1,100-mile Iditarod dog race, energy expenditure may approach 10,000 calories per day. For this reason, diets are adequate or inadequate only in relation to demands placed upon them. Infections may consume fuel by raising body temperature and/or mobilizing the immune system, or through incomplete processing of the diet, which is typical in gastrointestinal diseases. The body's first priority is to survive, and physical growth stagnates or takes a back seat under conditions of inadequate net nutrition (diet minus claims on the diet made by work and disease). If good times return, foregone growth may be recovered all or in part through a process of catch-up, whereby velocity exceeds that typical for a given age. Malnutrition that is acute but severe retards growth and may lead to permanent stunting, depending upon its duration, severity, and quality of conditions thereafter. Chronically poor net nutrition inevitably stunts adult height by as much as three to five inches, and possibly more in extreme situations.

It is useful to compare the slave heights with those from other populations that lived in the nineteenth century and with modern height charts. The slaves had an unusual age profile of physical growth, whereby the children were extraordinarily small (among the tiniest ever measured), but the teenagers had vigorous catch-up and adults were reasonably tall. The typical slave child was severely stunted, and would have caused alarm in a modern pediatrician's office. On average, these children fell below the first percentile of modern height standards, and were smaller than today's children living in slum areas of Lagos, Nigeria or urban areas of Bangladesh. At 67.2 inches, the adult men were similar in height to European upper classes of the early to mid-nineteenth century and were only slightly smaller than middle class whites who lived in the North.

As noted in the entry on mortality, many slave newborns had low birth weight affected by seasonal stress in the diet, disease, and work of the mother. Children who survived the hazardous first month of life faced an abbreviated period of breast-feeding followed by a low-protein diet of pap and gruel. Considerable stunting persisted until age 10, when the children usually began regular work in the fields. Other things equal the work reduced net nutrition, so something must have improved. The diet of workers included regular rations of pork and corn, which more than offset the nutritional demands of work and enabled catch-up growth. Thus, children who were constantly hungry probably looked forward to the nutritional benefits that came with joining the adult workforce.

Why did slaves have this peculiar pattern of physical growth by age? The answer seems to lie in slavery itself because children and adults in free populations of the past, and in those around the world today, overwhelmingly attain similar percentiles of modern height standards. If the children are (or were) small, the adults are (or were) similarly small. American slaves were different, and it is known that slave owners had enormous control over diet and work. Because planters owned all the future labor of their young slaves, one might think they had an economic incentive to provide good net nutrition. Apparently not as nutritionists know that adequate protein is important for normal physical growth, yet slave owners discovered, probably through trial and error, that a high protein diet for children was unprofitable. The standard ration of one-half pound of pork per day was reserved for working slaves, according to slave-owner letters to the editors of southern agricultural journals and instructions to overseers. The protein boost and other nutritional benefits that began with entry into the adult labor force were key to the catch-up growth that propelled teenage slaves upward through the percentiles of modern height charts. The cost of pork was too high relative to the benefits, given that humans are a tough species with a large capacity for catch-up growth if better times occur by early adolescence. Taller slaves were more productive in the fields and were worth more, but the additional cost of protein in childhood needed to achieve this made a poor investment even if one allows for lower child mortality that would have followed a better diet. In sum, economic incentives weakened the slave family. Adults knew, and children soon learned, that parents had limited ability to protect young slaves from hunger. Thus, the good care and feeding of children found in free populations involves parental devotion beyond the calculus of economic costs and benefits.

Richard H. Steckel

See also Childcare; Economy; Family; Food Preparation and Cooking; Gardening; Mortality and Life Expectancy.

Suggested Reading

Richard H. Steckel, "A Peculiar Population: The Nutrition, Health, and Mortality of American Slaves from Childhood to Maturity," *Journal of Economic History* 46 (1986): 721–41.

Domestic Slave Trade

Dey sold my mother, sister an' brother to . . . a slave speculator, an' dey were shipped to de Mississippi bottoms in a box-car. I never heard from my mother anymore.

—Patsy Mitchner, former bondwoman
(Born in Slavery: Slave Narratives from the Federal Writers' Project, 1936–1938 North Carolina Narratives, Volume XI, Part 2, 119)

The Transatlantic Slave Trade between Africa and the European colonies, and later independent nations like the United States, is estimated by historians to have resulted in the forced migration of 8 to 12 million African slaves. Best estimates indicate that 5 percent to 7 percent of these slaves arrived in Colonial British North America, later the United States, while the vast majority were shipped to Brazil, Cuba, and Caribbean islands. The exact sex ratio of males to females is unknown, but the minority of slaves were women because New World planters desired strong workers and because the slaves purchased in

A slave auction in the South. Illustrated in *Harper's Weekly* on July 13, 1861. (Library of Congress.)

Africa were generally African tribal war captives. In the United States, however, the relatively milder slaveholding regimes, in comparison to the Caribbean, and seaboard plantation agriculture led to a natural increase in slaves, while the Caribbean depended upon continual slave imports. By the time of the American Revolution, the seaboard colonies had relatively balanced sex ratios and a growing population of slaves so that by 1800, there were one million enslaved men, women, and children in the United States.

The American Revolution unleashed tremendous changes in the holding and trading of slaves in the United States. The so-called "first emancipation" occurred in the North as slaveholding dwindled and then disappeared, in practice and by law. In the Upper South between the American Revolution and the American Civil War, a growing population of enslaved workers outpaced the agricultural need for labor on exhausted soil. During the same era, the southwestward expansion of the United States into Louisiana, Florida, and Texas opened up new land for the cultivation of cotton. Pressures in the North to emancipate slaves and pressures in the Upper South to sell excess slaves combined with Deep South and southwestern demand to drive prices up while compelling an enormous, second forced migration from the southeastern states to the southwestern states. This Domestic Slave Trade included higher ratios of women than the Transatlantic Slave Trade, and female slaves had distinct experiences within the Domestic Slave Trade.

> *Grandmother drowned herself in the [James] River when she heard that grand-pap was going away. I was told that grandpap was sold because he got religious and prayed that God would set him and grandma free.*
>
> —Mary Moriah Anne Susanna James, former bondwoman (*Born in Slavery: Slave Narratives from the Federal Writers' Project, 1936–1938 Maryland Narratives, Volume VIII*, 38)

Traders typically sent slaves overland, although many were shipped by sea as well. The primary destinations were southern urban centers of slave trading, such as Natchez, Mississippi or New Orleans, Louisiana. According to the historian of the Domestic Slave Trade, Steven Deyle, early traders would purchase men and women in the Upper South until enough slaves, anywhere from 40 to 100, could be chained together on a "coffle," or long chain of shackled or restrained slaves (Deyle 2005, 4). These coffles would then march, sometimes for six to nine weeks, from the slave exporting states such as Virginia to the slave importing states such as Louisiana. Along the route, slave traders might sell slaves when opportunities arose, but the majority of slaves were intended for the auctions in slave markets in the southwest. Traders and overseers of coffles tended to shackle and restrain those thought most likely to run away, and this usually meant males, especially those independent of family ties to others on the coffle. Women were less likely to be restrained by shackles unless they had a history of running away or resisting the traders. Women, instead, were more likely to be tied with ropes or strips of

Manifest of "Negroes, mulattos, and persons of color" bound for Mobile, Alabama, 1844. National Archives, Collector of Customs, U.S. Customs Service. The name, age, sex, and owner are noted for each slave. (National Archives.)

leather, or carried with children and the elderly on carts, on their journey to the southwest. Coffles were usually strictly segregated by sex, and antislavery critics and slave narratives both noted that the separation of women from the men left enslaved women on coffles vulnerable to sexual abuse.

Slaves waiting for sale, Virginia. (Mid-Manhattan Library Picture Collection/New York Public Library.)

Once at the markets, enslaved women found themselves on the auction block where women were invasively inspected by potential purchasers. The slaves, male and female, who made it to the slave markets in towns such as New Orleans, Natchez, or even Montgomery faced close scrutiny by potential purchasers, while casual passersby could not avoid the sights and sounds of the auction. Traders sought to improve the chances of sale by grooming and oiling the slaves or by providing them with fresh clothing. Slaves were often paraded before buyers and expected to show energy and liveliness or face punishment from the traders. Purchasers could physically inspect slaves before purchase and many of the inspections of the muscles, teeth, eyes, and throat clearly derived from the examination of nonhuman livestock. Generally, nineteenth century modesty compelled traders and purchasers to make examinations of women's reproductive organs, for fertility or disease, behind curtains, but the invasive searches occurred nonetheless, and infrequently without any pretenses of modesty.

The Domestic Slave Trade mostly provided for agricultural labor demands and "prime" field hands were generally strong, young males expected to labor on cotton production. There were, however, specialized markets for slaves of other skills such as carpenters, coaches, and blacksmiths; for women, the specialized skills most sought after were domestic skills in nursing, cooking, laundry, or housekeeping. Women were traded for their ability to work on cotton production, but many found themselves advertised and purchased for other specific forms of gender labor in keeping with nineteenth century notions of female roles in society.

One specialized form of labor, sex work, was known in the nineteenth century slave trade as the "fancy trade." Prostitution and concubinage were not uncommon in urban areas, and in New Orleans especially, the trade in "fancy" women included substantial prices for women declared "fancy," or attractive. Usually these enslaved women were of mixed ancestry with distant, or not so distant, white ancestors with complexions noted as "bright" or "fair." According to slave law in the United States, freedom or slavery descended via the maternal line and a mixed race person could remain enslaved even if he or she had more white ancestors than African or African American ancestors. A woman of half, quarter, or eighth, or even much less African ancestry might still find herself enslaved even if her complexion was light enough to hide her African ancestry. These light-complexioned enslaved women bought and sold in the "fancy trade" were almost exclusively purchased as sex workers. Free women of color and free "fancy" women also engaged in sex work in urban areas such as New Orleans, complicating clear notions of their free will, sexual exploitation, or community standards. Even these free women had limited opportunities for employment, and although many might have turned willingly to prostitution or concubinage, many others, especially those caught in the "fancy trade" had no choice.

Another form of specialized labor was simply breeding. Planters, traders, and agricultural advisors from the American Revolution to Emancipation espoused a general plan of wealth accumulation from the birth and maturation of slave children. Female slaves on the auction block or in print advertisements were frequently attributed characteristics which emphasized their fertility. Although many slaveholders found pregnant or nursing women to be detrimental to immediate labor needs, the general consensus was that a female slave could easily make up for her expense by providing slaveholders with additional slaves, to be used as labor or sold for profit. Slave traders emphasized fertility, slaveholders routinely encouraged serial and plural "marriages,"

Us passed de vary fiel' whar paw an' all my folks wuz wurkin, an' I calt out as loud as I could an' as long as I could see 'em, 'good-bye, Ma!' 'good-bye, Ma!' But she never heard me. Naw, sah, dem white mens [traders] wuz singin' so loud Ma could'n hear me! An' she could'n see me, caze dey had me pushed down out o' sight on de floe o' de buggy. I ain't never seed nor heard tell o' my ma an' paw, an' bruthers, an' susters from dat day to dis.

—Carrie Nancy Fryer, former bondwoman
(*Born in Slavery: Slave Narratives from the Federal Writers' Project, 1936–1938 Georgia Narratives, Volume IV, Part 1*, 327)

and countless masters impregnated slaves themselves through force. Deyle notes that although female slaves were generally purchased to fulfill some other specified labor such as cotton cultivation or housekeeping, the secondary use of female slaves for breeding was widespread enough to appear in slave trade advertisements (Deyle 2005, 154–77). Historian of the New Orleans slave market Walter Johnson notes that escaped slave John Brown recalled Critty's forced breeding when their master required her to take two husbands and that she was sold because of her infertility (Deyle 2005, 71–72).

Slave narratives frequently recount the details of the Domestic Slave Trade. For female slaves, and for males as well, the destruction of family bonds and the selling of children were especially traumatic. Sexual exploitation by masters or opportunistic white men is a recurring theme in the narratives by women, such as that by Harriet Jacobs. According to her narrative, Jacobs' master threatened to sell her children if she did not submit to his repeated rapes. Others described the sexual exploitation that occurred on the forced migration of coffles into the Deep South. Solomon Northup, a freeborn mulatto who wrote about his experiences after being kidnapped and sold into slavery, described the deception practiced by a master to trick Eliza, a woman expecting emancipation, but who found herself on the auction block. William Wells Brown describes an attempted rape by his master of enslaved Cynthia while on a steamboat, presumably carrying the slaves to auction (Johnson 1999, 39, 63).

Abolitionists seized on the sexual exploitation of slave women, in their captivity and in the Domestic Slave Trade. Abolitionists sensationally presented this sexual exploitation to reading audiences in the nineteenth century; indeed reforms as distinct as campaigns against alcohol, against prostitution, and against slavery utilized sensational language to highlight violence and sexual crimes resulting from the vice of slavery or drink. The narratives of ex-slaves in combination with the print advertisements of slave traders, slave hunters, and masters seeking runaways provided abolitionists with ample material to depict the South as little more than a brothel where race mixture, rape, and murder were routine characteristics of slave holding. These sensationalized claims, although fairly accurate, sought to strike directly at slaveholders and to deny Southerners any claims to Christianity or honor. The sexualized auction of women in slave markets and the tales of their rape and concubinage routinely appeared in antislavery literature in the 1820s to emancipation.

Enslaved women shared many of the same horrifying realities that enslaved men faced, while they also participated with men in resistance to slavery and community building despite enslavement. Women, however, also faced distinct conditions because of their sex and gender. Women were expected to perform specialized work, usually gendered housework or childcare. Women also were much more likely to be exploited for breeding and were frequent targets of sexual abuse and exploitation, a reality that appears in both the heartrending ex-slave narratives and in the sensationalized antislavery literature of the era.

Nicholas Patrick Cox

See also Branding; Breeding; Economy; Fancy Girls; Middle Passage; Prices.

Suggested Reading

Steven Deyle, *Carry Me Back: The Domestic Slave Trade in American Life* (New York: Oxford University Press, 2005); Walter Johnson, *Soul by Soul: Life Inside the Antebellum Slave Market* (Cambridge: Harvard University Press, 1999); Jacqueline Jones, *Labor of Love, Labor of Sorrow: Black Women, Work, and the Family, from Slavery to the Present*, 2nd ed. (New York: Basic Books, 2009); Deborah Gray White. *Ar'n't I a Woman?: Female Slaves in the Plantation South*, rev. ed. (New York: W.W. Norton, 1999).

E

Economy

During their leisure time, enslaved women engaged in a number of activities for the purpose of acquiring cash or producing surplus products for barter or sale. Some skilled women engaged in self-hire, while urban enslaved women directly operated in the marketplace as vendors; others produced surplus food or consumer goods with market value. These economic endeavors enabled enslaved women to supply themselves and their families with food, clothing, and luxury items beyond the meager rations provided by enslavers. Yet, regardless of the specific item being purchased, the ability to earn money and exchange goods gave all black women who participated in this economy an important amount of self-determination over their otherwise rigidly controlled lives.

Earning Money and Producing Surplus Products

According to longstanding custom, the enslaved were only required to work six days a week for enslavers; usually Sunday was designated as their day of leisure. Additionally, enslaved laborers were allowed to pursue their own interests once their designated daily task was completed (under the task system) or after they had labored a specific number of hours (under the gang system). Although the majority of this "free time" was consumed by cooking, eating, childcare, sewing, laundering, and gardening, many enslaved women carved out time to earn cash or produce surplus goods for barter.

Both skilled and unskilled workers could directly sell their labor during this free time. Particularly during the harvest, enslaved people would insist that owners pay cash for extra time in the fields, or exchange that time for additional leisure time in the future. They also might sell their labor to neighboring planters who lacked adequate field hands. But skilled bondwomen possessed an even greater capacity for earning money during their free time. Whether negotiated directly with the hiring party or through the intervention of enslavers, talented seamstresses, gifted cooks, respected female folk doctors, and experienced midwives, all entered into employment contracts exchanging cash for their expertise. In urban areas, even laundresses could hire out their labor, particularly to middle-class whites who could not afford to purchase or hire an enslaved person on a full-time basis.

While some enslaved women earned money directly through the labor market, others produced desired commodities for sale or barter. Black women often cultivated gardens and raised animals not only for their own consumption, but also with the intention of generating a surplus. Poultry, pigs, eggs, and fresh produce all served as valuable items for exchange—either with other enslaved people, with enslavers' households, or for an outside market. Some enslaved people even used their garden plots to grow rice or cotton, whose sole purpose was as a market commodity.

Exchanging Goods

Once they had generated surplus commodities, bondwomen could exchange these goods in a variety of ways. Some bondpeople simply engaged in a barter economy within their own communities or with enslaved people on neighboring plantations. However, this greatly limited the commodities available for acquisition. More commonly—particularly in the most rural areas—enslavers agreed to purchase enslaved people's surpluses in exchange for commodities more difficult to acquire. For example, bondwomen might provide all the eggs required by the enslaver's household in return for sugar, flour, or extra fabric. Some larger plantations even set up the equivalent of a store where bondpeople could trade their surpluses for desired items.

Not all enslaved people, however, depended on enslavers for this trade. The closer enslaved people lived to a town or urban area, the more likely they were to exchange their products on the open market. Although enslaved men were often central to transporting goods between rural and urban areas, in many cases, rural female suppliers negotiated for the sale of their products directly with the urban bondwomen who predominated as market vendors. In addition to facilitating economic opportunities for bondwomen, these urban markets came to serve a central role as the intersection of communication and information exchange between rural and urban enslaved communities.

In growing cities such as Savannah, Georgia, and Charleston, South Carolina, much of the fresh produce, meats, and dairy products being consumed by white urbanites were the product of enslaved people's surpluses. Additionally, the sale of cakes and confectionaries was likewise controlled by urban bondwomen. Enslaved women initially entered urban markets to sell produce on behalf of enslavers, who also often permitted them to buy and sell goods for their own profit—paying the enslaver a set portion in return for this privilege. Much to their chagrin, whites could not purchase any of these desired commodities without engaging in intense negotiations with the enslaved women vendors themselves.

Spending Money and Acquiring Goods

For most bondwomen, earning money or accumulating surpluses for barter was not an attempt to raise funds to purchase freedom for themselves or their children; slave prices were often well beyond their earning capacity. Rather, most bondwomen used money or goods for exchange as a means of ameliorating the conditions of daily life for themselves and their families. Improvements to food, clothing, and (mainly for urban bondpeople) shelter were their primary concerns, although a small percentage of these purchases went towards recreation, religious practices, or other luxury goods used to express affection and respect.

The vast majority of surplus funds—perhaps up to 80 percent by the accounts of some historians—were spent on clothing. Although bondwomen sometimes purchased ready-made clothes, most desired fabrics in order to sew clothing for themselves. Additionally, enslaved women sought fabrics with which to adorn and personalize their otherwise bland attire as well as supplement to the minimal cloth rations provided by slaveholders. Enslaved people also took pride in their appearance at religious services, desiring dress clothes, which were an obvious departure from their daily work attire.

While enslaved people could partially supplement their meager food rations through hunting and fishing, foraging, raising pigs and poultry, and cultivating garden plots, several desired products that could only be obtained through barter or purchase. In particular, tea, coffee, sugar, and flour greatly improved their mealtime experiences, even if these items added little or no nutritional value to their diets. Bondwomen also sought cooking utensils to aid in their meal preparation. Again, while some utensils and cooking vessels could be fashioned from local materials, heat-resistant pots and pans were necessities only acquired through exchange. A much smaller percentage of their surplus funds were spent on luxury items such as liquor and tobacco, or tokens of affection for their loved ones. And while the spending practices of rural and urban bondwomen were relatively similar, housing expenditures were mainly confined to urban bondpeople—particularly those who labored under hiring contracts. The renting of private rooms—with the permission of the enslaver—supplied a certain level of autonomy and privacy, which was otherwise lacking in enslaved people's residential arrangements.

Sharon Ann Murphy

See also Clothing; Female Slave Network; Folk Medicine and Healing; Food Preparation and Cooking; Gardening; Hiring Out; Labor, Skilled; Midwives; Seamstress Work; Urban Slavery.

Suggested Reading

David Barry Gaspar and Darlene Clark Hine (eds.), *More Than Chattel: Black Women and Slavery in the Americas* (Bloomington and Indianapolis: Indiana University Press, 1996);

Ellen Hartigan-O'Connor, " 'She Said She did not Know Money': Urban Women and Atlantic Markets in the Revolutionary Era," in *Early American Studies* (Fall 2006); Betty Wood, *Women's Work, Men's Work: The Informal Slave Economies of Lowcountry Georgia* (Athens: University of Georgia Press, 1995).

Education

I nebber went tur schul a day in mah life, ma [rr]ied 'for freedum and w'en I got free, had ter wuk all de time ter mak a libin' fer mah two chillen.

—Precilla Gray, former bondwoman (*Born in Slavery: Slave Narratives from the Federal Writers' Project, 1936–1938 Tennessee Narratives, Volume XV,* 24)

Enslaved women benefited greatly from both formal and informal avenues of education. Their pursuit of knowledge represented a broader communal desire to become an educated people.

Legislation determined the availability of formal education opportunities. The majority of southern states prohibited the formal education of enslaved people by 1833 (Williams 2005, 14–15). A small number of free whites and blacks willingly defied the law and social ostracism by opening illegal schools. Women, like Susie King Taylor of Georgia, utilized this option. Taylor learned to read when her owner allowed her to live with her free grandmother in Savannah, Georgia. She studied her disguised schoolbooks with other enslaved children in the homes of two free black women, Susan Woodhouse and Mary Beasley. Schools for urban free blacks also often extended education to enslaved African Americans with and without their owners' permission. Women took advantage of the schools that existed in Savannah, Georgia; Charleston, South Carolina; Fayetteville, New Bern, and Raleigh, North Carolina; and other southern cities in Virginia, Florida, Tennessee, and Louisiana (Franklin and Moss 1988, 126). Unlike other southern states, Texas lacked legislation prohibiting the education of enslaved people. Therefore, schools for free blacks and the enslaved existed in rural and urban settings. Houston and other cities, for example, offered schools devoted to educating enslaved women. Formal education accounted for approximately 5 percent of state's slave population being literate by the eve of the Civil War (Winegarten 1995, 22).

Legislation and the lack of formal educational opportunities never deterred bondwomen from becoming educated. Informal education typified the experiences of enslaved women. Utilizing a web of secrecy, enslaved women sometimes obtained an education through sympathetic owners, clergy, playmates, or directly from their young charges. Most commonly, women obtained education from other enslaved men and women and outside of the enslavers' direct observations in the slave community. For instance, Mattie Jackson learned to read from her mother,

Mattie Jackson

Upon achieving freedom, Mattie Jackson as well as other female slaves pursued literacy. Having learned rudimentary literacy skills from her mother under slavery, Jackson sought educational advancement. According to Jackson,

> It appeared as though I had emerged into a new world, or had never lived in the old one before. The people I lived with were Unionists, and became immediately interested in teaching and encouraging me in my literary advancement and all other important improvements, which precisely met the natural desires for which my soul had ever yearned since my earliest recollection. I could read a little, but was not allowed to learn in slavery. I was obliged to pay twenty-five cents for every letter written for me. I now began to feel that as I was free I could learn to write, as well as others; consequently Mrs. Harris, the lady with whom I lived, volunteered to assist me. I was soon enabled to write quite a legible hand, which I find a great convenience. I would advise all, young, middle aged or old, in a free country, to learn to read and write. If this little book should fall into the hands of one deficient of the important knowledge of writing I hope they will remember the old maxim: "Never too old to learn." Manage your own secrets, and divulge them by the silent language of your own pen. Had our blessed President considered it too humiliating to learn in advanced years, our race would yet have remained under the galling yoke of oppression. After I had been with Mrs. Harris seven months, the joyful news came of the surrender of Lee's army and the capture of Richmond. (pp. 22–23)

Source: Jackson, Mattie J. *The Story of Mattie J. Jackson: Her Parentage, Experience of Eighteen Years in Slavery, Incidents During the War, Her Escape from Slavery: A True Story* (Lawrence [Mass.]: Sentinel Office, 1866), Documenting the American South. University Library, The University of North Carolina at Chapel Hill, 1999.

Ellen Turner. Jackson recalled practicing her reading skills with any scraps of printed material with her mother at night. Jackson's acquisition of an education typified the experiences of most enslaved women who learned from a literate relative or another enslaved person. Due to its secretive nature, scholars have been unable to accurately estimate the number of bondpeople who acquired an informal education. It is believed that a small percentage of the total enslaved population successfully became educated.

Women eked out an education in order to fulfill a communal desire to become educated. The institution of slavery denied their physical freedom and attempted to thwart their intellectual freedom. Thus, obtaining an education granted them a degree of freedom. Some used their knowledge to help escape slavery, temporarily and permanently. For instance, forging passes allowed women to visit separated family members and spouses at nearby plantations or to permanently escape slavery by running away. Enslaved women wanted an education not merely for themselves, but for their family and community. The desire to become an educated people remained constant even after freedom in 1865.

Hilary N. Green

See also Runaways; Resistance; Laws; Literacy; Taylor, Susie King

Suggested Reading

John Hope Franklin and Alfred A. Moss, Jr., *From Slavery to Freedom: A History of Negro Americans*, 6th ed. (New York: McGraw-Hill, Inc, 1988); Heather A. Williams, *Self-Taught: African American Education in Slavery and Freedom* (Chapel Hill: University of North Carolina, 2005); Ruthe Winegarten, *Black Texas Women: 150 Years of Trial and Triumph* (Austin: University of Texas Press, 1995).

Elderly Women

> *When my mother became old, she was sent to live in a little lonely log-hut in the woods. Aged and worn out slaves, whether men or women, are commonly so treated. No care is taken of them, except, perhaps, that a little ground is cleared about the hut, on which the old slave, if able, may raise a little corn. As far as the owner is concerned, they live or die as it happens; it is just the same thing as turning out an old horse.*
>
> —Moses Grandy, *Narrative of the Life of Moses Grandy; Late a Slave in the United States of America* (London: C. Gilpin, 1843), 51.

During the era of slavery in the United States, from the colonial period to Emancipation in 1865, life expectancies for all Americans were much shorter without the advantages of modern medicine. This was particularly true for enslaved people who lived under a harsh system of forced labor with meager resources, inadequate healthcare, and few protections from the physical and psychological violence of the institution. When applied to enslaved people, then, "elderly" refers to those who were aged or "old" for that time, which could have been from around age 40 to the more advanced years of the seventies, eighties, and nineties.

Among enslaved communities and families, elderly women typically enjoyed a venerable status. Respect for elders was a priority among enslaved people, reflecting a cultural retention that survived from West African societies organized around generational age sets in which community members' wisdom and experience determined their status and esteem. Elderly enslaved women were sometimes repositories of African culture, carrying on traditions and handing down knowledge acquired from their own or their immediate ancestors' past. This included folklore, labor patterns (such as rice cultivation and basket-weaving methods), cultural pathways (such as music and food preparation techniques), indigenous religious beliefs or conjuring, and traditional healing practices that incorporated the use of herbal remedies and emphasized spiritual well-being in addition to physical health.

Because of the disabilities, bodily decline, and lower stamina that often result from aging, most elderly women did not undertake intense physical labor such as agricultural work. Instead, they were sometimes assigned lighter tasks in the domestic space of the slaveholders' home or on "trash gangs" with pregnant women and children. They also provided valuable labor for the enslaved community. These duties usually included sewing, mending, weaving, cooking, gardening, laundering clothes, and cleaning the slave quarters. Some served as midwives, nurses, and heal-

Elderly former bondwoman, pictured here ca. 1902. (Library of Congress.)

ers for both whites and blacks. Often, elderly women "minded" or cared for enslaved children while their parents labored. As a result of this practice, they played a significant role in socializing children by conveying their wisdom to younger generations and teaching important life skills to resist and cope with enslavement. This provided an important modicum of protection and stability to enslaved children in an otherwise uncertain environment. For these reasons, elderly women were crucial figures in the female slave network and sometimes managed to shield young women from sexual harassment and exploitation. Harriet Jacobs' grandmother, who bought her own freedom and commanded the respect of the wider community, is one example of an elderly woman whose status enabled her to provide some limited protection to her granddaughter.

Elderly enslaved women were sometimes accorded some respect from their captors as individuals who had, perhaps, served as a nurse or lifelong house servant to the white family; these women were referred to as "Mammy." This service did

Some of de old women, and women bearin' chillun not yet born, did cardin' wid hand-cards; den some would at de spinnin' wheel and spin thread, three cuts make a hank. Other women weave cloth and every woman had to learn to make clothes for the family, and they had to knit coarse socks and stockin's.

—Gracie Gibson, former bondwoman (*Born in Slavery: Slave Narratives from the Federal Writers' Project, 1936–1938 South Carolina Narratives, Volume XIV, Part 2,* 114)

not guarantee respect or kindness, however, and some enslavers saw elderly bond-women as liabilities whose care and expenses could not be recouped through productive labor. Those who enslaved were sometimes known to emancipate aged and "useless" bondpeople who could not be sold as a way to avoid supporting them, leaving them to eke out whatever means they could to survive without the protection of their families and communities. The abandonment of elderly slaves became so prevalent that by the 1820s, southern states implemented laws to curtail this practice as recently freed, elderly blacks with no support system moved to cities and became public "burdens" or "vagabonds." This had a significant impact on elderly women, and on the enslaved communities from which they came; these communities would no longer benefit from their many contributions.

Jenifer L. Barclay

See also African Women and African-born Women; Conjurers; Emancipation; Female Slave Network; Folklore and Folktales; Folk Medicine and Healing; Health, Disabilities, and Soundness; Jacobs, Harriet; Labor; Laws; Mammy Stereotype; Midwives; Slave Quarters, Life in.

Suggested Reading

Stacey K. Close, *Elderly Slaves of the Plantation South* (New York: Routledge, 1996); Anne Patton Malone, *Sweet Chariot: Slave Family and Household Structure in Nineteenth Century Louisiana* (Chapel Hill: University of North Carolina Press, 1992); Leslie J. Pollard, "Aging and Slavery: A Gerontological Perspective," *The Journal of Negro History* 66, 3 (Autumn 1981): 228–34; Deborah Gray White, *Ar'n't I a Women? Female Slaves in the Plantation South* (New York: W.W. Norton & Company, 1985).

Emancipation

Better stay free if you can stay straight. Slabery time was tough, it like looking back into de dark, looking back into de night.

—Amy Perry, former bondwoman (*Born in Slavery: Slave Narratives from the Federal Writers' Project, 1936–1938 South Carolina Narratives, Volume XIV, Part 3*, 253)

The Emancipation Proclamation, which President Abraham Lincoln issued on January 1, 1863, freed all bondpeople in the Confederate territory, but it did not include enslaved blacks in parts of Louisiana, West Virginia, Missouri, Kentucky, and Delaware, because those states were not entirely under Union control. The Emancipation Proclamation recognized what enslaved people had been working for; it made official that "the war for the Union must become a war for freedom" for bondpeople and strengthened the morality of the Union cause ("Emancipation Proclamation" 2011). It was not until January 31, 1865, with Congress passing the thirteenth amendment to the Constitution, that slavery was officially abolished in the United States.

Group of "contrabands" at Foller's house at Cumberland Landing, Virginia, photographed by James F. Gibson, ca. May–August 1862. (Library of Congress.)

Once emancipated, formerly enslaved women played a significant role in the transition from slavery to freedom, reframing definitions of marriage and family, free labor, and womanhood to suit their familial and community needs, and directly engaging in the political struggles of the era. Scholars studying women's transition from slavery to freedom in the United States have explored the interconnections between race and gender, resulting in a significant reconsideration of the debate over emancipation and citizenship, whereby newly freed African American women serve as central political actors taking advantage of the changing postwar economic and political conditions.

The particular ways black women took aim at the institution of slavery varied during the Civil War. Well before the U.S. federal government devised an official policy on emancipation, enslaved women in low country South Carolina, as an example, challenged the slave system by slowing production and resisting new forms of mistreatment. Considering their options carefully, black women were opportunistic, observant, and anxious. Some staged dramatic escapes while others remained on their plantations well after the military upheaval ended. For mothers, the welfare and protection of their children weighed heavily on their decision to remain on the plantation or flee. Life in settlement camps proved chaotic and crowded for freedpeople. Military mobilization and wartime chaos upset social ties that held communities together under slavery and the care and responsibility of children, the ill, and the elderly typically fell to women. In areas where whites had fled and large numbers of black men joined the Union army, women combined their skills and supported one another by taking orphans into their homes, setting up living quarters, and caring for injured and ailing soldiers. Freedwomen's distinctive networks emerged in the Trent River Settlement near New Bern, North Carolina as well as the Combahee River region of South Carolina, where freedwomen transformed a small area for themselves into a Sea Island settlement.

Once a colored man . . . came to teach school. The white folks beat and whipped him and drove him away in his underwear. I wanted so hard to learn to read, but I didn't even know I was free, even when slavery was ended.

—Hannah Davidon, former bondwoman from Kentucky (*Born in Slavery: Slave Narratives from the Federal Writers' Project, 1936–1938 Ohio Narratives, Volume XII*, 28)

Freedwomen whose husbands returned from the Civil War marked their transition into free society by registering their legal status as married women, as required under the state law and the Freedmen's Bureau. These weddings were among the most elaborate and cherished moments in the aftermath of the war. Men borrowed suits and women hired seamstresses; one North Carolina freedwoman marked the occasion with "six bridesmaids." Freedwomen's decisions about marriage and family had a profound effect on the free labor system. Exempt from middle-class definitions of femininity, freedwomen who elected to withdraw from the labor force endured harsh criticism from their white employers who considered them to be "lazy" and "idle." In the low country—an area that contained some of the largest plantations, and before the war, some of its most stable, and culturally autonomous slave communities—freedwomen organized their labor according to their own community ideals, informed by their experiences in slavery. Working to meet obligations and responsibilities within their nuclear families as wives and mothers as well as their broader extended families as sisters, aunts, grandmothers, and neighbors, freedwomen regularly remained on plantations and assumed a frontline role in plantation battles over the shape of post-emancipation labor. In southwest Georgia, however, black fathers spoke for their family and kin groups arranging for family units to return to the plantation in the company of close kin. Single black women who contracted their own labor agreements ran the risk of ending up mired in debt. Unlike the low country; this labor system favored the skills of "No. 1 hands"—laborers capable of working uninterrupted, six days of the week, fifty-one or fifty-two weeks of the year. Planters docked the wages of workers, but especially female agricultural laborers, who failed to perform at the same level as men. Planters, however, did not have a monopoly on the free labor system. Married women and women who could summon support of a male head of household fared better than single women in wage negotiations in this region. Moreover, freedwomen regularly complained about planters who pushed them off the land before paying them their wages.

The responsibility to work weighed heavily on newly freed African American women in urban areas. Those who were not employed were labeled "vagrants" and punished in ways similar to that of African American and white men. For example, freedwomen were required to perform manual labor in the streets of Houston, Texas, a punishment typically reserved for vagrant and disorderly men. In Louisiana, agents of the Freedmen's Bureau requested permission to recruit black women to work when they could not find enough able-bodied black men. Southern white employers were not accepting of African Americans' rights to contract the terms of their labor after emancipation. Apprenticeship enabled former masters, desperate for laborers, to reverse some of the effects of emancipation by forcing the children of freedmen and women into extended labor contracts. Historian Karin Zipf explains that African American women vigorously challenged the apprenticeship system through the local courts. Black women argued that apprenticeship was a violation of their domestic relations. In addition to pressing their claims in local courts across the South, many turned to the Freedmen's Bureau, which was established in 1865, to monitor the transition to a free labor system and to protect black rights during and immediately following the Civil War.

The transition to free labor was particularly trying for black women. In bondage, enslavers prized enslaved women for their reproductive and physical labor. Desperate by the torment of survival, single black women made painful decisions about their children. In 1868, a pregnant freedwoman was sentenced to life in prison for beating her young son to death as

THE PARTING "Buy us too."

Sea Island School on Helena Island, South Carolina, established in 1862 (published by the Pennsylvania Freedmen's Relief Association). Numerous organizations sprung up after emancipation to educate freedmen, women, and children. (Library of Congress.)

they walked along the road at the end of the day. The same year, a freedwoman facing unemployment in Halifax County, Virginia was sentenced to hang for killing her newborn after her employer threatened to fire her if she had another child. In an effort to have the woman's death sentenced commuted, a Freedmen's Bureau officer noted that the woman sacrificed one of her children for the good of the five older ones.

Newly freed African American women took advantage of changing postwar social, economic, and political conditions by engaging directly in the political struggles of the era. Well before the Federal government extended juridical citizenship and then suffrage to newly freed African Americans in Little Rock, Arkansas, historian Hannah Rosen found black men and women engaged in political debate and decision making. They crafted new political rituals and staged public assemblies of a far different flavor than the antebellum political community in Arkansas. Black women and children were key participants in these public ceremonies. Public gatherings of this sort challenged widespread conservative assertions that blacks were unfit for citizenship and membership in the nation's political community. Above all, Elsa Barkley Brown has found that African Americans "understood the vote as collective," and black women were welcomed participants in voting decisions in black communities across the South. Black women further unraveled the hierarchal social relations bound up in the institution of slavery by appropriating the symbols and ceremonies of elite whites in support of their own dignity and humanity. According to historian Thavolia Glymph, public displays of this sort unnerved white women as they struggled to accept black family life was no longer "legitimized by ownership" (Glymph 2008, 213–23). Black women regularly clashed with whites who were unwilling to expand their prewar definitions of womanhood to include newly freed African American women. Newspapers across the South portrayed black women as aggressive, unrestrained, and pathological. In claiming their freedom, newly freed African American women fought against labels attached to them by former slaveholders, challenging sexual stereotypes, and laying claim to public space. The North Carolina *Raleigh Register* and the Tennessee *Memphis Daily Appeal* regularly featured newspaper articles highlighting black women with aggressive public behavior shortly after the war, distancing them from images of respectable womanhood.

Taking direct aim at constructions of womanhood that excluded black women, African American women challenged racial segregation on railway cars by law. In 1883, three women brought a case before the U.S. District Court because they were refused access to the ladies' car on the railway. In a separate but related incident, activist and reformer Ida B. Wells had her clothes torn when she tried to board the ladies' car. Wells pursued the case in court and won $500. During the aftermath of the Memphis Riots of 1866, black schools, churches, and innumerable homes were burnt down. Freedwomen courageously spoke about the rape and sexual violence they experienced before a congressional committee investigating the riots. Finally, black women were also at the forefront of grassroots political struggles aimed at community betterment. Calls for redress took the form of education, land distribution, and economic relief in the form of individual cash payments. In the late nineteenth century, black women like Callie House worked rallied for a federally funded program for former slaves and their families.

Brandi C. Brimmer

See also Civil War; Family; Gender Conventions; Laws; Manumission; Marriage and Cohabitation.

Suggested Reading

Nancy Bercaw, *Gendered Freedoms: Race, Rights, and the Politics of Household in the Delta, 1861–1875* (Gainesville: University Press of Florida, 2003); Brandi C. Brimmer, "All Her Rights and Privileges: African-American Women and the Politics of Civil War Widows' Pensions" (PhD dissertation, UCLA, 2006); Elsa Barkley Brown, "Negotiating and Transforming the Public Sphere: African American Political Life in the Transition from Slavery to Freedom," in *The Black Public Sphere: A Public Culture Book* (Chicago: University of Chicago Press, 1995), 111–50; Catherine Clinton, "Reconstructing Freedwomen," in *Divided Houses: Gender and the Civil War*, eds. Catherine Clinton and Nina Silber (New York: Oxford University Press, 1992), 306–19; Laura F. Edwards, *Gendered Strife and Confusion: The Political Culture of Reconstruction* (Urbana: University of Illinois Press, 1997); Mary Farmer-Kaiser, *Freedwomen and the Freedmen's Bureau: Race, Gender, and Public Policy in the Age of Emancipation* (New York: Fordham University Press, 2010); Thavolia Glymph, *Out of the House of Bondage* (Cambridge: Cambridge University Press, 2008); Martha Hodes, *White Women, Black Men: Illicit Sex in the Nineteenth Century South* (New Haven: Yale University Press, 1997); Tera Hunter, *To Joy My Freedom: Southern Black Women's Lives and Labors after the Civil War* (Cambridge: Harvard University Press, 1997); Susan E. O'Donovan, *Becoming Free in the Cotton South* (Cambridge: Harvard University Press, 2007), 162–207; Elizabeth Ann Regosin, *Freedom's Promise: Ex-Slave Families and Citizenship in the Age of Emancipation* (Charlottesville: University of Virginia Press, 2002); Hannah Rosen, " 'Not That Sort of Women': Race, Gender, and Sexual Violence during the Memphis Riot of 1866," in *Sex, Love, Race: Crossing Boundaries in North American History*, ed. Marthes Hodes (New York: New York University Press, 1999), 267–93 and *Terror in the Heart of Freedom: Citizenship, Sexual Violence, and The Meaning of Race in the Postemancipation South* (Chapel Hill: University of North Carolina Press, 2009); Julie Saville, *The Work of Reconstruction: From Slave to Wage Laborer in South Carolina, 1860–1870* (Cambridge: Cambridge University Press, 1994); Leslie A. Schwalm, *A Hard Fight for We: Women's Transitions from Slavery to*

Freedom in South Carolina (Urbana: University of Illinois Press, 1997); Karin L. Zipf, "Reconstructing 'Free Woman': African-American Women, Apprenticeship, and Custody Rights during Reconstruction," *Journal of Women's History* 12 (Spring 2000): 8–31; "Emancipation Proclamation." 2011. National Archives. http://www.archives.gov/exhibits/featured_documents/emancipation_proclamation/index.html.

F

Family

At the turn of the nineteenth century, theorists mistakenly predicted a dwindling enslaved population. They believed that the peculiar institution in the United States would come to an end as a result of the Transatlantic Slave Trade closing in 1808. However, these predictions never materialized because of the strong family units enslaved blacks formed and a host of other realities. Closing the slave trade did not send the Republic's black population plummeting. In fact, between 1800 and 1860, the enslaved population quadrupled by natural increase from one to four million over just three generations. In total population, the black proportion decreased as the population of the United States grew by annexation, immigration, and natural reproduction from 5.3 million in 1800 to 31.4 million in 1860. Blacks came to be the majority of the population along the south Atlantic coast and in the lower Mississippi Valley. This demographic trend marked a major turning point in American history. Instead of dissolving or merely hanging on, the institution of slavery flourished.

All through cold, bitter winter nights I remember my mother getting up often to see about us and to keep the cover tucked in. She thought us sound asleep, and I pretended I was asleep while listening to her prayers. She would bend down over the bed and stretching her arms so as to take us all in, she prayed with all her soul to God to help her bring up her children right.

—David Goodman Gullins, former bondman (*Born in Slavery: Slave Narratives from the Federal Writers' Project, 1936–1938 Georgia Narratives, Volume IV, Part 2, 81–82*)

The unique demographic vitality of the enslaved population in the southern United States required a social base—stable families that provided physical, emotional, and cultural support for childbirth and childrearing. The enslaved community had long been denied the legal sanctity of marriage before freedom. Bondpeople's desire for families went hand in hand with the slaveholding economy. For slaveholders, blacks represented capital investment, and each birth meant an increase in wealth. Enslaved families were also a means of social control for the slaveholder. For example, family ties and responsibilities could deter a person from running away.

Family separations occurred regularly and were a source of anxiety for all bondpeople. One historian estimated that separations occurred in the Upper South about one in three first slave marriages. Separations occurred when slaveholders rented out enslaved workers, moved them to another plantation, loaned them to creditors, carried them on extended trips, or became part of the state upon the enslaver's death. Familes also experienced separation as a form of punishment particularly when there were changes in the slaveholding family's finances. Although it occurred, the separation of *very* young children from their families was unusual. Sometimes, a slaveholder would transfer a bondman's wife or child into the "Big House" to work as a "servant." In some cases, this environment disrupted enslaved family bonds and caused tension among relatives and friends. In addition, because more women worked as domestics, cooks, washers, and personal maids, enslaved women and youth were vulnerable to sexual exploitation or random acts of physical abuse. While wives were less likely to be raped than single women, bondmen were powerless to prevent white men from sexually exploiting black females.

Despite these strains on the enslaved family, the reasons for a significant population increase are manifold and complicated. The prevailing ethos of paternalism offers a means of comprehending this change. Scholars have often mistakenly construed paternalism as white kindness and black accommodation. Paternalism was based on the careful calculation of the balance of power between slaveholder and the enslaved, white-held presumptions of right and wrong, and economic self-interest; kindness rarely entered into the equation. Bondpeople knew that it was only the threat of coercion, which permitted cooperation; violence—or the threat of violence—was ubiquitous in slavery, and the institution could not have existed without it. While no southern state recognized slave marriage, most slaveholders advocated marriage among their bondpeople because it encouraged morality, stability, and a means to increase their population. While whites in the colonial era offered their enslaved workers a barn or shed for housing, by the antebellum period, slaveholders would customarily provide black families with a small wooden cabin to reinforce the sense of a nuclear family.

Enslaved family units shielded bondpeople from the worst cruelties of slavery, and it was these family units that oftentimes help bondpeople fight against insurmountable odds. Enslaved blacks developed complex family structures that included two-parent, single-parent, and extended family groupings consisting of biological and fictive kin (those who were not related, but who acted as family). Families tended to be large, with the average number of births being seven. Enslaved couples had to ask for permission to marry; this usually was not a problem if partners lived together on the same farm or plantation. Yet, when an enslaved man from one plantation married a woman from another, he had to ask for a pass to visit his family. Although slaveholders worried that the travel might give bondmen ideas of independence, most thought the benefit outweighed the risks and these abroad "marriages" and families were fairly common. In fact, some enslaved couples preferred to live on different estates from their partners in order to create emotional distance that shielded them from witnessing any cruelties inflicted upon their loved ones.

The two-parent household was common in a variety of locations, but deviations from this social structure were often due to the place, size, or crop(s) produced. For example, two-parent slave families commonly lived apart on small farms. In these settings, the father lived on one plantation, and the mother and children lived together on another. The children often viewed their mother as the head of household because fathers were usually granted a weekly pass and had little control over the frequency of such visitations. Despite such challenges, relationships between husbands and wives and parents and children often endured for many years. Even though family members could rarely stop the beating or selling of their children or partners, they sought to shield and protect each other from these types of abuses. For example, wives and mothers helped their children complete agricultural tasks, supplemented inadequate food rations, and took punishments for them. Husbands and fathers also intervened on behalf of their spouses and children, and sometimes prevailed or redirected white anger upon themselves.

Some historians believe that fathers acted as the heads of their families and were considered as such by their wives, children, and the larger slave community. In their homes, some scholars maintain, both enslaved men and women strove to uphold the father's position as both a provider and a protector despite slaveholders' control and rationing of necessities like clothes and food. Other scholars posit that male-female relationships in the slave quarters are best characterized as either matrifocal (headed by the mother) or egalitarian. For example, women who labored as hard as men in the fields, often continued working late into the night completing household chores. While they prepared food, cleaned, made and laundered clothing, men also contributed by fishing and trapping animals. Both husbands and wives worked in the family's garden plot, if they had one.

Historians have long debated the dynamics of slave families. Many scholars have examined slave families that comprised two parents and asked: aside from the white slaveholder, was there a "head" of the slave family? Although female-headed households were not unheard of in slavery—either by abroad marriages or through the separation of family members—some evidence suggests that enslaved households, at least culturally, remained patriarchal. A long line of scholars have noted that white males were in charge of antebellum society and family units were further subsumed under their leadership. The male was the head of household by law and custom, and as heads of household, white men also oversaw life on the plantation. They had authority over white women and children as well as enslaved blacks. This was true even as the roles of the wife and mother became more delineated in the nineteenth century, especially regarding the care of young children. Thus, antebellum southern culture looked to the enslaved father as the head.

Enslaved family at the Gaines' house, ca. 1861 or 1862. (Library of Congress.)

Using the legal definition of patriarchy, the black family was patriarchal only relatively at best. Black fathers were not the legal head of their families—the slaveholders were. In the 1600s, states adopted the Virginia law, which declared that "all children born in this country shall be held bond or free only according to the condition of the mother." The law meant that black mothers transfered their enslaved or free status to their children. This excluded black men from patriarchy and invalidated any patriarchal structure to enslaved families. As state laws prohibited bondpeople from owning property or taking part in public life, black men were excluded from participating in or reaping any of the political and economic benefits from patriarchy. This exclusion of enslaved men put them on an equal level with enslaved women, as neither gender held economic power over the other. Since neither black men nor women controlled their labor, this semblance of gender equality might have prompted many bondwomen to view themselves as equal to their male counterparts.

In 1998, sociologist Orlando Patterson examined the contemporary black family. He blamed slavery for what was argued as a continuous trend of broken family units, fatherless children, and matriarchal households. Patterson's analysis revisits a historical debate that reached a pinnacle with the publication of Senator Daniel Patrick Moynihan's 1965 report, *The Negro Family: The Case for National Action*. Moynihan's report caused widespread concern over entrenched black poverty and what was defined as the "Black Matriarchy." While no one has been able to satisfactorily define the "Black Matriarchy," scholars imply that an abundance of female-headed households simply constitutes this type of familial organization. Likewise, they argue that historical and contemporary claims of a "Black Matriarchy" are more accusatory and uncritical explanations for unresolved social ills than accurate descriptions of black family life. Some seek to counter this argument with descriptions of the black family as patriarchal. However, the debate surrounding the structure and organization of enslaved families has set up a false dichotomy. Recent works by historians such as Herbert Gutman, Anne Malone, Larry Hudson, and Brenda Stevenson have demonstrated that these concepts are on a continuum and that historians need additional examinations of local slave communities to further understand how families actually survived and resisted the traumas of slavery.

Orville Vernon Burton and Beatrice Burton

See also Courtship; Domestic Slave Trade; Gardening; Marriage, Abroad; Marriage and Cohabitation.

Suggested Reading

Orville Burton, *In My Father's House Are Many Mansions*: *Family and Community in Edgeville, South Carolina* (Chapel Hill: University of North Carolina Press, 1985); Herbert George Gutman, *The Black Family in Slavery and Freedom* (New York: Vintage Books, 1977, c1976); Larry E. Hudson, *To Have and To Hold: Slave Work and Family Life in Antebellum South Carolina* (Athens: University of Georgia Press, 1997); Ann Patton Malone, *Sweet Chariot*: *Slave Family and Household Structure in Nineteenth Century Louisiana* (Chapel Hill: University of North Carolina Press, 1992); Brenda E. Stevenson, *Life in Black and White: Family and Community in the Slave South* (New York: Oxford University Press, 1996); Michael Tadman, *Speculators and Slaves: Masters, Traders, and Slaves in the Old South* (University of Wisconsin Press, 1989).

Fancy Girls

Fancy girls have been documented throughout the history of the South. The term refers to bondwomen who were selected on the basis of their physical appearance and were intended as sexual partners for white men. In most of the extant accounts of fancy girls, their appearance is noted as very light-skinned, as a result of many centuries of miscegenation between people of African, Native American, and European descent. While not all fancy girls were selected by this criterion, the sexual exploitation of racially mixed women in the United States was particularly expressed through this trade. Although rape and coercive sex did not distinguish between dark-skinned women and those that were almost white in appearance, the evidence of any African blood whatsoever justified, in the eyes of whites, the

Mary and Emily Edmonson, ca. 1850–1860. (Library of Congress.)

right of white men to dominate those who were unprotected under the law and often considered promiscuous and inferior by contemporary standards.

The "fancy" trade in the United States had several negative consequences upon mixed-race women. It often separated young girls from their families because of a white man's inclination for a steep profit. In one notable narrative, Eliza, the former mixed-race mistress of her enslaver, was sold with her daughter, Emily. The family was further divided when Emily was sold away from her mother. Although the man who purchased Eliza wanted her and her daughter, the slave trader refused because he knew that " 'there were heaps and piles of money to be made of her ... There were men enough in New Orleans who would give five thousand dollars for such an extra handsome, fancy piece as Emily would be ... No, no he would not sell her then' " (White 1985, 38). Not only were women and girls of mixed racial heritage susceptible to extreme sexual exploitation due to their physical appearance, their mothers were also vulnerable to losing their daughters to this insidious "trade in flesh." Young girls were not protected by their tender ages; youth, often coupled with light skin, was even more of a stimulant in their sexual exploitation. As light-skinned Harriet Jacobs shared in her narrative, *Incidents in the Life of a Slave Girl,* when she reached her adolescence, several men had offered to purchase her at high prices (Jacobs 1987, 19). Her enslaver chose to keep her on the pretense that he could not sell his daughter's servant. However, when Jacobs turned 15, she noted that she entered "a sad epoch in the life of a slave girl" (Ibid., 27). She wrote that the slaveholder's true intentions became known as he "began to whisper foul words in my ear" (Ibid.).

An anonymous writer recalled that in an auction of "nigger wenches," slave traders unabashedly presented their female victims as "warranted virgins," excellent as potential concubines, and valuable for "the manufacture of light colored slaves" (Toplin 1979, 190). Men were willing to pay four to five times the amount that a standard field worker would bring for these women who might become their sexual companions. In his work on the Domestic Slave Trade, Walter Johnson analyzed the role that racial ideology played in the minds of slaveholders. There was a world of meaning embedded within the appearance and skin color of African people, and Johnson states that, "whiteness was doubly sold in the slave market" (Johnson 1999, 155). While dark skin was associated with productivity, strength, and endurance, whites connected lighter skin with delicacy, intelligence, and gentility. This was often a crucial factor in determining who would labor in slaveholders' houses or fields. However, white men played out a fantasy in pursuing these "fancy pieces" by exploiting women who were white in appearance, and who personified the sexual availability of slaves. Johnson explains that the association of enslaved people's light skin with delicacy and modesty were merely "projections of slaveholders' own dreamy interpretations of the meaning of their own skin color" (Ibid., 155).

Historian Edward Baptist further describes fancy girls as pornographic symbols in the minds of their purchasers and rapists. He remarks that light-skinned women "were products of the long encounter between white exploiters of labor and black sources of labor, productive and reproductive" (Baptist 2001, 1647). Mixed race women hence symbolized a commodity and a sexual fetish, and by raping these women, Baptist posits that white men "had sex with their own history" since these sorts of acts had initially created this class of women. Thus, light-skinned "fancy girls" represented their right to force all women of African descent into bending to their sexual domination and raw power.

Nicole Ribianszky

See also Concubinage; Domestic Slave Trade; Gender Conventions; Girlhood; Miscegenation; Narratives; Prices; Sexuality; Violence, Sexual.

Suggested Reading

Edward E. Baptist, " 'Cuffy,' 'Fancy Maids,' and 'One-Eyed Men': Rape, Commodification, and the Domestic Slave Trade in the United States," *American Historical Review* 106, 5 (December 2001): 1619–50; Harriet A. Jacobs, *Incidents in the Life of a Slave Girl: Written by Herself*, ed. Jean Fagan Yellin (Cambridge: Harvard University Press, 1987); Walter Johnson, *Soul by Soul: Life Inside the Antebellum Slave Market* (Cambridge: Harvard University Press, 1999); Robert Brent Toplin, "Between Black and White: Attitudes toward Southern Mulattoes, 1830–1861," *The Journal of Southern History* 45, 2 (May 1979): 185–200; Deborah Gray White, *Ar'n't I a Woman?: Female Slaves in the Plantation South* (New York: W.W. Norton & Company, 1985).

Female Slave Network

The female slave network represented a series of networks enslaved girls and women formed among allies, friends, and patrons for resistance, communication, support, and social interaction. Female slave networks sought to protect members from physical threats as well as communicate news and information. Networks differed depending upon whether they were formed in urban or rural settings and in domestic, industrial, or agricultural working environments. By forming networks, women helped to maintain family and interpersonal relationships over distances, exchange information, moderate the effects of separation and sale, protect against domestic and sexual violence, and to forge a degree of female solidarity. Female slave networks were not merely defensive. Some assisted women in courtship, disseminating health information about birth control, maintaining religious communities, and organizing social events such as parties.

Slavery isolated and constrained women more than men because bondwomen were less likely to work on transportation networks and in public places. During childhood, women and men often worked alongside one another in the fields and in some southern factories, but more women occupied domestic service positions, leaving them isolated in the households of slaveholders or temporary employers. Motherhood compounded the burdens of enslavement. After a hard day's labor in a field or factory, mothers still had to take care of children. When bondpeople became too old to work in fields, they were then tasked with looking after younger children. Bondwomen enlisted fellow enslaved workers, family members, free women and men, and even slaveholders into networks to help them respond to such challenges. These networks also protected enslaved girls and women from sexual abuse, even though they were at a distinct power disadvantage. Enslaved women—more than men—were subject to sexual exploitation at the hands of slaveholders, overseers, and others. Bondwomen formed alliances to protect themselves and relatives, especially blood kin, from the worst abuses. Women sought protections within such networks and used them to shelter other enslaved girls and women from abuse. For example, a network of allies headed by Harriet Jacobs' grandmother protected her from her enslaver's sexual advances by keeping her hidden in an attic for several years before making it possible to run away.

Enslaved females were operatives on the Underground Railroad and used their networks to help runaways or assist in other forms of truancy. Harriet Tubman is the most famous example of a woman who operated a large-scale network to help bondpeople run away. Bondwomen routinely harbored runaways, and in turn, they received shelter when they ran away. One catalyst for truancy was violence, the threat of violence, or sexual abuse, to which women were particularly vulnerable. Running away, even temporarily, served to protest or prevent abuse, and women relied on the help and support of other enslaved women to help them carry out their objectives. Women empathized, offered support, and mobilized quickly. Sometimes truancy involved mothers hiding their children in woods or placing them with other members of their network to avoid an imminent sale. These covert activities provided solidarity despite physical distance and severe constraints.

Enslaved women's networks of resistance differed in urban and rural locations. Bondwomen in cities such as Richmond and New Orleans sometimes created complex networks for protection and communication, which involved allies in churches, factories, and other social settings. The church functioned as a network hub, connecting many women together within a city or neighborhood. Some women who were hired out bargained for working conditions that included visiting privileges of their friends and relatives. Employers' consent to allow members of networks to interact with a domestic servant could help mitigate abuse because it worked against the enforced isolation that these work environments created. In sparsely populated areas such as the frontier and mountain South, however, enslaved women had fewer opportunities to create protective networks and were more vulnerable as a result. In rural agricultural areas, especially the Cotton South, women and men often performed the same type of labor since there was little gender separation in the fields. Agricultural workers, therefore, were not as isolated as domestic workers.

No matter their type of labor, enslaved women took part in communications networks such as the clandestine "grapevine," where they exchanged surveillance and news often over considerable geographic distances. Women who were separated from family members or hired out to perform work would also use communications networks to make sure their remaining children received adequate care and instruction if possible. While females largely mediated these networks, enslaved males played a significant role in maintaining them as well. Enslaved men often formed the main lines of clandestine communications since they performed work in the transportation trades and took goods to market on wagons and riverboats, worked on railroads, or loaded and unloaded cargo. Women often enlisted enslaved men in helping to communicate over long distances and they often took advantage of these commercial networks to conduct secret businesses on the side. In addition, a select group of bondwomen served as market women or "hucksters" and had received permission to sell goods in urban markets. These women worked with their male contemporaries to participate in trading networks.

Often such communications networks could have profound local influences. Historian Laura Edwards has found that enslaved women maintained "gossip networks" that diffused cultural knowledge, often about the reputations of whites, into the broader community. That knowledge gained acceptance as it was repeated first by bondpeople and then by free people. Reports that originated with bondwomen could often become valid in court cases. Enslaved women therefore could influence legal proceedings even though they were barred from giving evidence because of their enslaved status. Slaveholders could be enlisted unwittingly in female slave networks when they spread gossip or repeated it as sworn testimony.

Enslaved women also formed networks that facilitated other types of social interactions, such as secret dances, parties, and courtship opportunities. In rural areas, female slave networks were critical to maintaining social connections across plantation and farm boundaries. Bondpeople organized clandestine parties for which they made and shared luxury goods such as decorative clothing, hair, and headdresses. They often availed themselves at night for gatherings, sometimes traveling miles away from their homes to gatherings where they danced, played music, sang, worshipped, carried on friendships and courtships, and exchanged gossip, news, and information. Sometimes, the secret dance or religious meeting would be the only way spouses could see each other, particularly if slaveholders barred interactions with other farms and plantations, or if they were part of a marriage abroad. Some arrived home at dawn and, although exhausted; they were forced to work a long day in the fields or factories.

Female slave networks also delivered medical knowledge and healthcare, especially in the realms of sexual health and childbirth. Enslaved females shared information on contraception and abortion and located a midwife for pregnant women, who often preferred slave healers to white physicians. Women often kept abortions secret because slaveholders would punish women for having them. Abortions meant that the enslaver would lose a property interest in the child of a bondwoman. Many enslaved women preferred to rely on local knowledge rather than white physicians, and slave healers were sometimes expert in the use of folk remedies, spiritual medicine, and in understanding human anatomy and psychology.

The female slave network served to connect enslaved girls and women who were especially vulnerable to isolation and abuse under slavery. Members of networks relied on one another for support, protection, news, information, and in the creation and maintenance of human relationships. Historians have debated the extent of the female slave network. First recognized by historian Deborah Gray White in the 1980s, recent scholarship has uncovered evidence of the female slave network existing and operating in many contexts and extending into all aspects of bondwomen's lives.

Calvin Schermerhorn

See also Abortion; Contraception; Courtship; Domestic Slave Trade; Free Women; Hair and Headdresses; Health, Disabilities, and Soundness; Hiring Out; Marriage, Abroad; Midwives; Motherhood; Resistance; Runaways; Tubman, Harriet; Underground Railroad; Urban Slavery; Violence, Sexual.

Suggested Reading

Stephanie M. H. Camp, *Closer to Freedom: Enslaved Women & Everyday Resistance in the Plantation South* (Chapel Hill: University of North Carolina Press, 2004); Laura F. Edwards, "Status without Rights: African Americans and the Tangled History of Law and Governance in the Nineteenth-Century U.S. South," *The American Historical Review* 112, 2 (April 2007): 365–393; Sharla Fett, *Working Cures: Healing, Health, and Power on*

Southern Slave Plantations (Chapel Hill: University of North Carolina Press, 2002); Calvin Schermerhorn, *Money over Mastery, Family over Freedom: Slavery in the Antebellum Upper South* (Baltimore: Johns Hopkins University Press, 2011); Philip Troutman, "Grapevine in the Slave Market: African American Geopolitical Literacy and the 1841 Creole Revolt," in *The Chattel Principle: Internal Slave Trades in the Antebellum Slave Market*, ed. Walter Johnson (Cambridge: Yale University Press, 1999); Deborah Gray White, *Ar'n't I a Woman?: Female Slaves in the Plantation South*, 2nd ed. (New York: W. W. Norton, 1999).

Folk Medicine and Healing

Folk medicine and healing describes the ways in which enslaved people, particularly women, treated each other medically when they experienced various forms of illness. In enslaved communities, women under bondage primarily served as healers for both black and white men and women. Unlike white men who were physicians, enslaved women were not educated in medical schools. They learned their trade as apprentices under older, more experienced enslaved nurses and midwives and often worked under their plantation mistresses as nurse assistants. Black women's medical knowledge was both rooted in the supernatural world and in their physical environments. Therefore, enslaved women were almost entirely dependent upon the use of plants, roots, and herbs in their healing practices. During the 1930s, the Works Progress Administration (WPA), a federal program instituted by President Franklin D. Roosevelt, sent government workers to record the histories of formerly enslaved people. These oral histories shed light onto folk medicinal practices and the hidden lives of women who lived under slavery.

> In de old days we made lots of our own medicine and I still does it yet. We used polecat grease for croup and rheumatism. Dog-fennel, butterfly-root, and life-everlasting boiled and mixed and made into a syrup will cure pneumonia and pleurisy. Pursley-weed, called squirrel physic, boiled into a syrup will cure chills and fever. Snake-root steeped for a long time and mixed with whiskey will cure chills and fever also.
>
> —Polly Colbert, former bondwoman (*Born in Slavery: Slave Narratives from the Federal Writers' Project, 1936–1938 Oklahoma Narratives, Volume XIII*, 82–83)

Bondwomen believed that "healing depends on the ability of the healer to draw on the power to control, protect, or attack . . . to orchestrate the flow of the natural, the spiritual, and relational aspects of life" (Mitchem 2007, 17). As many of their oral testimonies attest, folk medicine and healing sought to treat the body's physical ailments and to use the religious and magical world to cure or fix unnatural disorders. In many enslaved communities, supernatural healing was called "roots work."

Working with roots and herbs was one method through which bondwomen carried on an aspect of African cultural practices. Some female enslaved healers would order their patients to wear special roots like asafetida in pouches around their necks as a form of protection from either illness or evil. This custom has origins in several West African nations like Ghana, Nigeria, and Sierra Leone, the origins of the majority of enslaved people brought to America. Enslaved women also borrowed medicinal recipes from their Native American and white neighbors. For example, both blacks and Native Americans relied on blackberries to help treat stomach ailments such as dysentery. The knowledge gained from understanding the secrets of healing from whites and Native Americans allowed black women a semblance of authority on farms and plantations.

Folk medicine created a space for enslaved black women to exert power within their communities. Bondwomen and white medical men were frequently at odds over how sick black bodies needed to be treated and cared for by medical personnel. As a result, when black women utilized folk healing and medicine, they asserted that they knew what was best for other enslaved people. Bondpeople held black nurse and midwife occupational roles in great esteem and trusted their nonintrusive and nonsurgical methods of healing. Many times, slaveholders would use medical care as a form of punishment against the enslaved. Blacks sometimes feared they would die at the hands of white doctors and surgeons if either surgery or the ingestion of harsh and toxic medicines was required.

The reproductive care of enslaved women arose out of the needs of both the slaveholding and enslaved population. Bondwomen's healing knowledge was especially regarded when it came to their midwifery work with pregnant women. "Granny midwife" was a term commonly used to describe the elderly enslaved women who worked with parturient women. Dellie Lewis reminisced about the ways her grandmother assisted pregnant women during childbirth under slavery. In an interview with a WPA worker, she disclosed that her grandmother used a blend of "cloves and whiskey to ease the pain" of delivery for her patients (Yetman 1972, 47). In another example, Julia Brown of Atlanta stated that her granny midwife put an axe under her mattress to stop the pains after birth. Most enslaved nurses used "roots and bark for teas of all kinds" to cure illnesses (Williams 2004, 78), and bondwomen appreciated these women's remedies because they were gentler on their bodies than surgery.

Slave nurses were crucial to the economy of slavery. They mended physically sick bodies as well as interpreted the unknown through their medical work. At the beck and call of both whites and blacks, midwives and nurses had awesome professional responsibilities. However, these enslaved women managed to heal their charges with a greater success rate than southern white male doctors and achieved status within their communities by highlighting the supernatural aspects of their labor.

Due to the records of the WPA, the passing down of medical knowledge by formerly enslaved people through oral histories and continuous practice, black folk medicine and healing still exists. In communities like the Sea Islands in South

Carolina and coastal Georgia, there is a thriving subculture of "root" doctors and herbal specialists who are regarded by local blacks with a mixture of awe, fear, and respect. Black folk healing continues to be intertwined with the physical and spiritual realms and deeply connected to religious life, cultural practices, family relationships, and social activism.

Deidre Cooper Owens

See also Childbirth; Community; Elderly Women; Health, Disabilities, and Soundness; Midwives; Plantation Mistresses.

Suggested Reading

Stephanie Y. Mitchem, *African American Folk Healing* (New York: New York University Press, 2007); Horace Randall Williams, ed. *Weren't No Good Times: Personal Accounts of Slavery in Alabama* (Winston-Salem, NC: John F. Blair, Publisher, 2004); Norman Yetman, ed. *Voices from Slavery* (New York, Chicago, and San Francisco: Holt, Rhinehart and Winston, 1972).

Folklore and Folktales

The cultural values of the enslaved community were embodied in a rich oral tradition that was an important part of slave life. Most of the slave folktales that have been collected are trickster stories that center on a cunning male protagonist—Br'er Rabbit in the animal tales and Jack or John in other tales—with female characters appearing only as foils. A few surviving folktales feature women or girls as major actors; however, a comprehensive collection of women's folktales has yet to be made.

Since most enslaved Africans were prevented from learning to read and write, they developed a profound storytelling tradition. These folktales were widely known in the antebellum South, and they amused generations of nineteenth-century Americans—both white and black. One of the persistent misunderstandings of these stories is that they were light and nonsensical tales that bondpeople merely told to pass the time or for amusement. Contemporary scholars, however, recognize that this folklore represents a serious oral literature produced by the enslaved community that embodies a counterideology to prevailing notions of racism and white supremacy.

African American folktales performed the same functions as any other genre of literature. Although the tales were usually quite humorous, enslaved blacks used them to explore the most central and urgent issues of their lives. They used folktales to inspire, educate, socialize children, maintain solidarity within their communities, rebuke and satirize enslavers, protest the conditions of bondage, resist the dehumanization of slavery, accommodate to the inevitabilities of slavery, communicate encoded messages, suggest solutions to common dilemmas, and to explain how things came to be.

It is a profound achievement of African American culture that folktales could achieve all of these purposes with such subtlety and ambiguity in full view of white society without attracting suspicion or condemnation. This, in itself, gives insight into the nature of slave culture and black consciousness in the antebellum South. Antebellum slave culture was consistently subtle and indirect. African American folktales suggests that storytellers were extremely careful with their words and crafted their symbols and meanings with a delicate nuance and shrewd complexity that illustrates that enslaved blacks held their secrets in plain sight.

Most of the animal stories are trickster tales. These are consistently the stories of how a small, weak, but cunning male creature (such as a rabbit) outsmarts another much larger, more powerful, but rather stupid male animal (a fox, perhaps) who in the natural course of things should be eating the smaller creature. The little trickster animal is marked by his capacity for bragging, lying, and trickery as well as his strutting, egotistical, and self-assured personality. The larger animal is portrayed as dull, slow, rather unsure of himself, and easily tricked. The identification of the smaller animals with the enslaved and the larger ones with the slaveholder must have been obvious to the black community in antebellum times, but it never seems to have occurred to slaveholding whites. There were some tales that were never told in the presence of whites. While the themes and personalities of these stories were similar to the animal tales, they explicitly told how a bondperson outsmarted his or her enslaver.

Women and girls appear in many of these stories, though seldom as protagonists. This may indicate that the folktales collected so far represent the stories that enslaved men told, rather than those told by women. Nonetheless, the attitudes of the slave community toward women can often be observed in these collected tales. In the story of the Tar Baby, Brer Rabbit is caught by Brer Fox and almost killed after the fox fashions a doll made of tar in the shape of a woman. Brer Rabbit flirts with the Tar Baby and becomes upset when she does not reply to his greetings. Joel Chandler Harris's text of the story reads:

> "De Tar-Baby, she sot dar, she did, en Brer Fox, he lay low.
> " 'Mawnin'!' sez Brer Rabbit, sezee—'nice wedder dis mawnin',' sezee.
> "Tar-Baby ain't sayin' nothin', en Brer Fox, he lay low.
> " 'How duz you' sym'tums seem ter segashuate?' sez Brer Rabbit, sezee.
> ... en de Tar-Baby she ain't sayin' nothin'.
> " 'How you come on, den? Is you deaf?' sez Brer Rabbit, sezee. 'Kaze if you is, I kin holler louder,' sezee.
> "Tar-Baby stay still, en Brer Fox, he lay low.

" 'You er stuck up, dat's wat you is," says Brer Rabbit, sezee, 'en I'm gwine ter kyore you, dat's w'at I'm a gwine ter do,' sezee. . . . 'I'm gwine ter larn you how ter talk ter spectubble folks ef hit's de las' ack,' . . .

"Brer Rabbit keep on axin' 'im, en de Tar-Baby, she keep on sayin' nothin', twel present'y Brer Rabbit draw back wid his fis', he did, en blip he tuck 'er side er de head. . . . (Harris 1955, 7)

When Brer Rabbit hits the Tar Baby, he becomes stuck. As he continues to struggle with her, he becomes completely immoblized by tar and the fox is able to capture him. This tale is rich with multiple meanings, but it includes some warnings about women. Although Brer Rabbit manages to escape, he has placed himself in mortal danger through his egotistical behavior and his violence against women.

Another folktale entitled "The Ways of De Wimmens" may have originated during slavery. In this story, Adam and Eve are created equal by God, but they are always arguing because Eve wants to control Adam. Adam complains to God that Eve has an advantage because when she cries, she can make him do whatever she wants since he feels so "low down and dirty" when she does it. He asks God to make him stronger than Eve. When his request is granted, he rushes home and fights with Eve, beating her into submission. Adam then proclaims himself the head of the house and boss of Eve. Eve is angered by Adam's controlling demands and consults the devil. He advises her to ask God for some keys hanging on a nail. When she receives them, she runs home and locks the doors. When Adam returns and asks for food, Eve tells him that the kitchen door is locked and she cannot cook anything. Adam with all his strength cannot knock down the door. Eve tells him to go out and chop the wood and she will try something. The story continues:

"Wood choppin is you work," say Adam, "since I got most strength [and can tell you what to do]. But I do hit dis once, an see can you open de do."

So he git de wood and when he comes back, Eve has de do open. An from den on out Eve kept de key to de kitchen and made Adam haul in de wood.

Well, after supper Adam say, "Come on honey, less you and me hit de froghair."

"Can't," say Eve. "De baidroom do is locked."

"Dadblame!" say Adam. "Reckson you can trick dat do too, Eve?"

"Might can," say Eve. "Honey, you jes git a piece of tin and patch dat little hole in de roof, and while you's doin hit, maybe I can git the baidroom do open."

So Adam patched de roof an Eve she unlocked de baidroom do. From den on she kept DAT key and used hit to suit herself.

So dat de reason, de very reason, why de mens THINKS dey is boss and de wimmens KNOWS dey is boss, cause dey got dem two little keys to use in dat slippery sly wimmen's way. (Hughes and Bontemps, 63–64; Hurston 1935, 31–34)

In this story, Eve comes out the winner. In the 1930s, Zora Neale Hurston presents the tale as being told by women, hence demonstrating women's participation in the telling of tales and the imparting of symbolic lessons and meanings. Despite the emphasis on women, the story remains male-centered. Men are deemed responsible for heavy household duties, and women's power is relegated to sex and cooking. Hurston recorded an alternate version of this tale which also gave women the key to the door of Adam's "generations" or heirs. Thus, the tale identifies a sexual division of labor and marks women as sly and slippery. Since no comprhensive collection of women's folktales has been made, a full understanding of the folklore of enslaved women will have to await further research.

Anthony Lee

See also Community; Conflict, Intraracial; Gender Conventions; Narratives.

Suggested Reading

Roger D. Abrahams, ed., *African American Folktales: Stories from Black Traditions in the New World* (New York: Pantheon Books, 1985); Arna Bontemps and Langston Hughes, Popo and Fifina (New York: Oxford University Press, 1931; 1993); Thurman Garner, "Black Ethos in Folktales," in *Journal of Black Studies* 15, 1 (September 1984): 53–66; Henry Louis Gates, *The Signifying Monkey: A Theory of African-American Literary Criticism* (New York: Oxford University Press, 1988); Joel Chandler Harris, *The Complete Tales of Uncle Remus* (Boston: Houghton Mifflin Company, 1955); Zora Neal Hurston, *Mules and Men* (New York: HarperCollins, 1935).

Food Preparation and Cooking

Maw didn't work in de field. She say she done been hurt when she got a whippin' when she ain't growed [when she wasn't grown, i.e., still a child] and her back ain't good no more. Old Missy say, "Eva, you come in de kitchen and make some chittlin's, and iffen you cooks good, you can work in my kitchen." Maw, she make dem chittlin's and dey's damn good, so she gits to cook den.

—Willis Woodson, former slave
(Howell, Donna, ed., *I Was a Slave: True Stories Told by Former Slaves in the 1930s*, 16)

Food preparation and cooking were integral to the enslaved African American community. Food provided the daily nourishment needed to sustain life, represented a sense of community and identity, and offered collective and individual enjoyment. For enslaved women, cooking symbolized a form of cultural work that enabled them to provide for their families, creatively resist slavery, and forge a distinct culinary tradition.

Enslaved female house and field servants and cooks prepared meals for their families and plantation owners. They were praised for transforming meager rations into innovative culinary dishes. The typical slave diet included, but was not limited to, vegetables, cowpeas, cornmeal, peanuts, lima beans, millet, okra, beans, rice, seafood, chicken, salt meat, sweet potatoes, turnips, collards, milk, and a variety of fruits and breads like cornbread and buttermilk biscuits. Black women cooks combined a variety of vegetables and meats and blended African and European imported spices to enhance the taste of food. For example, leafy green collards, beans, okra, rice, and meats like beef and pork were used to thicken soups and stews. Spices were used to season pork, poultry, seafood, and rice dishes. On large plantations, slave cooks had access to spacious kitchens and cooking utensils such as various-sized cast iron pots, tin plates, skillets, and frying pans. Food preparation on small plantations, as suggested by historian Charles Joyner, was a crude affair.

In their quarters, enslaved women used whatever they could to prepare and consume food. They prepared meals over open-hearth fireplaces with one or two big pots or frying pans. Handmade wooden spoons, forks, and knives and broken pottery were used as utensils. Some enslaved families lacked eating utensils and consumed food with their hands. With one or two iron pots and frying pans, enslaved women prepared common meals like ashcakes. Ashcake is a flat corn cake wrapped in cabbage leaves and baked in hot ashes on a hearth. With limited cookware, enslaved women also prepared one-pot meals such as sofki. Sofki is a base of ground corn and hickory nuts combined with any available vegetable or meat. On plantations in South Carolina and Georgia, rice was a common ingredient in one-pot meals. Rice was boiled with fish, pork, and vegetables including black-eyed peas. A popular one-pot rice dish known as Hoppin' John combined rice with black-eyed peas, spicy sausages, ham hocks, and tomato sauce. One-pot meals benefited the enslaved family because they were easy to prepare, lasted for several days, and allowed enslaved cooks to utilize all parts of added meats, spices, and vegetables.

Enslaved women's unique culinary styles were symbolic of and inspired by African cooking traditions. The cooking of certain foods including yams, sesame seeds, okra, sorghum, and legumes as well as and methods of food preparation such as frying in deep oil, steaming plants, and baking in hot coals or ashes symbolized a sense of familiarity and identification with Africa. In various parts of the South, enslaved females prepared African-inspired dishes such as red rice and fufu, a type of pancake prepared by boiling water and stirring flour. They also prepared coosh-coosh, a fried dish made with cornmeal, onions, and peppers. African inspired dishes and cooking styles included

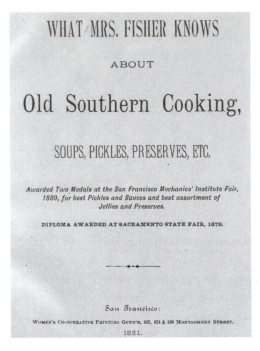

WHAT MRS. FISHER KNOWS

ABOUT

Old Southern Cooking,

SOUPS, PICKLES, PRESERVES, ETC.

Awarded Two Medals at the San Francisco Mechanics' Institute Fair, 1880, for best Pickles and Sauces and best assortment of Jellies and Preserves.

DIPLOMA AWARDED AT SACRAMENTO STATE FAIR, 1879.

San Francisco:

WOMEN'S CO-OPERATIVE PRINTING OFFICE, 420, 424 & 430 MONTGOMERY STREET,
1881.

Title page of *What Mrs. Fisher Knows About Old Southern Cooking*, 1881, possibly the first published cookbook by an African American woman. (Fisher, Abby, *What Mrs. Fisher Knows About Old Southern Cooking*, San Francisco: Women's Cooperative Printing Office, 1881.)

meals for planters' homes. Enslaved cooks combined African cuisine with that of European cooking traditions and introduced southern whites to deep-fried foods as well as a series of spicy foods and one-pot meals such as gumbo and jambalaya.

LaShawn D. Harris

See also Community; Diet and Nutrition; Female Slave Network

Suggested Reading

Herbert C. Covey and Dwight Eisnach, *What the Slaves Ate: Recollections of African American Foods and Foodways from the Slave Narratives* (Santa Barbara: Greenwood Press/ABC-CLIO, 2009); Charles Joyner, *Down by the Riverside: A South Carolina Slave Community* (Urbana: University of Illinois Press, 2009); Deborah Gray White, *Ar'n't I a Woman?" Female Slaves in the Plantation South* (New York: W.W. Norton, 1999).

Free Women

Free women of African descent, also referred to as free black women or free women of color, were present in North America from the earliest times of European exploration and settlement, which began with the Spanish. Slavery was often quite real to them, having at one time been enslaved themselves, having friends or family that were not free, actively or covertly struggling against the system, or in some rarer cases, owning slaves of their own. Freedom for women of African descent was a circumscribed state and they occupied a stratum that was not enslavement, yet not full freedom. In other words, they were free in a society in which most blacks were slaves, but did not enjoy all of the rights and privileges that whites did. In all places in North America, there were certain restrictions placed upon free black communities. Additionally, freedom was not technically actualized through legal channels for many women, yet they were not bound to owners and "acted" as if they were free. Scholars have termed free black women "quasi slaves" and have estimated that this elusive population represented as much as 20 percent of the African American population.

The earliest known free woman of African descent, Isabel de Olvera, surfaces in documentation from New Mexico in 1600 where she claimed to be "a free woman, unmarried, and the legitimate daughter of Hernando, a Negro, and an Indian woman" (Taylor and Moore, 33). However, there is evidence that African women were in North America as early as 1526 in the present-day states of Florida, New Mexico, and California. Their individual status as free or enslaved is unclear, but it can be reasonably presumed that there were some free women among them. These women are recorded as domestics and agricultural workers.

African American woman wearing a hat and holding a parasol, ca. 1861–1870. (Library of Congress.)

In British North America, the traditional date for the first documented Africans is 1619 in Jamestown, Virginia. At that time, slavery was not defined as a lifelong institution for African women and it was possible for women to serve an indenture and gain their freedom. Isabella Johnson is a prime example of this. She and her husband, Anthony Johnson, eventually accumulated land and servants of their own, both black and white, and passed a legacy of hundreds of acres of land to her children. After key legislation passed in the 1640s and 1660s, slavery became a lifelong, racially specific institution in which status was passed through the mother. Free people of African descent came to suffer racial discrimination and laws were passed which subjected them to differential treatment than whites. In spite of this, the population of free women continued to grow and flourish until slavery was abolished in 1865.

Several factors accounted for their increase, and the reasons for freedom were varied. In all of the areas of Spanish, British, French, and Dutch American colonial rule, there were avenues open to women to gain their manumission from slavery. They could be freed for performing meritorious service such as nursing a sick owner, saving an owner's life, or by "serving faithfully" for a number of years.

One could also emancipate slaves in a last will and testament or by deed. The French and Spanish legal systems offered more options for freedom than the British and later American ones. For example, an owner could free a slave by marrying them within the Church. This would automatically emancipate the bondperson and any children of the marriage. Under the Spanish, the right of enslaved individuals to purchase themselves from their slaveholders, or *coartación*, was guaranteed even if the owners were not amenable to this. The courts stipulated that an enslaved individual could pay a regulated price for his or her freedom. This undoubtedly added significantly to the free population.

There were certain regional differences that distinguished free women's experiences from one another. Scholars have divided the United States into three regions—the North, the Upper South, and the Lower South—to discuss how freedom affected women of African descent. The nature of the emancipations affected these three different regions in terms of community size, occupation, and phenotypes. After the American Revolution, many owners recognized the hypocrisy of the ideal of liberty coexisting with slavery and freed large numbers of slaves, especially in the North and the Upper South. It was at this time that most northern states began gradually phasing out slavery and legislated for gradual emancipation of the enslaved. The North supported large communities of free blacks, mainly in urban centers like Boston, Philadelphia, and New York City. These populations would eventually increase naturally. Communities in the North tended to be the result of indiscriminate manumission and not due to familial or personal ties as in the Lower South. Thus, free blacks in this region were more racially homogenous and did not share the mixed race heritage of many free people of color in the Lower South, where some historians have estimated 75 percent of them to be mainly of mixed African and European ancestry.

Despite racial hostility, negative stereotyping, and poverty, many free black women in the North were able to build institutions in the community. There was a rich tradition of women organizing schools for black children. Free black women were also instrumental in forming churches. They were also free to become involved in the abolitionist movement and women like Sojourner Truth and Jarena Lee spoke out strongly against slavery. The free black community was viewed with much more suspicion in the South and there were more severe limitations placed upon them, including the inability to gather in groups, testify against whites in court, and openly publish and speak out for abolition. There was a substantial level of interaction between free blacks and the enslaved in the Upper South, and activities intended to subvert slavery took place, albeit more secretively than in the North.

The Lower South was largely untouched by the rhetoric of the American Revolution which often led to mass manumissions of enslaved communities. The numbers of free black people were considerably smaller in this region; most emancipations took place selectively and often were the result of relationships between white men and women of African descent, or the children who were born to them. Refugees displaced by the Haitian Revolution flooded into states like South Carolina and Louisiana and also inflated these communities. The communities of free people of color tended to be in urban areas and they were considered in many ways to be a buffer group between the enslaved and whites. They often held themselves aloof from enslaved people and practiced endogamous marriages to keep property holding within small, elite groups.

Free women of color quite often were freed due to their relationships with men, more often than not, white men. Many women experienced involuntary sexual coercion with white men, which was the reason for the genesis of their free status. At other times, white men freed their mixed-race children while allowing their mothers to continue in slavery. The results of these associations with white men ranged from the attainment of freedom, to children being freed, to the inheritance of property. There are accounts of free women inheriting a small cabin on a tiny plot of land to others that included hundreds of acres, thousands of dollars in money and household effects, multiple dwellings, and bondpeople.

Sexual relationships with white men were not limited solely to enslaved women. The long-lived practice of *plaçage* in New Orleans placed young free women of color into a position of dependence and support by white men. White men were encouraged from young ages to contract with the family of a free woman of color and make living and support arrangements for her and any children they might have, prior to getting married to a white woman, and even continuing on after. This practice, which essentially became an institution, provided an alternative to legal marriages, which were prohibited between any whites and people of African descent, free or enslaved, in Louisiana. Children were produced out of these common-law, or "left-handed marriages" and there was very little social stigma attached to them in the free community of color. In addition to these formal arrangements, there are examples of free black women cohabiting with white men not only in New Orleans, but also all over the Lower South.

The relationships free black women had with men included a variety of forms. Marriages between free black men and free black women were common, especially in the North where the communities of African Americans and the pool of eligible men were larger. In the South, however, although it is somewhat difficult to document, free women were married to enslaved men. Marriages like these may not have been supported by the men's owners due to the fact that any children the couple might have would be born free, based on their mother's status. There are some rare cases of free women offering themselves back into slavery to be near their husbands and other family members. Finally, in some cases, there are records of marriages between free women of color and white men. These types, however, were often subject to the state and local laws and community opprobrium.

Free women of color in all classes, time periods, and phenotypes were susceptible to physical abuse waged against them and suffered under this force. The mere circumstance of one's freedom, as well as the fact that some free women of color were educated, property-owning, and law-abiding, however, did not protect them from outright, forceful violence. There are accounts of free women of color coming under assault and being beaten, not only by men with whom they were intimate, but by men they encountered casually or in business.

It is critical to note that violence did not merely translate into a physical attack against a woman and abuse was not limited to only this type of maltreatment. Reenslavement, kidnapping, or imprisonment directed against their persons or that of their families constituted an ever-present, implicit threat and, thus, a psychological form of violence. The most vulnerable of free women of color were also the majority: poor, illiterate, and propertyless. Observing patterns of occupational and residential segregation—which often had the effect of exposing free women to poverty, disease, and crime—are helpful in considering the various means through which violence was waged against free women of color. They were subjected to police harassment, the threat of deportment from the state, and in more ways than not, the whim of the larger white community who surrounded them. They were also confined to occupations, which did not pay lucratively such as laundering, domestic labor, seamstressing, peddling goods at the market, and boarding rooms. Consequently, this overarching matrix of violence affected them in complicated ways and required them to create strategies to combat it or at the very least, survive it.

Another critical aspect to consider that differentiated women's experience of violence from that of men's was their position as mothers. Throughout much of the time period, free women of color outnumbered men, including those who headed their own households with children. Poor free women of color often had to acquiesce to their children being bound out as apprentices until they were adults. This often was a thinly veiled form of slavery in which children were beyond their protection, including from sexual exploitation. The specter of kidnapping was a grave threat laden with violence against not only the children themselves, but against the mothers who had to worry about it. Due to increasingly restrictive laws governing manumission of bondpeople over time in the South, some mothers were forced to purchase and hold their own children as slaves. They had to contend with the weighty knowledge that if they were to die, there was a chance that their daughters and sons could be sold off into slavery. Free women of color took their responsibilities as mothers seriously and endeavored to have their children educated, bound out to learn trades, and if possible, left them property.

The common beliefs that black women, free and enslaved, were hypersexual and promiscuous, coupled with women's difficulties in eking out a living in a society that limited their economic opportunities, lent fuel to the fire that many free women of color were prostitutes. The vicious character assassination on free women of color was actually a form of violence because they all contributed to the fact that free blacks were debased as human beings and were not deserving of all the protection of the law and even at its mercy.

These beliefs of the inferiority of women of African descent, together with the loss of sympathetic whites, could spell disaster for free women of color and result in the loss of property. Property was a way that women could buttress themselves against being completely at the mercy of white society. Some free women of color held thousands of dollars in real estate, businesses, sumptuous household furnishings and goods, and lavish attire and jewels. However, this was a not a failsafe measure. Whites frequently preyed upon women of African descent, by contesting the wills of their friends or relatives who bequeathed property or freedom to them or by exploiting legal technicalities. Free women of color found themselves victims of trickery and dangerous deception upon the deaths of people who protected free people by their standing in the community.

The tactics that free women of color had at their means to resist this violence were varied in type and effectiveness. At times, they would physically resist their tormentors. Other strategies included vacating the area, quitting jobs, or withholding affection. It has also been documented throughout the Americas that women of African descent, including enslaved women, utilized the court system to protest injustices and struggle for their rights. Lucy Terry Prince and Elizabeth Key might be among the most famous of free black women who prevailed upon the justice system. Another way that free women sought to protect themselves was by acquiring property and accumulating wealth to avoid exposing themselves to compromising situations. Complicating this, free women of color living in cities like New Orleans and Charleston in the Deep South sometimes supported the prevailing economic system by also becoming slaveholders and externally adopting the dominant society's attitudes. Some light-skinned free women of color tried and passed as white. These seemingly contradictory behaviors could be viewed as acts of resistance. Since women of African descent were the most vulnerable population to acts of violence, being absorbed into the white population and becoming accepted as an undiscovered component of a racist society simultaneously subverted the system, as well as afforded free women of color another layer of protection. The experiences of free black women during slavery could be viewed as a dress rehearsal for what life would be like for them once the Thirteenth Amendment abolished slavery: they lived in a netherworld between enslavement and freedom, but managed to hold onto their dignity and carve out lives and build community.

Nicole Ribianszky

See also American Revolution; French America; Key, Elizabeth; North, The; Prince, Lucy Terry; Slaveholders, Free Black Women; South, The; Truth, Sojourner.

Suggested Reading

Ira Berlin, *Slaves Without Masters: The Free Negro in the Antebellum South* (New York: Vintage Books, 1971); James Oliver Horton, "Freedom's Yoke: Gender Conventions among Antebellum Free Blacks," *Feminist Studies* 12, 1 (1986): 51–76; Wilma King, *The Essence of Liberty: Free Black Women during the Slave Era* (Columbia: University of Missouri Press, 2006); Dedra McDonald, "To Be Black and Female in the Spanish Southwest," in *African American Confront the West, 1600–2000* eds. Quintard Taylor and Shirley Ann Wilson Moore (Norman: University of Oklahoma Press, 2004), 32; Loren Schweninger, *Black Property Owners in the South, 1790–1915* (Urbana: University of Illinois Press, 1990).

Freeman, Elizabeth

Birth Date: ~1742
Death Date: 1829

Elizabeth Freeman tested the meaning of the ideals of freedom and equality that stood at the heart of American Revolution. In 1781, she filed suit against her owner and initiated a case which established a precedent that would dismantle the legality of slaveholding in Massachusetts. Freeman was born in Claverack, New York in 1742 and was also known as Mum Bett. She spent nearly 40 years in service to John Ashley of Sheffield, Massachusetts. While intervening during a violent confrontation between her sister and her owner's wife, Freeman fled the Ashleys' home after she was struck with a heated kitchen shovel. John Ashley appealed to the courts for her return. However, in 1781 with the legal assistance of Theodore Sedgewick, Freeman and an enslaved man, Brom, who also worked for the Ashleys, petitioned the court for their right to freedom. The core argument of *Brom and Bett vs. Ashley* rested on the premise that the newly adopted state constitution of Massachusetts declared freedom and equality for all persons irrespective of race, class, status, or gender.

There are a number of reasons which explain what compelled Freeman to sue for her freedom. The most obvious would have been to escape the exploitation and brutality of enslavement to exercise greater control over her life and labor. However, Freeman's case was also one in a series of legal petitions brought by enslaved men and women in New England during the Revolutionary era to both assert their individual right to the freedom upon which the Republic was founded and to abolish slavery as an institution. All of these cases demonstrated the extent to which the ideals of the American Revolution provided a language of inalienable rights that enslaved people believed should also extend to them.

The jury ruled in favor of Elizabeth Freeman's petition and ordered her former owner to pay both her and Brom 30 shillings along with court costs. She became the first enslaved black woman freed under the Massachusetts state constitution of 1780. In subsequent court rulings, most notably in the *Commonwealth vs. Jennison* decision of 1783, the Massachusetts court legally abolished slavery. Following her case, Elizabeth Freeman worked as a paid housekeeper in the home of her lawyer, Theodore Sedgewick. She later took up nursing and midwifery and moved into her own home with her only daughter in Stockbridge, Massachusetts. She remained here until her death in 1829. Freeman's legacy of advocacy for the rights of black Americans to freedom and equality lived on in the work of her great-grandson, civil rights pioneer W.E.B. Dubois.

Kennetta Hammond Perry

See also Abolitionism; American Revolution; Emancipation; Laws; North, The; Violence, Racial.

Suggested Reading

Sidney Kaplan and Emma Kaplan, *The Black Presence in the American Revolution* (Amherst: University of Massachusetts Press, 1989); Gary Nash, *The Forgotten Fifth: African Americans in the Age of Revolution* (Cambridge, MA: Harvard University Press, 2006); "The Massachusetts Constitution, Judicial Review and Slavery: The Mum Bett Case," http://www.mass.gov/courts/sjc/constitution-slavery-d.html.

French America

Louisiana was probably the only place in the antebellum South where, at her death in 1837, Madame Couvent, an 80-year-old enslaved women born in Africa, could have left a legacy large enough to build a school for poor black Catholic orphans. Although this example is far from normative, it serves as a window into the discrete nature of slavery and gender in nineteenth-century Louisiana. Its settlement by the French may account for this exception in the antebellum South.

From 1699 to 1763, France possessed about one-third of the present-day United States, a vast territory expanding from the Great Lakes to the Gulf Coast and from the Mississippi River to the foothills of the Rocky Mountains. This extensive area was traded to Spain with the Treaty of Paris of 1763 before it was secretly retroceded to France with the Treaty of San Ildefonso in 1800. Although officially belonging to Spain for more than three decades, it remained Gallic in terms of culture and languages, even after it was ceded to the United States with the 1803 Louisiana Purchase. It was this original Gallic imprint that left its distinct mark on the slave system.

The French Company of the Indies first introduced enslaved Africans into Louisiana in 1719. Although Louisiana, especially Lower Louisiana, was a slave society, it never thrived under French rule. With little interest in its most remote colony, the French only sent one more shipment of enslaved Africans into Louisiana after 1731. The increase in the enslaved population during the first French period was mostly natural, which led to the formation of an important creole slave society, a feature that determined the nature of slavery in Louisiana. By 1763, there were only roughly 4,500 slaves in the territory, all creolized within a French and Catholic social system.

The Spanish reinstituted the slave trade, a move that re-Africanized the colony. By 1803, Lower Louisiana comprised more than 24,000 enslaved Africans. French and Spanish colonial rule shaped the interracial relationships and left a clear imprint on the territory after its purchase by the United States. Both colonial powers were Catholic, which led them to maintain a relatively relaxed vision of race relations. Under Spanish law and tradition, slavery was not necessarily a permanent status, hence Louisiana developed into a three-tiered society with a numerically and economically significant group of free people of African descent. Since there was a great gender imbalance among the French people that settled in Louisiana in the early colonial period, relationships between Frenchmen and Indian and African women were not infrequent. The relative openness of racial mixing reshaped the slave system in the French territory.

Although marriage between the races remained illegal, *liaisons* were frequent between white men and women of color, whether the women were enslaved or free. Such close relationships were common on Louisiana's plantations, although they did not necessarily entail the freeing of the enslaved women or racially mixed children born of those relationships. The sexual exploitation of enslaved women was also common in New Orleans, where the urban environment encouraged close contact between the races. One particular feature of New Orleans was its slave trading markets that promoted the sale of "fancy girls"—a tradition that both degraded enslaved women and offered them escape from the hard labor of the plantation system. The codified system of *plaçage*, a system that officially "placed" free women of African descent with white men, was especially peculiar to New Orleans. This open racial mixing gave birth to a very distinct system of racial classification, which differentiated people of color according to the degree of black and white blood in them—griffe (3/4 black), mulatto (1/2 black), quadroon (1/4 black), and octoroon (1/8 black) among others. This racial classification induced a hierarchical organization, which had repercussions on the status of enslaved and free women of African descent.

Beyond racial mixing, Louisiana society, profoundly Catholic and Gallic, also had effects on the slave system. This does not mean that slavery was better or more bearable in French America. However, Louisiana society extended rare privileges to enslaved blacks such as social promotion and educating bondpeople including that of enslaved women. Enslaved women, like their male counterparts, were allowed a certain degree of participation in colonial Louisiana's economic life. It was most remarkable in New Orleans, where women were allowed to move about relatively freely in order to attend to their duties. Enslaved women were allowed to go to the market to sell or purchase goods, to walk the streets hawking their goods, and to travel about the city when they were seamstresses, laundresses, or hair-dressers. It was not unusual for these women to retain a part of their wages, and many were able to live outside the view of their masters and mistresses.

Besides enjoying an economic freedom superior to that of their counterparts in the Anglo-Saxon South, a number of black women managed to free themselves and their children. The possibility to purchase one's freedom as well as the free-dom of one's friends and relatives was introduced under Spanish rule and was known as *coartación*. This offered enslaved women the rare occasion to access both freedom and the relatively privileged status of women of color.

Women of African descent in Louisiana were introduced into the Catholic Church and indeed became its most numerous and devout practitioners. It was a factor that paved their way to social promotion. This process began during French rule when the Ursulines offered religious instruction. This was particularly done through an organization called the Children of Mary and was followed by the Sisters of the Holy Family, the first black women's religious order in Louisiana under the lead of Henriette Delille and Juliette Gaudin. This specific French Catholic tra-dition was reinforced by the arrival, in the twenty years surrounding the Louisiana Purchase, of several thousand refugees—whites, slaves, and free people of color in almost equal numbers—from the former French colony of Saint-Domingue, who were actively involved in promoting education and religious instruction among people of color, free and enslaved. Their presence reinforced the traditions left by the French colonial Louisiana Creoles. The free refugees of color were espe-cially active in the management of Mme Couvent's legacy and of the Catholic Indigent Orphan's Institute that was created with this legacy in the third district of New Orleans.

Although French rule formally ended in the American South in 1803, the prin-ciples it had introduced in the slave system pervaded Louisiana's society for sev-eral decades before the Civil War.

Nathalie Dessens

See also Free Women; Religion.

Suggested Reading

Emily Clark and Virginia Meacham Gould, "The Feminine Face of Afro-Catholicism in New Orleans, 1727–1852," *William and Mary Quarterly* 59 (2002): 409–48; Nathalie Dessens, *From Saint-Domingue to New Orleans: Migration and Influences* (Gainesville: University Press of Florida, 2007); Virginia R. Domínguez, *White by Definition: Social*

Classification in Creole Louisiana (New Brunswick: Rutgers University Press, 1986); Lois Virginia Meacham Gould, "In Full Enjoyment of Their Liberty: The Free Women of Color of the Gulf Ports of New Orleans, Mobile, and Pensacola, 1769–1860" (PhD dissertation, Emory University, 1991); Gwendolyn Midlo Hall, *Africans in Colonial Louisiana*: *The Development of Afro-Creole Culture in the Eighteenth Century* (Baton Rouge: Louisiana State University Press, 1992); Kimberly Hanger, *Bounded Lives, Bounded Places: Free Black Society in Colonial New Orleans, 1769–1803* (Durham: Duke University Press, 1997); Arnold R. Hirsch and Joseph Logsdon, *Creole New Orleans: Race and Americanization* (Baton Rouge: Louisiana State University Press, 1992); Daniel Usner, *Indians, Settlers, and Slaves in a Frontier Exchange Economy: The Lower Mississippi Valley Before 1783* (Chapel Hill: University of North Carolina Press, 1992).

G

Gardening

Gardening provided a sense of communal, economic, and material ownership for enslaved African Americans. During slavery, bondpeople worked in gardens or provision grounds as a required task and for subsistence in their "leisure time." While gardens were central to supplementing meals, the use of provision grounds and yards as communal workspace also allowed enslaved workers, and especially bondwomen, to cultivate community.

There is little scholarship dedicated to bondpeople's keeping and maintenance of gardens. Scholars initially suggested a gendered division of labor that made bondwomen responsible for planting and tending the garden while bondmen hunted and fished. However, recent scholarship indicates that men and women shared these duties. Gardening not delegated by the slaveholder was done as time permitted, either at night after a long day in the fields or on Sundays. The geographic location of the plantation determined the size, location, and vegetation of gardens. Slaveholders allocated space to the enslaved often for the sole purpose of growing their own food and keeping livestock. In the Chesapeake region of Maryland and Virginia, gardens for the enslaved were small and typically comprised squash, sweet potatoes, Indian peas, cucumbers, and melons. In the low country region of South Carolina and Georgia, the enslaved population was larger and slaveholders provided bigger provision grounds. Bondpeople planted a more diverse range of plants, which included root crops from Africa like tannier as well as millet, sorghum, sesame, and African peppers. Legumes were also cultivated and incorporated into bean-based soups and stews—a primary means of supplementing enslaved dietary needs.

Any surplus gained from these gardens allowed bondpeople to participate in an informal economy of trade, barter, and exchange. Bondpeople could achieve a small degree of economic and material autonomy by selling goods at local markets or to their slaveholders. Gardening allowed women to partake in the material and economic well-being of their families. It allowed them to provide nutritional foods, cultivate community through the development of space, and continue the practice of African traditions through the planting of certain crops.

Terry P. Brock

See also Community; Economy; Family; Food Preparation and Cooking; Slave Quarters, Life in.

Suggested Reading

Patricia A. Gibbs, "Slave Garden Plots and Poultry Yards." Colonial Williamsburg. http://research.history.org/Historical_Research/Research_Themes/ThemeEnslave/SlaveGardens.cfm; Philip D. Morgan, *Slave Counterpoint* (Chapel Hill: University of North Carolina Press, 2006); John Michael Vlach, *Back of the Big House: The Architecture of Plantation Slavery* (Chapel Hill: University of North Carolina Press, 1993); Web sites: http://www.twinleaf.org/articles/aagardens.html and http://research.history.org/Historical_Research/Research_Themes/ThemeEnslave/SlaveGardens.cfm; Richard Westmacott, *African-American Gardens and Yards in the Rural South* (Knoxville: University of Tennessee Press, 1992).

Garner, Margaret

Birth Date: 1833
Death Date: ~1858

Margaret Garner was an enslaved woman who chose to commit infanticide rather than allow her daughter to be re-enslaved. For her actions, abolitionists made her a cause célèbre. Garner's decision became the subject of Toni Morrison's Pulitzer Prize-winning 1987 novel *Beloved*. Her tragic story also inspired Morrison to write the libretto for the opera, *Margaret Garner* (2005), which featured music by composer Richard Danielpour.

In 1856, Margaret Garner and her husband Simon Garner Jr. (also known as Robert) decided that their family would no longer live as bondpeople. Margaret, Robert, and 15 other fugitives—including Simon's parents and the Garner's four children—made the bold albeit perilous decision to cross the frozen Ohio River to "free" country. According to an editorial in Canada's *Provincial Freedmen*, the group successfully reached the free state of Ohio. While nine of them made it to the Underground Railroad and fled to Canada, the Garners were pursued and soon surrounded by 11 armed men that included their enslaver, Archibald K. Gaines, Kentucky slave hunters, and a deputy U.S. marshall. The Garners' resistance to recapture was both praised and sanctioned by black and white abolitionists across the nation. In an effort to stop the encroaching men from seizing his family, Robert Garner fired three shots from his stolen revolver and wounded an officer, but was overtaken. In an equally determined effort to evade re-enslavement, Margaret Garner struck her two sons on the head with a shovel, grabbed a butcher knife, and killed her two-year old daughter, Mary. She tried to kill the other child before she was stopped.

The Garners's arrests attracted the attention of local and national abolitionists. At the heart of the debate surrounding the Garner trial was the question whether Margaret Garner should be tried for murder or "destruction of property." Her lawyer, John Joliffe, instructed the court to charge Margaret with murder and the

Harper's Weekly engraving after Thomas Satterthwaite Noble's painting of Margaret Garner as the "Modern Medea," 1867. (Library of Congress.)

other adults as accessories to murder with the hope that they would be tried in a free state and possibly, thrown on the mercy of a sympathetic court. The Garners, however, were remanded to slavery, under the dictates of the Fugitive Slave Act. Sympathetic abolitionists attempted to purchase the Garner family, but they were rebuffed by Gaines, who defiantly refused to sell them to abolitionists who would surely grant them their freedom.

Determined to keep Margaret Garner out of reach of the abolitionists, Gaines boarded the Garners on a ship to Louisville, Arkansas. The ship began to sink, and Garner jumped off the vessel with her surviving ten-month old daughter. It is not clear whether she was trying to jump onto the boat that had come to the first ship's rescue or whether this was, indeed, another suicidal attempt. Her daughter drowned, but Margaret was saved and reportedly happy that her youngest daughter had also escaped re-enslavement.

Margaret Garner's act of resistance was powerful ammunition against proslavery theorists who argued that blacks were content to be enslaved. Garner's act and other reports of women who killed their enslavers, overseers, themselves, or their children forced readers to speculate on the everyday experiences that would drive them to take such rebellious and desperate measures. The black press enthusiastically praised the Garners' actions. For example, an editorial printed in the *Provincial Freedmen* asserted that Margaret Garner's efforts embodied Patrick

Henry's revolutionary call, "Give me liberty or give me death." According to her biographer, Steven Weisenburger, Margaret Garner's contemporary importance as a symbol of the antislavery cause rivaled that of Anthony Burns' and Dred Scott's.

Alexandra Cornelius-Diallo

See also Abolitionism; Infanticide, Laws; Resistance; Runaways; Underground Railroad.

Suggested Reading

Levi Coffin, *Reminiscences of Levi Coffin, the Reputed President of the Underground Railroad* (Cincinatti, 1876, rpt. New York: August Kelsey, 1968); Mark Reinhardt, *Who Speaks for Margaret Garner?* (Minneapolis: University of Minnesota Press, 2010); Sarah P. Remond, "Speech by Sarah P. Remond," Delivered at the Music Hall, Warrington, England, January 24, 1859 in *The Black Abolitionist Papers. Vol. 1 The British Isles, 1830–1865*, ed. C. Peter Ripley (Chapel Hill: University of North Carolina Press, 1985), 437–38; Steven Weisenburger, *Modern Medea: A Family Story of Slavery and Child-Murder from the Old South* (New York: Hill and Wang, 1998); www.margaretgarner.org, "Margaret Garner"; Julius Yanuck, "The Garner Fugitive Slave Case," *Mississippi Valley Historical Review* 40 (June 1953): 47–66.

Gender Conventions

Gender conventions refer to sets of ideas or ideologies about what society deems to be the standard behaviors and dominant traits of men and women. Over time these conventions appear as natural and fixed, representative of an imagined essence of manhood and womanhood. They include thoughts about masculinity and femininity, the gendered division of labor, standards of appearance, appropriate sexuality, and many other "norms" that society expects conformity with and socializes children into. In response to changes in the economic, political, and social landscape, these conventions shift gradually over time. Factors, such as race and class, also influence these gender "rules." For enslaved women, negative views of blackness and African ancestry during the era of racial slavery in the United States shaped the gender conventions assigned to them by the wider society. These gender ideologies produced and sustained many stereotypes and fictitious representations of black women such as the Mammy and Jezebel figures against which whites imagined their supposed racial superiority. These pernicious images survived for decades after the end of slavery despite enslaved peoples' attempts to forge their own more positive ideas about gender.

Early encounters between Europeans and Africans set the tone for the gender conventions that whites would later ascribe to enslaved women in the United

States. Travel narratives from the 1600s and 1700s demonstrate that European men, accustomed to perceiving women as delicate and frail in their own societies, imagined African women as hypersexual and physically hardy because of their "exotic" appearance and the types of agricultural labor they undertook. They viewed African women as lascivious, unemotional "beasts of burden" who could complete strenuous physical labor and effortlessly bear children with little or no pain. This mischaracterization contributed to rationalizing and justifying their enslavement. Such falsehoods informed perceptions of black womanhood for centuries afterward and coalesced into rigid gender conventions by the antebellum era (1820–1860) in the United States.

During this period, gender conventions for enslaved women must be understood in relation to those for white women, often referred to as the Cult of True Womanhood. This set of ideas maintained that white women of "good character" (such as plantation mistresses) were pious, sexually pure, submissive or deferential to their husbands, and happily confined to the domestic space of the home. Most whites at this time believed that enslaved women (and by association free women of color) were the antithesis of these qualities and inherently unable to live up to these same standards because of their race and "uncivilized" African heritage.

For example, Americans considered wifehood an essential tenet of "true" womanhood, but for enslaved women this gender convention was almost impossible to attain. This resulted from laws that refused to officially recognize marriage between enslaved people (protecting only slaveholders' rights and ability to sell their "property") and from abroad marriages that often compelled enslaved women to live independent of their husbands. Practices such as these permitted whites to envision enslaved women as immoral and outside of the bounds of respectability that monogamous, heterosexual marriage guaranteed for white women. This convenient belief was tied to deliberate misperceptions of enslaved women as sexually promiscuous, which directly limited their ability to fulfill other standards of "true" womanhood such as embodying the allusion of sexual purity.

These notions also stimulated mischaracterizations of enslaved women's roles as mothers, another central component to antebellum ideas about womanhood. Since slaveholders considered enslaved children property that inherited the status of "slave" through the mother, there was an incentive to minimize the validity of enslaved mothers and encourage them to bear many children, whether through "marriage" or outright forced breeding. This perpetuated slaveholders' opportunistic logic that denigrated enslaved women for their supposed immorality and lasciviousness. The types of physically strenuous labor that slaveholders assigned to women further reinforced these ideas. Unlike delicate "true" women, enslaved women's forced labor enabled whites to perceive them as more masculine and outside the purview of the protective, chivalrous gender conventions enjoyed by "vulnerable" white women. These widespread ideas about womanhood also dictated the terms of beauty, or what physical characteristics society prized as desirable and pleasing. Because whites largely controlled the development of these gender conventions, certain physical attributes such as skin color, hair texture, facial features, clothing, and other accoutrements of appearance were designated "beautiful" based on white standards alone.

Despite the predominance of white gender conventions, enslaved people often tacitly resisted these damaging ideas by designing their own standards about the roles and attributes of women within their communities. These often included a greater acceptance of women's independence and a marked sense of egalitarianism between men and women. These notions combined with a community-centered ethos that valued the collective contributions of women to enslaved communities and engendered the development of protective mechanisms such as the female slave network. In other ways, these revised gender conventions encouraged enslaved women to reject white notions of beauty by incorporating their own visions of this quality into clothing, hairstyles, and other personalized aspects of appearance.

Jenifer L. Barclay

See also African and African-born Women; Breeding; Clothing; Female Slave Network; Free Women; Hair and Headdresses; Jezebel Stereotype; Labor, Agricultural; Labor, Nonagricultural; Labor, Skilled; Laws; Mammy Stereotype; Marriage and Cohabitation; Motherhood; Plantation Mistresses; Representations; Sexuality.

Suggested Reading

Hazel Carby, *Reconstructing Womanhood: The Emergence of the Afro-American Woman Novelist* (New York: Oxford University Press, 1987); Jennifer Morgan, *Laboring Women: Enslaved Women, Reproduction and Slavery in Barbados and South Carolina, 1650–1750* (Durham, NC: Duke University Press, 1995); Deborah Gray White, *Ar'n't I a Woman?: Female Slaves in the Plantation South* (New York: W.W. Norton and Company, 1985).

Girlhood

On the eve of the Civil War, there were roughly one million enslaved girls under the age of 16. A unique construction of girlhood, shaped by the convergence of race, age, and gender under slavery, influenced the everyday lives of girls for whom parents, slaveholders, fictive kin (unrelated by blood but close influences), and friends played a central role.

But I now entered on my fifteenth year—a sad epoch in the life of a slave girl. My master began to whisper foul words in my ear. Young as I was, I could not remain ignorant of their import.

—Harriet Jacobs, *Incidents in the Life of a Slave Girl* (44)

Children constituted one-quarter to one-third of the enslaved people imported from West and Central Africa. Though more males like Olaudah Equiano would chronicle their abductions, both Phillis Wheatley and Florence Hall documented their traumatic experiences at the hands of slavers. While fewer girls were captured overall, the *Margarita* and the *Maria* were among two eighteenth-century British vessels that had carried shiploads of girls and boys from Africa to America. While adult males were crammed into the holds of ships, 41 girls shared the quarterdecks of the British ship, *Brookes*, with other bondwomen. Though unfettered while onboard, enslaved girls nevertheless faced sexual dangers during the lengthy transatlantic voyages. Sailors commonly engaged in

Plantation scene from a nineteenth-century woodcut by Alexander Anderson depicting a woman at work accompanied by four children. (Library of Congress.)

unchecked sexual exploitation of enslaved females, and a British slave ship captain was tried for the death of a 15-year-old girl who refused to dance naked in 1792. Following a mutiny aboard the *Amistad* in 1839, a handful of enslaved girls ages seven to eleven years of age were among the very few ever to return to Africa.

Far more girls were born into slavery following the 1662 Virginia Assembly declaration, later adopted by other colonies, that made children the property of their mother's owners regardless of their father's status. Since fathers often resided on other plantations, half of all enslaved girls lived apart from their male parents. Threatened by the likelihood of separation from female kin, enslaved girls were typically named after grandmothers, aunts, and cousins. That was done according to African naming traditions that reinforced generational continuity and community. Enslaved girls were also named after "fictive kin," that is, individuals who were not biologically related, but functioned as family members. •

At birth, half of all enslaved infants weighed less than 5½ pounds due to the poor health of their mothers who were typically overworked and underfed. Coarse ground corn boiled into "mush" as well as salt pork or bacon, molasses, and sweet potatoes, slowed the growth and endangered the health of enslaved girls and boys, who suffered from diseases and vitamin deficiencies that led to rickets, beriberi, scurvy, and lockjaw. In addition to persistent hunger, other hardships included extreme heat and cold. Coarse linen shifts (two per year), no shoes, stockings, or outerwear provided little protection from the cold or rain. With no running water and few furnishings besides candles, boxes, and barrels in crudely built cabins, enslaved girls slept on burlap-covered straw on dirt floors. While the enslaved daughters of plantation owners sometimes received more clothing and food and better shelter, half of all bondwomen did not survive their girlhood. Those who did spent much of their time with other children under the age of 12—both enslaved and free, boys and girls—playing with handmade toys, pretending to cook and serve food, playing in the yard, swimming in streams, gathering nuts and berries, and playing "hide and seek." Enslaved girls also played "ring games" and jumped rope, sometimes transforming the traditional games learned from whites into ones with transgressive meanings. While jumping rope, one enslaved girl sang, "My old mistress promised me/Before she dies she would set me free/Now she's dead and gone to hell/I hope the devil will burn her well."

From their parents and other adults, enslaved girls acquired useful skills and cultural traditions. Mothers taught daughters household tasks such as spinning thread, weaving cloth, churning butter, and making soap and clothing. Girls also learned religious songs, beliefs, and practices as well as secular traditions involving music and dance. Encoded in songs and stories were lessons about how to endure slavery, resist assimilation, and maintain self-respect. For example, African animal trickster tales were adapted to the realities of American plantation life. These tales entertained the young while imparting survival skills. While wily rabbits and other animal figures were often males, the female figure in the *Tar Baby* taught girls to "say nothing," avoid victimization, and endure physical abuse. The prescriptive ideals about gender and childhood that prolonged girlhood dependency and elevated innocence in antebellum America were largely the preserve of white girls in bourgeois families. Enslaved girls and boys under the age of 12 cared for younger children (both enslaved and free), ran errands, fed chickens, collected eggs, milked cows, tended livestock, churned butter, swatted flies, rocked cradles, gathered wood, toted water, and carried out a number of other tasks. While some mistresses took kindly toward some enslaved girls, others violently abused them in ways that violated the doctrine of domesticity and notions of childhood.

As enslaved girls entered adolescence, they often joined pregnant women and older bondpeople on "trash gangs" where they learned such skills as raking, hoeing, and weeding in preparation for their adult role as field workers. Although one girl began midwifery training at 13, there were few skilled jobs for females. Consequently, enslaved girls had fewer opportunities to earn money to buy necessities or freedom. Instead, they often learned how to fake illness and work slowly or haphazardly from other more experienced bondpeople, which was a common form of everyday resistance.

Adolescent girls had greater opportunities to socialize after church services, during seasonal celebrations, and at dances. Although they had few material resources to draw upon, they tied ribbons in their braided hair, used honeysuckle and rose petals for perfume, dried chinaberries for blush, and used soot for eye shadow. Young bondwomen who engaged in premarital sex without recrimination and social stigma within the slave community typically bore their first child between the ages of 16 and 19. Knowing that their child would become property generated deep ambivalence in these young mothers.

Harriet Jacobs documented the sexual abuse that adolescent girls like her were forced to endure in *Incidents in the Life of a Slave Girl* (1861). While idealized "southern belles" were exalted for their virtue, licentious slaveholders and overseers justified sexual violence against African American girls they perceived as "naturally" sexual. Unwanted pregnancies often resulted from rape by slaveholder, their sons, overseers, and other males who forced enslaved girls to submit or be sold. The presence of mixed-race children on plantations kindled the suspicions of mistresses who were more likely to strike young bondwomen than the husbands upon whom wives were forced to depend.

Slaveholders who abused, punished, and sold bondpeople typically mediated the role of enslaved parents and other protectors. The low life expectancy (about 21 to 22 years as compared to 40 to 43 years for whites) meant that about half of all enslaved children lost a parent during their childhood. Although often unable to intervene when enslaved girls were sexually abused or beaten, family members and fictive kin provided support and guidance when and wherever they could. In an effort to protect her granddaughter from an abusive overseer, one bondwoman asked her master to move her to another part of the plantation. When he refused, she angrily released all the cattle from the pen. Though enslaved girls were less likely than boys to run away, Harriet Jacobs escaped to her grandmother's house where she hid undetected for nearly seven years before fleeing North and gaining her freedom.

Miriam Forman-Brunell

See also Courtship; Diet and Nutrition; Domestic Slave Trade; Family; Gender Conventions; Health, Disabilities, and Soundness; Laws; Life Cycle; Miscegenation; Motherhood; Overseers; Owners; Plantation Mistresses; Pregnancy; Resistance; Runaways; Sexuality; Violence, Sexual; Wheatley, Phyllis.

Suggested Reading

Edward Ball, *Slaves in the Family* (New York: Ballantine, 1998); Elizabeth Fox-Genovese, *Within the Plantation Household: Black and White Women in the Old South* (Chapel Hill: University of North Carolina Press, 1988); Harriet Jacobs, *Incidents in the Life of a Slave Girl* (Boston, 1861); Wilma King, *Stolen Childhood: Slave Youth in Nineteenth-Century America* (Bloomington: Indiana University Press, 1995); Wilma King, *African American Childhoods: Historical Perspectives from Slavery to Civil Rights* (New York: Palgrave Macmillan, 2005); Steve Mintz, *Huck's Raft: A History of American Childhood* (Boston:

Harvard University Press, 2006); Stephanie Shaw, "Mothering under Slavery in the Antebellum South," in *Mothers & Motherhood: Readings in American History*, eds. Rima Appel and Janet Golden (Columbus: Ohio State University Press, 1997), 297–318; Deborah Gray White, *Ar'n't I a Woman? Female Slaves in the Plantation South* (New York and London: W.W. Norton & Co., 1985): 92–103; David Wiggins, "The Play of Slave Children in the Plantation Community of the Old South," in *Glory Bound: Black Athletes in White America* (Syracuse: Syracuse University Press, 1997), 3–20; "The Atlantic Slave Trade and Slave Life in the Americas: A Visual Record," Virginia Foundation for the Humanities and University of Virginia, http://hitchcock.itc.virginia.edu/Slavery/detailsKeyword.php ?keyword=girl&recordCoun=26&theRecord=23

Gullah Culture

The term "Gullah" refers to the cultural legacy of African slaves brought from the Gold Coast of West Africa and found in the coastal region of Georgia and South Carolina, particularly in the Sea Islands off the coast of South Carolina. It is the most intact African culture among African American communities today. In many parts of Georgia, the Gullah culture is referred to as Geechee. The Gullah culture is characterized by its use of a creole language and arts and crafts traditions that heavily borrow from West African cultures.

Gullah culture has been preserved through time due to a combination of geography and climate. The Sea Islands and parts of South Carolina were known for their rice production; malaria and other native disease thrived in the widespread areas of standing water where mosquitoes could breed. As a result, many plantation owners would leave their plantations during months with high rates of infection. Owner absenteeism thus left the enslaved population with the opportunity to develop and maintain their own culture without interference from slaveholders. Prior to the abolition of the Transatlantic Slave Trade in 1808, Africans brought to Georgia and South Carolina predominately came through the Port of Charleston. With the assemblage of so many African cultures in one place, and because of the relative isolation from other enslaved populations, African cultures were shared and molded into the Gullah culture.

Gullah culture has traditions that include language, arts and crafts, cooking, and various folk beliefs regarding medicine, nature, and the spirit world. The Gullah people speak in a creole language, which is an amalgamation of African dialects and English. The Gullah are also known for their basket-weaving traditions, originally used to hold and carry vegetables. Today, sweetgrass weaving is a highly prized folk art. Gullah cooking is heavily seafood-based and rice, greens, and okra are also staples of the Gullah diet. Several folk medicine remedies include using spiderwebs as bandages and placing a piece of moss in one's shoe to counteract high blood pressure. Gullah worship services are characterized by the "ring shout," a ritualistic dance performed to the beat of singing, clapping, shouting, and pounding. If a person in a Gullah town died, a drum beat would announce the death.

The mainstays of Gullah culture today, however, are under constant threat. Development of Gullah land and historic sites are threatening the existence of the culture, particularly in the Sea Islands, where the most intact form of the Gullah culture is found today. The Gullah people are making efforts to preserve their culture and currently there are books printed in the Gullah language as well as "homecoming" events in West Africa. Many of the arts and crafts traditions are thriving as well, including the Sea Island's famous basket-weaving. Today, it is that part of the Gullah culture that is most recognizable around the country. It is hoped that with these preservation efforts the Gullah culture will continue to live.

Katherine M. Johnson

See also African Women and African-born Women; Creoles; Decorative Arts; Folk Medicine and Healing; Food Preparation and Cooking.

Suggested Reading

Mason Crum, *Gullah: Negro Life in the Carolina Sea Islands* (New York: Negro Universities Press, 1968); Marquetta L. Goodwine and Clarity Press Gullah Project, *The Legacy of Igbo Landing: Gullah Roots of African American Culture* (Atlanta: Clarity Press, 1998); Patricia Jones-Jackson, *When Roots Die: Endangered Traditions on the Sea Islands* (Athens: University of Georgia Press, 1987); William S. Pollitzer, *The Gullah People and Their African Heritage* (Athens: University of Georgia Press, 1999); Lorenzo Dow Turner, *Africanisms in the Gullah Dialect*, Southern Classics Series (Columbia: University of South Carolina Press, 2002).

H

Hair and Headdresses

Discussions of African American women's hair and hairstyling methods have been and continue to be fraught with controversy. Contemporary debates concerning black women's hair as an embrace of an African past or conversely, a desire to imitate a white aesthetic are rooted in the ways African and African American women in the Americas sought to care for and style their hair during their enslavement. While the control of black women's bodies was at the center of slavery's brutality, enslaved women were for the most part able to choose the ways in which they styled their hair. African American women created and sustained an intricate system of hair care and beautification rituals even in the midst of their enslavement, that was at once an homage to their African heritage and an adaptation to their circumstances in the United States.

The first enslaved women in the Americas—who originated primarily from West and Central Africa—were connected to a culture that used hairstyles and headdress to denote social status, economic position, and ethnic identity. Women, in particular, were admired for growing long and thick hair which was seen as a sign of economic prosperity and fertility; lack of grooming was associated with loose morals and mental deficiency. Beautification rituals emphasized communal engagement, with women spending hours braiding one another's hair and sharing their hand-carved combs and hair picks.

Unfortunately, when Europeans encountered African women within the context of the Transatlantic Slave Trade, they used the physical attributes of Africans, namely their darker skin and tightly curled hair, as a marker of difference and as part of the justification for their enslavement. Travel diaries of European explorers are replete with descriptions of black women's hair and overall appearance as both alluring and repulsive. The intricate hair designs so heralded in West African society were often ridiculed and patronizingly compared to clumps of straw.

Once in the New World, enslaved women, attempting to replicate many of the beauty rituals from their African homeland, became adept at modifying what was available in their new environment for their roles as enslaved laborers. For example, on typical days when bondwomen worked in the fields, they usually tied a simple bandanna on their heads to protect themselves from the sun and perspiration. These headdresses were not only functional, but they were also fashionable, replete with bright colors and bold patterns derived from dyes and modified quilting techniques. The aesthetic properties of the bandanas often raised ridicule from white observers who found the multicolored patterns gaudy and foolish. However, on special occasions like church services and weddings, such headdresses were usually abandoned revealing hair that had been carefully wrapped and threaded with cloth and strings. In other words, when enslaved women did have some time away from their required labor, they groomed their hair using modified items like metal-toothed cards normally used to comb sheep's hair as well as commonly used household items like axle grease as a conditioning agent for their hair. Similar to their West African ancestors, hair grooming was a communal activity involving women and young girls.

Finally, slave narratives recount examples of slaveholders and mistresses manipulating and cutting the hair of enslaved women as forms of punishment. Enslaved women and girls whose hair closely resembled the hair of their white mistresses often invoked special ridicule and contempt.

Tiffany M. Gill

See also Narratives; Punishment.

Suggested Reading

Ayana D. Byrd and Lori Tharps, *Hair Story: Untangling the Roots of Black Hair in America* (New York: St. Martin's Press, 2001); Shane White and Graham White, *Stylin': African American Expressive Culture from Its Beginnings to the Zoot Suit* (Ithaca: Cornell University Press, 1998).

Health, Disabilities, and Soundness

You know in dem days, dey didn't have many doctors. Well, I was always good when it come to de sick, so dat was mostly my job. I was also what you call a midwife, too. Whenever any o' de white folks 'roun' Hanover [Virginia] was going to have babies, dey always got word to Mr. Tinsley dat dey want to hire me fer dat time. Sho', he let me go. 'Twas money fer him, you know. He would give me only a few cents, but dat was kinda good o' him to do dat . . . Sometimes I had three an' four sick at de same time. Marster would tell me I was a valuable slave.

—Mildred Graves, former slave (Howell, Donna, ed., *I Was a Slave: True Stories Told by Former Slaves in the 1930s*, 28)

At its heart, racial slavery was a system of forced labor so slaveholders placed an inordinate value on enslaved people's health, the state of their bodies and, to a lesser extent, their minds (so that they could effectively labor). The worth of healthy individuals was reflected in their higher prices while those with severe or prolonged illnesses and various physical or psychological disabilities were assumed to be useless as laborers and perceived by slaveholding whites as financial burdens. Enslaved people, however, did not see themselves or their family and community members as worthless because of their ill health or disabilities.

Healers from within the slave community, often women, practiced their own forms of folk medicine that focused on not only the body, but also spiritual aspects of sickness that white medical professionals dismissed or ignored. Moreover, nondisabled bondpeople often valued the daily contributions of those with disabilities since they helped alleviate the difficulties of enslaved life and sustain a sense of community.

"Disability" is defined as a permanent or temporary physical or psychological health condition that impairs or limits an individual, preventing him or her from participating in what many consider the "normal" activities of everyday life. In addition to the embodied aspects of disabilities, society attaches many stereotypes, beliefs, and attitudes to those deemed "disabled" that change over time. Throughout history, nondisabled people typically pitied those with disabilities, believing that they could not lead happy, fulfilling lives because of their affliction and were in constant need of charity and assistance. Depending on the severity and visibility of a disability, nondisabled individuals also sometimes experienced anxiety or fear when confronted with another's bodily difference. In some cases, this manifested itself in the belief that disabilities were "monstrosities" and the mark of God's punishment for an individual's sins or those of their parents. With the advent of professional medicine coupled with the reformist spirit of the antebellum era (1820–1860) that characterized movements such as abolition and women's rights, ideas about disability shifted toward the notion that disabled persons could be rehabilitated or made "normal" through surgery, rudimentary prosthetics, and other techniques that physicians devised and implemented.

Many types of visible and invisible disabilities sometimes affected enslaved women, men, and children and occurred at different times throughout the life cycle. Some were conditions that enslaved people were born with such as blindness, deafness, missing or deformed limbs, mental retardation, or other disabilities resulting from congenital illnesses. In other cases, enslaved people became disabled as a result of injuries or illnesses. Sometimes, the labor that slaveholders forced bondpeople to complete caused temporary or permanent disabling injuries. These ranged from debilitating skeletal and muscular conditions that resulted from overexertion or repetitive motions to those that were sustained in the use of equipment and machinery that sometimes led to injuries such as the accidental amputation of limbs. In other cases, severe physical punishments led to disabilities or, in fact, set out to intentionally cause them. Through the eighteenth century, for instance, runaways were sometimes punished by having a foot or leg amputated to prevent them from absconding; in other cases, they were permanently disabled by being shot or mauled by dogs when fleeing.

Illnesses and unhealthy living environments also led to some disabilities. For enslaved people, the unsanitary, cramped space of inadequate slave quarters sometimes facilitated the spread of contagious diseases such as scarlet fever, typhoid fever, and dysentery that could result in disabilities. Poor living conditions also contributed to the growth of various parasites such as hookworms, roundworms, and tapeworms that bondpeople were sometimes infected with (this was especially prevalent in the warm environment of the South and among those who were in close contact with livestock and the land). Prolonged exposure and infection could lead to permanent bone and muscle deformities, retarded mental development, and infertility. Inadequate diet and nutrition also sometimes led to disabilities, particularly among children who developed conditions such as rickets (caused by a lack of vitamin D and calcium) that softened bones and caused deformities in extreme cases. Psychological disabilities including mental retardation and insanity, as well as neurological disorders such as epilepsy (a condition that abolitionist Sojourner Truth reportedly suffered from), also sometimes affected enslaved people. Many whites, however, argued that enslavement mitigated black insanity by providing for enslaved people's needs and relieving them from the burden of emotional stress thought to trigger this generalized condition. The processes of aging also resulted in some disabilities such as the onset of blindness, deafness, debilitating rheumatism, dementia, and other conditions associated with elderly individuals. These factors, in general, certainly had an adverse effect on the health of enslaved women and girls.

Some health and disability-related concerns directly involved enslaved women alone. Poor maternal diet and overwork, for instance, increased infant mortality rates and congenital disabilities among enslaved children. Pregnancy itself was also a significant health risk for all women through the nineteenth century and certainly for enslaved women. In addition to the obvious factors that made pregnancy difficult prior to the advances of modern medicine (such as a lack of knowledge about sterile environments, anesthesia, and antibiotics), slaveholding whites often viewed enslaved women as being physically "hardier" than white women because of stereotypes and gender conventions of the day. As a result, bondwomen were often forced to continue physical labor throughout their pregnancies and resume work shortly after giving birth. In some extreme cases, they were even brutally punished while pregnant which sometimes caused death, severe fetal injury or death, or permanent disabilities for both mothers and children who survived such abuse. In addition to pregnancy, or as a consequence of it, some bondwomen experienced gynecological problems such as prolapsed uterus, incontinence, menstrual cycle disorders, and infertility. Their enslaved status marked them as appropriate "subjects" upon which nineteenth century medical physicians performed rudimentary, experimental surgeries. J. Marion Sims—also known as the "father of gynecology"—performed repeated, intrusive, and painful operations on bondwomen without anesthetic in his quest to perfect treatment for internal injuries to women's reproductive organs that occurred as a result of childbirth. His most well-known patient was Anarcha, a young bondwoman who endured over 30 surgeries in a period of five years.

Slaveholders almost universally relied on the concept of "soundness" to express the degrees to which an enslaved person's body and mind met the standards of optimal health. This, in turn, determined the amount and type of labor that an enslaved person could perform and their subsequent monetary value as property. Soundness encompassed enslaved people's appearance, physical abilities, and even the less visible quality of their "character" or "temperament." Slaveholders sometimes believed that an enslaved person's character could be ascertained by interpreting physical marks such as scars from previous punishments that potentially indicated unruly or rebellious behavior. For enslaved women, the emphasis on these intangible, subjective characteristics was likely exacerbated by men's tendency to view all women as being predisposed to an irrational lack of emotional control and "feeble-mindedness." Also, since slaveholders valued women for their ability to both labor and reproduce the enslaved labor force through pregnancy, their reproductive health and ability to bear children was a significant element in assessments of their soundness. Slaveholders often considered female infertility a "defect" that diminished a woman's value since they could not be used as "breeders." Ideas about barrenness also informed racist notions about individuals with mixed-race parentage, derogatively called "mulattoes" throughout the era of slavery, who were often believed to be defective and sterile because of the "unnaturalness" of miscegenation.

Slaveholders typically deemed individuals with physical or psychological disabilities as "unsound," viewing them as useless and sometimes even as liabilities and expenses. Soundness, then, was an important component in the sale of enslaved people. Sellers often guaranteed the soundness of enslaved people in warranties that purchasers sometimes disputed in court when their recently acquired "property" exhibited signs of concealed illness, disease, or disability that rendered them less valuable than the price paid. There were some instances, however, in which slaveholders profited in unusual ways from enslaved people with disabilities. For example, one southeastern North Carolina slaveholder, Jabez McKay, sold his enslaved, one-year-old conjoined twins Millie-Christine for $1,000 in 1852 to be exhibited in freak shows and other popular antebellum American and European venues, retaining a contractual right to one quarter of all proceeds made from the twins' exploitation.

In contrast to slaveholders' routine devaluation of them, enslaved people with disabilities often provided important labor and valuable social support to their families and communities precisely because their disabilities precluded them from performing forced labor for profit. Enslaved women with disabilities—some disabled as a result of their advanced age and others who were born or became disabled—often took on or were assigned tasks that benefitted the enslaved community. These included mending and sewing clothes, caring for children, nursing the ill, and cooking. In some cases, their disabilities determined the type of labor slaveholders compelled them to undertake, such as cases in which an individual was perhaps permanently "lame," but could nevertheless complete work within the home such as cooking, serving, and cleaning. Because enslaved women with disabilities tended to have a diminished market value and were less likely to be sold, they sometimes provided a stable presence within enslaved families and communities that otherwise faced the ever-present threat of separation and sale. As a result, disabled bondwomen could potentially provide some small modicum of continuity and act as bulwarks against the injurious effects of slavery, particularly for the enslaved children over whom they often watched.

Occasionally, disabilities shaped the outcome of situations in which bondwomen would otherwise have faced very harsh circumstances, providing them with an unusual mechanism of defense or a unique opportunity to resist. One enslaved woman, for example, committed arson and a local court ordered her owners to sell her away from her family as punishment for this crime. Because she experienced epileptic fits in jail, however, she was unable to be sold and therefore avoided this sentence for an undetermined period. In another case, one enslaved woman, Ellen Craft, feigned multiple disabilities as part of an ingenious, multilayered disguise that enabled her and her husband, William, to escape from slavery in 1848. They describe this harrowing journey in their classic narrative *Running a Thousand Miles for Freedom*.

While being labeled as "valueless" by slaveholders perhaps left disabled women with some small opportunities to provide support for their communities and families and avoid or resist some of slavery's harshest elements, disabilities also had other consequences. On some occasions, slaveholders outright abandoned them, leaving them to fend for themselves with little or no means of self-support, as was the case with the frail grandmother of famed abolitionist and fugitive slave Frederick Douglass. In such instances, they were often cared for by enslaved relatives who shared their already meager food rations and supplies with them. This reflected a pervasive, community-centered slave ethos that women played a crucial role in, as demonstrated in the female slave network. This ethos, stemming from a worldview or cosmos that differed in many ways from that of European Americans, might also have led enslaved people to perhaps regard some disabilities less as conditions to be pitied and more as sources of spiritual power because of surviving African cultural retentions.

Jenifer L. Barclay

See also Breeding; Community; Conjurers; Diet and Nutrition; Domestic Slave Trade; Elderly Women; Female Slave Network; Folk Medicine and Healing;

Gender Conventions; Girlhood; Labor, Agricultural; Life Cycle; Miscegenation; Pregnancy; Prices; Punishment; Resistance; Runaways; Slave Quarters, Life in; Truth, Sojourner.

Suggested Reading

Dea Boster, "An 'Epeleptick' Bondswoman: Fits, Slavery and Power in the Antebellum South," *Bulletin of the History of Medicine* 83, 2 (Summer 2009): 271–301; Sharla Fett, *Working Cures: Health, Healing and Power on Southern Slave Plantations* (Chapel Hill: University of North Carolina Press, 2002); Ariela Gross, *Double Character: Slavery and Mastery in the Antebellum Southern Courtroom* (Princeton: Princeton University Press, 2000); Ellen Samuels, " 'A Complication of Complaints': Untangling Disability, Race, and Gender in William and Ellen Craft's *Running a Thousand Miles for Freedom*," *MELUS* 31 (Fall 2006): 15–47; Todd Savitt, *Medicine and Slavery: The Diseases and Health Care of Blacks in Antebellum Virginia* (Chicago: University of Illinois Press, 1978); Harriet Washington, *Medical Apartheid: The Dark History of Medical Experimentation on Black Americans from Colonial Times to the Present* (New York: Anchor Books, 2006).

Hemings, Sally

Birth Date: ~ 1773
Death Date: 1835

Sally Hemings was an enslaved woman legally owned by and the concubine of Thomas Jefferson, one of the most prominent founding fathers, author of the Declaration of Independence, and third president of the United States. Named Sarah at her birth in about 1773, Hemings was the daughter of enslaved Elizabeth (Betty) Hemings and possibly fathered by John Wayles, Elizabeth's owner and Jefferson's future father-in-law. Upon his death in 1774, Wayles bequeathed Elizabeth and her children to Jefferson and, by 1776, the entire Hemings family moved to Monticello, Jefferson's sprawling estate located in the mountains of Charlottesville, Virginia. After the death of his wife Martha Wayles Jefferson in 1782, Jefferson spent several years in Paris as commissioner and minister for the United States. In 1787, he requested that his daughter join him abroad and she was accompanied by her servant, Sally, who was approximately 14 years of age at the time. At some point after their return to Virginia in 1789, the older, widowed Jefferson and the much younger, enslaved Hemings began an intimate relationship that lasted 38 years and produced six children: Harriett, who died in infancy; Beverley born in 1798; an unnamed child who also died in infancy; Harriett born in 1801; Madison born in 1803; and Eston born in 1808. During this time, Hemings labored as a household servant primarily acting as a lady's maid to Jefferson's daughters, caring for children, and sewing, among other types of domestic labor. While Jefferson never publically or privately acknowledged his relationship and children with Sally, he outright manumitted or willfully neglected to pursue members of only the Hemings family when they ran away—preferential treatment suggesting that they likely were his children.

In 1802, during Jefferson's second term as president, journalist James T. Callendar disclosed local speculation about Jefferson and Hemings in a Richmond newspaper, initiating a national scandal about their relationship given Jefferson's prominent political position, slaveholding status, and the controversial issue of miscegenation, or biracial relationships. Many of Jefferson's white descendants and other staunch supporters vehemently denied these accusations and the possibility of a sexual and/or romantic liaison between Jefferson and Hemings, both at the time and since then, claiming that another member of the Jefferson family fathered Hemings' children. The controversy continues to haunt historians despite DNA evidence released by Dr. Eugene Foster on October 31, 1998, which demonstrates Jefferson's near-certain paternity of Eston, Hemings' youngest child. In addition to scientific evidence, the Thomas Jefferson Memorial Foundation also employed documentary evidence in a 2000 report to prove that Jefferson was always in Hemings' presence during the conception periods of each of her six pregnancies, that other notable locals knew about and acknowledged their relationship, and that oral histories passed down through generations of the Hemings family consistently maintained that he fathered Sally Hemings' children.

The Hemings-Jefferson relationship exemplifies one of many complicated forms of sexual violence or exploitation that enslaved women routinely faced, considering the extremely imbalanced power relations between the two. Some scholars romanticize their relationship and assume that it was completely consensual and loving. Others, however, emphasize the tremendous disparities between Hemings and Jefferson and argue that the entire affair was forced or, at best, one that Hemings only consented to because she had little recourse or opportunity to resist. Indeed, as Harriet Jacobs' *Incidents in the Life of a Slave Girl* makes clear, some enslaved women endured their owners' unwanted sexual advances, daily harassment, and coercive threats that left them feeling virtually powerless to refuse sexual encounters with them. It is difficult to say what the precise dynamics were between Hemings and Jefferson and the circumstances surrounding their relationship, but the fact remains that profound social, economic, and political inequalities existed between the enslaved Hemings and her wealthy, powerful, and famous owner. The heated controversy over their relationship and the paternity of Hemings' children remains contentious to this day, demonstrating that enslaved women were central to the history of the nation despite attempts both past and present to erase or ignore them and their legacy.

Jenifer L. Barclay

See also Concubinage; Jacobs, Harriet; Labor, Skilled; Miscegenation; Motherhood; Pregnancy; Violence, Sexual.

Suggested Reading

Annette Gordon Reed, *Thomas Jefferson and Sally Hemings: An American Controversy* (Charlottesville: University of Virginia Press, 1997); Annette Gordon Reed, *The Hemingses of Monticello: An American Family* (New York: W.W. Norton and Company, 2008); The Thomas Jefferson Memorial Foundation, "Statement on the TJMF Research Committee Report on Thomas Jefferson and Sally Hemings" (January 2000).

Hiring Out

Arguably one of the least-noted aspects of slave hiring in the United States is the hiring out of female slaves. Much of the historiography suggests that most hired bondpeople were primarily urban and skilled males because enslaved women's childbirth and childcare responsibilities precluded them from being hired out. Enslaved women, however, were hired out just as much, if not more often, than enslaved men. Bondwomen were hired out in both urban and rural contexts and usually with little difficulty. The hiring out of black women was not an institutional aberration, but a routine aspect of slavery in the Upper South and other regions with diversified economies and rapidly increasing enslaved populations.

> *Muh first marster en missis wuz Amos and Sophia Holland en he made a will dat we slaves wuz all ter be kep among de fam'ly en I wuz h[i]red fum one fam'ly ter 'nother. Wuz owned under de 'will' by Haddas Holland, Missis Mary Haddock en den Missis Synthia ma'ied Sam Pointer en I libed wid her 'til freedum wuz 'clared.*
>
> —Precilla Gray, former bondwoman
> *(Born in Slavery: Slave Narratives from the Federal Writers' Project, 1936–1938 Tennessee Narratives, Volume XV, 24)*

Enslaved women's hiring-out experiences differed from that of their male counterparts. Hired-out men were usually sent to hirers on their own, but slaveholders often paid local white men to keep close watch on hired-out bondwomen from their place to a slave-hiring-day site for auction or directly to a hirer's residence. Women's movements were thus scrutinized by slaveholders and slave hirers and sometimes involved their transportation in wagons, carts, railroad cars, or boats with white men present at each point along the journey.

Pregnancy and childbirth also made bondwomen's hiring-out experiences unique. Many enslaved women were pregnant or had very young children when they were hired out. Pregnancy and/or possession of young children often was precisely the reason why they were hired out by enslavers who wished to shift to others the responsibility for bondpeople deemed relatively unproductive consumers of food and clothing. Women and young children were hired out as a family unit for several consecutive years because slaveholders regarded them as being capable of little labor. Given prospective hirers' reluctance to hire bondwomen, who were pregnant or with young children, slaveholders frequently had to pay other whites to hire women they deemed insufficiently productive to feed and clothe. Enslavers sometimes hired out such bondwomen in exchange for their food and clothing only. Like many other slave-hiring arrangements, these transactions were sometimes done at auction where pregnant women and those with small children were set up to the lowest bidder who was then paid by a slaveholder to take them. White diarists' descriptions of hiring days note price ranges for enslaved women and men, as well as for women and children kept by other whites for slaveholders who were unable to provide for them. Slaveholders paying others to take women and children off their hands for a year or more was a routine practice. Whereas childbearing bondwomen normally commanded high prices on the slave-buying market, their procreative capacity often reduced their value on the slave-hiring market. The difference stemmed from the fact that slave hirers realized no long-term gain from slave women's children to offset the women's diminished ability to labor because of pregnancy and/or child-care responsibilities.

Women who were hired out with their young children as a family unit faced arduous days in a hirer's charge. They were forced to divide their time between labor for the white family and care of their own new children. There was not sufficient time for both activities, and bondwomen who failed to meet hirers' expectations were often whipped or sold. Additionally, these hired-slave women found that their children were hired out apart from them once the children had been judged old enough to bring their own hire, which generally occurred when the children were about ten years of age.

Many hired-out women who cared for their young children were attended by an enslaved midwife when they gave birth at a hirers' residence. These midwives were hired from other slaveholders for that specific purpose, and their importance to the larger slave community cannot be exaggerated. Hired midwives created important communication links between bondpeople on different plantations. These channels served as an important complement to interplantation visits during the holidays, and to interplantation visits made by usually more mobile enslaved males who ran errands for their owners or visited their wives. While bondmen typically had greater opportunities for unsupervised mobility than their female counterparts, hired midwives commanded sufficient white respect to travel and sometimes be paid for their services, and so forged a special niche for themselves within the slave-hiring system.

Hired enslaved women's lives were also shaped by their occupation in an employer's charge as well as the location of their job site. In rural locales, as well as even when they were not pregnant or with infant children, many hired women worked as field laborers on small farms where divisions of labor were not very pronounced. White male hirers' gender assumptions also led them to employ enslaved women in their homes as house servants. In cities, the general absence of agriculture created a very highly developed sexual division of labor among hired slaves. Advertisements placed by white city dwellers who wished to hire bondwomen always occupied much space in newspapers, and many rural slave-holders hired out enslaved women to work in cities. In 1860, over 1,500 bond-women labored for hirers in Richmond, Virginia's First and Second Wards alone. As in rural areas, most urban hired women's occupations as house servants created especially divergent levels of mobility between themselves and hired bondmen. House servants were normally required to remain on call at all times, and this meant that any visiting occurred most often as the result of hired bondmen's travel to homes where hired enslaved females lived and worked. Bondwomen's white hirers, however, fearful of such socializing among bondpeople, frequently refused to permit hired men to visit the women they held on hire. Hired bondwomen often responded to such white prohibitions and other actions with arson directed against hirers' residences, as well as with attempts to place poison in the food they prepared for their white hirers. Hired enslaved women who engaged in such forms of resistance risked being whipped, hanged, or sold.

The hiring out of enslaved women was an integral part of slavery in the United States. Slaveholders hired out large numbers of bondwomen based on the economic nexus of labor expectations and women's life cycle. Slave hiring, therefore, enabled enslavers to mesh their perceptions of slave women as laborers and as women. Consequently, pregnancy and child care duties actually enhanced enslaved women's likelihood of being hired out by slaveholders who wished to avoid expenses, and who thereby forfeited any claim to the paternalist label. Hired-out bondwomen's experiences, including opportunities for, and the nature of, their resistance, were also conditioned by their occupation and location and whether they were pregnant or had small children.

John J. Zaborney

See also Childbirth; Childcare; Family; Female Slave Network; Gender Conventions; Historiography; Labor, Skilled; Life Cycle; Pregnancy; Resistance; South, The.

Suggested Reading

Sharla M. Fett, *Working Cures: Healing, Health, and Power on Southern Slave Plantations* (Chapel Hill: University of North Carolina Press, 2007); Jacqueline Jones, " 'My Mother Was Much of a Woman': Black Women, Work, and the Family Under Slavery," in *Our American Sisters: Women in American Life and Thought*, eds. Jean E. Friedman, William G. Shade, and Mary Jane Capozzoli (Lexington, MA: D.C. Heath and Company, 1987),

169–202; Midori Takagi, *"Rearing Wolves to Our Own Destruction": Slavery in Richmond, Virginia, 1782–1865* (Charlottesville: University Press of Virginia, 1999); Deborah Gray White, *"Ar'n't I a Woman?": Female Slaves in the Plantation South* (New York: W.W. Norton & Company, 1985); John J. Zaborney, "Slave Hiring and Slave Family and Friendship Ties in Rural, Nineteenth-Century Virginia," in *Afro-Virginian History and Culture*, ed. John Saillant (New York and London: Garland Press, 1999), 85–107.

Historiography

The trajectory of historical writing on a particular topic is known as *historiography* or the history of what historians have said about past events, people, institutions, and so forth. History is not a static, monolithic thing, but a multitude of stories that emerge from the act of historical thinking—the ways that historians piece together evidence and sources in new ways to challenge the dominant narratives of those who preceded them. This process is influenced to varying degrees by each historian's own background, identity, life experiences, and even the social, political, economic, and cultural context in which they generate knowledge about the past. As with all subjects of historical inquiry, the history of enslaved women possesses its own arc of scholarship that reflects these many factors.

During the era of slavery in the United States, some of enslaved women's distinct experiences were discussed by abolitionists and slaveholders (often inaccurately) as well as by women themselves, like Harriet Jacobs, Sojourner Truth, Elizabeth Freeman, Elizabeth Keckley, and Susie King Taylor. In the post-Emancipation decades—particularly after the collapse of Reconstruction in 1877 and the official start of *de jure* racial segregation with the infamous 1896 *Plessy vs. Ferguson* case—professional and lay historians displaced, ignored, erased, or re-remembered these realities to soften the painful legacy of slavery and the Civil War for newly reunited white Americans still working to heal a deep national wound. Slavery was romanticized as a kind and gentle institution in which presumably childlike bondspeople of all ages were content and well cared for by beneficent masters. Demeaning representations of enslaved women (such as the Mammy and Jezebel stereotypes) provided false evidence for these egregious beliefs as well as others pertaining to enslaved women's sexuality and supposed worth only as laborers. The brutalities of physical and sexual violence, breeding, concubinage, the detrimental effects of slavery on families, motherhood, pregnancy, childcare, marriage, and health, in addition to how women resisted enslavement in gender-specific ways were inconvenient truths written out of history.

By the late 1950s, a new generation of scholars—guided by the social and political impulses of the Civil Rights and Black Power movements that spanned into the 1970s and also inspired by a New Left trend to write history "from the bottom up"—questioned the validity of many myths about slavery. Rejecting the notion that it could only be known through the racist filters of slaveholders and their sympathizers, these groundbreaking historians focused instead on the complexities of everyday life for enslaved people: the relationships and social roles they forged within their families and communities, the wide range of resistance they carried out on a regular basis, their varied labor experiences, and the ways they found unity through cultural expressions like music and folklore and a sense of collective history through African cultural retentions. These scholars creatively gleaned the voices and perspectives of the enslaved from traditional plantation records, abolitionist materials, fugitive slave narratives, and other sources once dismissed as "unreliable," such as ex-slave interviews.

Pivotal works of this time include: Kenneth Stampp's *The Peculiar Institution: Slavery in the Antebellum South* (1956); Stanley Elkins's *Slavery: A Problem in American Institutional and Intellectual Life* (1959); John Blassingame's *The Slave Community: Plantation Life in the Antebellum South* (1972); Eugene Genovese's *"Roll, Jordan, Roll": The World the Slaves Made* (1972); Leslie Howard Owens's *This Species of Property: Slave Life and Culture in the Old South* (1976); and Lawrence Levine's *Black Culture and Black Consciousness: Afro-American Folk Thought from Slavery to Freedom* (1977). This scholarship revised racist historical interpretations of slavery and some even employed historical knowledge to engage pressing social issues and domestic policies of the day. Herbert Gutman's 1972 work *The Black Family in Slavery and Freedom, 1750–1925*, for instance, responded to Daniel Patrick Moynihan's well-intentioned, but fundamentally racist 1965 government report, "The Negro Family: The Case for National Action." Intended to promote liberal policies of racial equality and justice, Moynihan nevertheless mischaracterized black families as dysfunctional and so beleaguered by the legacy of slavery that they remained a "tangle of pathology" well into the twentieth century, a view that Gutman set out to disprove through historical research. Collectively, these innovative scholars had a profound and lasting impact on the study of American slavery, but their scholarship was not without fault. Most analyzed enslaved life only from the universal, default male perspective.

Second wave feminism—which grew out of and gained strength from the impassioned calls for social justice and racial equality that swept the nation in the 1960s and 1970s—inspired historians to also recover the forgotten lives and contributions of women in the past. The movement, however, primarily reflected the social, political, and economic interests of middle-class white women who ignored the added complexity of race in the lives of African American women. As a result, the historical experience of enslavement escaped the notice of most white feminist scholars in much the same way that those interested in racial slavery overlooked the institution's effects on women. While some turned their attention towards "herstory" in the United States during the era of racial slavery—such as Barbara Welter's classic 1966 essay "The Cult of True Womanhood: 1820–1860"—much of this work entirely overlooked nonwhite women.

Pushing back against these racial blind spots in feminist scholarship, black women and a handful of progressive white women narrowed their historical inquiries more specifically on bondwomen. Scholar and activist Angela Davis wrote perhaps one of the earliest articles about them, "Reflections on the Black Woman's Role in the Community of Slaves" (1972). Influenced by her activity in the militant Black Power movement and commitment to Marxist theory, she argued that stereotypes of domineering black women saturated even enlightened scholarship on slavery, that enslaved women paradoxically benefitted their families through household labor that historically oppressed white women, and that the conditions of their bondage forced them into a position of equality with men which further perpetuated mischaracterizations of them as overbearing matriarchs. Historian Gerda Lerner also spotlighted enslaved women's complicated history by compiling some of their writings, speeches, memoirs, and other primary sources in multiple chapters of her 1972 collection, *Black Women in White America: A Documentary History*. By 1979, Darlene Clarke Hine raised additional concerns in her essay "Female Slave Resistance: The Economics of Sex" that discussed sexual abstinence, contraception, abortion, and infanticide. The emphasis these early scholars placed on enslaved women gradually came to influence broader feminist studies such as Susan Brownmiller's pivotal 1975 work *Against Our Will: Men, Women and Rape*. A classic in the canon of feminist scholarship, Brownmiller examined rape historically, made clear its function as a tool of political oppression, and dedicated an entire chapter to the sexual assault of bondwomen in the antebellum South.

By the 1980s, a troubling economic recession and national longing for an imagined "simpler time" produced a reactionary backlash against the progressive politics of civil rights and social equality for women, African Americans, and other minorities. Conservative President Ronald Reagan won a landslide electoral victory in 1980 and a resurgence of Christian evangelism politicized the "traditional" nuclear family. Feminist concerns like birth control, abortion, and divorce came under attack at the same time that pernicious new stereotypes emerged about African American women like the so-called "Welfare Queen" and the supposed urban epidemic of "crack babies," or newborns addicted to crack cocaine presumably because of their mothers' lack of maternal concern and criminal proclivities. These dramatic changes in social attitudes only galvanized historians committed to advancing knowledge about both African American women and the history of racial slavery.

In 1984, Dorothy Sterling produced a noteworthy compendium of primary sources that contained the voices of both enslaved and free black women in *We Are Your Sisters: Black Women in the Nineteenth Century*. Paula Giddings and

Jacqueline Jones also wrote extensive histories of black women in the United States through the twentieth century, each with considerable analyses of slavery, in *When and Where I Enter: The Impact of Black Women on Race and Sex in America* (1984) and *Labor of Love, Labor of Sorrow: Black Women, Work and the Family from Slavery to the Present* (1985). Deborah Gray White, however, revolutionized the field in 1985 by publishing the first full-length monograph devoted entirely to them, *Ar'n't I a Woman?: Female Slaves in the Plantation South.*

The importance of White's work cannot be overstated because she established a sweeping framework for future discussions about enslaved women by honing in on both sexual exploitation as well as sexual agency; stereotypes and inherently contradictory racial and gender ideologies; major milestones and specific difficulties that marked various phases of bondwomen's life cycle; and their development of a female slave network from which they gained strength from one another even as they sometimes experienced animosity and intraracial conflict. As the 1980s waned, scholars complicated this history even more by considering bondwomen's lives in relation to other southern women like plantation mistresses or by providing a contrast through studying free black women as Elizabeth Fox Genovese and Loren Schweninger did, respectively, in *Within the Plantation Household: Black and White Women of the South* (1988) and "Property Owning Free African American Women in the South, 1800–1870" (1990). These developments unfolded alongside other profoundly influential trends, particularly Joan Scott's dramatic re-conceptualization of the very meaning of women's history in her seminal essay "Gender: A Useful Category of Historical Analysis" (1986). Scott challenged historians to move beyond simply restoring women to historical narratives and, instead, to recognize how gender—socially-constructed ideas of masculinity and femininity—structures various relationships and can be critically utilized as an analytical tool in the production of historical knowledge. Scott's tremendous contribution to the historical profession propelled the historiography of enslaved women into another phase, especially as American society shifted once again by the final decade of the twentieth century and into the new millennium.

In the 1990s, a majority of Americans gradually retreated from the previous decade's ideological rigidity and selective moralizing as the economy returned to a more buoyant state. Democratic President Bill Clinton was elected in 1992 and initiated important conversations about race in which he promoted multiculturalism, diversity, and tolerance. This was unsurprising in light of a gripping national scandal about race, sex, and power that occurred immediately before to the start of his presidency. The 1991 Senate confirmation hearings of conservative, then-potential Supreme Court Justice Clarence Thomas—accused of sexual harassment by his colleague, lawyer Anita Hill—symbolized for many the difficult and painful circumstances in which African American women often find themselves because of the intersection of race, gender, and class as well as the ubiquity of age-old stereotypes used to delegitimize and invalidate them. The 1990s also stand out as a decade in which academics frequently transgressed disciplinary boundaries, historians more fully embraced the "cultural turn," and ethnic studies programs—particularly African and African American Studies—enjoyed considerable success and broad support. All of these factors shaped the production of historical knowledge about enslaved women, making it more complex and nuanced.

By the early 2000s, Americans had fully entered into the "Internet Age" and technological advances coupled with the international forces of globalization made the world appear smaller, more connected, and easier to access. This phenomenon produced a heightened awareness of transnational linkages between and among people that prompted historians to ask new questions about similar issues in the past. These additional factors further impacted how historians of enslaved women approached various topics and framed their studies.

Nell Painter's "Soul Murder and Slavery: Toward a Fully Loaded Cost Accounting" (1995), for example, drew on insights from modern psychology to consider the internal ramifications of slavery on both whites and blacks, but particularly for physically, psychologically, and sexually abused enslaved children and women. Stephanie Shaw's "Mothering under Slavery in the Antebellum South" (1994) provided an in-depth analysis of motherhood that neither romanticized it nor stripped enslaved mothers of their agency. Instead, she pragmatically considered how, by simply caring for their children, enslaved mothers reinforced the system of slavery even as many directly or indirectly rattled its foundations through abortion, infanticide, or teaching children to be self-sufficient and loyal to their own communities and families.

Other studies focused specifically on the family and, in doing so, examined gender and race relations between bondwomen and men and between blacks and whites in addition to mirroring a greater social acceptance of nontraditional family structures, such as Brenda Stevenson's *Life in Black and White: Family and Community in the Slave South* (1996) and Ann Patton Malone's *Sweet Chariot: Slave Family and Household Structure in Nineteenth Century Louisiana* (1996). Two significant collections of essays also stand out as characteristic of the trends that influenced historians of enslaved women in the 1990s. Darlene Clark Hine, Wilma King and Linda Reed edited *"We Specialize in the Wholly Impossible": A Reader in Black Women's History* (1995), which contains important chapters written by John Thornton, Herbert Klein, Paul Lovejoy, Sylvia Jacobs, and Rhoda Reddock that more fully connect enslaved women in the United States with Africa and the African Diaspora. The notion of Diaspora also marks another significant collection of essays edited by David Gaspar and Darlene Clark Hine, *More than Chattel: Black Women and Slavery in the Americas* (1996), which assessed the extent to which scholars integrated gender into studies of New World slavery.

Many full-length studies expanded on these themes and advanced the field in new directions throughout the 2000s. Historian Sharla Fett grappled with diasporic issues using the lens of bondwomen's culturally-derived medical knowledge and their struggle to retain control over their own and their family and community's healthcare practices in *Working Cures: Health, Healing, and Power on Southern Slave Plantations* (2002). Jennifer Morgan and Kathleen Brown pushed back the standard chronological boundaries of histories of enslaved women in the United States to the colonial era and produced poignant gendered analyses in their respective works, *Laboring Women: Reproduction and Gender in New World Slavery* (2004) and *Good Wives, Nasty Wenches, and Anxious Patriarchs: Gender, Race, and Power in Colonial Virginia* (2006). In addition to these aspects, Morgan's work also critically engaged the ways in which African-descended women in the New World were important transmitters of African cultural knowledge, underscoring the importance of cultural retentions, but also suggesting the role of multiculturalism in the story of American slavery. Tiya Miles furthered discussion of this phenomenon in her analysis of the fusion of African and Native American cultural pathways within families and the role bondwomen took on in this process in *Ties that Bind: the Story of an Afro-Cherokee Family in Slavery and Freedom* (2006). Culture also played a significant role in Stephanie Camp's 2004 study, *Closer to Freedom: Enslaved Women and Everyday Resistance in the Plantation South*, though it was more in terms of how bondwomen took control of the interior spaces of their own minds, bodies, and private quarters to create a "rival geography" in opposition to the spaces that slaveholders sought to constrict them to. Daina Ramey Berry's *Swing the Sickle for the Harvest Is Ripe: Gender and Slavery in Antebellum Georgia* (2007) shifts the focus to the gendered division of labor, challenges its standard definitions, and highlights overlooked social spaces that bondpeople enjoyed even within the system of forced labor.

Biographies and microstudies about specific people also furthered the historiography of enslaved women, particularly in the 1990s and 2000s. By detailing the specifics of select women's lives, historians made clear that they were often microcosms of the complicated themes writ large in the lives of all bondwomen. Some notable studies in this category include Melton A. McLaurin's *Celia: A Slave* (1991); Nell Irvin Painter's *Sojourner Truth: A Life, A Symbol* (1996); Annette Gordon Reed's *Thomas Jefferson and Sally Hemings: An American Controversy* (1997); Jean M. Humez's *Harriet Tubman: The Life and the Life Stories* (2003); Jean Fagan Yellin's *Harriet Jacobs: A Life* (2004); Milton C. Sernett's *Harriet Tubman: Myth, Memory and History* (2007); Annette Gordon Reed's *The Hemingses of Monticello: An American Family* (2008); Lea VanderVelde's *Mrs. Dred Scott: A Life on Slavery's Frontier* (2009); and Emile Piper and David Levinson's *One Minute a Free Woman: Elizabeth Freeman and the Struggle for Freedom* (2010).

It is also true that historians outside of the United States have contributed important works dealing with enslaved women that stand out as unique because of their very different backgrounds. British scholars have all provided interpretations from a non-American perspective, such as Betty Wood's *Women's Work, Men's Work: The Informal Slave Economies of Lowcountry Georgia* (1995) and more recent studies like Emily West's *Chains of Love: Slave Couples in Antebellum South Carolina* (2004); Rebecca Fraser's *Courtship and Love among the Enslaved in North Carolina* (2007); and Damian Alan Pargas's *The Quarters and the Fields: Slave Families in the Non-Cotton South* (2010). Also, scholars who focused on gender in the era of the Transatlantic Slave Trade and within the African Diaspora in areas such as the Caribbean left an indelible mark on the historiography of enslaved women in the United States. Notable works of this ilk include Hilary Beckles' *Natural Rebels: A Social History of Enslaved Black Women in Barbados* (1989), Marietta Morrissey's *Slave Women in the New World* (1989), and Barbara Bush's *Slave Women in Caribbean Society, 1650–1838* (1990).

The historiography of enslaved women has shifted considerably since the 1970s and 1980s, but forthcoming publications, recent articles, and dissertations reflect many of these nuanced understandings even as they are refracted through the contemporary issues and new challenges of the time. Amani Marshall's dissertation, for instance, continues a conversation about gender and resistance, "Female Fugitives: Enslaved Women's Resistance in South Carolina and Georgia, 1820–1865" (2006), as does his recent article " 'They Will Endeavor to Pass for Free': Enslaved Runaways' Performances of Freedom in Antebellum South Carolina" (2010). Jessica Millward's forthcoming study, *Charity's Folk: Enslaved Women, Families, and Freedom in Pre-Civil War Maryland*, as well as Courtney Moore's dissertation-in-progress, "The Rites of Passage for the Adolescent Female Slave in the Antebellum South, 1800–1861," both take up questions of family and the social roles and rituals of enslaved women. Other recent studies capture the confluence of gender with transnationalism, the African Diaspora, and the Atlantic world such as Sowande' Mustakeem's 2008 dissertation, " 'Make Haste & Let Me See You with a Good Cargo of Negroes': Gender, Health, and Violence in the Eighteenth Century Middle Passage" and his 2011 article " 'She Must Go Overboard and Shall Go Overboard': Diseased Bodies and the Spectacle of Murder at Sea" as well as Jessica Johnson's dissertation, "Black Atlantic Women: Entrepreneurship, Kinship, Religion and the Struggle for Freedom in Senegal, Gulf Coast Louisiana and Saint-Domingue, 1715–1848" (2009).

Dierdre Cooper Owens takes a slightly different path in breaking new ground with her comparative analysis of two distinctly racialized groups of women in the United States in her dissertation, " 'Courageous Negro Servitors' and Laboring Irish Bodies: An Examination of Antebellum-era Modern American Gynecology" (2009). Jenifer Barclay is also adding to the growing field of African American medical history with her disseration on enslaved people with disabilities. The related body of scholarship on free black women—which allows, through comparison, greater insight into enslaved life—also continues to grow as evidenced by Anrita Myers forthcoming study of free women in South Carolina, *Negotiating Women: Race, Gender, and Freedom in the Nineteenth Century South* and Nik Ribianszky's 2011 dissertation, " 'To Seek Shelter She Knows Not Where': Freedom, Movement, and Gendered Violence Among Free People of Color in Natchez, Mississippi, 1779–1865."

Jenifer L. Barclay

See also Abortion; African and African-born Women; Breeding; Celia; Childcare; Community; Concubinage; Conflict, Intraracial; Contraception; Emancipation; Family; Female Slave Network; Free Women; Freeman, Elizabeth; Health, Disabilities, and Soundness; Infanticide; Jacobs, Harriet; Jezebel Stereotype; Keckley, Elizabeth; Labor, Agricultural; Labor, Nonagricultural; Labor, Skilled; Life Cycle; Mammy Stereotype; Marriage and Cohabitation; Motherhood; Pregnancy; Representations; Sexuality; Taylor, Susie King; Truth, Sojourner; Violence, Racial; Violence, Sexual.

Suggested Reading

Stephanie Camp and Edward Baptist, eds., *New Studies in the History of American Slavery* (Athens, GA: University of Georgia Press, 2006); David Gaspar and Darlene Clark Hine, eds., *More than Chattel: Black Women and Slavery in the Americas* (Bloomington: Indiana University Press, 1996); James Oliver Horton and Lois E. Horton, *Slavery and Public History: The Tough Stuff of American Memory* (New York: The New Press, 2006); Jennifer Morgan, Daina Ramey Berry, Stephanie Camp, Leslie Harris, Barbara Krauthamer, Jessical Milward, and Deborah Gray White, "Roundtable on the Twentieth Anniversary of the Publication of *Ar'n't I a Woman?*" *The Journal of Women's History* 19, 2 (Summer 2007), 138–69.

I

Incidents in the Life of a Slave Girl

See Jacobs, Harriet

Infant Mortality

See Infanticide; Mortality and Life Expectancy

Infanticide

Cultural definitions of infant and infanticide are variable. Infanticide generally involves the murder of a child under the age of two. It is usually committed immediately after birth, and the perpetrator is usually one of the parents, particularly the mother. Suffocation, abandonment, and drowning are the most common methods of committing infanticide.

Infanticide was practiced, though rarely, by some enslaved women in the United States. There were many motives to induce its occurrence. A woman born into slavery in the United States could expect that she would be subjected to violence and exploitation throughout her lifetime. Southern laws did not recognize the rape of an enslaved woman as a crime and sexual abuse of bondwomen was common. Infanticide was one method to deal with unwanted pregnancies resulting from sexual abuse. Evidence of real and perceived cases of infanticide practiced by enslaved women is found in court documents. An enslaved woman in Virginia was convicted of killing her mixed-race infant. She claimed, "she would not have killed a child of her own color" (quoted in King 1996, 160).

Some enslaved women committed infanticide to free their children from a life of bondage. The case of Margaret Garner, who ran away from slavery with her family in 1856, is the most notorious incident. Garner murdered her two-year-old daughter when she realized the recapture of her family was imminent. She did this because she did not want her children to live as slaves. An enslaved woman in South Carolina allegedly killed her newborn to prevent her enslaver from selling him, as he had sold her three previous children (Schwartz 2006, 210). These acts of intentional infanticide can be viewed as an extreme form of resistance in which the women exercised control over their children within a system in which they had no rights to them.

Some instances of infanticide involving enslaved infants were committed by slaveholders, their wives, overseers, and slave traders. Former bondpeople remembered these incidents and shared them with Works Progress Administration interviewers in the 1930s. One enslaver in Kentucky allegedly killed an infant to improve the chances of selling his mother (Ibid., 211). A Texas slave trader forced a woman to abandon her infant on the side of a road on the way to auction (Ibid., 7). A former bondperson in Georgia recalled that a slave owner's wife decapitated an enslaved woman's child because her husband fathered the child (Fox-Genovese 1998, 325).

Court records indicate that accusations of infanticide committed by enslaved women were far more common than actual incidence. Recent historical and medical research suggests that many children who were supposedly suffocated by a mother were actually victims of Sudden Infant Death Syndrome (White 1985, 88). Neonatal tetanus and other diseases caused by poor living conditions and enforced neglect caused by labor requirements also contributed to high infant mortality that enslavers sometimes perceived as infanticide. If a slaveholder suspected infanticide, the bondperson could be punished harshly, sometimes with fatal results. It was an issue of economics for the slaveholder; infanticide meant a loss of property. However, it meant much more for enslaved women. Infanticide among enslaved mothers was not a common act committed by women with no maternal feelings for their children, but rather an atypical, compassionate act of protection or resistance, or a means of self-survival.

Lori Lee

See also Garner, Margaret; Mortality and Life Expectancy.

Suggested Reading

Elizabeth Fox-Genovese, *Within the Plantation Household: Black and White Women of the South* (Chapel House: University of North Carolina Press, 1998); Wilma King, "Suffer with Them till Death," in *More than Chattel: Black Women and Slavery in the Americas*, eds. David Barry Gaspar and Darlene Clark Hine (Bloomington: Indiana University Press, 1996); Marie Jenkins Schwartz, *Birthing a Slave* (Cambridge: Harvard University Press, 2006); Deborah White, *Ar'n't I a Woman: Female Slaves in the Plantation South* (New York: W.W. Norton & Company, 1985).

Islam

The religion or *din* (pronounced *deen* meaning faith) of Muslims, also called Moslems, is commonly defined as peace or surrender/submission to the oneness of G-d. Muslims believe the final or seal of the prophets was Prophet Muhammad of Arabia. Islam was the "largest monotheistic religion introduced into post-Columbian America following Catholicism" (Diouf 1998, 2). A significant number of the first enslaved Africans brought to the Americas were Muslims from West Africa, mainly the Senegambia region. Many Muslim bondpeople were settled in coastal South Carolina and Georgia, specifically among the Gullah people. The religion of Islam was systematically repressed under American Christianity and slavery. As a result, explicit Islamic practices gradually disappeared, thus making Christianity the main uncontested religion of Africans and their descendants during enslavement. The total numbers of Muslims among African captives brought to the America are difficult to determine, however, scholars' estimate that 20 percent of the enslaved population were initially Muslims and of that estimate, 15 to 20 percent were female. Muslim women were identifiable by their diet, clothing, names, prayer beads, and rituals. They also stood out because of their literacy skills. Most Muslim women were able to read, write, and speak fluent Arabic. Literacy was strongly encouraged among Muslims in order to read the Quran (Koran), their primary religious text.

Slavery made the adherence to Islamic rituals difficult and near impossible to maintain. Although enslaved Muslims did not have access to the Quran (Koran) or other spiritual texts, worshippers continued to practice their religious faith. Under the institution of slavery, Muslim women continued to adhere to Islamic dietary restrictions and dress. They cooked a variety of foods especially during *Ramadan*, the month of fasting. The most well-documented food among enslaved Muslims was "saraka cakes," rice cakes given out as charity, also called *zakat* (Diouf 1998). Muslim women's clothing set them apart from other enslaved women. They were described as wearing distinctly tied head wraps around their heads, which were sometimes called veiling, and covered everything except the women's faces. Their manner of dress consisted of layered clothing such as skirts and shawls in order to maintain the guideline of modesty required of all Muslim women. They were also observed making prayers at various intervals during the day, typically two to three times. While Islamic doctrine requires Muslims to make a total of five daily prayers, work demands and religious intolerance frequently precluded enslaved worshippers from doing so.

Today, there are an estimated 4.5 million persons of African descent who belong to the religion of Islam in America. Scholars have discovered a great deal about the Muslim slave population in general, however, more work is underway that will help illuminate the daily life and experiences of enslaved Muslim women.

Bayyinah S. Jeffries

See also Clothing; Food Preparation and Cooking; Gullah Culture; Literacy; Religion.

Suggested Reading

Allan D. Austin, *African Muslims in Antebellum America* (New York and London: Routledge, 1997); Sylviane A. Diouf, *Servants of Allah: African Muslims Enslaved in the Americas* (New York and London: New York University Press, 1998); Aminah B. McCloud, *African American Islam* (New York and London: Routledge, 1995).

J

Jacobs, Harriet

Birth Date: 1813
Death Date: 1897

Harriet Ann Jacobs, an ex-bondwoman who later became an abolitionist and reformer authored one of the most significant slave narratives, *Incidents in the Life of a Slave Girl* (1861). This narrative embodies a bondwoman's perspective, a voice long overlooked in the history of slavery, particularly on the issue of sexual exploitation. Since Jacobs wrote *Incidents* under the pseudonym Linda Brent and gave the actual people fictitious names, it was considered a white-authored fiction until the 1987 edition proved that it was indeed an autobiography written by a black woman.

Incidents is Jacobs' memoirs of her life as a female house slave in the South and a fugitive in the North, highlighting her struggle against sexual oppression and her long-lasting fight for freedom. Jacobs had a relatively fortunate girlhood; she lived with her family until she was six years old and was taught how to read by her mistress who took her in after her mother's death. Jacob's painful adolescence began before she turned 12. When her mistress died, she bequeathed Jacobs to her little niece whose parents virtually became her slaveholders.

Her middle-aged enslaver, Dr. Flint, sexually harassed her and ordered Jacobs to be his concubine when she was 15. In order to avoid his assaults, she became sexually involved with a young white neighbor Mr. Sands, by whom she had two children. This infuriated Dr. Flint, who threatened her again with concubinage. Jacobs resisted and was sent away to his son's plantation. Learning about Dr. Flint's plan to sell her children, Jacobs decided to escape to the North, hoping that Dr. Flint would give up on her and her children and that Sands would buy and free them. She was sheltered by her neighbors, looking for a chance to escape, but Dr. Flint's persistent search for Jacobs kept her from leaving town. She hid herself in a tiny attic crawlspace in her grandmother's house for almost seven years. At age 29, she escaped to the North and was reunited with her children, who had been bought by Sands and sent North. After years of working as a nurse in New York in constant fear of capture, Jacobs finally gained freedom through her sympathetic employer, Mrs. Bruce, who ironically purchased her.

Incidents also portrays the lives of other enslaved women like Jacob's grandmother Martha who devoted her life to protect her offspring, her great-aunt Nancy who went through numerous miscarriages through overwork, and her friend Betty who helped her mistress shelter Jacobs. *Incidents* is not only a valuable historical document on the lives of enslaved women, but it is also considered one of the earliest canonical works in African American literature.

Fumiko Sakashita

See also Abolitionism; Concubinage; Family; Girlhood; Narratives; North, The; Owners; Resistance; Runaways; Violence, Sexual.

Suggested Reading

Harriet A. Jacobs, *Incidents in the Life of a Slave Girl: Written by Herself*, ed. Jean Fagan Yellin (Cambridge: Harvard University Press, 1987); "Harriet Jacobs: Selected Writings and Correspondence": http://www.yale.edu/glc/harriet/.

Jezebel Stereotype

Jezebel was a stereotype of a sexually predatory and lascivious enslaved woman. A name taken from a character in the Old Testament (The Book of Kings), Jezebel in the Bible was portrayed as a strong and aggressive queen who dominated her husband, the king and worshipped false prophets. Later interpretations referred to her being a painted woman, deceptive, and associated with prostitutes. Within the context of American slavery, women refered to as "Jezebel" were sometimes characterized as having a light complexion from being mixed race, likely the result of a sexual encounter between the slaveholder and an enslaved woman. However, Jezebel was also applied to any woman of African descent and routinely depicted black women as wanton, promiscuous, and sexually aggressive in contrast to nineteenth-century notions of Victorian feminine purity.

The image of Jezebel was created and perpetuated by slave masters to justify the rape and sexual exploitation of enslaved women and girls by white men in their communities. Early modern European racialist discourses and initial interactions between Africans and Europeans laid the ideological foundation for perceptions of racial and gendered difference. Upon initial contact in Africa, Europeans wrote extensively of African women's bodies as they labored in the fields and tended their children. Europeans' cultural misunderstandings equated differences in African women's physical attire and marriage customs with sexual promiscuity and immorality. During the Middle Passage and on the American auction blocks, African women found themselves commodified and sexually appraised. During these dehumanizing processes, enslaved females were often sexually victimized by various men aboard slave ships, in plantation settings, and by owners, military men, and visitors in urban environments. In systems of plantation and urban slavery, the rape of black women was not punishable by law and black women had no recourse from sexual violence. Enslaved women faced sexual threats in most areas of their lives and slave owners profited from their reproductive capabilities.

On American plantations, overseers exerted violent threats against female field laborers for both slow productivity and resisting sexual advances. In close contact with the white household, black women who performed domestic work also faced routine sexual assault from white men and boys. Not able to defend themselves or seek protection from black male partners, enslaved women were often characterized as inviting and accepting of the sexual advances of white men. The Jezebel stereotype served to remove the onus of power and responsibility from the white male perpetrators for their sexual domination and exploitation of black women and disavowed the possibility enslaved women as sexual victims. For white women, the image of Jezebel as sexual instigator helped to rationalize their husbands' and relatives' infidelities and immoral behavior. Manifesting from centuries of gendered and racialist ideologies, the pervasive Jezebel stereotype of a hypersexual black woman served the interests of white patriarchal economic and sexual power.

Marisa J. Fuentes

See also Gender Conventions; Mammy Stereotype; Violence, Sexual.

Suggested Reading

Saidiya Hartman, *Scenes of Subjection: Terror, Slavery, and Self-Making in Nineteenth-Century America* (New York: Oxford University Press, 1997); Jennifer L. Morgan, *Laboring Women: Reproduction and Gender in New World Slavery* (Philadelphia: University of Pennsylvania Press, 2004); Deborah Gray White, *Ar'n't I a Woman: Female Slaves in the Plantation South* (New York: W.W. Norton & Company, 1985).

K

Keckley, Elizabeth

Birth Date: 1818
Death Date: 1907

By the age of four, Elizabeth Keckley described the Virginia plantation on which she lived as a "hardy school." There, she learned self-reliance, a lesson that would facilitate her survival in slavery, she and her son's eventual freedom, and her success as an entrepreneur. Keckley was born a cherished child to her parents, Agnes Hobbs and George Pleasant, but a slave to Colonel Armistead Burwell. Her first "duty," at four years old, was to care for the Burwell's infant child. Keckley's age, however, did not save her from the brutal beatings that resulted from her inability to care for the newborn. As the Burwell family grew and their stock of servants increased, Keckley's "young energies were taxed to the utmost." She struggled to help her mother make clothes for the growing plantation community while simultaneously continuing her own exhaustive chores. Keckley's father, who lived on a neighboring plantation and was allowed to visit only twice a year, was sent to Tennessee when Keckley was eight. She never saw him again.

At 14, Colonel Burwell sent Elizabeth Keckley to live with his minister son, Robert Burwell, thus separating her from her mother. Keckley, along with Burwell's family, moved to North Carolina where Burwell took over a church. Despite years doing "the work of three servants," Keckley could not escape the wrath of Burwell's wife. Mrs. Burwell retained Mr. Bingham, a local schoolmaster and church member, to repeatedly and severely beat Keckley. Unable to tame her into submission, Burwell gave Keckley to a family friend, Alexander Kirkland, who kept her as his concubine, which led to the birth of her only child, George. After Kirkland's death four years later, Keckley and her son George were sent to Colonel Burwell's daughter's family, the Garlands, in St. Louis, where Keckley reunited with her mother. Attempting to relieve their financially desperate situation, the Garlands aimed to hire out Keckley's mother. Devastated, Keckley gained permission to find work to spare her mother from doing so and quickly earned a reputation as a skilled seamstress and dressmaker.

For the next several years, Keckley worked relentlessly among wealthy whites and freedpersons. This exposure to freed blacks especially allowed her to meet

Undated image of Elizabeth Keckley, seamstress and author of *Behind the Scenes Or, Thirty Years a Slave and Four Years in the White House* (1868), who labored as First Lady Mary Todd Lincoln's dressmaker after buying her freedom. (*Documenting the American South*, University of North Carolina at Chapel Hill Libraries.)

and eventually marry the worldly James Keckley, who claimed himself a free man. Over time, their union caused Keckley to ponder her own right to freedom. Hugh Garland finally conceded and allowed Keckley to buy her and her son's freedom for $1,200, which she did in 1855. In 1860, Keckley left her husband, discovering he was neither a truly free man nor a "helpmate." She headed first to Baltimore and then to Washington, D.C., where she established herself as a sought-after modiste (dressmaker) for an elite clientele. Ultimately, Keckley's savvy entrepreneurship landed her a job in the White House as Mrs. Lincoln's personal dressmaker and confidante, which she discusses in her autobiography, *Behind the Scenes: Thirty Years a Slave, and Four Years in the White House* (1868). Little is known, however, of Keckley's post-White House years. From 1892 until she suffered a stroke in 1894, she headed the Domestic Science Department of Wilberforce University in Ohio.

Sometime after, Keckley ended up in the Home for Destitute Women and Children, an institution in Washington, D.C, that she helped found, and where she died in 1907.

Linda L. Rodriguez

See also Concubinage; Domestic Slave Trade; Marriage, Abroad; Punishment; Seamstress Work.

Suggested Reading

Frances Smith Foster, Historical Introduction to *Behind the Scenes* (Chicago: University of Illinois Press, 1998); Elizabeth Keckley, *Behind the Scenes: Thirty Years a Slave, and Four Years in the White House* (Chicago: University of Illinois Press, 1998).

Key, Elizabeth

Birth Date: 1630
Death Date: ~

In the seventeenth century, most early settlers in the British colony of Virginia came as indentured servants. They were bound to their masters for a period of years to pay for their passage to the New World. Labor was so scarce during most of the seventeenth century that many unscrupulous masters kept their servants beyond the agreed-upon term of service. To challenge their unlawful detention, some servants successfully brought freedom suits in the colonial courts. Elizabeth Key was one of those early legal petitioners for freedom in colonial America.

During this period there also were small numbers of Africans or their descendants in the Virginia colony. Historians continue to debate their legal status. Undoubtedly, a few were indentured servants and even fewer were free, but most were considered bondpeople. Disputes over the legal status of Africans and their descendants arose as early as the 1630s, but colonial administrators often handled these legal questions on an individual basis. There was no specific resolution of this question until 1670 after Elizabeth Key—the daughter of a married English settler, Thomas Key, and his female "negro" bondwoman—sued for her freedom in a Northumberland County Court.

When wealthy English settler Colonel John Mottrom died in 1655, the inventory of his estate listed two types of human property: servants and slaves. The remaining years of service were listed next to the name of each servant, but no years appeared next to the names of bondpeople, indicating that they were bound for their entire lives. Elizabeth Key was listed among the bondpeople. According to the 1655 trial records, Thomas Key gave Elizabeth, at the age of six, to Henry Higginson, a prominent and wealthy English settler. Higginson, her alleged godfather, promised to free her in nine years, but instead gave her to Colonel Mottrom who converted her into an enslaved person.

Key, with the assistance of William Grinstead, the English-born father of her two children, challenged her enslavement in the courts, arguing that she was a free-born practicing Christian who inherited her father's English subjecthood and, as a result, could not be enslaved for perpetuity. Thus, she claimed, the agreement between Thomas Key and Henry Higginson was a contract of indenture, not a contract for the sale of a bondperson. The Northumberland County Court ultimately ruled in her favor, only to have its decision overturned by the General Court. Disappointed, Grinstead took Elizabeth's case before the General Assembly, which, until 1680, served as both the legislative body and the highest appellate court in the Virginia colony. The General Assembly ruled in Key's favor and granted her freedom.

Elizabeth Key and William Grinstead married in 1659. When Grinstead died in 1661, Key married John Parse (Peirce), an English widower. In 1662, the Virginia General Assembly, seeking to avoid future status disputes, enacted a law providing that the condition of the child follows that of the mother. Therefore, if a child's mother is enslaved at the time of a child's birth, then that newborn is also considered enslaved. The legal status of the child's father had no bearing. This became a fundamental law of slavery throughout the colonies and later in the United States.

Taunya Lovell Banks

See also Free Women; Laws.

Suggested Reading

Taunya Lovell Banks, "Dangerous Woman: Elizabeth Key's Freedom Suit—Subjecthood and Racialized Identity in Seventeenth Century Colonial Virginia" (forthcoming *Akron Law Review* 41 (2007–2008), 1; Warren M. Billings, ed. *The Old Dominion in the Seventeenth Century: A Documentary History of Virginia, 1606–1689* (Chapel Hill: University of North Carolina Press, 1975), 165–69; Warren M. Billings, "The Case of Fernando and Elizabeth Key: A Note on the Status of Blacks in Seventeenth-Century Virginia," *William and Mary Quarterly* 3rd ser. 30, 3 (July 1973), 467–74.

L

Labor, Agricultural

Few bondpeople escaped agricultural labor in pre-Civil-War America, and of those who did, even fewer were women. On the rural farms and plantations, where a vast majority of slaves lived, opportunities for women to engage in nonagricultural labor were scarce, and slaveholders allocated many skilled occupations exclusively to men. Consequently, most enslaved women worked for most of their lives as field hands, producing staples such as tobacco, wheat, rice, cotton, and sugar. The specific nature of their labor varied across time and space according to the demands of the different cash crops that they were forced to cultivate. However, in most regions they performed tasks that could be accomplished by hand or with a hoe, as prevailing gender conventions convinced slaveholders that men more efficiently performed operations that required more complicated tools.

> There wasn't many men who could class up with [my mother] when it come to working. She could do more work than any two men.
>
> —Leonard Franklin, former bondman (WPA Slave Narrative Project, Arkansas Narratives, Volume 2, Part 2, 337)

> I been so exhausted working, I was like an inch-worm crawling along a roof. I worked till I thought another lick would kill me. If you had something to do, you did it or got whipped. Once I was so tired I couldn't work anymore. I crawled in a hole under the house and stayed there till I was rested. I didn't get whipped, either.
>
> —Hannah Davidon, formerly bondwoman from Kentucky (Born in Slavery: Slave Narratives from the Federal Writers' Project, 1936–1938 Ohio Narratives, Volume XII, 28)

As early as the mid-seventeenth century, the major staple crop produced in the Chesapeake (Virginia, Maryland, and Delaware) was tobacco. And although soil exhaustion and falling prices caused its production there to decline by the late eighteenth century, during the nineteenth century, tobacco expanded to other parts of the Upper South such as Kentucky and Missouri. Wherever it was produced, tobacco was a fickle plant that demanded a great deal of attention. After clearing and preparing the land by "chopping it up" with hoes in January and early February, field hands carefully sowed tobacco seeds in late February and March, then transplanted them into specially made "hills" and continuously weeded between April and August. When they were not planting, bondpeople were picking ground worms and caterpillars off of the fragile tobacco leaves, removing unwanted buds and shoots, or working in the provision grounds. In August, the hoes were "laid by" to harvest the first tobacco plants. The tobacco was cut, allowed to sweat overnight, and then hung from the rafters in the tobacco house in order to cure. The leaves were then stripped from the stalks, individually rolled, and packed into hogsheads. The harvest was usually over by early October, but tasks such as stripping, rolling, and packing the tobacco kept bondpeople busy into the winter.

Tobacco planters engaged bondwomen in almost all aspects of the crop's cultivation, organizing them into small squads where they worked alongside their male counterparts from sunup to sundown; during the harvest season they even worked by candlelight into the night. On large plantations squads were usually divided by gender, with the men working at a quicker tempo than the women and children. Felling trees and cutting tobacco represent two tasks done exclusively by enslaved men, otherwise, women did much the same work as their male counterparts. Even women in advanced stages of pregnancy were expected to work until childbirth and fulfill their normal labor quotas as early as two weeks later.

Slaves plant cotton on Sea Island, South Carolina. *Harper's Weekly*, April 17, 1869. (Library of Congress.)

By the late eighteenth century, most slaves in the Upper South found themselves also cultivating wheat and other small grains (such as corn, oats, rye, flax, and hemp) in addition to tobacco, and by the turn of the nineteenth century, some regions had shifted almost completely to grains and mixed farming. A sexual division of labor was more frequently employed in the new mixed economy, with women often relegated to the least specialized and most menial duties during certain seasons. For example, preparing the land for grain planting required plowing, a semiskilled occupation allocated exclusively to men. Men also mowed the wheat with scythes and made hay, and they were charged with carting the harvested grains to local mills, thus affording them more opportunities for physical mobility. Women, on the other hand, labored either with hoes (weeding, leveling ditches, making "hills" to receive the seeds), or their hands (sowing grains, gathering and treading out wheat, or cleaning stables).

The cultivation of rice in the eighteenth and nineteenth century low country (coastal South Carolina and Georgia) placed very different demands on field hands, keeping bondpeople busy year round. If new land was to be cleared, this was done in January and February, months otherwise spent burning the trash from the previous year's crop, repairing dykes, and digging and cleaning out ditches (the hated "mudwork"). By March, bondpeople were preparing the land for planting: the fields were plowed, then the lumpy soil was chopped and leveled, and trenches were dug to receive the rice seeds—the latter done with the hoe. In April, the rice was sowed by hand, after which the sluices (or "trunks") were opened and the rice fields were flooded until the plants sprouted. The water was then drawn off and bondpeople began hoeing in the muddy fields. This cycle of flooding, draining, and hoeing was repeated at least twice more until the last flooding in mid-July, which lasted for two months. While the fields were inundated, most labor was diverted to the plantation's provision grounds, where corn and other vegetables were cultivated. Still, planters forced many bondpeople to wade through stagnant water to rake off trash in the rice fields. By mid-September the rice was ready for harvesting, ushering in the most laborious season in the low country. Bondpeople cut rice using "rice hooks" (sickles), then tied the cut rice into sheaves and transported them to the threshing yards, where they separated the heads from the stalks by furiously beating them with flailing sticks. The grain was then separated from the chaff by winnowing, and the rice was "pounded" with long wooden pestles in mortars made of hollowed-out logs. Threshing and pounding were most often done by hand, but by the mid-nineteenth century, many planters had at least some of their rice processed at water- or steam-powered mills. By the end of November the harvest was over, and field hands began to prepare the land for another cycle of rice planting.

The complicated irrigation systems and machinery on the rice plantations required several trunkminders, boatmen, mill workers, and watchmen from the

Work Songs

To break the monotony of arduous field labor, bondpeople often resorted to music to both enliven their workday and to give them the strength to endure the general conditions of enslavement. Here is an example of a slave work song.

Hoe Emma Hoe

Caller: Hoe Emma Hoe, you turn around dig a hole in the ground, Hoe Emma Hoe.
Chorus: Hoe Emma Hoe, you turn around dig a hole in the ground, Hoe Emma Hoe.
Caller: Emma, you from the country.
Chorus: Hoe Emma Hoe, you turn around dig a hole in the ground, Hoe Emma Hoe.
Caller: Emma help me to pull these weeds.
Chorus: Hoe Emma Hoe, you turn around dig a hole in the ground, Hoe Emma Hoe.
Caller: Emma work harder than two grown men.
Chorus: Hoe Emma Hoe, you turn around dig a hole in the ground, Hoe Emma Hoe.
(Repeat)

Source: Colonial Williamsburg, Teacher Resources–Slave Work Songs, http://www
.history.org/history/teaching/enewsletter/february03/worksongs.cfm.

male ranks—but women worked almost exclusively in the fields performing the most fundamental tasks, often separate from men. While the men felled trees during winter, the women burned the trash from the previous year's crop, dragging the fire along with their hoes. When spring came, the women chopped the clods and dug the trenches; only the men plowed. Sowing rice by hand was considered women's work. And during the harvest season, women performed the exhausting tasks of threshing, winnowing, and pounding, but not rice cutting, which was done by men. However women and men did much of the same work including the "mudwork" as well as the endless hoeing. Only female slaves in advanced stages of pregnancy were regularly spared the most unhealthy aspects of rice cultivation. Due to high mortality rates in the region, slaveholders generally tried to keep pregnant women out of the swamplands as much as possible. Expectant mothers were therefore usually put to light work in the up-country provision grounds until shortly before childbirth; afterwards, they were afforded a "lying-in" period of about one month before being eased back into rice cultivation.

Low-country bondpeople worked according to the "task system," whereby each individual was assigned a certain task every morning that he or she had to complete by sundown the latest. For most field operations, a full task was one square acre, measured off by irrigation ditches. A typical daily task might consist of hoeing an acre of rice, for example. According to age and ability, bondpeople were usually assigned portions of a full task—adolescent, elderly, and pregnant bondpeople were often "half-task" or "three-quarter-task" hands, whereas able-bodied laborers were "full-task" hands. Gender was not necessarily a factor in task rating and adult women were usually assigned full tasks, the same as the men. Nonetheless, work gangs were often segregated by gender, so that in any given field a gang of women would be working at their tasks while the men would be working in another field somewhere else. The task system carried with it a number of advantages for bondpeople. Most importantly, it allowed field hands a unique degree of flexibility in determining their own work tempo, and by working quickly many were able to finish by the middle of the afternoon, after which some were afforded control of their "free" time. Family members often worked collectively to help each other finish their tasks early, and it was not uncommon for men to come to the assistance of their wives and daughters after they had completed their own tasks. This allowed low-country women more time to devote to childcare and domestic duties than women in other regions.

In the nineteenth century, the cultivation of cotton dominated most of the Lower South, creating a "Cotton Kingdom," which eventually extended from upland South Carolina all the way to Texas. While not necessarily a difficult crop to cultivate, cotton demanded unceasing labor and strict discipline for most of the year.

African Americans pick cotton in Georgia, ca. 1907. After emancipation, many former slaves continued the same type of back-breaking agricultural work. (Library of Congress.)

As in other parts of the South, the winter months in the cotton districts were devoted to clearing land and preparing the fields for planting. The stalks from the previous year's crop were cut, the ground was broken, and long furrows were opened with plows. Between March and early May, the ridges were split open with a small plow and the seeds were sown into the furrows by hand, then covered with earth by a hoe. Once the cotton plants sprouted, the endless process of thinning and weeding began, which kept bondpeople busy until July. This was accomplished with a hoe but often followed by a plow, which served to raise the ridges and keep the spaces between the rows free from weeds. When the hoeing ended in late July or early August, field hands were diverted to the plantation's provision grounds where they cultivated corn and peas. By late August, the first rows of cotton were ready for picking, a tedious and often physically painful task because the sharp edges of the cotton bolls frequently cut bondpeoples' hands. By the 1850s, daily quotas for cotton picking were as high as 200 pounds per day for able-bodied adults. Once picked, the cotton was dried and passed through the cotton gin to remove the seeds. After that, it was baled and covered with a tarpaulin before being transported to market. The cotton harvest lasted until early December in some regions.

As in other parts of the South, enslaved women in the cotton districts performed many of the same arduous tasks as men. Working in sex-segregated gangs from sunup to sundown under the close supervision of overseers and drivers, women sowed the cottonseeds by hand and repeatedly thinned and weeded the plants with their hoes. During the harvest season they furiously picked hundreds of pounds of cotton a day. Even women in their last week of pregnancy were expected to pick an average of three-quarters or more of the amount that was normal for other women. Indeed, in most tasks pregnant women were forced to work just as hard as the others until childbirth. Two weeks later, new mothers were back in the fields, although their productivity was usually lower than that of other bondpeople during the first two months of their return. Enslaved women on cotton plantations were sometimes assigned different tasks than the men, however. As elsewhere men felled trees and plowed, for example, although on small plantations even women were put to the plow. And in the winter many women were forced to "card, spin, and reel" the cotton they had picked during the harvest—a task which was considered women's work.

Sugarcane represented the other major staple of the nineteenth-century Lower South. Largely limited by climactic conditions to the southernmost parishes of Louisiana, sugarcane was the most exhausting of all American crops to produce. Its annual cycle began in early January, when the land was prepared by chopping it up and opening wide furrows with plows to receive the "seed cane"—literally stalks of cane that had been selected and treated the previous autumn. February was the month for planting, when the seed cane was placed lengthwise in the furrows and covered. When the seed was in the ground, a couple of weeks were devoted to other plantation tasks such as cleaning out drainage ditches, burning trash from the previous year's crop, repairing levees, clearing land, and chopping wood for fuel. When the first sprouts appeared, bondpeople began the repetitive cycle of hoeing and plowing, which kept them busy until the summer. In July, the hoes were laid by and the cane was left to mature. When they were not cultivating cane, bondpeople were cultivating corn or procuring wood for the laborious "grinding season," which commenced in October. The cane not only had to be harvested, but sugar and molasses had to be produced as well, and sugar plantations were as much factories as farms. In order to prevent rapid spoilage, the cane stalks had to be cut quickly and immediately rushed to the sugarhouse, where they were processed in industrial fashion by complicated machinery (which included boilers, conveyer belts, and steam engines). The grinding went on twenty-four hours a day, seven days a week, and lasted until Christmas, after which the cycle repeated itself.

Work on a sugar plantation was hard, and for most agricultural operations bondwomen toiled at an exhausting pace from sunup to sundown in sex-segregated gangs. They were often called upon to perform paid overwork on Sundays as well. Favoring labor over leave, sugar planters required pregnant women to work until shortly before childbirth, a practice that contributed to the appallingly high mortality rates and low birthrates in the region. After childbirth, women were usually allowed a month-long confinement period, after which they were eased back into cane cultivation. Men and women performed many of the same tasks on sugar plantations, including the endless hoeing, planting, ditching, and repairing levees—although even when performing the same tasks, they did so in separate gangs. As in other parts of the South, however, certain tasks were allocated exclusively to men. Only men plowed and only men felled trees, although women and children did engage in gathering driftwood for fuel. At harvest time, the men cut cane while the women and children gathered the stalks and transported them to the sugar-house. In the sugar-house (where bondpeople were required to work eighteen hours a day, seven days a week during the grinding season), virtually all of the skilled and managerial occupations—from sugar boiling to tending the machines—were assigned to men. Women worked in assembly line fashion, carting the stalks and loading the conveyer belts.

Performing much of the drudgery, women formed the backbone of agricultural labor during slavery. Their work differed across time and space, but in virtually all regions enslaved women were frequently relegated to the most menial and repetitive tasks in plantation agriculture—tasks most often accomplished with hoes or by hand.

Damian Alan Pargas

See also Childbirth; Childcare; Elderly Women; Gender Conventions; Labor, Non-agricultural; Mobility; Mortality and Life Expectancy; Pregnancy; South, The.

Suggested Reading

Ira Berlin, *Generations of Captivity: A History of African-American Slaves* (Cambridge: Harvard University Press, 2003); Daina Ramey Berry, *"Swing the Sickle for the Harvest Is Ripe": Gender and Slavery in Antebellum Georgia* (University of Illinois Press, 2007); Richard Follett, *The Sugar Masters: Planters and Slaves in Louisiana's Cane World, 1820–1860* (Baton Rouge: LSU Press, 2005); Lewis Cecil Gray, *History of Agriculture in the Southern United States to 1860*, 2 vols. (Washington: Carnegie Institution, 1933); Philip D. Morgan, *Slave Counterpoint: Black Culture in the Eighteenth-Century Chesapeake & Lowcountry* (Chapel Hill: University of North Carolina Press, 1998); Leslie A. Schwalm, *A Hard Fight for We: Women's Transition from Slavery to Freedom in South Carolina* (Urbana: University of Illinois Press, 1997); Brenda E. Stevenson, *Life in Black & White: Family and Community in the Slave South* (New York: Oxford University Press, 1996).

Labor, Nonagricultural

While the main employment of the vast majority of enslaved women was agricultural, 10 percent to 20 percent of bondwomen were primarily engaged in nonagricultural work. In both rural and urban settings, nearly all of this nonagricultural labor was concentrated in traditional female occupations: domestic work, cooking, childcare, nursing, midwifery, sewing, spinning and weaving, and laundering. Yet even among female agricultural workers, a substantial portion of their time away from the fields was often devoted to accomplishing these same activities for the benefit of their families and/or the wider slave community on the plantation. In urban areas, a small number of bondwomen were also engaged as vendors in local markets.

The extant evidence—namely hiring contracts, advertisements of bondpeople for sale or fugitive ads, and life insurance policies—indicates that few women worked in traditionally male crafts or in the emerging industries of northern and southern cities. The reasons for this gender stratification among nonagricultural occupations, particularly when similar gender divisions were virtually nonexistent for agricultural laborers, were twofold. First, the work of skilled artisans such as carpenters, smiths, and masons—for whom finding labor substitutes would be difficult—would be substantially disrupted by the exigencies of childbearing. In contrast, pregnant and lactating women could often continue working in the fields, although they might also be brought inside to form a temporary part of the nonagricultural workforce. For house servants, childbearing served as no more than a minor disruption to their normal work schedules. Second, the spinning, weaving, and sewing requirements of most plantations were extensive. Throughout the year, but especially during the winter months, enslaved women were needed to provide clothing and household linens for both the enslaved population and the white slaveholders. Thus, bondwomen could not be spared for other types of skilled occupations.

Nonagricultural Labor on Plantations: General Domestic Work

The most common type of nonagricultural labor in rural areas was general domestic work. Regardless of the size of the farm or plantation, the mistress was expected to manage the entire household. On small farms, the first bondperson hired or purchased was often a house servant who would work side-by-side the mistress in performing the innumerable tasks involved in running a household. The number of bondwomen employed, as well as the degree of specialization involved in their domestic duties, increased with the size of the plantation. On the largest plantations, mistresses were able to delegate most, if not all, of their household responsibilities entirely to bondpeople.

With the exception of cooks and nurses on the largest plantations, most domestic servants were expected to be adept at a wide variety of household tasks. Among the range of activities which fell under this heading were manufacturing candles, soap, dyes, and lye; dusting furniture, sweeping floors, and beating carpets; washing and ironing clothes; and waiting on tables. They also aided their mistresses in the preservation of fruits, vegetables, and meats for year-round consumption. Young enslaved girls were often expected to sleep on the floor of their mistress's room, and to rise early to start the morning fire.

In seeking out reliable, trustworthy, competent bondpeople to perform domestic tasks, the majority of mistresses believed that it was most effective to train young girls between the ages of six and twelve. While in some instances the mistress would train these girls herself, in most cases domestic knowledge was transmitted from one generation of bondwomen to the next. Commonly, the daughters of house servants would shadow their mothers from an early age, picking up skills and assisting in progressively more difficult tasks as they grew.

Nonagricultural Labor on Plantations: Skilled Occupations

One of the most specialized occupations for a bondwoman was as the household cook. On most plantations, the cook was entrusted with planning and preparing three meals a day for the family. Talented in the use of local herbs and spices, and employing recipes that had been passed down within the slave community for generations, the cook was granted a great deal of autonomy by her mistress—who was often much less knowledgeable in this area. Having acquired her skills after years of training at the side of an elder cook (who was often her own mother), these enslaved women were highly prized and achieved a rare level of prestige within the household. In addition to her autonomy, another advantage of this position was the easy access to food; unlike most bondpeople, cooks rarely lacked calories or variety in their diet. They likewise used their position to supplement the diets of their families and friends.

Another occupation central to the plantation household was caring for the children of the slaveholder. Mistresses commonly entrusted bondwomen with the day-to-day tasks involved with childrearing. As with most other domestic occupations, enslaved women often began caring for the slaveholder's children when they were quite young themselves, and learned their trade on the job. Yet, they often brought to the household their firsthand experience of childrearing in the slave quarters as well as knowledge passed down to them from older enslaved women. If a young bondwoman proved herself to be an able nurse, she might continue in that position over the long term, caring for each additional child as it was born, and eventually even caring for the slaveholder's grandchildren as well. During her childbearing years, the nurse might even breastfeed the slaveholder's children in lieu of her own offspring.

Enslaved women were also critical to textile production on the plantation. Although slaveholders imported large amounts of luxury cloth for their household consumption, a substantial portion of their textile needs (including the production of household linens) was still met through the use of homespun cloth. Additionally, an even larger percentage of slave clothing was produced entirely on the plantation. Although small plantations could only devote a room or shed to cloth production, the larger plantations would often construct an entire building devoted to spinning and weaving.

This high demand for cloth required the constant attention of enslaved women. Some bondwomen only participated in spinning, weaving, and sewing when their labor was not required in the fields, while others—particularly on the larger plantations—eventually specialized in cloth production. A talented seamstress (or mantua maker, as she was often called) might become as highly prized and respected as a cook or nurse. She was often placed in charge of directing the sewing of other bondwomen. The slaveholder might even hire out her skills to neighboring plantations, or she might be permitted to hire herself out and retain a portion of her earnings.

Nonagricultural Labor in the Slave Quarters

Enslaved women were also required to meet the domestic needs of the slave quarters. During the day, when bondpeople worked in the fields, childcare was a pressing need. Soon after giving birth, a new mother was expected to return to her position in the fields, leaving her newborn infant behind in the care of elderly bondwomen. These community elders were charged with caring for all enslaved infants and young children while their mothers toiled. When young enslaved girls grew to the age of six or seven, but before they were old enough to join their parents in the fields, they would often be expected to assist their elders in caring for the smallest enslaved children. On larger plantations, one bondwoman would likewise be assigned the sole task of preparing daytime meals for the entire community.

When a bondwoman returned from the fields each evening, her own labor now shifted to domestic tasks. In addition to resuming the care of her children, which might often need to be done as a single parent, her time would be devoted to cooking the family meal. Although slaveholders preferred the creation of communal kitchens in the slave quarters, most bondpeople resisted sharing meals (particularly the evening meal). They desired to prepare their meals individually, for consumption within the family cabins. Rations such as corn would often need to be ground by hand before they would be ready for use. Lacking kitchens, enslaved women cooked these meals over open fires. Yet like the cooks of the household, they often brought great skill and knowledge—passed down through the generations—to these meals. Employing family recipes, they supplemented their simple rations with local herbs and ingredients from their family gardens.

After preparing and consuming this meal, a bondwoman's evening would likely be consumed with making, mending, and laundering clothes. Slaveholders purchased few ready-made clothes for their bondpeople, most of which went to single enslaved men. Enslaved women, on the contrary, were annually allotted a certain amount of cloth, a needle, and some buttons, which they were then required to turn into clothing for their families. This combination of childcare, meal preparation, sewing, and laundering left bondwomen with precious little time to rest before returning to the fields in the morning.

Within the slave community, midwives and female folk doctors were the most highly respected among bondwomen. Like household cooks, they often learned the essentials of the trade—particularly healing techniques and the secret recipes for medicinal blends—from their own mothers or another female relative. Bondpeople depended on these women both to safely deliver babies and to provide herbal treatments for a variety of ailments. Since these skills were not always present on all plantations, a talented midwife might travel to several different plantations delivering babies. Not only did this allow her a greater degree of autonomy and mobility than most other bondwomen, but it also placed her at the center of the slave communication network as she transmitted news and messages from one slave community to the next.

Nonagricultural Labor in the Cities

By the early nineteenth century, the vast majority of bondpeople in the burgeoning cities of the South were female. And the majority of the labor of these urban bondwomen was likewise devoted to domestic tasks. The needs of the urban household did not differ much from those of the plantation household. Enslaved women lived in the slaveholder's house and were responsible for preparing all meals, cleaning the house, sewing and laundering clothes, taking care of children, tending to the needs of visitors, running errands, and performing any and all other tasks requested by the master or mistress. Even more so than in the rural areas, slaveholders increasingly viewed all domestic labor as demeaning for the mistress, requiring even the smallest tasks to be completed by their bondwomen. For urban whites who could not afford to purchase or hire a domestic bondperson for their complete household needs, they at least attempted to hire washerwomen or seamstresses as necessary to supplement their own labor.

The one occupation for enslaved women that was unique to urban areas was as market traders. Many slaveholders entrusted their bondwomen with the task of buying or selling goods on their behalf at the local markets. Some of these women seized the opportunity to sell other items as well, with or without their owner's approval. Their knowledge of how the market functioned enabled them to serve as middlemen between rural bondpeople seeking to sell surplus products, and the urban buyers of these products. Although urban whites often complained about the prominence of enslaved women working as vendors, these bondwomen played an increasingly important role in many urban markets of the South.

Sharon Ann Murphy

See also Childbirth; Childcare; Community; Economy; Family; Female Slave Network; Folk Medicine and Healing; Food Preparation and Cooking; Gardening; Gender Conventions; Girlhood; Hiring Out; Labor, Agricultural; Labor, Skilled; Midwives; Mobility; Owners; Plantation Mistresses; Pregnancy; Seamstress Work; Slave Quarters, Life in; Urban Slavery; Wet Nursing.

Suggested Reading

Elizabeth Fox-Genovese, *Within the Plantation Household: Black and White Women of the Old South* (Chapel Hill: UNC Press, 1988); David Barry Gaspar and Darlene Clark Hine (eds.), *More than Chattel: Black Women and Slavery in the Americas* (Bloomington and Indianapolis: Indiana University Press, 1996); Ellen Hartigan-O'Connor, " 'She Said She Did Not Know Money': Urban Women and Atlantic Markets in the Revolutionary Era," in *Early American Studies* (Fall 2006); Richard C. Wade, *Slavery in the Cities: The South 1820–1860* (New York: Oxford University Press, 1964); Deborah Gray White, *Ar'n't I a Woman?: Female Slaves in the Plantation South* (New York: W.W. Norton & Co., 1985); Betty Wood, *Women's Work, Men's Work: The Informal Slave Economies of Lowcountry Georgia* (Athens, GA: The University of Georgia Press, 1995).

Labor, Skilled

Many people have the perception that bondpeople were predominantly unskilled manual laborers. Although this may have been true for some newly imported bondpeople, it was not the case for those already residing for several years or born in the United States. Similarly, those bondpeople born into slavery elsewhere, "seasoned," and imported to mainland North America also came with significant labor skills. Historian Gwendolyn Midlo Hall lists eleven major skill categories and over 100 skill subcategories that pertain to the enslaved labor forces. Her data set encompasses the time period from 1725 to 1820. By the latter date, the majority of enslaved people living in the United States were indeed native born.

My mother nursed Mrs. Hall from a baby consequently the Hall family was very fond of her and often made the statement that they would not part with her for anything in the world[.] [B]esides working as the cook for the Ball family, my mother was also a fine seamstress and made clothing for the master's family and our family.

—Hannah Austin, former bondwoman (*Born in Slavery: Slave Narratives from the Federal Writers' Project, 1936–1938 Georgia Narratives, Volume IV, Part 1*, 20)

Skills common among bondwomen, in particular, were concentrated in the areas of domestic service and health care, with very few classified as "skilled artisans." Within the first category, subcategories included wet nurse, domestic, cook, laundry, personal servant, and child-care. These skills could be acquired rather easily by women who demonstrated an ability to fit into the household routines, especially those who were between the ages of 15 and 25, which were the prime childbearing years. A pregnant woman would find work in the fields difficult for at least part of her pregnancy. Thus, if she were able to perform domestic services, the loss of labor from a pregnant woman would be reduced and the availability of a wet nurse would be insured.

The extent to which slaveholders employed women in low skilled activities such as field hands depended on the area of the South in which she was located and the period of time during which she lived. During the late seventeenth and early eighteenth centuries, bondwomen would have been employed in planting tobacco and rice in the coastal states along the Atlantic seaboard. They would also have been employed in tending to these crops during the growing period. However, enslaved men would have been more likely to harvest rice and tobacco. As cotton growing expanded in the eastern area and spread westward, women would have been used in planting and "chopping" cotton, which was the hoeing and weeding of the cotton fields. Preparation of the land for planting for all of these crops would have been work relegated primarily to enslaved men. In the sugar growing areas of Louisiana, bondwomen would have had a more limited role for fieldwork and would have been valued more highly for their domestic skills and health care skills.

The gang system, which was employed primarily on cotton and rice plantations, relegated women to the role of seed planter or the one who tamped the dirt down after the seed or seedling was planted. A bondman would have been the one to go first and prepare the ground and a hole for planting, as this required much greater physical strength. In the gang system, each bondperson was relegated to the task in which he or she was relatively the most efficient. Doing so increased productivity and made the gang system on plantations successful. The gang system required little if any skilled labor from bondmen or women. However, at planting time many skilled bondpeople would be allocated to the planting process, as it needed to be completed within a particular time frame. The same was true of harvesting, as all bondpeople were able to pick cotton.

In skill areas other than domestic service, bondwomen were valued at relatively lower prices, as men were more easily transferred to fieldwork and were more productive when needed in the fields. That is, the secondary use of enslaved women with skills other than domestic service did not generate output with enough value to compensate for the gender productivity differentials that existed in these nondomestic categories. It was only in the area of domestic service skills that bondwomen were more highly valued than men.

In the crafts area of skills, women could easily be employed as cigar makers, seamstresses, bakers, confectioners, or spinners, but these would be the likely limits to artisan type work for bondwomen. In health care, women would likely possess the skills of a curer or healer, midwife, nurse, hospital worker, or bleeder (during the period of slavery bleeding someone was considered a means of removing the "bad blood" from an ill person).

All this is not to say that bondwomen never possessed skills outside these categories, but that the skill categories discussed above were the primary areas in which slaveholders employed them. Interestingly, these skills were similar to those possessed by free women who found themselves employed in nearly the same categories. The major exception would be the employment of free women in the field of education. Most slaveholders did not encourage bondpeople to become educated, let alone become educators, as this would have enhanced the chances of a slave successfully escaping.

William Hutchinson

See also Education; Folk Medicine and Healing; Free Women; Labor, Agricultural; Labor, Nonagricultural; Midwives; Pregnancy; Seamstress Work; Wet Nursing.

Suggested Reading

Robert W. Fogel, *Without Consent or Contract: The Rise and Fall of American Slavery*, vol. I (New York: W.W. Norton, 1989).

Laney, Lucy Craft

Birth Date: 1854
Death Date: 1933

The nationally renowned educator and civil rights activist, Lucy Craft Laney, was born into an extraordinary enslaved family in Macon, Georgia, in 1854. She was the sixth child in the family, which would eventually consist of 10 biological children, several cousins, and at least one orphan who was found wandering in the streets of Macon after the Civil War. Her father, Rev. David Laney, and her mother, Louisa Tracy Laney, nurtured Laney's large enslaved family in their private home. When Lucy Laney was born, David Laney was serving as an exhorter for the enslaved individuals who were owned by members of the white First Presbyterian Church. Laney, who was "held in high regard by his mistress," was allowed to choose his own profession and eventually became a master carpenter who, by 1836, was hiring out his own time in Macon, Georgia, and teaching other enslaved people carpentry. Laney's mother, Louisa, had been purchased by the wealthy Campbell-Tracy family from a band of Creek Indians. Her children swore that she was so young at the time that she did not know where she was born, who her parents were, or how old she was.

Lucy Craft Laney. (Daniel, Sadie Iola, *Women Builders*, Associated Publishers, Washington, D.C., 1931.)

Shortly after their marriage, Rev. David Laney and Louisa had their first child, David, who was born in 1842. Twelve years later, Lucy Laney was born. She grew up in this close, religious extended family and had the good fortune having a mother who encouraged her exceptional gift for learning. Surprisingly, Laney's mother could neither read nor write and her father could only read, but not write. Laney's own sister, Flora Campbell, also contributed to her education as, she had been the recipient of an excellent classical education herself. By the time she was four, Laney could read and could translate "difficult passages" of Latin by the time she was twelve, all of which was illegal in the state of Georgia.

After the Civil War, Laney attended the American Missionary Association's Lewis School in Macon, and was part of the first class to enter Atlanta University in 1869. Having graduated from the Normal Department in 1873, Laney began teaching in the emerging public schools of Augusta, Georgia. In 1880, she left Augusta and taught for three years in the Savannah Public Schools before

Haines Normal and Industrial Institute, Augusta, GA. (Daniel, Sadie Iola, *Women Builders*, Associated Publishers, Washington, D.C., 1931.)

returning to Augusta to open her own private school in the basement of Christ Presbyterian Church. She created an institution where she could teach the whole student—the head, the heart, and the hand—and where she would be in charge. This became an institution from which she would send young men to the best colleges in the North, and young men and women out to teach all over the South. In 1886, the state of Georgia licensed Laney's school, and she felt confident enough to travel to the General Assembly of the Northern Presbyterian Church (her father's affiliation after the Civil War) in Minneapolis to appeal for support of her school. There, she did not receive financial support but made many friends, including Mrs. Francine E.A. Haines, chairperson of the church's Women's Board of Missions to the Free People and for whom the school would later be named. Haines drew attention to the work that Laney was doing in desperate circumstances.

The first class graduated from the Haines Institute in 1888, and by 1889, Laney had received a large bequest from the Marshall estate via the Northern Presbyterian Church and constructed an impressive brick building, Marshall Hall. During the 1890s, Laney became nationally known as an educator and leader of "her people." She served as the Honorary Chairperson of the newly organized National

Association of Colored Women's Southeastern Division and delivered lectures at Dr. W.E.B. DuBois's Conferences at Atlanta University, which were widely published by the university. She also delivered a paper entitled "The Burden of the Educated Colored Woman" at the 1899 Hampton Conference. She also established Augusta's first kindergarten, a hospital for black citizens, and a nurse's training program that later evolved into the Lamar School of Nursing. By 1900, Laney's school enrolled a number of students and employed some 30 teachers. So distinguished was the faculty of Haines that Dr. W.E.B. DuBois chose to photograph Laney's teachers for the Negro Exhibit at the World's Fair in Paris in 1900.

As early as 1886–1887, Laney began publishing reports and articles in the nationally circulated *Home Missions Monthly* of the Woman's Executive Committee of the Northern Presbyterian Church and the *Church at Home and Abroad*. She penned articles on the Presbyterian Church's special mission to educate the freed people, the importance of "pure" homes and moral mothers, the progress of the "Negro" in America, and the evils of the convict lease system. She also travelled extensively, raising money for the Northern Presbyterian Church's schools for her people, "speaking to our different ladies' societies on behalf of our work among the colored people of the South, a mission for which she has a rare gift, apparently without knowing it" (Cowan 1893, 140).

Discipline in Laney's school was strict and the curriculum in the classics demanding. Laney taught the fifth year of Latin herself and sent her male students to the best colleges in the North with a sense that they were prepared to compete and succeed, knowing that they were the masters of the secret language of the educated. Recognizing the value of organizing, Laney founded the Augusta Women's Federate Clubs as part of the National Federation of Colored Women's Clubs in 1912 and the Augusta Chapter of the N.A.A.C.P. in 1917. In 1916, she attended the national Amenia Conference in Amenia, New York, as one of the few women present. She worked for temperance and suffrage and urged black Augusta women to register to vote when it became legal. Laney served on the Commission on Interracial Cooperation and in the 1920s joined other prominent black women, including Margaret Washington (wife of Booker T. Washington), Mary McLeod Bethune (who taught at Haines at the beginning of her distinguished career), Mary Jackson McCrorey (who was Miss Lucy's assistant principal from 1896 until her marriage in 1916), Janie Porter Barrett (who also taught at Haines), S.W. Crosthwait, and Lugenia Burns Hope (Laney taught John Hope when he was in grammar school in Augusta) to integrate the YWCA.

Realizing that racism was an international problem, Laney was a founding mother of the International Council of Women of the Darker Races, which was spearheaded by Mary Church Terrell and Madame C. J. Walker. Laney died on October 23, 1933, having "burned out not rusted out" just as she had wished. Thousands attended her funeral and her life was eulogized by nationally recognized race men and women, and the white citizens of Augusta. Her real legacy was the knowledge, dignity, and self respect which she imparted to her students, while acting as the "Mother of the Children of the People" to the end of her long and productive life. Thanks to then Governor Jimmy Carter, Laney's portrait hangs in the Georgia State Capitol rotunda, between Dr. Martin Luther King and Rev. Henry McNeal Turner.

Kent Anderson Leslie

See also Civil War; Education; Emancipation; Laws; Literacy.

Suggested Reading

E. P. Cowan, "Haines Normal and Industrial School," in *The Church at Home and Abroad*, Vol. 13–14 (Philadelphia: Presbyterian Church in the U.S.A. Board of Publication and Sabbath-School Work, 1893), 138–140; Asa C. Griggs, "Notes: Lucy Craft Laney," *Journal of Negro History* 19 (January 1934): 97–102; June O. Patton, "Lucy Craft Laney," *Facts on File Encyclopedia of Black women in America*, vol. 1 (New York: Facts on File, 1997); Jennifer Lund Smith, "Lucy Craft Laney and Martha Berry: Lighting Fires of Knowledge" in *Georgia Women: Their Lives and Times*, vol. 1., ed. Ann Short Chirhart and Betty Wood (Athens: University of Georgia Press, 2009).

Laws

Laws are the formal body of legal rules and regulations that governed enslaved women in America. Laws sanctioned and legitimated slavery, categorized enslaved women as property, established civil and criminal punishments, and regulated their religious, commercial, sexual, and reproductive lives. Initially, European laws governed the lives of enslaved women in the English, Dutch, French, and Spanish colonies in America. Later, domestic laws in the colonies and states governed the lives of enslaved women.

Transnational Laws

European colonial powers established transnational legal structures governing the lives of enslaved women. They included the *Geoctroyeerde Westindische Compagnie* (*GWC*, Dutch West India Company), the Spanish *Consejo de Indias* (Council of the Indies), and the French *Code Noir* (Black Code). Slave laws varied in scope. The *Code* was more comprehensive than the Dutch or English laws and included provisions for civil, commercial, and criminal activities. Laws in English colonies focused primarily on police measures and largely ignored commercial activities. Laws in Dutch colonies restricted employment and commercial activities, but granted other civil rights to enslaved women.

The Spanish *Consejo de Indias*, founded in 1524, was the supreme governing body for Spain's American colonies. The *Consejo* regulated judicial, financial, religious, commercial, military, and administrative issues. The Spanish *Siete Partidas* (Seven Parts), which was the Spanish civil code established in the thirteenth century, the 1526 *cédula* (royal proclamation), and the law of the Catholic Church were the governing laws in Spanish Florida (1565–1763 and 1784–1821). Enslaved women had the right to testify in court, protection from the most brutal abuse, remain with their families, and purchase their freedom. Slave status was not hereditary under this code. Enslaved women could generally raise their children until they reached 12 years of age. In the Spanish colony of Louisiana (1762–1802), the Spanish government inherited and substantially retained the French slave laws. Slave owners continued to privately enforce laws over enslaved women without significant government oversight.

The *Geoctroyeerde Westindische Compagnie*, a trading and colonizing company, governed Dutch colonies in the Americas (1621–1644) and regulated the lives of enslaved women in what are now Connecticut, Delaware, New Jersey, New York, and Pennsylvania. Slaves owned by *GWC* received additional rights that slaves owned by private owners did not receive. Slaves owned by *GWC* had some religious, family, labor, and legal rights. Enslaved women could sign legal documents, testify in court, and bring civil actions against whites. They could join, be baptized in, and married in the Dutch Reformed Church. Some slaves were allowed to earn wages when working after hours. Initially, most of the slaves in the Dutch colonies were owned by the *GWC*. Throughout this period, the *GWC* remained the largest slave owner in the Dutch colonies.

The 1685 French *Code Noir* was an official proclamation by King Louis XIV. The *Code* governed issues regarding enslaved women in French colonies in the Americas, including the territories that became Louisiana and Florida. Like later slave laws, the *Code* declared slaves to be property. It incorporated some religious and humanitarian values. The *Code* required that all slaves in French territories in the Americas be baptized as Roman Catholics and forbade slaves from working on Sundays. It also required the consent of slaves and their owners for slave marriages and instructed families with young children to be sold together. Slave status of children was attached to the enslaved status of their mothers at the time of their birth. The *Code* mandated that slave owners provide and pay for food and care for sick and elderly slaves.

The *Code* limited the freedom of movement of enslaved women, their ability to engage in commercial activities, and did not grant slaves rights to be a party to legal proceedings. It set forth civil and criminal punishments for slaves, including confiscation of goods, imprisonment, beating, whipping, branding, hamstringing, and death. The *Code* allowed the chaining and beating of enslaved women at their owner's whim, but prohibited maiming and torture.

Similarly, public officials often did not enforce and slave owners often did not respect enslaved women's legal rights. Enslaved women could not seek to enforce their rights themselves because they were deemed property and had no standing in legal proceedings. For example, the *Compangnie des Indes* (Company of the Indies) that governed the French slaves of Louisiana (1719–1731) did not enforce many rights granted to slaves in the *Code*. As a result, female slaves were forced to work on Sundays, were denied proper food, shelter, and clothing, and were raped. Pregnant women were beaten until they miscarried. In 1862, an Anglo American Bilateral Treaty established courts that had the power to hear cases addressing the status of slaves in the British colonies in the Americas. However, no cases were ever actually heard by the courts established under the Lyons-Seward Treaty (1862).

Slave Laws in English Colonies

Before the American Revolution (1775–1783), England held 13 colonies: Connecticut, Delaware, Georgia, Maryland, Massachusetts, New Hampshire, New Jersey, New York, North Carolina, Pennsylvania, Rhode Island, South Carolina, and Virginia. Early slave laws granted some rights that were withdrawn over time as economic concerns were given higher priority. Initially, slavery was not a lifelong status and Christian baptism was a legal path to freedom. Later laws repealed the right to achieve freedom through baptism, declared lifelong servitude for all black slaves, and linked slave status to race. Some colonies enacted laws that transferred slave status to children and wives based on the enslaved status of their mothers and husbands, respectively. This was a significant change from traditional common law, which assumed that the status of the child followed that of the father.

Massachusetts was one of the first English colonies to explicitly legalize slavery, including the enslavement of Native American, whites, and black women. Its 1641 Body of Liberties, which was also accepted by Connecticut and New Haven, governed the treatment of enslaved women in these regions for approximately 40 years. Initially, the Body of Liberties granted enslaved women a right to police protection, to legal counsel, and to give testimony in court. It did not address the legal status of children of slaves. Like slave laws in other colonies, many of these rights were later rescinded and the children of slaves could be sold into slavery.

Slave Laws in U.S. Territories

Some territories had harsher slave laws than the European colonies. In Louisiana, a U.S. territory from 1803 to 1811, the territorial legislature enacted a slave law in 1806 that stripped slaves of the rights they had previously been granted under the French *Code*. The 1806 law allowed enslaved women to be married without their consent and sold away from their husbands and children. The right to food and care when they were sick or elderly was also rescinded.

Antebellum State and Federal Laws

In 1783, the newly independent American states maintained the legal status of slavery and inherited long-standing and well-developed slave laws, which continued to govern the status of enslaved women. Slave laws enacted during the colonial period remained in effect unless they were repealed. Enslaved women were still legally property and did not have rights over their own bodies. Slave owners continued to control whether or not enslaved women had children and female slaves were still not guaranteed the right to raise their own children.

Teaching slaves to read or write remained illegal in South Carolina. This law was first enacted in the 1740 South Carolina Negro Act, which eliminated legal protections for slaves in the colony. South Carolina slave laws continued to reinforce the class status of slaves by regulating the types and quality of clothes that slaves were permitted to wear, a law that was first enacted under the Negro Act.

Government representatives, private companies, law enforcement officers, and private citizens retained the power to enforce slave laws. Slave owners and their employees played a key role in the day-to-day enforcement of slave laws and punishment of enslaved women. Enslaved women had no legal recourse and were subject to punishments that escaped the accountability of the public legal system.

Between 1783 and 1865, slave laws became increasingly restrictive. For example, the 1850 Fugitive Slave Act legally mandated the return of escaped slaves as federal law. This codified colonial practices evidenced in the articles of the 1643 New England Convention between Connecticut, New Haven, Massachusetts, and Plymouth, mandating the return of escaped slaves.

Abolishing Slavery

On December 31, 1865, the Thirteenth Amendment to the U.S. Constitution formally abolished slavery in the United States except as a punishment for a crime for which the party has been duly convicted.

Rachel J. Anderson

See also Abolitionism; Domestic Slave trade; Free Women; Literacy; Manumission; Scott, Harriet Robinson.

Suggested Reading

Robert I. Burns, S. J. (ed.), *Las Siete Partidas Vols. I–V* (Philadelphia: University of Pennsylvania Press, 2000); Alan Watson, "The Origins of the Code Noir Revisited," *Tulane Law Review* 71, 34 (1997); William M. Wiecek, "The Statutory Law of Slavery and Race in the Thirteen Mainland Colonies of British America," *The William and Mary Quarterly* 34 (1977); *Slavery in America* Web site: www.slaveryinamerica.org

Life Cycle

Enslaved women, despite their designation as property, experienced distinct phases within their life cycle. Physiological changes as well as unique experiences and responsibilities marked each developmental stage. The nebulous nature concerning age during the colonial and antebellum periods makes it is difficult to identify precise ages for each cycle, but there are generally accepted categories for each period. Childhood inaugurated slave life; beginning at infancy, it concluded around 10 or 12 years of age. Adolescence, which consisted of enslaved girls roughly 12 to 18 years old, marked the second transition. Age 19 to the late forties constituted the adult years. After years of labor, enslaved women, starting around 50 years of age, were ushered into their elderly years.

Childhood

At birth, infants entered the world inheriting their mother's slave status. If enslaved infants survived the first few days after birth, a name was selected. The naming process marked a significant rite for enslaved infants within the slave community. While some infants were named by their slaveholders, many were given names by their parents or other enslaved people. For many parents, naming a child was very important because it continued the connection with their African past, paid homage to relatives, and marked a modicum of authority they maintained over their children. For slaveholders, the naming process was significant for economic rather than sentimental reasons. Although enslaved infants were unable to contribute physically to the plantation economy, whites valued them because of the potential profit they would yield in coming years. Having written their name on slave ledgers and assigned a monetary value based on age, sex, and health, most white slaveholders divorced themselves from the care of black children. Upon receiving a name, enslaved infants remained under the care of their mothers and others within the community. As they grew they were able to frolic around the plantation, yet they were still unable to make a substantive contribution to it. Even as toddlers and children, enslaved girls were still unable to work and contribute to slaveholding profits. Therefore, girls were described as "charges" of the estate and subsequently relegated to the margins of slave society. Despite this marginalization by white slaveholders, childhood was an important phase of bondpeople's lives, marked primarily by recreation and the completion of small tasks around the plantation Big House or the farm.

Girls, particularly on larger estates, were typically confined to an age-segregated, unisex environment where they were under the supervision of older enslaved youth, nurses, or elderly bondpeople. At the slave nurseries, several children often gathered. Most scholars agree that care rendered to these children was poor at best, as elderly bondpeople were often assigned other tasks to complete such as spinning and older enslaved children were easily distracted from their childcare responsibilities by recreation. Hence, it was not uncommon for children to be severely or fatally injured while under the supervision of other enslaved persons. Under this inadequate care, boys and girls received their meals, played an array of games, and performed small jobs. Meals usually consisted of mush, milk mixed with bread flavored with molasses, corn bread with potlicker (the liquid from cooked greens), or possibly greens. Food was typically served in troughs where several children were expected to eat from it on their hands and knees.

Girls, while playing with black and white children, enjoyed a number of recreational activities. Games included line and ring games, jumping rope, and playing with marbles or dolls. Other recreational activities included organized games such as Tag, "You Can Catch Me," and "Hide and Seek." Simply running through the woods, climbing trees, or searching for fruit and flowers also constituted forms of play. These activities indicate that girls, despite being considered property, enjoyed a sense of normalcy if only temporarily. Moreover, the race and gender of enslaved girls' playmates as well as the nature of the games, indicated that during childhood notions concerning masculine and feminine roles as well as race were not as strictly enforced. But with time, and as children grew older, the blurred gender and racial lines became more clearly demarcated.

Aside from playing, enslaved girls completed light work tasks such as fanning flies, toting water, and sweeping the yard. Most enslaved women did not consider these tasks demanding. Like children today, recreation for enslaved girls consisted of imitating adult roles and requesting to assist in adult tasks. So it was not unusual for unknowing enslaved children to joyfully tote water or gather bark for cooking. But with the onset of puberty, enslaved girls were introduced to adult work responsibilities and slowly acclimated to their ensuing lives as adult bondwomen.

Adolescence

Adolescence for enslaved girls was characterized by more stringent racial and gender lines, the onset of menarche, introduction to work, increased attention to personal appearance, courting, and sexual abuse.

Unlike their girlhood experience, adolescents quickly discovered that racial and gender lines were more strictly enforced as they matured. Enslaved girls' young white playmates—entering adolescence as well—began assuming their roles as mistresses, while enslaved teenage girls began the process of learning what it meant to be enslaved. The nature of these roles meant that a clear line of demarcation was established in which race dictated each group's function within slave society. This established racial line separated childhood playmates, placing whites in a superior position and blacks at the bottom of the social order. In addition to losing their white playmates, enslaved girls began to experience physical changes as they increased in height and weight and began developing breasts. These physiological changes began around 13 years of age. Two years later, around 15 years of age, girls' menstrual cycles began. At the same time that these physical changes were occurring, enslaved girls were introduced to their work duties.

Many enslaved girls began their work responsibilities in the slaveholder's home. Acting as body servants, attending the needs of white children, and cleaning were among the female house slaves' endless tasks. Though most youth began work in the plantation home, only a few remained domestic slaves as adult women. The majority of adolescent enslaved females were sent to the fields. Trained by adult field hands, teenage enslaved girls were introduced to the working world by assignment to a trash gang by the slaveholder or overseer. In the fields, the girls' duties included raking, pulling weeds, or completing light hoeing. Once able to cultivate cash crops, young girls were sent to the physically taxing task as fractional hands. Many began as "quarter hands," which required them to produce one-fourth of the output of an experienced adult bondperson. With age and growth, the girls were eventually considered "full hands" and expected to meet the higher adult work quotas. Working within this mixed age and gender environment, adults and teens engaged in an array of learning experiences.

Aside from learning techniques associated with harvesting a specific crop or domestic duties, adolescent girls became acquainted with the rhythms, work ethics, and modes of resistance among bondpeople. Additionally, by working with pregnant women, nursing mothers, and elderly women, adolescent girls learned about the mysterious world of sex, labor, and childbirth that had not been a part of their early childhood experiences.

Despite their introduction to adult work and topics, enslaved girls, like modern teens, were also interested in clothes and boys. On most plantations, enslaved women received two clothing allotments per year. During fall they received a wool dress and in the spring they received a cotton dress. Upon receiving their dresses many girls customized them to fit their personalities. Changes included brightly dying them, or placing grapevines in the skirts to give it an ample, regal look. Once donned in their attire, many set out to catch the eye of a local beau.

Young enslaved females had their own ideologies concerning sex and courting. With the onset of puberty, some girls no longer viewed boys as playmates, but as objects of affection. To gain the attention of a particular boy, enslaved girls wore the ornate dresses when participating in dances and other teenage courtship rituals. Teens also concocted makeup from berries, adorned their hair with kerchiefs and ribbons, and designed jewelry made of nuts. They also perfumed themselves with honeysuckles, roses, and orchard flowers. By grooming themselves, teenage bond-women reflected the need for individuality and the desire to attract mates. Once presentable, enslaved females engaged in the courtship process with their young mates. Black and white adults had conflicting views concerning teen girls court-ing. Many enslaved parents worked diligently to delay courting because they real-ized that courtship could catapult teenage girls to an early awareness of sex. However, white slaveholders, desiring that enslaved girls begin to reproduce more slave labor, wholeheartedly supported slave courtship. Some even went so far as to arrange relationships between teenage boys and girls. Despite the divergent views concerning courtship among adults, it was an important part of the teen experience because introduction to young men made teenage girls aware of their budding sex-uality.

Unfortunately, sexual knowledge did not always come from voluntary sexual relations because the teenage years for enslaved girls generally marked the begin-ning of illicit sexual relations with white men. Most enslaved women noted that sexual abuse began during the teenage years, with the inception of physical devel-opment. This abuse varied from explicit sexual conversations to sadistic acts of rape. Some teenage enslaved girls were able to avoid engaging in sexual relations with their owners and overseers while others were not as fortunate. Despite the ways in which teenage girls acquired sexual knowledge, via voluntary or involun-tary experiences, this newfound knowledge concerning sexual relations oftentimes led to pregnancy and or marriage, rites that catapulted teenage girls into adulthood.

Adulthood

The ages 18 through 49 marked bondpeople's prime years as adults. Physically mature, adult bondwomen were able to maximize slaveholding profits through cul-tivating crops and reproducing enslaved progeny. Though work constituted a sub-stantial part of adult bondwomen's lives, motherhood and marriage were also two significant rites associated with this cycle. The nature of slavery, coupled with conflicting beliefs concerning premarital sex, meant that most enslaved women entered motherhood before marriage. Bondwomen, though valued for their labor, were also prized because of the potential increase their wombs yielded. As such, slaveholders strongly encouraged bondwomen to procreate. Engaging in sex with partners selected through courting experiences or arranged sexual relationships by slaveholders, most women bore their first child between 18 and 21 years of age. Motherhood was considered extremely important as it marked a rite of pas-sage from adolescence to adulthood and the inception of the slave family in which the mother played a central role. Additionally, motherhood brought security, as slaveholders would be less likely to sell fertile women. It also fostered greater intimacy among enslaved women as young mothers relied on older women for support with pregnancy, labor, and childrearing. But with these perceived gains, motherhood also brought increased workloads, as mothers were still expected to meet the labor goals of the slaveholder as well as the needs of their own children.

These responsibilities were further magnified for married bondwomen. Marriage, though arguably not as sacred for enslaved women as motherhood, was a significant part of the adult woman's life. Some women were forced into marriage while others selected mates through courtship. For bondwomen who entered motherhood before marriage, their mate may not have been the father of their children. Potential spouses were selected from the same plantation or neighboring farms. If married bondpeople were fortunate to live on the same plantation, they were in a better position to live as a family. Long-distance partners were forced to cultivate their relationships during weekends or on holidays. Despite the nature of the relationship or the frequency of the contact, enslaved spouses recognized that their marriage could be ended easily, and at the slaveholder's whim. As bondwomen continued to work for slaveowners, rear children, and nurture marriages, they continued to increase in age and decrease in physical aptitude.

Elderly Bondwomen

Enslaved women who were fortunate enough to overcome the physically taxing nature of slave labor and medical maladies of the time eventually entered their elderly years. During this phase of life, which generally started in one's fifties, elderly bondwomen saw a decrease in workloads and a change in the plantation household's perception of her status. Many slaveholders believed that these women's work capacity and monetary value began to decline around 50 years of age; therefore, slaveowners began to modify the roles that senior bondwomen played within the plantation household. Unable to maintain the strenuous pace of the field or slaveholding home, most older women worked on spinning, weaving, sewing, or caring for enslaved children as their parents labored on the plantation. Additionally, elderly women were called on to share their vast knowledge concerning folk medicine, childbirth, childrearing, and marriage.

Historically, elderly people in most societies, despite race, were valued within larger communities. This was often the case for older bondwomen as well. As reflected in white diaries, memoirs, and slave narratives, older bondpeople, despite decreased work output, were sometimes loved and revered by all in the community. Often referred to as "Aunt" or "Mammy," whites often felt a special affinity to older bondwomen because of their perceived loyalty and duty to the family. Members of the slave community, in keeping with African traditions that valued the elderly, respected them for their vast knowledge and wisdom and cared for them until death. Unfortunately, for those who were devalued because of their inability to contribute to the plantation economy found themselves deemed useless and subsequently banished to the margins of the plantation, sent to the country-side, or exiled to cities to conclude their lives in poverty or loneliness.

Bondwomen, though enslaved, engaged in rich experiences through each life phase. Transitioning from childhood, adolescence, adulthood, and through the senior years, these women endured significant rites that informed them of their lives as chattel within the peculiar institution. As they progressed through each rite, they were better able to endure the countless emotional, physical, and psycho-logical hardships associated with being deemed unfree in a free society and often formed strong bonds that contributed to the development of a female slave network.

Courtney Moore Taylor

See also Childcare; Clothing; Community; Courtship; Elderly Women; Family; Female Slave Network; Folk Medicine and Healing; Gender Conventions; Girl-hood; Labor, Agricultural; Labor, Nonagricultural; Labor, Skilled; Mammy Ster-eotype; Marriage, Abroad; Marriage and Cohabitation; Motherhood; Naming; Pregnancy; Sexuality; Violence, Sexual.

Suggested Reading

Stacey Close, *Elderly Slaves of the Plantation South* (New York: Garland Publishing, 1997); Paul Finkelman, ed., *Women and the Family in a Slave Society* (New York: Garland Pub., 1989); Elizabeth Fox-Genovese, *Within the Plantation Household: Black and White Women of the Old South* (Chapel Hill: University of North Carolina Press, 1988); Jacque-line Jones, *Labor of Love, Labor of Sorrow: Black Women, Work and the Family, from Slavery to the Present* (New York: Vintage Books, 1985); Wilma King, *Stolen Childhood: Slave Youth in Nineteenth-Century America* (Indianapolis: Indiana University Press, 1995); Stephen Mintz, *Huck's Raft: A History of American Childhood* (Cambridge: Bel-knap Press, 2004); Jennifer L. Morgan, *Laboring Women: Reproduction and Gender in New World Slavery* (Philadelphia: University of Pennsylvania Press, 2004); Marie Schwartz, *Born in Bondage: Growing Up Enslaved in the Antebellum South* (Cambridge: Harvard University Press, 2000); Deborah White, *Ar'n't I a Woman?: Female Slaves in the Plantation South* (New York: W.W. Norton & Company, 1985).

Literacy

Some bondpeople "stole" their education, others were educated by masters or taught by sympathetic whites, yet however they became literate, it is difficult to ascertain the full extent of enslaved literacy because in most southern states, cus-tom, if not legislation, prohibited the education of the enslaved. The best estimates suggest that in 1865 between 5 and 10 percent of freed people had achieved a degree of signature literacy, which is to say they could read and write. Of these 200,000 to 400,000 individuals, males were in the majority and although it is difficult to be certain why they were more likely to be literate than females, the evidence suggests that gender ideology shaped educational opportunity.

White expectations of gender roles often had a negative impact on educational opportunity for enslaved women. Slaveholders who saw some advantage in enslaved literacy were the source of many a bondmen's education, and such owners focused their efforts upon managers, overseers, and skilled artisans, roles that were generally, though not exclusively, reserved for men. Male slaves may also have had greater access to the educational underground. Slaves, free blacks, and even white Southerners established covert schools of one type or another, yet accessing this illicit network required a degree of mobility more frequently available to male as opposed to female slaves. Campaigns for Bible literacy also favored men over women. Evangelicals emphasized the unique revelation of reading scripture and encouraged masters to teach the enslaved to read, if not write, but gendered preconceptions shaped the outcome of these efforts. Such slaveholders who were persuaded to educate anyone usually preferred to educate an individual bondman as a lay preacher (a conduit of white male authority over scripture), rather than encourage more widespread scriptural literacy among their bondpeople.

Yet gender norms also afforded females sex-specific access to education. Where literacy was "stolen," white children were often unwitting educators because they could be persuaded to share or repeat their lessons without realizing they were violating the color line. The gendering of childcare duties therefore afforded bondwomen educational opportunities, and many such women also encouraged their own offspring to play at schools with white children in order to gain access to their books and learning. Gendered understandings of gentility also shaped educational opportunity in ways that favored enslaved women. Gender ideology constructed elite white women as educators and to fulfill this role, they sometimes chose to educate particular slaves. Female domestics, whose household roles informed white perceptions of them as more genteel and feminine than other bondwomen and whose sex rendered them less threatening to the Victorian parlor ideal than the African American male, might thus receive an education from a plantation mistress or her daughters.

Gender biases also help explain how bondpeople's uses of literacy sometimes differed according to sex. Comparatively few slave-authored letters survive, but as a corpus of evidence these letters suggest that bondwomen corresponded with other bondspeople more often than their male counterparts. Bondwomen were also more likely to receive letters from other slaves, whether male or female. While we must be cautious not to draw hard and fast conclusions from limited data, it is arguable that these differences reflect gendered ideas about sentimentality and sociability that were both imposed upon and appropriated by enslaved African Americans.

In the final analysis, however, although many African American women did acquire access to education during slavery, the gendered assumptions that shaped both slaveholder and enslaved worldviews tended to predicate against bond-women's acquisition of either signature or scriptural literacy. Such evidence not-withstanding, testimony both from oral and written recollections of slavery, and from the surviving slave-authored correspondence, suggests that enslaved African American women were not only eager to learn, but also very active in the educa-tional process. Moreover, the array of letters written by or to bondwomen demon-strate that they were at least as determined as their male counterparts to utilize literacy and letter writing as a means to develop and maintain social networks that fostered strategies for survival and even resistance.

Two Letters Written by Enslaved Women

The racism and sexism of American slavery rendered the bodies of enslaved women as objects defined not only by their ability to labor, but also by their sexual vulnerability and reproductive potential. Letters written by female slaves attest to their efforts to assert themselves in the face of this exploitation. For instance, in May 1853 Virginia Boyd wrote Rice G. Ballard from a Houston trader's yard, challenging the terms of her sale. Virginia had been a house servant on a plantation Ballard owned jointly with Samuel Boyd, father to Virginia's unborn baby and youngest child, but not to her teenage daughter. Though the exact details are unclear, fragmentary evidence suggests that when Boyd's wife discovered that Virginia was pregnant again, she demanded Ballard sell her and her offspring. While custom ensured that mother and infant would not be parted by sale, this did not stop Ballard separating Virginia from her eldest daughter, a market deci-sion that promised the best price. Virginia was desperate to prevent this separation and her letter was her last chance to do so. Her efforts to persuade Ballard to relent ranged from offering to work her "finger ends off" to raise money to buy her chil-dren, to questioning Boyd's honor as a "free-born American" prepared to "sell his own offspring," to demanding her children's freedom as recompense for providing Boyd with sexual "service and gratification." This description of Boyd's dishonor-able conduct also served as backdrop to her appeal to Ballard's honor, for as father to "a family of children" himself, he would surely "simpathize [sic] with others in distress." However, he did not, and in August, Virginia and her daughter were sep-arated when the sales went ahead, just as Ballard had specified.

Where Virginia drew on the discourse of masculine honor to plead her cause, another letter writer named Lavinia entreated her mistress, Phoebe Sarah Lawton, in the gendered language of motherhood. Written July 1849, Lavinia's letter was a plea on behalf of Aggie, her daughter. Aggie's husband Jimmy—described by Lavinia as an "audacious proud villain [who] wants a woman to wash his feet and be called dirty slut"—had left her for "a base woman ... the vilest of the vile ... a devil ... a Jesebel" named Juddy who had already born two children to another woman's husband before dropping him for Jimmy. Worse still, these acts of adultery and abandonment had been permitted, even facilitated, by members of the Lawton family. Lavinia therefore begged her mistress to "take pity on Aggie and use your influence in stopping this wretched business" and proposed that she "[v]iew this matter as you would if they were your children. Have they not souls as well as white people?" While this intervention was probably unsuccessful, it is nevertheless striking that like Virginia Boyd, Lavinia used her literacy to write directly to a white slaveholder, demanding acknowledgement of the common humanity of master and slave, and challenging the idea that female slaves' sexuality was available to be exploited, used, and discarded by either white or black men.

Ben Schiller

See also Education; Laney, Lucy Craft; Wheatley, Phillis.

Suggested Reading

Janet Duitsman Cornelius, *When I Can Read My Title Clear: Literacy, Slavery, and Religion in the Antebellum South* (New York: Columbia, 1991); Ben Schiller, "Learning Their Letters: Critical Literacy, Epistolary Culture and Slavery in the Antebellum South," *Southern Quarterly* 43, 3 (June 2008); Heather Andrea Williams, *Self-Taught: African American Education in Slavery and Freedom* (Chapel Hill: University of North Carolina Press, 2005).

Letter Sources

Virginia Boyd to Rice C. Ballard, May 6, 1853, Rice C. Ballard Papers, Southern Historical Collection, Wilson Library, University of North Carolina; Lavinia to Phoebe Sarah Lawton, July 1849, Papers of the Willingham and Lawton families, South Caroliniana Library, University of South Carolina.

M

Mammy Stereotype

Enslaved women who labored as so-called mammies made an indelible impression on American consciousness. Nourished by literature, slavery historiography, and popular culture, a mythology surrounded this group of enslaved women and obscured their realities from full illumination in their day and at present. From their menial positions as household servants, surrogate mothers, wet nurses, and cooks, "mammies" rose to prominence in slaveholding households and in the American imagination. However, while slaveholders exploited these women's labor, they also created and reinforced the mammy stereotype to further justify the workings of household slavery.

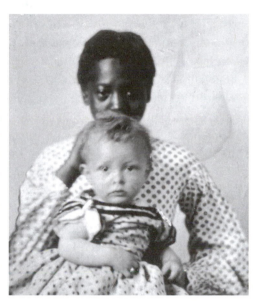

Young African American woman holding a white child, ca. 1855. (Library of Congress.)

Southern whites used the mammy figure to project the idea that the plantation was an extended family comprising happy slaves and whites. This myth helped to convince slaveholders themselves and outsiders that slavery was beneficial to society because it trained and sheltered blacks, who would revert to savagery without the civilizing influence of whites. The so-called defective traits of enslaved women could also be ameliorated under the constant supervision of the mistresses in the plantation household under this type of mythology.

Diaries and records left by planters, the South's wealthiest slaveholders, confirm this ideology by assigning positive attributes to enslaved women who served as mammies. Though slaveholders seldom praised enslaved people in general, mammies were often warmly complimented. Slaveholders often described them as "self-respecting, independent, loyal, forward, gentle, captious, affectionate, true, strong, just, warmhearted, compassionate, fearless, popular, brave, good, pious, quick-witted, capable, thrifty, regal, skillful, competent, sensible, careful, efficient, truthful."

The praise slaveholders bestowed on mammies exposes a contradiction between their belief in innate black inferiority and their unrestrained admiration for these enslaved women's competence. If enslaved people were mentally deficient and uncivilized, whites acted irresponsibly when they placed their households and their children in mammy's charge. What slaveholders hoped to prove with glowing accounts of "mammy" ultimately undermined the image of enslaved people they were attempting to portray. Instead of showing the civilizing influence of slavery on "subhuman" enslaved women, their praise for mammies exposed the ideology as an elaborate, self-serving fantasy. Under the weight of its contradictions, the fantasy should have disintegrated. It did not disintegrate, however, because the slaveholding class needed the gratitude of enslaved people to define themselves as moral human beings.

Slaveholders projected a genial image for mammies in order to claim loyalty from the enslaved women who toiled in their homes. However, in order to script this sentimental mammy myth, slaveholders had to suppress slavery's brutality— the details of which figure prominently in slave narratives. Frederick Douglass, for example, described his Aunt Hester's flogging as one of many instances of enslaved women's physical scourging. In addition, only on large plantations would there have been an enslaved woman whose duties exclusively consisted of child care. Many lower-class and smaller farmers were also captivated by this mythology, yet they required an enslaved woman to perform her housework in addition to field labor.

Indeed, mammy's touted devotion to her master and his family could have been contrived to secure a degree of power. Mammy's good-natured compliance in the slaveholding household could have given her leverage, which she might use to gain limited privileges for herself and her own family. It is entirely possible that a slave mammy's devotion to whites was a façade used to gain such concessions. Contemporary scholars and novelists have shown how bondwomen employed the mammy stereotype to exploit their position, gain new privileges, and promote the slave community's interests in addition to their own.

Veta Smith Tucker

See also Community; Family; Gender Conventions; Historiography; Jezebel Stereotype; Plantation Mistresses; Representations; Wet Nursing.

Suggested Reading

Octavia Butler, *Kindred* (Boston: Beacon Press, 1988); Ernest Gaines, *A Lesson Before Dying* (New York: Knopf, 1993); Eugene Genovese, *Roll Jordan Roll: The World the Slaves Made* (New York: Vintage, 1976); Toni Morrison, *Beloved* (New York: Knopf,

1987); Jessie Parkhurst, "The Role of Mammy in the Plantation Household," *Journal of Negro History* 23 (July 1983), 351–57; Deborah Gray-White, *Ar'n't I a Woman: Female Slaves in the Plantation South* (New York: W.W. Norton & Company, 1985).

Manumission

Manumission refers to the formal legal process of freeing enslaved people through legal deed or writ such as an owner's last will and testament or deed of manumission. To *manumit* means to grant freedom through legal deed or writ. The terms *manumission* and *emancipation* are often used interchangeably to discuss the freeing of enslaved persons. However, manumission refers to the process of producing a legal document in order to free an individual in a region where slavery is a legal institution whereas *emancipation* usually refers to freeing an entire population after the legal demise of slavery in a given locale

Manumission was a common practice in communities where slavery and servitude constituted part of the labor regime. Isabella Johnson, a manumitted indentured servant, and her husband Anthony established one of the first black settlements in seventeenth-century Virginia. Enslaved women Elizabeth Key and Elizabeth Keckley, both from Virginia and born a century apart, sued for their freedom, won, and were freed by formal documents of manumission. The American Revolution is often viewed as a hallmark date for increased slave manumissions. Scholars suggest that manumissions rose during this period for several reasons. First, religious denominations such as the Methodists and Quakers developed firm antislavery philosophies and therefore, forbid their congregants to hold slaves. Second, the egalitarian philosophies associated with the American Revolution such as the belief in equality for all mankind produced an environment that was critical of slaveholding. Third, the efforts of bondwomen (and men) used the language of liberty and freedom and sue for their own freedom.

Gradual emancipation laws in northern states also contributed to the rise in manumissions in post-Revolutionary Maryland. Vermont led the emancipation efforts by outlawing slavery in its 1778 state constitution. In 1780, Pennsylvania passed the "Act for the Gradual Abolition of Slavery"; this act abolished slavery within the state of Pennsylvania. However, the law also took into account the fate of children born to bondwomen prior to the formal passing of the law. Unborn children were required to serve as indentured servants or slaves until they reached the age of 28. Other states adopted all or parts of the Pennsylvania model. By 1804, all states north of Delaware made provisions to grant slaves freedom via gradual manumission, with abolishment of slavery as the end result. In states where slavery remained legal, laws developed to regulate the manumission of children until they reached a particular age. In New York, for example, male children

Charity Folks, Sr. (ca. 1757–1828) and Charity Folks Bishop (1795–1875)

Charity Folks, Sr., and her daughter Charity Folks, Jr., became two prominent members of the manumitted caste of Annapolis, Maryland. While enslaved as a domestic in the home of John and Mary Ridout, Charity Folks, Sr., had five children—Harriet, Hannah, James, Mary, and Charity, Jr. She maintained an abroad marriage with Thomas Folks, a bondman owned by a local shopkeeper. Thomas Folks was manumitted in 1794. Together he and Charity hired their time and negotiated for the freedom of Charity, her five children, and three grandchildren. Charity herself was released from bondage in 1797, when she was between 40 and 45 years old. In their wills, John and Mary Ridout made financial provisions for Charity: an annual allowance, material goods, and quite possibly a home. The exact nature of Charity's relationship with the Ridouts remains shrouded in mystery. Charity Folks, Sr., died in 1828, leaving property, including her house at 84 Franklin Street, to her three surviving daughters (Charity, Mary, Harriet) and to her granddaughter, Elizabeth. In 1874, a descendant sold the property at 84 Franklin Street to the Mount Moriah African Methodist Episcopal Church, which built their permanent meetinghouse on the site. Now part of the National Historic Trust, Mount Moriah was converted into the Banneker-Douglass Museum in 1984. This museum is Maryland's official repository for African American heritage.

Photograph of the document granting manumission of Charity Folks, Sr., from the Anne Arundel County Court Manumission Record, 1797–1807, Vol. 825, pp. 17–18. (Maryland State Archives.)

Charity Folks, Jr. was manumitted in 1807, when she was approximately 12 years old. In 1821, she married recently manumitted black William Bishop. The couple had seven children. Bishop was the executrix of both her mother's estate and that of her husband, who died in 1870. Charity Folks Bishop owned 16 pieces of real estate at the time of her death in 1875. The Folks/Bishop clan was one of the wealthiest and most influential families of color in Maryland during the nineteenth century and into the twentieth century.

were promised freedom when they reached the age of 28, and women were manumitted when they reached the age of 25.

These laws are often referred to as "postnati" arrangements as they provided stipulations for the child's labor once they were born. These arrangements often provided a manumission date for the child and established provisions for the former slave to enter into an apprenticeship with a tradesperson once freed. Training in a trade or profession also quelled white fears of a large manumitted black class dependent upon local county resources. Real or imagined fears of a free black underclass were also used as a justification to hold persons in bondage for longer periods of time than originally anticipated. For example, persons interested in membership in Methodist churches were to relinquish their human property as slaveholding conflicted with the basic tenants of the faith. Owners repeatedly applied to their local church boards citing that freeing their slaves had the potential to enlarge the free black class. Owners also suggested that manumitting their bondpeople conflicted with their inherent right to property.

It is important to underscore that manumission was not a northern phenomena, nor was it a practice that died out as the South became more dependent on slave labor. Rather, manumission had a long history in cities such as Baltimore, Richmond, Charleston, and New Orleans where the increasing free wage economy enabled women to buy themselves out of slavery. As in the North, the rates of manumitted women in southern communities increased in the late eighteenth century. A range of reasons account for the sharp increase in freed blacks in the American South. In urban areas such as Charleston, slaves competed with white wage earners in an open market. In Maryland, the nature of crop cultivation changed as wheat replaced tobacco as the chief product. Whereas harvesting tobacco required a year-round labor force, wheat did not. The transition to wheat also perpetuated a revolving cycle of planter debt, whereby many owners sold their slaves or hired them to others to meet their financial obligations. These factors, coupled with the increasingly urban nature of cities such as Charleston and Baltimore, suggest that the profitability of permanent chattel slavery decreased. Despite the upsurge in manumissions, southern slaveholders preferred manumitting blacks on an individual basis rather than abolishing slavery forever.

Considerable attention is often given to the ability of enslaved women to exploit their sexual relations with slave owners in order to earn their freedom or that of their children. There is some indication that this is true. President Thomas

Jefferson freed the children of his mistress Sally Hemings in his will; he did not, however, manumit Sally Hemings. In Louisiana, manumission and the plaçage system almost developed hand in hand. Owners manumitted their enslaved mistresses and maintained their residences. Despite popular scenarios such as that of Sally Hemings, the exact numbers of enslaved women who used their sexual relationships with their owner to achieve their own manumission or that of their children, remains hard to determine. In fact, a sexual relationship was just one avenue an enslaved woman used to access manumission. Enslaved women were quite astute in negotiating manumissions. Market women in Charleston, for example, used a portion of their earnings to buy their freedom. Other enslaved women negotiated with their owners when they were hired out to work for someone else. After being manumitted from slavery, some women become landowners and acquired a degree of financial security. Manumitted women did not forget those who remained in bondage, however. They worked to purchase the freedom of their fictive and biological kin. In some cases, they were successful; in other cases, they were manumitted while their family members remained in bondage for the duration of their lives.

Manumission was not without its consequences. The freedom of manumitted women was often in put in jeopardy if they did not have enough money to purchase freedom papers. In Virginia, as in other states, manumitted slaves had to leave the state within 30 days or face re-enslavement. Moreover, the fear of a large free black population influenced some planters to manumit their bondpeople under the provision that they relocate to Canada, Liberia, or the West Indies. Whatever their fate, manumitted women lived the remainder of their lives outside of the reach of the owner's whip. However, they never forgot their experiences in bondage.

Jessica Millward

See also Abolitionism; Emancipation; Free Women; Hemings, Sally; Keckley, Elizabeth; Key, Elizabeth.

Suggested Reading

Ira Berlin, *Slaves Without Masters: The Free Negro in the Antebellum South* (1975; reprint New York: New Press, 1992); Jane Dabel, *A Respectable Woman: The Public Roles of African American Women in 19th-Century New York* (New York: New York University Press, 2008); Leslie Harris, *In the Shadow of Slavery: African Americans in New York City, 1626–1863* (Chicago: University of Chicago Press, 2003); Darlene Clark Hine and David Barry Gaspar, eds., *Beyond Bondage: Free Women of Color in the Americas* (Urbana: University of Illinois Press, 2004); Wilma King, *The Essence of Liberty: Free Black Women during the Slave Era* (Columbia: University of Missouri Press, 2006); Suzanne Lebsock, *The Free Women of St. Petersburg: Status and Culture in a Southern Town, 1786–1860* (New York: W.W. Norton & Co., 1985); Jessica Millward, *Deliverance from the*

Chaldeans: Gender and Slave Manumissions in Maryland, 1770–1830, Race in the Atlantic World Series, 1700–1900 (Athens: University of Georgia Press); Annette Gordon Reed, *Thomas Jefferson and Sally Hemings: An American Controversy* (Charlottesville: University Press of Virginia, 1997); T. Stephan Whitman, *The Price of Freedom: Slavery and Manumission in Baltimore and Early National Maryland* (Lexington: University of Kentucky Press, 1997).

Maroon Communities

Maroons were fugitive bondpeople who had escaped, joined other enslaved runaways, and lived on their own in settlements inaccessible to slaveholding authorities. Their communities existed in places such as mountaintops, rainforests, and swamps in tropical and semitropical regions in the Western Hemisphere. Maroon communities are important to the study of women because females were essential to community survival.

Primarily phenomena of the colonial slavery era in mountain areas of South America and the Caribbean, in the United States, maroon communities were located in swamps and marshes of the South. Because these places of refuge became established settlements sustained by farming, hunting, and fishing, long-term communities evolved that lasted for a few years to generations.

At great peril, enslaved women served several roles in facilitating the development of maroon communities. Some women in the slave quarters assisted others who fled. Many women runaways were truants who returned to the slave quarters, but others became fugitives who escaped from rural areas to urban areas where they could avoid discovery, or to obscure locations where they could establish permanent settlements with other fugitives. When apprehended, however, fugitive women and others who had assisted them endured brutal punishment.

Although slaveholders advertised in newspapers for fugitive women, and at times named the women and described how they had escaped, ads could not tell us whether the runaways became maroons. However, a maroon community could not survive for very long without women to bear the children needed for future generations. Women not only bore the children, but also farmed the land, while the men hunted and fished, and helped the men defend their settlements when attacked.

The establishment and survival of large maroon societies in semitropical locations was a more difficult feat than those found in the tropical and rain forest regions of the Americas. In the United States, smaller groups of fugitives attempted to subsist on the fringes of developed areas near places such as the Dismal Swamp located between Virginia and North Carolina. The swamp is a unique wilderness of forest wetlands that European Americans believed to be uninhabitable by European settlers and their descendants. As a result, the Dismal

Swamp provided inaccessible refuge for about 200 maroons and their offspring who lived there for several generations. Maroon survival was facilitated by an illegal trade maintained with whites living on the borders of the swamp.

The women of these communities also participated in warfare against invaders. For example, authorities uncovered the maroon community of Cabarrus County, North Carolina in 1811. Militia attacked the maroons and the community was destroyed. Two of the four fugitives captured during the ensuing battle were women. In an 1818 case, one member of a group of over 30 militants captured in a Princess Anne County, Virginia raid was an elderly woman. Although authorities did not acknowledge her to be the leader, the deference other fugitives showed her suggests that she was. In another case near Mobile, Alabama, a group of men, women, and children put up a strong fight against authorities, but their lack of sufficient weapons resulted in their defeat and the destruction of the maroon settlement.

Maroon survival was important to bondwomen of all ages, which explains why so many fought tirelessly to defend their settlements. Female leadership in maroon communities, though difficult to establish from the accounts that have survived in the United States, should not be viewed as a surprising phenomenon. Similar survival and resistance strategies worked for women of African descent throughout the African diaspora during slavery.

Rosalyn Terborg-Penn

See also Community; Elderly Women; Punishment; Resistance; Runaways; Truancy.

Suggested Reading

Stephanie M. H. Camp, " 'I Could Not Stay There': Enslaved Women Truants," *Slavery and Abolition* 23, 5 (December 2002), 1–20; Jane Landers, "Maroon Women in Colonial Spanish America: Case Studies in the Circum-Caribbean from the Sixteenth through the Eighteen Centuries" in *Beyond Bondage: Free Women of Color in the Americas*, eds. David Barry Gaspar and Darlene Clark Hine (Urbana: University of Illinois Press, 2004); Timothy Lockley, *Maroon Communities in South Carolina* (Columbia: University of South Carolina Press, 2009); Rosalyn Terborg-Penn, "Black Women in Resistance: A Cross-Cultural Perspective," in *In Resistance: Studies in African, Caribbean and Afro-American History*, ed. Gary Y. Okihiro (Amherst: The University of Massachusetts Press, 1986).

Marriage, Abroad

In an August 2011 *New York Times* op-ed entitled "Putting an Antebellum Myth to Rest," historian Tera Hunter untangles the historical debates about enslaved marriages. She explains that "couples were not entitled to live under the same roof" and that some enslaved partners lived "miles apart." A substantial percentage of slaves instead participated in what were called *abroad marriages*, where wives

> My pappy . . . had to git a pass to come see mammy . . . [but his owners] took a notion to sell him to Arkansas. My mammy weep 'bout dat but what could her do?
>
> —Sena Moore, former bondwoman
> (WPA Slave Narrative Project, South Carolina Narratives, Vol. XIV, Part III, 209)

and husbands were owned by two different slaveholders and lived on separate farms or plantations. (It should be noted that although enslaved people were not legally allowed to marry, marriages were nonetheless found throughout the enslaved population.) Abroad marriages were most prevalent in regions of the South dominated by small-scale slavery, such as the backcountry and border states, but these unions occurred in all parts of the South and on all sizes of slaveholdings. Historians have estimated that abroad couples accounted for one-third of slave marriages in South Carolina and over half in Missouri, for example.

The few bondpeople residing on smaller holdings forced enslaved men and women to look elsewhere for marriage partners, so many plantation slaves chose abroad matches. Motivated by more than demographics, enslaved individuals exercised their personal and cultural preferences when selecting mates. American bondpeople found, however, a limited number of suitable, nonrelated, potential spouses on some plantations, because, as was true in many African cultures, they followed rules of exogamy that made marriage taboo with close-blood kin such as first cousins. In addition, enslaved men and women exerted autonomy through their choice of marriage partners. Likewise, men living abroad on other estates enjoyed the expansion of their social life and the break in their routine provided by traveling to visit their families. For some enslaved men, living away from their wives shielded them from witnessing the potential abuse of their wives and children at the hands of slaveholders.

Slaveholders acknowledged the legitimacy, although not the legality, of abroad marriages only after prospective husbands and wives gained the consent of both of their slaveholders. Some planters forbade bondpeople to marry away from the home plantation, but most slaveholders gladly sanctioned abroad marriages because they recognized that, at the very least, their economic best interests depended on it. On the most basic level, slaveholders hoped to increase their work force through the marriage of bondwomen and the eventual births of their children. Slaveholders of enslaved men also accepted abroad marriages even though they did not reap the benefits of the slave family's reproduction and suffered most of the inconveniences and risks associated with men's increased mobility. Some slaveholders reasoned that enslaved men who forged ties to women and children would be more content in their enslavement and less likely to flee. In addition, they relied on their slaveholding neighbors to extend visitation privileges to the husbands of their enslaved women. In the final analysis, small slaveholders permitted these unions knowing that the fate of slavery depended on the allowance of cross-farm marriages and the mobility of abroad enslaved husbands.

Slaveholders of both enslaved men and women recognized these unconventional marriages as legitimate and helped sanction them by providing their bondpeople with weddings and allowing visitation privileges. Custom dictated that enslaved men could regularly visit their wives, but couples relied on their owners to recognize these rights. Bondmen were usually given passes to visit their families once on the weekend and occasionally once during the week. Depending on the distance traveled, enslaved men often arrived to visit their families on Saturday evening and left before sunrise on Monday morning. Couples usually lived within a few miles of one another, although some men journeyed a much greater distance to spend a few short hours with their families. The time needed to travel between their homes often determined how frequently husbands were allowed to visit. Some visited every night, while those at greater distances came much less often than even the traditional weekly visit.

Enslaved men in general, even those with resident wives, struggled to protect and support their families in light of slaveholders' power. Abroad bondmen could provide their wives and children with only limited economic assistance, physical protection, and emotional support because they spent time infrequently with them. The material quality of life enjoyed by slave families was directly influenced by the contributions made by all household members. Abroad enslaved men were not at their families' cabins long enough to be of much assistance with basic household chores and most were unable to supplement their families' diets in the same manner as resident husbands and fathers. Abroad bondwomen may have taken some pride in their ability to manage their households without their partners, but there is no indication that they found the experience liberating.

Abroad marriages exposed enslaved women to increased risk of sexual abuse as well. The close living and working conditions found on small slaveholdings led to the sexual abuse of bondwomen by male members of the slaveholding household more often than on plantations, but the absence of abroad husbands also may have been a contributing factor. Enslaved men could do little to protect their wives, since their physical presence might have served as a deterrent for some slaveholders.

Interviews with former bondpeople suggest that relationships between enslaved children and their fathers were compromised by abroad marriages. Years later, many spoke at great length about their mothers and merely mentioned in passing that their fathers lived elsewhere. The brief nature of fathers' visits may have made it difficult for some enslaved children to forge strong emotional bonds with their fathers. Mothers tended to children's physical and emotional needs, as well as disciplined and taught them, on a daily basis.

Abroad bondwomen also were susceptible to heartbreaking deception by their frequently absent spouses. Some abroad men were involved with and occasionally even married to two women simultaneously. A few abandoned their first wives, but others continued to visit both women. The sporadic visiting habits of many abroad husbands easily concealed these relationships. Some enslaved men and women may have knowingly participated in polygamous relationships as a continuation of African marriage practices, but other abroad wives either did not know of the other women or were opposed to their husbands' decisions to take additional wives.

Abroad slave families were also more vulnerable to separation due to migration, estate divisions, and sales, and especially since they were dependent on the life circumstances and temperaments of two slaveholders. Slave marriages were not legal unions and could be severed at their owners' discretion. Husbands and wives were often permanently separated when their spouse was sold or an owner moved away. If the distance was greater than that which could be traveled in a few hours, the separation was usually recognized as a divorce by both the slaveholding and the slave communities. A few owners honored the marriages of abroad slaves, but most were unwilling or financially unable to purchase an enslaved individual in order to unite a family. The pervasive system of slave hiring significantly increased the number of abroad marriages as well. Hiring arrangements separated even some couples living together on the same farm or plantation.

In contrast, the inherent flexibility of abroad marriages protected many slave families from permanent separation. Abroad marriages were little disturbed by estate divisions or sales if enslaved persons were transferred to local owners. Enslaved couples merely continued to visit one another as they had previously done. The distance traveled to visit loved ones may have become more formidable, but most enslaved men believed it worth the effort to spend a little time with their families.

Most abroad families did not have the luxury of daily contact, but many created long-lasting relationships regardless of the difficulties facing them. Historical sources reveal the existence of strong bonds of marriage and family during slavery. Given the alternative of isolation, most enslaved men, women, and children accepted the limitations of abroad families and relished the time they spent with one another. Although these relationships were challenging to maintain, vital emotional ties existed between many abroad men and women and between enslaved children and their fathers, regardless of the distance that often physically separated them. Many enslaved husbands and wives tenaciously made difficult marriage arrangements work over a long period of time. The thousands of abroad slave couples that chose to live together and legalize their marriages after the Civil War is evidence of the vitality of many unions.

Diane Mutti-Burke

See also Civil War; Domestic Slave Trade; Emancipation; Family; Laws; Marriage and Cohabitation; Mobility.

Suggested Reading

Diane Mutti-Burke, " 'Mah pappy belong to a neighbor': The Effects of Abroad Marriages on Missouri Slave Families," in *Searching for Their Places: Women in the South Across Four Centuries*, eds. Thomas H. Appleton, Jr., and Angela Boswell (Columbia: University of Missouri Press, 2003); Stephen Crawford, "Quantified Memory: A Study of the W.P.A. and Fisk University Slave Narrative Collections" (PhD dissertation, University of Chicago, 1980); Paul Escott, *Slavery Remembered: A Record of Twentieth-Century Slave Narratives* (Chapel Hill: University of North Carolina Press, 1979); Eugene Genovese, *Roll, Jordan, Roll: The World the Slaves Made* (New York: Pantheon Books, 1974); Herbert G. Gutman, *The Black Family in Slavery and Freedom, 1750–1925* (New York: Pantheon Books, 1976); Tera Hunter, "Putting an Antebellum Myth to Rest," *New York Times*, OP-ED, August 1, 2011; Brenda E. Stevenson, *Life in Black & White: Family and Community in the Slave South* (New York: Oxford University Press, 1996); Emily West, *Chains of Love: Slave Couples in Antebellum South Carolina* (Urbana: University of Illinois Press, 2004); Deborah Gray White, *Ar'n't I a Woman?* (New York: W.W. Norton & Co., 1985).

Marriage and Cohabitation

Although enslaved marriage was not legally sanctioned, many bondpeople considered themselves married, sometimes even with the approval of slaveholders and with marriage ceremonies. For women who married men on their own plantations, cohabitation in the same household was possible. Women who lived with their husbands benefited from his presence; he offered protection, spousal support, physical intimacy, and extra food. Slaveholders usually allotted bondmen one day per week to go fishing or hunting around the farms. This extra food was essential to staving off malnutrition and supplementing rather limited diets. Many slaveholders also encouraged and expected their married bondpeople to live together. Cohabitation increased the possibility of pregnancy, maintained commonplace gender conventions, and created an environment that emphasized the importance of family. Cohabitation records suggest that oftentimes it was the act of living together that deemed a couple "married" since bondpeople were not afforded the legal status of marriage in the eye of the law.

Enslaved women tended to marry at a very young age, sometimes as young as 12 or 13. Slaveholders could avoid problems associated with forced marriages if the girl was young enough to have not yet developed romantic feelings for a man. Marrying at an early age also lengthened the amount of time bondwomen spent in their childbearing years. Slaveholders put a great deal of pressure on enslaved girls who had reached sexual maturity to give birth as soon as possible, recognizing that early marriages and pregnancies meant a longer timeframe within which women could potentially be giving birth to children. Slaveholders did not

Marriage and Cohabitation | 197

hesitate to ensure that they were getting their money's worth from their bond-women, both in terms of physical labor, but also in terms of replenishing the supply of their human chattel. If anything, marriage and cohabitation helped facilitate both processes.

Despite cohabitation, slave marriage rituals reflected their lack of legal sanction and were shaped by the nature of the relationship between the husband and wife. If

My pappy didn't 'low other slave men to look at my mammy. I see him grab Uncle Phil once, throw him down on de floor, and when him quit stompin' Uncle Phil they have to send for Dr. Newton, 'cause pappy done broke Uncle Phil's right leg.

—Henry Gladney, former bondman
(Born in Slavery: Slave Narratives from the Federal Writers' Project, 1936–1938 South Carolina Narratives, Volume XIV, Part 2, 129)

a man and woman willfully decided to marry and if they received permission from the slaveholder(s), a small ceremony might have been conducted. Slaveholders who approved of a particular match might have provided the couple with nicer

Undated photograph of an elderly slave couple in Mercer County, Kentucky. (Schomburg Center for Research in Black Culture/New York Public Library.)

clothing and a small meal to celebrate. More common, the slaveholder made a public pronouncement that the couple was married. Less common was a written certificate stating the union. Many bondpeople turned to their churches for the ceremony and a blessing, spiritually recognizing their marriage as official.

The lack of formality of these marriages led to the development of unique traditions, including the tradition of "jumping the broom." Jumping the broom refers to the act of a husband and wife jumping over a broom laid on the ground directly after being married. Since slave marriages could not be legally recognized, jumping the broom became the ritual that marked the official beginning and recognition of a slave marriage. The tradition behind the ritual claims that whoever jumps over the broom the highest would be the decision-maker of the household. The legitimacy this ritual afforded the marriage was the primary motivation for its use, particularly since many married couples could not cohabitate. Though marriage and cohabitation were viewed as the ideal arrangement for many couples, the reality of enslavement oftentimes rendered both impossible.

Katherine M. Johnson

See also Childbirth; Community; Courtship; Domestic Slave Trade; Family; Laws; Life Cycle; Marriage, Abroad; Pregnancy; Punishment.

Two African Americans photographed in the early twentieth century. (Library of Congress.)

Suggested Reading

Rebecca J. Frazer, *Courtship and Love among the Enslaved in North Carolina* (Oxford: University of Mississippi Press, 2007); Elizabeth Fox-Genovese, *Within the Plantation Household: Black and White Women of the South* (Chapel Hill: The University of North Carolina Press, 1988); Eugene D. Genovese, *Roll Jordan Roll: The World the Slaves Made* (New York: Pantheon Books, 1974); Herbert G. Gutman, *The Black Family in Freedom and Slavery* (New York: Pantheon Books, 1976); Brenda E. Stevenson, *Life in Black and White: Family and Community in the Slave South* (New York: Oxford University Press, 1996); Emily West, *Chains of Love: Slave Couples in Antebellum South Carolina* (Chicago: University of Illinois Press, 2004); Deborah Gray White, *Ar'n't I a Woman?: Female Slaves in the Plantation South*, 2nd ed. (New York: W.W. Norton, 1999).

Medical Experimentation and Surgery

The unique impact of the institution of enslavement on the bodies of black women led to the development of the medical specialty of gynecology in the United States. Slavery as an institution relied upon the labor of enslaved blacks. However, the status of enslaved women made them particularly susceptible to sexual abuse, degradation, and medical experimentation carried out for the purposes of ensuring their reproductive capacity as "breeder." The role of breeder women (to bear children who would carry the legal status of their enslaved mother) and its resulting health consequences set the stage for surgical medical experimentation on the bodies of enslaved women.

In Montgomery, Alabama from approximately 1845 to 1849, three enslaved women—Anarcha, Betsey, and Lucy—and at least six or seven unnamed others were subjected to repetitive experimental surgeries to close openings between their vagina and bladder without anesthesia to dull their pain. The law deemed bondpeople as chattel property subject to ownership and white society accepted the social science of the day, which believed that blacks could tolerate pain more so than whites. The women suffered from a medical condition called vesico-vaginal fistula, or tears that form between the vagina and the urinary tract or bladder allowing urine to flow uncontrollably, often a result of experiencing a difficult childbirth.

Anarcha, reportedly about 17 years of age, lived on the Wescott plantation, only a mile from Montgomery and had been in labor for 72 hours after being diagnosed as "hopelessly incurable" and "unfit for duties required of a servant" after developing a fistula a few days after delivery (assisted by Dr. J. Marion Sims with the use of forceps). Betsey, a servant of Dr. Harris from Lowndes County, was reportedly 17 or 18 years old, with a fistula after the birth of a child. Lucy, reportedly about

18 years old, was a servant of Tom Zimmerman of Macon County, with a fistula after the birth of a child. Dr. J. Marion Sims is credited with finding a cure for vesico-vaginal fistula after securing the bondwomen from their enslavers and conducting experimentation on them in his backyard hospital. Sims's initial reluctance to take these types of cases eventually defined his medical career, created a field of specialty in the study of gynecology, and led to various surgical inventions and instruments still used today. The numerous experimental surgeries performed on the enslaved women serve as the foundation for Sims's historical reference as the so-called "father of American gynecology."

On Anarcha Westcott's thirtieth operation in May 1849, Sims's use of fine silver wire to suture (mend together) the fistulas instead of the traditional silk thread was deemed a successful surgery. This was followed by Betsey's and Lucy's cures within two weeks of that of Anarcha. The four-year period of experimental surgeries conducted by Sims on the enslaved women resulted in surgical inventions such as the "Sims's speculum" (a duckbilled instrument used for medical examinations of the vagina and cervix) and gynecological innovations such as "Sims's position" (patient lies on the left side in a semi-prone hand-knee position for examination purposes) as well as developing surgical instruments such as the S-shaped silver urinary catheter (prototype of today's self-retaining urinary catheter) to drain the bladder after surgery.

Anarcha, Betsey, Lucy, and the unnamed others were given large doses of opium (highly addictive though routinely used during this era as a therapeutic sedative) as part of Sims's postoperative regimen, each taking turns as the other one healed from the experiments. Sims noted in his 1852 medical journal article, *On the Treatment of Vesico-Vaginal Fistula*, that "[i]t [opium] calms the nerves, inspires hope, relieves the scalding of the urine, prevents a craving for food produces constipation, subdues inflammatory action and assists the patient, doomed to a fortnight's horizontal position, to pass the time with pleasant dreams, and delightful sensations, instead of painful forebodings, and intolerable sufferings." Though an account from the enslaved black women is not recorded during the four-year period of Sims's trial and error to find a cure for vesico-vaginal fistula, the women undoubtedly formed a sense of community defined both by the physical restraints of enslavement, routine opium postoperative procedures, and repetitive surgical invasions on a rolling basis, as they assisted each other. Anarcha, Betsey, Lucy, and other unnamed enslaved black women served as subjects of medical experimentation which yielded reproductive knowledge and was the basis for the medical specialty of gynecology in the United States.

Deleso A. Alford

See also Breeding; Community; Health, Disabilities, and Soundness; Violence, Sexual.

Suggested Reading

W. Michael Byrd and Linda A. Clayton, *An American Health Dilemma: A Medical History of African Americans and the Problem of Race: Beginning to 1900* (New York: Routledge, 2000); Deborah Kuhn McGregor, *Sexual Surgery and the Origins of Gynecology: J. Marion Sims, His Hospital, and His Patients* (New York: Garland Publishing, Inc., 1989); J. Marion Sims, *The Story of My Life* (New York: D. Appleton and Company, 1884); Deleso Alford Washington, "Critical Race Feminist Bioethics: Telling Stories in Law School and Medical School in Pursuit of " 'Cultural Competency'" 72 *Alb. L. Rev.* 961 (2009); Harriet A. Washington, *Medical Apartheid: The Dark History of Medical Experimentation on Black Americans from Colonial Times to the Present* (New York: Doubleday, 2006).

Middle Passage

The Middle Passage refers to the oceanic crossing that enslaved women, men, and children endured on slave ships sailing from West Africa across the Atlantic Ocean and into various seaports within the Americas and the Caribbean from the 1400s to the mid-nineteenth century. It was called this because it was the middle part of a three-part European trading at the time. The ships began in European countries with the first passage, where they carried various goods ranging from tobacco, sugar, pork, gunpowder, iron, cloth, and rum to Africa, which were used to help barter for the purchase of human cargo represented through African men, women, and children who had been captured for enslavement in distant plantations. Once docked overseas, sailors transported Africans (those who had survived) off the boats onto American and Caribbean soil for interested buyers to bid upon and trade for tobacco or sugar, which was taken back to Europe.

Before the Middle Passage began, enslaved females, much like bondmen, were captured and marched from the interiors of Africa towards the coastal shores of West Africa in order to be offered for sale to arriving merchants and ship masters. Once there, captives were commonly stowed within gender specific slave dungeons and coastal barracoons, resulting in the separation of females and males during their temporary holding. The duration of their shoreline placement, ranging from weeks to several months depended greatly upon local outbreaks of war, overseas demand, and most importantly, the negotiation of sale agreed upon between local traders and arriving slave ship captains. Sailors typically carried a variety of goods aboard ships to use as a way of bartering for the procurement of African people. These items ranged from such items as glass beads, to silk, rum, and even guns. Once a slave trader took interest in the purchase of a bondperson, physical and mental assessments were first conducted to assess their overall health and potential value. During this process, both men and women were commonly

Branding of an enslaved woman prior to boarding a slave ship. (Eon Images.)

scrutinized through rather degrading and sexually exploitative means on the basis of determining the labor they could potentially generate for future planters. However, female captives—young girls, teenagers, and adult women—were inspected on the basis of two factors: (1) physical labor they were capable of exerting within the house and the fields of distant plantation communities within the New World; and (2) reproductive labor with regards to the children they could possibly produce.

After captives were selected and negotiations concluded for their final sale, arrangements were made for their immediate transport aboard the ship of the captain who bought them. Once purchased, bondwomen and men became the "human cargo" itemized alongside various material items including tobacco, sugar, pork, cloth, and rum. Yet, considerable diversity existed among different bondpeople lodged within ships. This pertains to the different African ethnicities represented such as Fante, Bakongo, Yoruba, Ewe, Akan, Melimba, Angola, and Igbo as well as variation according to both gender and age. The captives most highly desired by planters were males between 15 and 30 years of age. Adult male captives are commonly referenced within ship manifests alongside younger men regularly listed as "men-boys" and "boys." Ship captains also detailed a broad range of female captives among the ship "cargo," ranging from adult women, "women-girls," and "girls."

Slaves taken from a vessel captured by the HMS *Undine*. Illustrated in *The Graphic*, London, June 7, 1884. (Library of Congress.)

In addition to these groupings, elderly captives, nursing infants, young children, and new mothers also found themselves placed aboard slave vessels.

Once sold, bondpeople were ushered aboard wooden slave ships in preparation for the oceanic crossing known as the infamous "Middle Passage" that resulted in their transport across the Atlantic Ocean and into various seaports within the Caribbean and Americas. Immediately following their coastal removal, European seamen regimented the separation of female and male captives on ship. Due to lingering fears of rebellion, they moved bondmen in chains to the bottom holding of the vessel. Conversely, they placed females and children without chains into a separate location—often the quarter-deck—which was in many cases near the crewmen's sleeping quarters. Although sailors held considerable anxieties about male captives' potential disobedient shipboard behavior, they viewed women and children as much less of a threat, rather docile in nature, and less likely to engage in physical rebellion.

Set out at sea, both captives and sailors were subject to a host of factors detrimental to their health. In particular, for those enslaved however, unsanitary and crowded conditions aboard ships further worsened their susceptibility to acquire various diseases and become enfeebled. Throughout different slaving voyages bondpeople regularly died from the effects of a range of deadly diseases such as flux, apoplexy, malaria, smallpox, or yaws. The mortality of bondwomen especially stemmed from the attack of many of these and other ailments. As females they were also likely to perish from the loss of a child through miscarriages, which slave-ship surgeons commonly listed as a cause of death.

Throughout much of the passage, violence remained a regular occurrence for both sailors and captives. For bondwomen, violence manifested in the unending threats of rape they confronted from crewmen employed aboard vessels. Their proximity to sailor's quarters often facilitated this reality as well as the separation of bondmen within bottom holdings, which prevented them from assisting female captives in their attempts to fight back. As a result of these aggressive behaviors, it was not uncommon for bondwomen to become both impregnated as well as psychologically scarred prior to their arrival within distant plantation communities. Unwilling to endure the cycle of bondage nor the constant attempts of sexual abuse, many women boldly fought back. They did so through a variety of means including abortion, poisoning the crew's food, jumping overboard, committing acts of suicide, as well as engaging in physical combat.

Bondmen were commonly feared and in many cases are regularly referenced as the primary actors who participated in these open acts of violence through rebellion; however, female captives were oftentimes critical to the success of these bloody intentions. Unchained throughout much of the voyage and held in quarters typically close to the storage room, this permitted bondwomen the opportunity to serve as spies as well as to sneak various types of ammunition down to the bottom holding where their male cohorts were stowed. Although they assisted in preparations for rebellion, female captives also fought alongside men in the quest for their freedom, risking the possibilities of death as well as harsh punishments of whipping, beheadings, and other methods of torture committed against them by sailors in view of the entire ship.

By the time of their port arrival and placement within the system of auction block sales, bondwomen as well as bondmen had already undergone life-altering experiences of slavery at sea. Forced to recreate ties of kinship and family, many women in particular endured threats of sexual abuse, while also bearing witness to the complex challenges of motherhood. As such, they entered plantation slavery physically, emotionally, and most importantly psychologically damaged by the Middle Passage.

Sowande' Mustakeem

See also Branding; Domestic Slave Trade; Health, Disabilities, and Soundness; Mobility; Resistance; Violence, Racial; Violence Sexual.

Suggested Reading

Emma Christopher, *Slave Ship Sailors and Their African Cargo, 1730–1807* (London: Cambridge University Press, 2006); Sowande' Mustakeem, "Far Cry from Fantasy

Voyage: The Impact of the Middle Passage on Slave Societies across the Atlantic World," *Islas: Official Publication of the Afro-Cuban Alliance, Inc.* Year 2, 8 (Fall 1007), 28–34; Sowande' Mustakeem, " 'I Never Have Such a Sickly Ship Before': Diet, Disease, and Mortality in 18th-Century Atlantic Slaving Voyages," *Journal of African American History* 93 (Fall 2008), 474–96; Marcus Rediker, *The Slave Ship: A Human History* (New York: Viking Press, 2008); Stephanie Smallwood, *Saltwater Slavery: A Middle Passage from Africa to American Diaspora* (Cambridge: Harvard University Press, 2007); Eric Taylor, *If We Must Die: Shipboard Insurrections in the Era of the Slave Trade* (Baton Rouge: Louisiana University Press, 2007).

Midwives

Midwives are skilled caregivers who aid in the child-birthing processes for women both during the prenatal and postnatal period. During the antebellum era, enslaved midwives or "granny mothers," as they were fondly referred to, provided a traditional brand of medical care to other enslaved women as well as to many white mistresses on slave plantations. Slaveholders viewed midwives' skills as important to the reproductive capacities of enslaved women they viewed as property. Despite their commoditized labor, midwives held invaluable wisdom that offered opportunities for agency and resistance within the overall enslaved community.

Midwives, typically beyond childbearing age, provided guidance to women in a holistic manner. They understood women's fertility cycles, advised women on proper nutrition and care during pregnancy, and provided folk medicines and spiritual support to women. Midwives were often knowledgeable about a variety of health issues beyond childbirth, possessing what many called "motherwit—a blend of God-given wisdom, commonsense, and the instruction of older women" (Fett 2006, 75). Outsiders of the community rarely understood this wisdom. Former bondwoman Maria Jackson of Georgia recalled her work as a midwife. "My job" she explained "was to cotch the babies, and see dat everything was alright" (*American Slave Narratives: An Online Anthology*, http://www.xroads.virginia.edu,

> *My white folks give me to de doctors in dem days to try en learn me for a nurse. Don't know exactly how old I was in dat day en time, but I can tell you what I done. Couldn't never tell how many baby I bring in dis world, dey come so fast. I betcha I got more den dat big square down dere to the courthouse full of 'em. I nurse 13 head of chillun in one family right here in dis town. You see, dat all I ever did have to do. Was learnt to do dat. De doctor tell me, say when you call to a 'oman, don' you never hesitate to go en help her en say you save dat baby en dat mother both. Dat what I is always try to do.*
>
> —Sara Brown, former slave
> (Howell, Donna, ed., *I Was a Slave: True Stories Told by Former Slave in the 1930s*, 29)

accessed February 2012). Midwifery is clearly identified as a crucial component of African American's survival of the institution of slavery.

Midwives were afforded mobility opportunities that were atypical for enslaved women. Their duties sometimes allowed them to move between plantations. Oftentimes, they were hired out to neighboring slave owners. Midwives' labor was viewed as an important service to her enslaver. Her major role was to oversee the safe and efficient reproduction of slaves, thus increasing his property and economic capital. This precarious position also left her vulnerable when enslaved infants did not survive.

The knowledge and mobility of midwives cultivated a sense of agency and was a means of resistance for midwives and those for whom she cared. Her holistic teachings of body and spirit empowered younger enslaved women to have a sense of ownership over their bodies. Midwives not only humanized the reproductive processes of black women and their bodies, but also created a nurturing environment for the enslaved community. The wisdom of midwives within enslaved communities was critical to the transmission of practical skills, sacred understandings as well as familial lineages and histories that foregrounded the spirit of resistance.

Rashida L. Harrison

See also Abortion; Childbirth; Childcare; Community; Contraception; Folk Medicine and Healing; Health, Disabilities and Soundness; Life Cycle; Mobility; Pregnancy; Resistance.

Suggested Reading

Sharla M. Fett, "Consciousness and Calling: African American Midwives at Work in the Antebellum South," in *New Studies in the History of American Slavery*, eds. E. E. Baptist and S. M. H. Camp (Athens: the University of Georgia Press, 2006), 65–86; Sharla M. Fett, *Working Cures: Healing, Health, and Power on Southern Slave Plantations* (Chapel Hill: University of North Carolina Press, 2007); Gertrude J. Fraser, *African American Midwifery in the South* (Cambridge: Harvard University Press, 1998) Marie Jenkins Schwartz, *Birthing a Slave: Motherhood and Medicine in the Antebellum South* (Cambridge: Harvard University Press, 2006).

Miscegenation

Miscegenation, a word rarely used by scholars or the general public in the twenty-first century, refers to the mixing of races, usually through interracial marriage or sex. In the nineteenth century, the term was synonymous with "amalgamation," a word that has completely faded out of use with regard to race.

Miscegenation created challenges to customs and law in the United States prior to the Civil War, particularly in the South, as race was legally and socially constructed as a binary, one was either black or white, and that status often was the crucial marker of slavery or freedom, citizen or property. On a more basic level, miscegenation often was a product of the power imbalance between whites and blacks. In 1643,

> There was a world of yellow people then. My mother said her sister had two yellow children; they were her master's.
>
> —Rachel Fairley, former bondwoman
> (WPA Slave Narrative Project, Arkansas Narratives, Volume 2, Part 2, 261)

Virginia passed a law establishing that African women would be taxed while English women would not, effectively making no distinction between female slaves and men in terms of productive capacity. This law was among the first to create a foundation of racial difference between whites and blacks and also discouraged free men from marrying African women as they would have to pay additional taxes. By 1662, Virginia law determined that the status of slave or free would follow the mother rather than the father. The implications of this law were profound as they assured that all children born of enslaved women would be enslaved for life regardless of the father's status. Essentially, this not only legalized the sexual exploitation

Photograph from 1863 showing Rebecca Huger, Charles Taylor, and Rosina Downs, fair-skinned emancipated slaves from New Orleans brought to the North by abolitionists. (Library of Congress.)

of enslaved women, but also made it profitable if a slaveholder and one of his bond-women had a child. Enslaved women often were presented with a difficult choice: give in to sexual desires of white men or face punishment.

While it is certainly questionable if a situation in which one person owns another could lead to a consensual relationship, some enslaved women found ways of using sexual relationships to their advantage. Slaveholders or overseers might promise to grant enslaved women something in return for sex, perhaps even free-dom, and these deals could be too enticing to turn down. Without a doubt, some enslaved women used these relationships to their advantage across the South from the colonial period through the Civil War. Unfortunately, the power imbalance between whites and blacks and the functions of slavery led to a trade in "fancy girls" or "fancy maids," light-skinned women and girls, usually of mixed race, who were essentially sold as concubines to wealthy slaveholders. This trade often centered in southern cities, particularly New Orleans, where planters might oper-ate two separate households. Fancy girls invariably sold at the highest prices.

Despite the level of exploitation fostered by the institution of slavery, miscege-nation in the nineteenth century was almost always characterized by racist assumptions that black women were insatiably promiscuous. While broader American or Southern society might have frowned upon white men for using slav-ery as a cover for sexual relationships, the unions were not uncommon nor did they go unnoticed. White men and women, however, placed the blame on black women. Often white men viewed black women as temptresses while white women saw them as little more than prostitutes. This racist logic excused married white men for straying from their wives and provided white women a scapegoat for mar-riages that were in trouble.

Additionally, this stereotypical and flawed presentation served to elevate the position of white women as morally superior to others while completely degrading black women. Of course, not all married white women simply accepted sexual relationships between their husbands and enslaved women. When these relation-ships were discovered, bondwomen could find themselves the victims of terrible retribution. In addition to punishing their husbands, white women could exact revenge on their rivals with physical and psychological torment. White wives might insist that their husbands' paramours be sold away, splitting families and communities. If children were involved, they might be singled out by plantation mistresses for especially brutal treatment since they were living reminders of their husbands' infidelity. Still others argued that the treatment of enslaved women elevated white women both from menial labor and from the sexual exploitation and desperation of white prostitutes in places like the North where free labor had taken hold.

By the antebellum period, miscegenation frequently was at the heart of both the abolitionist and proslavery movements. Though the two sides opposed one another on the morality of slavery, both usually shared assumptions about racial difference and both considered miscegenation a problem. Abolitionists could claim that enslaving African American women led to the corruption of morals among young white men who were encouraged by slavery to experiment on them sexually. Proslavery thinkers agreed that interracial sex could be a problem, but only because it could corrupt the "purity" of the white race. Many proslavery writers warned that mulattoes were doomed individuals—the "tragic mulatto"—an idea that made its way into works of fiction in the nineteenth century and film in the twentieth, as they would be shunned by both blacks and whites. Some contended that, like mules, mulattoes were sterile.

After the Civil War, white concerns about miscegenation remained, but took on a different character, as slavery no longer legally enforced a system that granted white men a monopoly on patriarchy. Interestingly, anxieties over miscegenation shifted from white male relationships with black women, to white women's interactions with black men. Without the legal power of slavery backing white manliness, extralegal actions, particularly lynching, was used to discourage such relationships between black men and white women. Well after the Thirteenth Amendment (1865) ended slavery, laws against interracial marriage remained in place across the country. In Alabama, men and women judged to be of different races living together either in marriage or more informally could be sentenced to the penitentiary for two to seven years. The U.S. Supreme Court unanimously ruled antimiscegenation laws unconstitutional in 1967 in a case known as *Loving vs. Virginia*.

Timothy R. Buckner

See also Civil War; Concubinage; Fancy Girls; Hemings, Sally; Laws; Plantation Mistresses; Punishment.

Suggested Reading

Martha Hodes, *White Women, Black Men: Illicit Sex in the Nineteenth Century South* (New Haven: Yale University Press, 1999); Deborah Gray White, *Ar'n't I a Woman?: Female Slaves in the Plantation South* (New York: W.W. Norton, 1985).

Mobility

Bondwomen experienced physical and geographic mobility in a significantly different manner than bondmen. In general, women had far fewer opportunities to move beyond the plantation area, where some enslaved men carried messages or accompanied slaveholders on travels. As a result, women had fewer opportunities to build intercommunity networks or learn about the surrounding landscape. Additionally, women's mobility was often constrained by childrearing or by the many physical disabilities caused by the conditions of enslavement. Nevertheless, bond-women found multiple and creative ways to practice resistance within their circles of mobility, as well as to exceed those boundaries by practicing valued professions such as midwifery and healing.

All bondpeople contended with legal, physical, and social limitations on their movement. As early as 1690, colonies such as Virginia enacted laws requiring bondpeople to carry written passes, or "tickets," whenever in public without a white companion. Such passes listed the names of the bondperson, his or her destination and purpose, and the amount of time covered by the pass. The pass system regulated bondpeople's movements in order to contain and repress both physical and political liberty. By the nineteenth century, informal militias known as slave patrols were established to police the movements of both free and enslaved African Americans. If a black person could not produce a pass, he or she could be legally killed, beaten, or jailed and then sold at auction. Patrols also entered slave cabins at night to make sure all residents were present, and some patrollers frequented churches, taverns, and other public gathering places hoping to catch bondpeople without a pass.

Passes were more often used by men, but bondwomen who were highly valued or trusted were sometimes given passes to travel, to obtain medical care, to run errands, and to attend multiplantation socials. These were almost always domestic rather than agricultural laborers as bondwomen with special skills were generally able to exercise the greatest geographic mobility. In particular, healers and midwives were often able to travel substantial distances both within and between plantations. Such arrangements, generally preferred by slave owners over the expensive option of bringing in white physicians for bondpeople's medical needs, also gave greater power to such women in terms of both geographic liberty and elevated communal status. This mobility allowed skilled bondwomen to visit friends and family on other plantations, carry news and messages, and help to plan escapes or revolts.

The use of passes to control bondpeople's mobility was a major factor in the legal prohibition of literacy for enslaved persons. Teaching a bondman to read or write was punishable by law in all slave states, and many narratives by enslaved persons describe the struggle to acquire literacy as central to both escape and the achievement of full personhood. Bondpeople with these forbidden skills often used them to subvert the system of controlled mobility. Harriet Jacobs, for example, provides both one of the most striking historical examples of constrained physical mobility for an enslaved woman—as she lived for seven years as a fugitive confined in a tiny attic crawlspace—and one of the most remarkable stories of empowered literacy—as she used letters to manipulate her previous owner and arrange for her children's freedom and eventually, her own.

Abroad marriages between bondpeople on different plantations were another important area of mobility. In accordance with both white and black gender ideals, men were usually the ones who traveled to neighboring plantations to visit wives and children. In their travels, men had more opportunities to familiarize themselves with the landscape, to acquire useful skills, and to come into contact with notions of freedom and citizenship, and many husbands brought this knowledge home so that women could also share the hope of a different life. For example, William Craft was able to use his travel and work experience to plan a successful escape with his wife, Ellen Craft. Their escape also depended on Ellen's ability to disguise herself as a white man, thus bypassing the need for a written ticket for William.

While abroad marriages did not generally provide significant geographic mobility for bondwomen, they did open a wider worldview which contributed not only to plans for escape, but also to the subtler forms of everyday resistance practiced by many enslaved women. These acts included feigned illness to avoid backbreaking work, keeping forbidden objects in slave quarters, spiritual and cultural practices, and sneaking out at night to meet for personal rendezvous or social gatherings. Perhaps, because of the greater likelihood of rebellion fostered by abroad marriages, some plantation owners forbade their bondpeople from marrying out.

Bondpeople's movements were also directly and physically limited through cruel forms of punishment such as the use of yokes and chains, the practice of mutilation, and brutal beatings, which often resulted in permanent physical impairment. In addition, bondwomen were physically debilitated by the demands of constant childbearing, with many women bearing 10 or 15 children before reaching middle age. Slaveholders sometimes relocated pregnant women from fieldwork into the plantation domestic sphere. There, they cared for infants or performed other less physically demanding, but still essential, roles in the plantation economy. These relocations further limited women's mobility, but also provided a less strenuous environment within which to practice everyday resistance.

Attachments to children were another major factor affecting bondwomen's mobility. Many women saw their children sold away under the brutal conditions of slavery, and those who kept their children close were naturally unwilling to leave them even to seek freedom. However, it was nearly impossible to escape and travel to the North with small children. On the other hand, the threat of a sale that would separate mothers from children was sometimes the impetus for daring attempts at escape. Responsibility for children, as well as the aforementioned factors, also led to greater numbers of enslaved men than women leaving southern plantations during and immediately after the Civil War to fight for the Union Army or travel to the North for freedom.

Finally, increased mobility was not always a positive factor in bondpeople's lives. Being sold to another slaveholder often involved separation from family and community even as it entailed geographic movement and a wider sphere of action. Additionally, enslaved people sold into the deeper South, "down the river," generally faced harsher physical conditions and diminished possibilities for escape. Contrary to slaveholder claims of devotion to their bondpeople, enslaved persons who were ill, disabled, or elderly were frequently sold or abandoned once they were perceived as useless. Due to the greater physical debilitation experienced by enslaved women, they were more likely to be abandoned or discarded in this manner. Fugitive slave narrator Lewis Clarke described a bondwoman who was punished by being forced to drag a log chain for several days. The woman never recovered and was unable to be sold since she was henceforth viewed as an idiot. This example demonstrates the intertwining of personal, social, and geographic mobility under the brutal conditions of enslavement.

Ellen Samuels

See also Health, Disabilities, and Soundness; Hiring Out; Labor, Skilled; Marriage, Abroad; Runaways.

Suggested Reading

Daina Ramey Berry, *Swing the Sickle for the Harvest is Ripe: Gender and Slavery in Antebellum Georgia* (Urbana & Chicago: University of Illinois Press, 2007); Stephanie Camp, *Closer to Freedom: Enslaved Women & Everyday Resistance in the Plantation South* (Chapel Hill: University of North Carolina Press, 2004); Sharla Fett, *Working Cures: Healing, Health, and Power on Southern Slave Plantations* (Chapel Hill: University of North Carolina Press, 2002); Harriet Jacobs, *Incidents in the Life of a Slave Girl* (Boston, 1861. Reprint Clayton, DE: Prestwick House, Inc., 2006).

Mortality and Life Expectancy

The percentage of children who die in the first year of life (infant mortality rate) and the average length of life (life expectancy at birth) are key health indicators of any society. By modern standards, the figures of the nineteenth century were horrific for all countries. As far as we can tell, in 1800 no country had a life expectancy above 38 years and yet with the exception of Swaziland (32 years), today even the poorest countries in Africa, Asia, and South America have a life expectancy above 38 years, and the average for the world as a whole is about 67 years.

Thus, there has been considerable progress over the past two centuries, but comparisons across countries and social groups for the nineteenth century are quite informative about the relative state of health for American slaves. In these comparisons, American bondpeople did poorly. The benchmark usually chosen is the free white population of the mid-nineteenth century, for which life expectancy was about 39 years and the infant mortality rate about 22 percent. The raw data needed to calculate mortality rates and life expectancy for slaves are thin, but that which is available from records kept by plantation owners suggests a life expectancy in the neighborhood of 25 years and an infant mortality rate of approximately 35 percent. If mortality rates are tabulated by age, it is clear that the excess mortality of slaves was concentrated among children, especially those below age 5. The mortality rates of white and slave adults were approximately equal. Therefore, most of the black-white difference in life expectancy of about 15 years is attributable to the poor health of enslaved children.

Why did enslaved children have such high mortality rates? The difficulties began *in utero*, or prior to birth. The ability of pregnant bondwomen to nourish the fetus depended upon the quality of nutrition received, which fluctuated by season of the year. It is useful to think of the human body as a biological machine, which consumes fuel (food) that it expends by breathing and keeping warm (basal metabolism), by work or physical activity, and by fighting infection or disease. For this reason, nutrition and mortality rates are highly connected. The diet improved in summer, when fresh produce was readily available, and continued at a high level through the autumn, when livestock was typically slaughtered, and went downhill thereafter until spring. The most demanding work, from which pregnant women had little relief, was in the plowing and planting season of mid-winter to early spring, and then again during the harvest of mid-August to late autumn. The most prevalent seasonal disease was malaria, which peaked from mid-summer to early autumn. Because the fetus is most vulnerable to nutritional conditions during the first trimester, unborn offspring endured a type of roulette whereby children conceived from mid-winter through mid-spring faced the harshest nutritional conditions (their mothers had the worst diet and the hardest work), which created congenital birth defects and high rates of neonatal mortality (the first month). Children commonly remained unnamed until they passed through this hazardous phase and had a plausible chance of living.

Infants who managed to live through the first month of life faced other obstacles to survival. Records kept by plantation owners on the amount of cotton picked by women relative to date of delivery are particularly informative. Work in the fields was so valuable that pregnant women continued to pick cotton at normal rates until a couple of weeks before delivery, and resumed at near-normal rates within a couple of months after delivery. These women must not have had time to breastfeed their children. Instead the infants were housed in nurseries tended by older women assisted by girls too young to work in the fields. During the day, the infants were fed pap or gruel from unwashed utensils, which were often contaminated by bacteria that caused diarrhea and other gastrointestinal diseases. The plantation records are rife with notes on infant deaths from these causes.

Numerous studies on health and mortality show a strong connection between nutritional status and mortality. Poorly nourished children have weakened immune systems and are more vulnerable to illness, and once sick, are more likely to die. This synergy between nutrition and survival operated for slave children who were old enough to eat solid food. Instructions to overseers and letters from plantation owners published in southern agricultural journals make clear that meat protein (the major source was pork) was largely reserved for working slaves. The young and the old were excluded from regular rations that consisted of one-half pound of pork per day. Parents could have shared meat rations with their children, if the rations were allocated to the family. Perhaps, one-half the southern plantations had this system and the others had central kitchens that prepared food. In either case, slave owners knew that meat protein was essential for hard work, and if parents chose to share, their work would have lagged in the field and they would have faced the lash or other punishment.

Mortality rates of slaves relative to whites declined dramatically after age 10, when most slaves began regular work in the field. The physical effort consumed more fuel (food), which would have increased mortality rates if nothing else changed. These new entrants into the work force had better diets, and especially more meat protein, which was important for a healthy immune system and physical growth. As discussed in the entry on diet and nutrition, this unusual pattern of slave health and physical growth was actually profitable for slave owners. Thus, the peculiar institution shaped many important aspects of slave life.

Richard H. Steckel

See also Diet and Nutrition; Food Preparation and Cooking; Health, Disabilities, and Soundness; Labor, Agricultural; Pregnancy.

Suggested Reading

Richard H. Steckel, "A Dreadful Childhood: The Excess Mortality of American Slaves," *Social Science History* 10 (1986), 427–65.

Motherhood

Enslaved women on the American mainland produced wealth in products and were strongly valued for their capabilities to reproduce and nurture. These women, however, were often denied extensive time to care for their own children and other members of their enslaved communities. Also, slaveholders sometimes sexually exploited enslaved women and treated them as commodities to furnish their profit and insure their economic status. Furthermore, the exploitation of enslaved women is counted among the primary devastations of slavery. All of these factors made motherhood a deeply complicated and often wrenching experience for enslaved women.

In both the North and South, enslaved women worked and lived under various oppressive conditions. Many factors such as geographic location, demography, social relations, religion, ethnicity, social hierarchy, and the type of work and service performed helped to define the particularities of their lives. Although their experiences were far from monolithic, many attitudes and practices directed toward enslaved women were buttressed by ideas about the supposed inferiority and subhuman status of people of African descent. The cruelty and insensitivity of slaveholders is most evident in their attitudes toward motherhood, particularly regarding the separation of enslaved families

When dey's hoein' cotton or corn, everybody has to keep up with de driver, not hurry so fast but workin' steady. Some de women what had suckin' babies left dem in de shade while dey worked. One time, a big, bald eagle flew away with it. De mama couldn't git it and we never heared of dat baby 'gain.

—Mattie Gilmore, former slave
(Howell, Donna, ed., *I Was a Slave: True Stories Told by Former Slave in the 1930s*, 28)

Woodcut by Alexander Anderson entitled "Slave scene." Illustration shows children and a woman carrying a wooden bucket on her head at a plantation. (Library of Congress.)

including, at times, the very offspring produced by enslaved women and slave-holders.

Yet, both enslaved women and slaveholders supported motherhood perhaps not always based on the same assumptions about its ideals and practices in relation to bondpeople. While white women were increasingly revered as wives and mothers, enslaved women were continuously viewed as producers of material wealth, both in people and things, and were given similar tasks as men. Some slaveholders, for benign reasons, worked to keep mothers and children together. Their efforts, however, were sometimes thwarted when enslaved women ran away or sought other avenues out of slavery. For example, many of these women sought or helped their families gain freedom through legal and other means, even when this meant physical separation from their relatives and friends.

Contradictions and Ambiguities

Slavery, perhaps, hindered more than encouraged maternal desires and aspirations in enslaved women. Some bondwomen became mothers without having any expressed desire to become mothers. Still, others welcomed motherhood and reared their children, at times, with the help of relatives and other members of enslaved communities, with hopes for a better future. Bondwomen's ideas about motherhood were also influenced by African-derived cultural principles and prac-tices such as those evident in protective rites relating to mothers and children.

Some enslaved women were troubled by the prospect of rearing enslaved chil-dren. A 1662 law passed in Virginia and practiced throughout slavery dictated that the condition of the child followed that of the mother. Thus, the thought of contrib-uting to the production of a cadre of unfree laborers may have led some enslaved women to practice preventive measures against pregnancy and other acts of resis-tance. These included abortion, running away with their children, and even engag-ing in desperate measures such as infanticide. For instance, in January 1856, bondwoman Margaret Garner escaped from Kentucky to Ohio with her family. When pursued, she tried to protect her children from a return to slavery. She killed her two-year old daughter, but was prevented from killing the other children. Garner's story inspired Toni Morrison's novel *Beloved* (1987) and the opera Margaret Garner produced in 2007.

Some enslaved women did not welcome childcare duties of either white or black children. Slaveholders' demeaning efforts to seek absolute control of enslaved people's lives, treating them as inferiors, dependents, and perpetual chil-dren, most likely provided more discouragements in the arena of motherhood and childcare. Yet, enslaved women may have felt empowered when they exercised decision-making power in matters relating to motherhood such as planning their own pregnancies and in managing family members.

Slaveholders prioritized enslaved women's reproduction over productive labor, yet their profit-making impulses demanded that bondwomen serve as productive laborers as well. These mothers were forced to adjust their childrearing activities to the economic needs of slavery as well as to the whims of individual slaveholders. For instance, the practice of weaning infants may have been affected more by the economic priorities of slaveholders than cultural factors within enslaved communities and the personal preferences of enslaved mothers. Slavery required these women to work long hours and they had to leave their babies early in the development stages as well as other young children who needed nurturing. Enslaved laborers had to adopt motherhood and childcare responsibilities to these considerations or confront authorities, as many did, to change these mostly unjust and exacting demands and expectations.

Enslaved women provided for their families by augmenting the provisions that slaveholders gave them. That these women supplemented dietary and other necessities through sales and exchanges, and by relying on gardening, hunting, and forging activities are all strong indications that supplies from slaveholders were often inadequate. Findings of dietary animal bones, seeds, tools, and other remains from archaeological excavations support the documentary data for interpreting enslaved people's efforts to provide for their own material needs.

Female-headed households, strong mothers, and archetypes of powerful grandmothers were evident during slavery and are still important factors for understanding African-descendant families in America today. African American men, on the other hand, have been presented, more or less, as passive or angry victims consumed by the overt powerlessness of their conditions for slavery worked to make them insignificant others in the general well-being of enslaved people. Moreover, their time and labor were appropriated for someone else's profit and welfare, and not for the security and prosperity of their families. Bondmen suffered as the laws and customs of slavery rendered them mostly defenseless to protect African American women and children from cruelties and exploitation, sexual and otherwise. All these situations profoundly impacted the nature of African American men's contributions and shaped the meaning of mothering under slavery.

Enslaved men, however, resisted their marginalization and engaged in many levels of involvement and influence in parenting, far beyond their willing or unwilling biological roles. Many of these men were indeed strong fathers or male figures. In fact, the nuclear family norm seldom best described bonded families' relational supports and networks. Enslaved people also had both relatives and non-relatives as part of household units, and parents and other caregivers raised enslaved children. These extended familial networks give credence to the African-derived saying that "it takes a whole village to raise a child."

The Social Landscape of Enslaved Motherhood

Some slaveholders planned the location of slave housing and other living arrangements in main houses to accommodate the requirements of nursing mothers and caretakers, all while maximizing the labor of the enslaved. Therefore, they generally considered the needs of pregnant and nursing women, but usually these concessions and indulgences were aimed at minimizing adverse impacts on their investment in human capital. On some plantations, slave quarters were grouped or placed close to each other so as to lessen the distance mothers would travel to leave children with day caregivers, who were usually elderly women and older children. Placing childcare in the hands of elderly women provided mixed blessings for enslaved communities, for these children probably learned important life lessons from these women who mothered them in the absence of their biological mothers. However, the aged and poor health conditions of some caregivers negated such benefits as they, too, needed nurturing and hardly endured duties to nurture infants and young children.

While childcaring arrangements close to work areas allowed enslaved mothers shorter travels, these women still spent considerable time traversing these distances. At times, they had to hurry to have more time to spend with their children as well as to stave off punishment for tardiness from overseers and other managers. Enslaved people with living areas near or within the slaveholder's residence, commonly called the "Big House," probably had less travel-distance for childcare duties and perhaps, had more opportunities for mothering their own children. Overall, work at the "Big House" seldom favored the enslaved, for some women had to leave their children behind at the quarters with siblings or other relatives. Apparently some mothers, in defiance, harbored children close to their work areas. Thus, they engaged in everyday forms of resistance prompted, more or less, by the exigencies of motherhood. In urban areas, enslaved women shared living spaces with, or lived in close proximity to, their legal owners. These living conditions generally resulted in reduced time off and less occasions for socializing than those times allowed or taken by other enslaved people, like occupants at slave quarters.

Bonds of Motherhood

Enslaved women officiated at the births of children, both white and black. They worked alongside white women in midwifery, wet-nursing, and other childrearing activities. Despite these intimate interactions, white women seldom identified with the sufferings of enslaved women, but generally worked to uphold their own superiority as designated by law and social practice. Children, too, were not immune in the relations of motherhood for they identified with others, free and enslaved, across racial lines based on activities in this arena.

Some slaveholders noted how helpful their enslaved nurses and caregivers were with children and adults and rewarded them for their service. The domesticity and management skills of enslaved women, particularly within white households, became variously associated with the "mammy" figure. Stock images of the "mammy" represented enslaved women as devoted to mothering white children and prioritizing the needs of slaveholders while ignoring children of their own and others in enslaved communities. Some portrayals complemented them with strength, imagining them as feisty to confront and sometimes successfully opposing slaveholders and other oppressors. Many of these renditions oversimplified and polarized the experiences of enslaved women. The reality of their lives only bordered on these representations, which fail to capture the complex nature of the interactions and negotiations these women enacted in motherhood and as they contributed to the resilience of their own communities.

However hard enslaved women worked and nurtured their own children, slaveholders complained and were dissatisfied with them. In fact, some slaveholders—including slaveholding women—treated bondwomen with cruelty and exacted difficult and excessive labor from them even when these workers were pregnant. A pregnant bondwoman was not exempted from punishments like whippings but, generally, special considerations were undertaken to protect the unborn child or children. One method was to prepare a hole to accommodate the mother's stomach in which she was placed prone and whipped. Punishments and other derogatory practices were enforced to keep enslaved people subdued while slaveholders exacted continuous economic and social benefits from them without concerns about compensation. For example, Fanny Moore recalled her mother praying for the protection of her children and when "de overseeah" put a "cowhide' on her "ole black back," her mother responded with a grin and said "I's saved. De Lawd done tell me . . . No matter how much yo' all done beat me an' my chillum [,] de Lawd will show me de way." She ended this act of resistance noting that "some day we nevah be slaves" (Slave Narratives: A Folk History of Slavery in the United States, www.gutenberg.org).

Health and Well-Being

Generally, enslaved women on the North American mainland had higher fertility rates than bondwomen in the Caribbean or South America. The enslaved population increased naturally especially after the abolition of the slave trade in 1808, thus allowing some slaveholders a continuous supply of laborers for their own enterprises and a steady supply of human chattels for a booming Domestic Slave Trade as well. Yet, mortality among enslaved children was a problem. Both bondpeople and slaveholders dealt with the deaths of children from illnesses like dysentery, typhoid, malaria, and smallpox, and yet the enslaved population was most adversely affected. Bondwomen fought, however, for the survival of their children and defined their own pathways within the confines of slavery, for example, preferring to treat their family members with their own folk remedies rather than prescribe to the conventional medicine dispensed through slaveholders and overseers.

Moreover, childbirths and child illness sometimes interfered with the daily operations of plantations. Production suffered when ill children could not work and mothers, midwives, and other healers were then called away to nurture these children back to health. The absence of these laborers impacted work routines and production because of the diverse and important roles women played on plantations and other slaveholdings. For instance, in addition to being regular field and domestic laborers, midwives also served as nurses, doctors, and morticians. They specialized in the treatment of women and children and promoted the health and well-being of the enslaved communities.

In spite of the apparent fertility of enslaved women, their health, too, concerned both slaveholders and enslaved people alike. Among the common stresses that women faced in raising children and caring for others were nutritional deficiencies, parasites, respiratory diseases, dysentery, childbirths, violence, and occupational hazards. Work situations often included inadequate rest-times and strenuous work loads during pregnancies; adverse living conditions, including drafty and pest-ridden cabins; and poor provisioning practices of most slaveholders and their management teams. These practices considerably affected the daily health and well-being of enslaved communities.

Slaveholders, too, interfered in the daily lives of enslaved women in many ways. They attempted to coordinate bondwomen's sexual unions, selected partners in marriages, ordered birth attendants, and directed the terms of childrearing by selling and bequeathing children and other relatives. They also directed physicians and other white health practitioners, including midwives, to oversee deliveries of babies, and to administer medicine to enslaved mothers and children. These interventions and controlling practices opened the way for more intrusive medical methods and increased the risks of illnesses for enslaved women and their children. Some mainstream medicinal practices displaced traditional methods that were less stressful and trusted by enslaved people. They also supplanted the roles of enslaved midwives and healers. The wishes of enslaved women were often ignored as doctors sought financial and career gains by providing services to slaveholders and working on their behalf. Throughout the nineteenth century, medical doctors increasingly developed skills in matters relating to the healthcare of women, including reproduction, by experimenting and practicing on enslaved women in inhumane ways (Schwartz, 2006).

Although enslaved people accepted remedies emanating from management, different aspects of mainstream medicines, and white doctors' treatments, they generally preferred healers from within their enslaved community and/or practiced self-healing. Enslaved women, for example, sought human and divine means to influence fertility and to ensure the health of children by using protective charms and amulets of beads, shells, and other materials; through prayers, naming practices, pharmaceutical potions, and plant and food remedies. Overall, enslaved people's search for health and well-being in motherhood and other areas of their lives had contradictory consequences. In many ways, they promoted individual and communal development but, at the same time, helped to sustain an enslaved labor force and the vicious cycle of exploitation.

Conclusion

Motherhood empowered some enslaved women to fight against the evils of slavery. These women opposed slaveholders' directives and supplanted them with their own orders and ways of doing things, negotiated feeding arrangements for their children, and fought for improvements in their working and living conditions. Enslaved women also worked to gain other concessions within the system like prolonging the time children would have before becoming full-time laborers, controlling information about illnesses, and helping others practice various levels of absenteeism, malingering, and other forms of resistance. Motherhood and child-caring activities, while fraught with traumatic and painful situations, were also interlaced with opportunities for women to play leading roles in building family and community.

Yvonne Edwards Ingram

See also Abortion; Breeding; Childbirth; Childcare; Community; Contraception; Diet and Nutrition; Domestic Slave Trade; Elderly Women; Family; Folk Medicine and Healing; Health, Disabilities, and Soundness; Infanticide; Laws; Life Cycle; Mammy Stereotype; Medical Experimentation and Surgery; Midwives; Pregnancy; Punishment; Representations; Resistance; Violence, Sexual.

Suggested Reading

Yvonne Edwards Ingram, "Medicating Slavery: Motherhood, Health Care, and Cultural Practices in the African Diaspora" (Doctoral Thesis. Ann Arbor, MI: UMI ProQuest Information and Learning Company, 2006); Marie Jenkins Schwartz, *Birthing a Slave: Motherhood and Medicine in the Antebellum South* (Cambridge: Harvard University Press, 2006); The Garner Fugitive Slave Case. http://www.motopera.org/mg_ed/educational/FugitiveSlaveCase.htm.

N

Naming

A name defines a person and, when honorable in nature, it is worn with pride because it symbolizes a person's heritage and identity. The concept of naming was inherently

controversial for enslaved people in the United States since, as they were sold and resold to numerous owners, they were subjected to the humiliating practice of continuous renaming.. While some enslaved people appear in the historical record as nameless souls, others have rather descriptive names.

Scholars who write about slave naming patterns identify several categories including African, animal, classical, biblical, place, and descriptive names. Evidence of African names appears in most New World regions; for example, women with African names included Aba, Fanny, Macaba, and Sabina. Scholars who have studied slave trade ship registries have catalogued the names of Igbo and other African ethnic groups. Bondwomen with biblical names include Mary, Mariah, Martha, Esther, and Leah. Enslaved women with classical names included Venus, Delia, and Celia to name a few. Place names for women included Charlotte, Virginia, America, Florida, and Savannah. Regardless of the naming category, it is clear that bondpeople cared about what they were called and, if given the opportunity, renamed themselves.

One can look at the naming of Phillis Wheatley as an example of how some slaveholders carelessly chose certain names for bondpeople. John Wheatley, the man who purchased young Phillis, was said to have named her after the schooner that brought her to America as a child to be sold into slavery. She also received her purchaser's last name. Even when she published her first book, *Poems on Various Subjects, Religious and Moral* (1786), she included after her byline a description of herself as the "Negro servant to Mr. John Wheatley of Boston, in New England." Though intellectually free and defiant in showing her writing gifts, Wheatley revealed that she could only claim total ownership of her gifts by acknowledging her "owner," the man who allowed her to literally "make a name for herself."

The renowned abolitionist Sojourner Truth, on the other hand, underscores the importance of a bondwoman choosing her own name and eschewing the one initially assigned to her by previous slaveholders. Formerly known as Isabella Baumfree, Sojourner Truth received her new name in a dream or vision after she was freed. That same dream unveiled to her a new life mission, which was to help emancipate bondpeople throughout America. In this case, her name became a signifier of a moral position and a revolutionary act she planned to undertake.

The presence or absence of names and surnames as well as if a surname was that of a current slaveholder's also suggests something of the contentiousness of slave naming practices and its gendered aspects. In slave records for New Jersey, women's names often are not even listed. Only the names of "Free Negroes" or "Negroes" who owned property and were taxed were included in the township of Upper Freehold New Jersey's municipal records. Wench Betty, who was allegedly murdered by her owner in this New Jersey township, is one of the few enslaved women listed who has a last name, but it is illegible in court records. Upon examining manumission and slave birth records, several township women are listed with a first name only and, where a surname for a bondman is listed, it is often the surname of the slave-owning family.

Certain geographic areas could also reflect distinctive slave naming patterns. Scholarship about the Ball plantations of South Carolina, for instance, catalogued the naming practices for children that followed routine patterns with names that included holidays such as Christmas and Easter; or names after months, such as March, January or June. But Gullah-speaking African Americans of the South Carolina and Georgia lowcountry had feminine, African names such as Fatimata, Hawa, Kadiatu. In some of these communities, children received an "English" name to use in public and a private name for use in the slave community. As with most slave communities, however, bondpeople in these regions also participated in naming children after relatives and fictive kin such as mothers, grandmothers, aunts, and other influential figures. In order to understand enslaved naming patterns, one must look to the written record and consider that some bondpeople changed or had their names changed often. Regardless of such inconsistencies, naming patterns were an important part of enslaved identity.

Sue Kozel

See also Life Cycle; Motherhood; Truth, Sojourner; Wench Betty, Murder of; Wheatley, Phillis.

Suggested Reading

Molefi Kete Asante. *The Book of African Names* (Trenton: Africa World Press Inc., 1991); Cheryl Ann Cody, "There Was No 'Absalom' on the Ball Plantations: Slave-Naming Practices in the South Carolina Low Country, 1720–1865," *The American Historical Review* 92, 3 (June 1987), 563–96; Harold Courlander, *A Treasury of Afro-American Folklore: The Oral Literature, Traditions, Recollections, Legends, Tales, Songs, Religious Beliefs,*

Customs, Sayings, and Humor of Peoples of African Descent in the Americas (New York: Marlowe, 1996); File 34201 (The) State v. Barcalow, Monmouth Murder. *Inquisitions + Arthur Barcalow with Testimony*. New Jersey State Archives, New Jersey Government, Trenton, New Jersey; Henry Louis Gates, Jr., *The Trials of Phillis Wheatley: America's First Black Poet and Her Encounters with the Founding Fathers* (New York: Basic Books, 2003); Joseph E. Holloway, "African-American Names," *Slavery in America*. http://www.slaveryinamerica.org/history/hs_es_names.htm; G. Ugo Nwokeji and David Eltis, "The Roots of the African Diaspora: Methodological Considerations in the Analysis of Names in the Liberated African Registers of Sierra Leone and Havana," *History in Africa* 29 (2002), 365–79; M. C. Onụkawa, "The Chi Concept in Igbo Gender Naming," *Africa: Journal of the International African Institute* 70, 1 (2000), 107–17; Phillis Wheately, *Poems on Various Subjects, Religions and Moral*, Reprint 1786 (New York: AMS Press, 1976); Deborah Gray White, *Ar'n't I a Woman?: Female Slaves in the Plantation South*, 2nd ed. (New York: W.W. Norton, 1999).

Narratives

Slave narratives by women occupy a special place in the long history of slave narration because enslaved women suffered additional burdens based on gender. As the emancipated slave Harriet Jacobs observed, those qualities of beauty and femininity long honored in all cultures became a special curse for enslaved women because these attributes often led to sexual abuse by slaveholders, overseers, and occasionally bondmen. Often, enslaved mothers resorted to infanticide, such as Sethe in Toni Morrison's fictional work, *Beloved*, which was based on the true history of Margaret Garner, an enslaved mother who was tried and convicted of the murder of her child. Slave narratives written by women describe many abusive episodes, highlighting the additional burdens that enslaved women were forced to bear.

In addition to the cruelties of the plantation owners and overseers, enslaved women were also frequently mistreated in their marriages and domestic relationships. They were held responsible for the bearing, rearing, and feeding of their children, whether through slave marriages (which were not recognized by law) or through illicit, forced relations with overseers, owners, or enslaved men other than their husbands. Moreover, enslaved women were often co-workers with their male counterparts, serving as field hands as well as domestic servants. After a full day's work in the field, bondwomen were also required to return to a primitive dwelling to mend clothes for her family, prepare meals from scratch, and tend to domestic chores before enjoying any rest or leisure.

Some examples of the cruel and unequal treatment of bondwomen appear in accounts written by men. Frederick Douglass, for example, was particularly sympathetic to the plight of bondwomen in his 1845 autobiography, *The Narrative of*

In addition to published narratives during the nineteenth century, fieldworkers from the Works Progress Administration interviewed former slaves in the 1930s, giving readers firsthand accounts of U.S. slavery. Pictured here is Patsy Moses of Waco, Texas, photographed on November 15, 1937, at age 74. (Library of Congress.)

the Life of Frederick Douglass, an American Slave. He graphically describes the flogging of Aunt Hester and the brutal beating of Hetty, a deformed and disabled bondwoman, as examples of the sadism of owners and overseers who exploited their power in relation to enslaved women even more than they were able to exert over bondmen. Slave mistresses, such as Sophie Auld, also appear powerless in relation to their husbands and the male characters in the narratives. However, it is the bondwoman's narrative itself that carries the most significant accounts of the perils of enslaved women. Some examples are Harriet Ann Jacobs's *Incidents in the Life of a Slave Girl* (1861), *The History of Mary Prince, a West Indian Slave* (1831), and *The Memoir of Old Elizabeth, a Coloured Woman* (1863).

These documents share a typology of slave narrative conventions, and they also have a double agenda of narrating the personal experience of a particular enslaved person while citing the horrors and brutality of antebellum slavery so that the dominant white culture would be forced to grant emancipation. This "double vision" governs most slave narratives, regardless of gender. Most antebellum slave narratives also carry the providential metaphor as an informing structural principle. The guidance and salvation of many enslaved people were credited to God's Providence as much as to the individual's ingenuity or courage. As literature, the slave narratives recapitulate elements of earlier spiritual autobiographies, illustrating the experience of the narrator through parallels to the ancient Israelites, who were persecuted and enslaved by the Egyptians. Both groups looked forward to a better life in the next world. For example, Negro spirituals—the folk songs of slave culture—were imbued with these Biblical parallels. The Israelite deliverance from suffering in Egypt was perceived to be a foreshadowing of God's deliverance of southern bondpeople from a more contemporary, but equally merciless ordeal. "Crossing over Jordan," "We are Climbing Jacob's Ladder," and "Swing Low, Sweet Chariot" reinforced the conviction that somehow

God would provide deliverance and that the rewards of a better everlasting life would await the faithful believer.

Because the conventions of slave narratives were widely appropriated by slave narrators, veracity and authenticity became a persistent problem. Introductions were frequently penned by well-recognized white supporters, including leading abolitionists such as William Lloyd Garrison and Lydia Maria Child, to counter accusations of fabrication and misrepresentation that were often raised by reviewers. "Written by Himself" or "Written by Herself" thus accompanies many slave narrative titles, as in the cases of Douglass and Jacobs. Ironically, it is the very conventions of slave narration that often determine the effectiveness of the rhetorical strategies employed by an individual author. Some slave narratives were "ghostwritten" by people sympathetic to the abolitionist cause, but it must be remembered that all slaves were forbidden to learn to read or write by most southern slaveholding state statutes. Thus, the term has a different meaning from its current usage. As William Andrews observed, "the fact that both the narratives of Prince and Jackson were ghostwritten by persons sympathetic to the abolitionist cause requires us to remember that the power to write their own stories as they saw fit did not come to female slaves as early as it did to male slaves" (Andrews 1988, xxxiv).

Most importantly, these narratives share conventions of storytelling that form the core of their rhetorical strategies for terminating the "peculiar institution" of slavery. Much like slave narratives written by men, these works employed a number of similar literary devices in their attempts to successfully and faithfully describe the experience of enforced servitude. These rhetorical devices were employed not to render all slave narratives alike; rather, they were a formula for successful narration of the imprisoned slave's experience and the successful recuperation of that experience by writing the self into being. In most of the antebellum accounts, the following characteristics appear regularly:

1. a journey motif, in which the narrator's personal experience was metaphorically paralleled by the struggle for freedom;

2. a sense of the narrator's isolation in a hostile environment, which imposes barriers that must be crossed in the journey to freedom such as slave laws, educational limitations, and prohibitions against literacy;

3. the presence of multiple voices as the adult narrator recapitulates earlier experiences in slavery and then provides commentary, both moral and interpretative, from a contemporary retrospective viewpoint;

4. several prominent episodes along the way during which transformations occur, such as gaining an awareness of the importance of literacy to the achievement of freedom;

5. a litany of the horrors of slavery, including flogging and auction scenes. (Jacob's account includes a particularly horrible and dramatic version of the auction scene, in which seven children are taken, one by one, away from a mother, who later is reduced to madness by her ordeal.);

6. the narrative movement of a stressful pursuit, in which predator and prey are always closely allied in an intense chase, closely paralleling the predator/ prey configuration found in sentimental novels, which the northern white female readership of these slave narratives would have been quite familiar;

7. an emphasis on the slave's family, including attempts to establish a primitive genealogy, where possible. Often for the slave, this effort was fruitless because most slaves were not aware of their parents. Douglass, a mulatto product of an enslaved mother and a white father, never discovered his father's true identity and yet the opening paragraph of his 1845 narrative contains a moving account of his efforts to establish his genealogy. Similarly, Jacobs has her alter ego, Linda Brent, establish clearly the relations between herself, her grandmother, and her children by Mr. Sands. Family ties were especially important for Jacobs and other female slave narrators such as Mary Prince and the maintenance of family relationships is a dominant theme in these narratives.

These rhetorical strategies and conventions are commonly shared; however, they should not mean that the introducers were either authors or editors, or that the abolitionists created these figures and their narratives as a means to the end of terminating slavery. Rather, the slave narrators became instruments of abolitionist rhetoric and communication, just as William Lloyd Garrison's anti-slavery newspaper, *The Liberator* (1831–1865), gave voice to the abolitionist crusade. Slave narratives are the "insider's voice" in the abolitionist cause for freedom. Harriet Beecher Stowe, whose fictional work *Uncle Tom's Cabin* (1852) had sold nearly five million copies by 1861, along with Ralph Waldo Emerson, Henry David Thoreau, Walt Whitman, and John Greenleaf Whittier were literary voices opposing slavery.

The "Abolitionist Crusade" (1831–1865) was led by political abolitionists such as William Lloyd Garrison, Wendell Phillips, Lydia Maria Child, and Charles Sumner, all white opponents of the "peculiar institution." However, the slave narrators provided antebellum readers with a unique perspective for examining American culture in its formative stages. When many of these documents were written, beneath the long shadow of the *Declaration of Independence* and its charter pronouncement that "all men are created equal," the United States was barely half a century old. As Frederick Douglass would remind his audience in "What to the Slave is the Fourth of July" (1852), the short life of the United States was "only at the beginning of your national career" and already it was mired down in philosophical inconsistencies that threatened its future. Like many of the literary opponents of slavery, Douglass was also keenly sensitive to the rights of women in the United States—not only enslaved women, but the disenfranchised women of European American society. Reform movements were active during the nineteenth century and American slave-women narrators were pressing both the abolition of slavery as an institution and the emancipation of women who were also viewed as slaves. The causes of both were fused in the female slave narrative.

For example, women and slaves were often conflated in the reform literature of the nineteenth century. And a female slave narrative, such as the Jacobs's or Prince's accounts, would intensify this rhetorical strategy to render a narrative specifically designed to appeal to northern white women and mothers. Mary Boykin Chesnut, the wife of a prominent southern politician, viewed marriage itself as slavery: "All married women, all children and girls who live in their father's house, are slaves." The Jacobs's and Prince's slave narratives provide many examples that reinforce this critical observation. And Stowe describes the status of women as slaves in sections of *Uncle Tom's Cabin*, especially in Chapter IX. She describes a scene in which Senator and Mary Bird argue vigorously about the 1850 Fugitive Slave Law, for which the senator has recently voted. She also develops the character of Uncle Tom to exhibit those qualities of nurturing and strength associated with the slave mother. Stowe's novel and Jacobs's narrative both show the redemptive power, integrity, and strength of enslaved women and the feminized central character, Uncle Tom.

Jacobs's *Incidents in the Life of a Slave Girl* is a slave narrative written several years before its publication, just prior to the outbreak of the Civil War. It is technically a "sentimental novel" with fictional names thinly disguising the real persons they represent. However, its powerful narrative voices (there are multiple voices throughout) clearly show the author's consistent dedication to the end of chattel slavery, especially the brutal treatment of bondwomen, through the rhetorical strategy of combining the sermonic voice of direct address to the reader with a graphic tale of brutality and sexual abuse. As in Samuel Richardson's *Clarissa* (1748) and *Pamela* (1740) or in Charlotte Bronte's *Jane Eyre* (1847), the sentimental theme of a young, attractive woman being intensely pursued by an older, lecherous male predator is developed within the context of a narrative of spiritual and moral growth. Throughout Jacobs's account, the sanctified figure of the grandmother looms large, not only as a nurturing presence and a safe haven from Dr. Flint, but also as a moral force and a guiding symbol of integrity. As with most slave narratives, male and female, the power of the enslaved mother is present in both Jacobs's and Prince's accounts. As William Andrews observes,

> as early as Prince's story, [1831,] female slave narrators portrayed the enslaved black woman as a person of near indomitable dedication to the

highest principles of human dignity and individual freedom . . . Thus the slave mother, or some comparable black maternal figure, more than the female narrator herself, plays the hero's role in most early black women's autobiographies. The mother inspires within her daughter the hope of freedom and provides an example of a woman who will not give in to despair. Sometimes the mother [or grandmother] furnishes material as well as moral assistance to her daughter, when she strikes for freedom (Andrews 1988, xxx).

Generally, the slave-as-mother looms large in these accounts, and grandmothers are especially sanctified for qualities of integrity, endurance, and moral support. These maternal figures in women's slave narratives serve the dual purpose of relating the horrors of slavery to free, predominately female readers and appealing directly to the mothers in the readership, who would naturally sympathize with the anguish of enslaved mothers who lost their children at slave auctions, a particularly brutal feature of these stories.

For example, both Jacobs and Prince show how slavery violated the sacred bonds of family. Jacobs provides a searing example in a chapter entitled "The Slave's New Year's Day." She writes,

Hiring-day at the south takes place on the first of January. On the 2nd, the slaves are expected to go to their new masters. On a farm, they work until the corn and cotton are laid. They then have two holidays. Some masters give them a good dinner under the trees. This over, they work until Christmas eve . . . then comes New Year's Eve; and they gather together their little alls, or more properly speaking, their little nothings, and wait anxiously for the dawning of day. At the appointed hour, the grounds are thronged with men, women, and children, waiting, like criminals, to hear their doom pronounced (Jacobs, Chapter III).

In the Mary Prince account, an idyllic childhood with her immediate family was abruptly divided by an auction and her account of this event is memorable:

At length the vendue master who was to offer us like sheep or cattle, arrived, and asked my mother which was the eldest . . . He took me by the hand and led me out into the middle of the street, and, turning me slowly around, exposed me to the view of those who attended the vendue. I was soon surrounded by strange men, who examined and handled me in the same manner that a butcher would a calf or a lamb he was about to purchase . . . I was then put up for sale . . . I then saw my sisters led forth, and sold to different owners; so that we had not the sad satisfaction of being partners in bondage. When the sale was over, my mother hugged and kissed us, and mourned over us, begging of us to keep up a good heart, and to do our duty to our new masters. It was a sad parting; one went one way, one another, and out poor mammy went home with nothing (Andrews 1988, 233).

In Jacobs's account, a slave auction results in the suicidal madness of an enslaved mother, who had all of her children taken from her in a single auction. Jacobs explains:

On one of these sale days, I saw a mother lead seven children to an auction block. She knew that some of them would be taken from her, but they took all. The children were sold to a slave-trader, and their mother was bought by a man in her own town. Before night, her children were all far away. She begged the trader to tell her where he intended to take them; this he refused to do. How could he, when he knew he would sell them, one by one, whichever he could command the highest price? I met that mother in the street, and her wild, haggard face lives today in my mind. She wrung her hands in anguish and exclaimed, "Gone!! All gone!! Why don't God kill me?" I had no words wherewith to comfort her (Jacobs, Chapter III).

The thirty years that separate the Prince's and Jacobs's narratives do not erase the relation of common experience, one in the United States and one in the West Indies. In standard autobiographies, the primary characteristic or theme is that of self-definition. But in these two slave accounts, the definition of the persona is intrinsically linked to the narrator's impulse toward personal freedom. This conflation of the desire for freedom and the identity of the subject of the autobiography pervade all slave narratives; indeed, the power of this central theme governs one of the most complex paradoxes in all slave narration. There is powerful irony in slave narratives because the slave narrator is compelled to recall her former state, even a former self, just as she has reached that "promised land" of freedom and has achieved that purpose toward which the entire objective of the experience has been directed. Thus, "[t]he slave, happily ceasing to be a slave, describes his or her slave self to preserve it just as it is about to cease to be a condition under which the self lives" (Niemtzow 1982, 96). This persona is quite different from other contemporary autobiographical figures, such as Benjamin Franklin (who assumes several different personae) in *The Autobiography of Benjamin Franklin* (1791, English trans., 1793), one of the most popular autobiographies of the early nineteenth century. Slave narratives are the life accounts of victims, who achieve the status of the heroic by overcoming, enduring, and often triumphing over unimaginable circumstances.

After the Civil War and the passage of the Thirteenth Amendment to the United States Constitution in 1865, which granted freedom to the slaves, other female slave narratives appeared, notably *From the Darkness Cometh the Light, or*

Struggles for Freedom (1891) by Lucy A. Delaney; *A Slave Girl's Story* (1898) by Kate Drumgoold; *Memories of Childhood's Slavery Days* (1909) by Annie L. Burton; and *The Story of Mattie J. Jackson* (1866). Like the antebellum female slave narratives, these accounts also exhibit those conventions and rhetorical strategies designed to bring the horrors of slavery to the attention of the reading public both in the United States and in Great Britain. There is less emphasis on the rhetoric of abolition and more on the brutal horrors of slavery as an American institution; however, the conventions and typology of the narratives remain much the same.

Mason Lowance, Jr.

See also Abolitionism; Breeding; Delaney, Lucy A.; Domestic Slave Trade; Education; Elderly Women; Emancipation; Family; Garner, Margaret; Health, Disabilities, and Soundness; Infanticide; Jacobs, Harriet; Laws; Literacy; Motherhood; Overseers; Punishment; Violence, Sexual.

Suggested Reading

William L. Andrews, ed., *Six Women's Slave Narratives* (New York: Oxford University Press, 1988); Annette Niemtzow, "The Problematic of Self in Autobiography: The Example of the Slave Narrative," in *The Art of Slave Narrative: Original Essays in Criticism and Theory*, eds. John Sekera and Darwin T. Turner (Macomb: Western Illinois University, 1982).

North, The

Enslaved African women were introduced to the northern colonies of mainland North America beginning in the early seventeenth century. As a result, northern women labored as bondpeople and bore children primarily during the colonial era. Slavery was abolished gradually in the North following the American Revolution. New Jersey was the last northern state to completely abolish slavery in 1847. Although Delaware was originally part of Pennsylvania, once separated in the early eighteenth century, it became a border colony like Maryland, which did not abolish slavery until after the Civil War. Consequently, of the 13 original colonies, the following seven jurisdictions were considered the northern colonies: Massachusetts, New Hampshire, Connecticut, and Rhode Island in New England; New York, New Jersey, and Pennsylvania in the middle colonies. Enslaved women in the North were important to the development of the diversified colonial economy, the resistance against slavery, and the cultural survival of African-born and Creole bondpeople (those born in America).

By the 1690s, the black female population totaled over 4,000, with half that number living in New York. The state-by-state breakdown was as follows: Massachusetts (400), Connecticut (200), Rhode Island (250), New Hampshire (100), and

New York (2,170). The numbers of enslaved women began to escalate in the early 1700s, with New Jersey (2,581) and Pennsylvania (circa 3,000) totaling nearly 6,000 together.

During the early colonial era, gender and generational imbalances created intolerable conditions for the enslaved women, which inhibited healthy family life and reproduction. Although the scarcity of enslaved women—one for every two men—appeared to give women better chances to establish marital relations, poor health and overwork resulted in African-born women having few children and at older ages. A generation later, Creole enslaved women in the northern colonies bore more children and at younger ages than their African-born mothers. Natural increase among black women did not appear to rise until the second and third decades of the eighteenth century. By this time, the male/female ratio was about even and the enslaved population increased significantly along with new imports arriving from English Caribbean colonies.

Silvia Dubois. Portrait from her book, *Silvia Dubois, (now 116 years old): a biografy of the slav who whipt her mistress and gand her fredom.* (Schomburg Center for Research in Black Culture/New York Public Library.)

On the eve of the Revolution, there were over 15,000 black women living in the seven northern colonies. Although some of them had gained freedom through manumission, self-purchase, or purchase by another family member, the vast majority was enslaved and there were more free black males than females in the region. One explanation came from Venture Smith, an African-born former bondperson from Rhode Island. He purchased himself, his two sons, and another bondman before his pregnant wife Meg, from whom he had been separated when their daughter and eldest child was one month in age. Smith finally purchased his daughter Hannah's freedom in 1775, after redeeming his wife from slavery and two more enslaved men. Smith was motivated to redeem enslaved men for economic reasons rather than familial ones, because he needed males to labor for him.

Unlike the southern colonies, where large farms and plantations grew staple crops, a diversified economy characterized the North. In the former Dutch colony of New Amsterdam, large plantations developed from the area known as the borough of the Bronx in New York City north throughout the Hudson River valley. Dutch landowners used bondpeople, both men and women, to plant and harvest wheat and other staple crops. In the New England colonies, as well as in New York and other middle colonies, women labored in the fields part-time by plowing, planting vegetables, and gathering crops. However, their primary tasks were found in dairy and cattle raising industries. Enslaved women also served as mill workers, like Isabella (Sojourner Truth), who spoke Dutch and worked in a gristmill in Ulster County, New York. Most enslaved women, like Isabella, also performed domestic work, cooking, cleaning, butchering animals, white washing, waiting tables in taverns, nursing and rearing their owners' children.

Silvia Dubois was an example of a woman who performed a variety of tasks while working alongside her mother, Dorcas Compton. Dubois was born in New Jersey in 1768. Working conditions were grueling and their respective owners were cruel. The man who owned Dorcas forced her to go back to work three days after she had delivered a child and beat her because she could not perform proficiently. The woman who owned Sylvia beat her often for no apparent reason. Sylvia labored in both New Jersey and Pennsylvania as a farm worker, ferryman, and a domestic in a tavern.

In cities such as New York, Boston, and Philadelphia, skilled enslaved women became proficient in spinning, knitting, and weaving, thus rivaling white women in needle trades. In rural areas, enslaved women often lived directly in households with their parents or their husbands, but this was rarely the case in urban areas, where they were separated from their primary family members and often suffered emotionally because of isolation and over work.

Enslaved women in northern colonies resisted the unhealthy working conditions and isolation under which they worked. Several acts of rebellion, including arson and running away, occurred especially in New York, the colony with the largest enslaved population by the eighteenth century. During the 1708 and 1712 New York City slave revolts, women were reported to be the main arsonists. In 1793 at Albany, Bet and Deane were apprehended as they attempted to set fire to buildings in the city. Both women were hanged, as was their male accomplice. Runaway attempts were also reported. For example, in 1758 on the Van Cortland plantation of Westchester County, Bridget conspired with six other enslaved females to runaway beyond the British lines, but they were caught and punished. The most famous of New York enslaved women who escaped from her owner was Isabella, who once she gained her freedom changed her name to Sojourner Truth. Born in 1796, the year before gradual emancipation was legislated in the state, Truth would have been one of the last women emancipated by the law in 1827. By July 4, 1827, Truth should have been freed after she completed spinning the wool and the heavy harvesting. However, her owner had murdered an enslaved male who indicated that he was leaving the farm after the harvest because he was legally free. The murder intimidated the other illegally enslaved workers, but Truth decided to sneak away with her infant, especially after her owner sold her son outside of the state illegally. She sought asylum and received it, then went to court and successfully gained the release of her son.

Other enslaved women had used the courts to gain freedom. In 1766, Jenny Slew brought suit successfully against her Massachusetts owner. The court awarded her damages as well as her freedom. However, the case was an individual one, which did not bring freedom for all those enslaved, especially women. Enslaved men in militias were more likely to gain freedom when they brought freedom suits after fighting in the Continental Army. However, this would change when in 1781 Elizabeth Freeman, known as Mum Bett, sued successfully for her freedom in Massachusetts. New York-born in 1744, Mum Bett was sold and toiled in Sheffield, Massachusetts. With the help of Theodore Sedgewick, she was able to obtain legal counsel and filed suit against her owner for illegally detaining her and a male slave named Brom. Freeman's lawyer based his argument on a newly enacted 1780 state constitution provision that declared that all persons were born free and equal. The Freeman and Brom lawsuit paved the way for ending slavery in Massachusetts.

Despite the harsh environment, enslaved black women provided not only kinship ties for their children and extended family, but passed customs and language through communal networks that spanned two or three generations by the eighteenth century. Some excelled in storytelling and in the arts. For example, the illiterate Lucy Terry (Prince) composed a poem, "Bars Fight," describing the Indian raid she witnessed at Deerfield, Massachusetts in 1746. The poem has been called the most accurate account of the raid. Terry and others transmitted the poem orally until it was first published in 1855. African-born, Terry was captured as a child, sold in Bristol, England, and then transported to Rhode Island for sale again. She not only composed the poem, but, once free, also advocated for black rights. For example, Terry fought for her son to attend the Free School that did not accept black children; because of Terry's efforts, her son was eventually admitted.

The most well-known enslaved female writer in the North was Phillis Wheatley, who was a Revolutionary War era poet. She became the first black female to write a book of poetry, *Poems on Various Subjects, Religious and Moral*, which was published in 1773. Like Lucy Terry, Phillis was a child when she was captured in West Africa. She was sold in Boston to the Wheatleys, whose daughter noticed Phillis trying to write and taught her how to read the Bible. As did Lucy Terry (Prince), Phillis Wheatley married. However, a life of poverty ensued, as her former owner and benefactor died and apparently her husband, John Peters, could not take care of his wife and children, all of whom perished. Phillis died at the age of thirty, unattended in Boston shortly after the birth of her third child. Both Lucy Terry (Prince) and Phillis Wheatley (Peters) left legacies as poets, who, despite enslavement, made a way to express creative talent and to become free.

For two hundred years enslaved women in the northern colonies of North America endured harsh climates, hard work, physical and emotional abuse, but managed to adjust to slavery in order to make a way for themselves, their children, and their communities. Performing diverse tasks may very well have enabled them to become proficient in the many ways that enabled survival for generations to come. Despite the many casualties, survivors carried the culture from generation to generation, as their foremothers had done.

Rosalyn Terborg-Penn

See also African and African-born Women; Childbirth; Childcare; Community; Creoles; Domestic Slave Trade; Economy; Female Slave Network; Freeman, Elizabeth; Labor, Agricultural; Labor, Nongricultural; Labor, Skilled; Laws; Literacy; Manumission; Pregnancy; Prince, Lucy Terry; Punishment; Resistance; Runaways; Seamstress Work; Wheatley, Phyllis.

Suggested Reading

Vincent Carretta, ed., Unchained *Voices: An Anthology of Black Authors in the English-Speaking World of the 18th Century* (Lexington: The University Press of Kentucky, 1996); Sylvia Dubois, *A Biography of a Slav Who Whipt Her Mistres and Gand Her Freedom*, Jared C. Lobdell, ed. (New York: Oxford University Press, 1988); John Hope Franklin and Alfred A. Moss, *From Slavery to Freedom: A History of African Americans*, 8th ed. (New York: McGraw Hill, 2000); Benjamin Quarles, *The Negro in the Making of America* (New York: Simon and Schuster, 1996); Brenda Stevenson, "Slavery," in *Black Women in America*, 2nd ed., vol. 3 (New York: Oxford University Press, 2005): 135–50; Sojourner Truth, *Narrative of Sojourner Truth*, Margaret Washington, ed. (New York: Vintage Books, 1993); A. J. Williams-Myers, *A Portrait of Eve: Towards a Social History of Black Women in the Hudson River Valley* (New Paltz, NY: Center for The Study of the African Presence in the Hudson River Valley, 1987).

O

Overseers

One of the most important relationships in an enslaved woman's life was that which she developed with the plantation overseer, the white manager of the plantation. Since the vast majority of bondwomen worked as agricultural laborers under the watchful eye of the white male manager hired by their owners, this figure proved to be a central and often menacing influence in their lives. Theirs was a relationship fraught with tension from the start, not only because of the relative power of the overseer and vulnerability of the enslaved woman, but also because of the slaveholder's contradictory expectations for both a lucrative harvest and happy, healthy bondpeople. The particulars of each relationship between an enslaved woman and an overseer depended on a variety of factors such as the personalities of the individuals in question, as well as the historical, geographical, economical, and social circumstances in which they lived and worked. However, there are some general themes that characterize the interaction of overseers and bondwomen over time and place, all of which reveal the ways in which the former loomed heavily over the lives of the latter.

Southern slaveholders realized that their economic success was dependent on the productive labor of the human beings whom they held in bondage. As such, slave management was one of their priorities. Those owners who put 30 or more bondpeople to work on a single plantation most often relied on the assistance of an overseer who administered the day-to-day operation of the business. Usually from a family of modest or poor financial standing, uneducated, and generally stereotyped as a coarse and cruel outsider by slaveholders and bondpeople alike, the overseer nonetheless exerted considerable power in both the fields and the slave quarter. Bondwomen, the majority of whom spent the entirety of their lives in these two spaces, resisted but could rarely escape the influence of this often feared and usually despised agent of the slave system.

Denied the consideration given white women by white men, enslaved women were typically sent to the fields with their male counterparts to cultivate the crops that would fatten the wallets of their owners. Like bondsmen, they worked hard in the frigid cold, rain, and boiling sun, often at the expense of their health. Pushing them to exert themselves even further was the overseer who rode through the fields often with whip in hand on the lookout for loafers. Since the planter held him responsible for the quality and quantity of the crop, the overseer was inclined to push bondpeople to their limits. He did so occasionally with the promise and distribution of rewards, but more commonly he used verbal threats and physical violence. Some enslaved women followed the orders and endured the intimidation and beatings of overseers for fear of the consequences were they to do otherwise. However, many bondwomen resisted the pace and duration of the workday set by the overseer, as well as his means of enforcement. They did so in a variety of ways.

Enslaved women frequently challenged the overseer's ability to control their labor by exercising methods of resistance common to both men and women, such as breaking agricultural implements, feigning sickness, speeding up their pace when the overseer was present, and slowing down when he was not. Some took more extreme measures. The historical record reveals numerous instances in which bondwomen retaliated against an overseer's physical beatings in kind and, on rare occasions, even conspired with enslaved men to commit murder. And while it was usually more difficult for them to do so because of their responsibility for young children, bondwomen, like bondmen, attempted to remove themselves from the overseer's influence by running away temporarily or permanently.

Despite the similarities between men and women's resistance to their authority in the field, overseers often complained that enslaved women were more difficult to control than enslaved men. One reason for this may have been that bondwomen, who were often consigned to work in sex-segregated gangs, sometimes banded together to resist the authority of overseers. Another reason may be that enslaved women requested or demanded that their loads be lightened during pregnancy and early maternity, conditions in which most enslaved women labored for much of their lives. While many overseers kept their sights on the bottom line and ignored the appeals of pregnant bondwomen and new mothers, thereby risking the health of the women and their babies, their employers had much to gain financially by the natural reproduction of their labor force. As such, many overseers were compelled to heed the demands of the women whom they futilely tried to control. Yet, while pregnancy may have given enslaved women a modicum of power over their labor and the man charged with regulating it, their very womanhood made them vulnerable to a more personal form of violation at the hands of the overseer.

Black women, who were assumed by the larger society to be sexually promiscuous, always faced the threat of sexual abuse on the plantations where they lived in bondage. The perpetrators were usually male slaveholders, their kin, and overseers. While many enslaved women escaped being the victims of rape and many white men refused to engage in such acts of violence, the evidence that such offenses occurred frequently on southern plantations was ever present, particularly in the presence of the many mixed-race children who were born to bondwomen each year. Those women who worked in the fields under the supervision of overseers were especially vulnerable to attack by men who saw access to the bodies of bondwomen as one of their privileges and as a potent expression of their power over them. Bondwomen whose husbands lived on distant plantations were put at increased risk of sexual exploitation, for the absence of one's spouse made it more convenient for a vicious overseer to exercise his assumed prerogative. Yet, even women who lived with their husbands were not safe from sexual abuse. While enslaved husbands presented an obstacle to a potential rapist, more often than not bondmen were reminded of their lack of power in the slave system when overseers punished them, often severely, for attempting to protect their wives.

When the efforts of enslaved women and their husbands to physically resist or prevent a rape proved unsuccessful, it was common for enslaved women to appeal to their owners for help. While it was not unusual for male slaveholders to reprimand or dismiss overseers who violated their female property, the appeals of enslaved women usually garnered the most sympathy from plantation mistresses. While the latter were unlikely to rebuke their husbands or sons for raping bondwomen (in fact, many slaveholding women directed their anger at the victims), they often did not hesitate to intervene on behalf of enslaved women who were attacked by overseers. Typically seeing these hired men as crude inferiors, white women were known to personally fire them or to exercise their socially prescribed moral authority on their husbands by encouraging them to discipline or dismiss the offending employee.

In the fields and the quarters, enslaved women interacted with overseers in a daily battle of push and pull, as both sought to protect their interests and assert their power in the face of a system that subjected both parties to the will of the slaveholder. Yet in an effort to depict themselves as benevolent lords, slaveholders frequently delegated the most unpleasant tasks of slaveholding, namely supervision and discipline, to overseers. As such, these men came to best represent the evils of slavery to those who suffered its injustices. Bondwomen fought daily against these agents of the slave system to defend not only their autonomy in the fields, but also their bodies, their families, and their dignity.

Nikki Berg Burin

See also Domestic Slave Trade; Female Slave Network; Gender Conventions; Health, Disabilities, and Soundness; Jezebel Stereotype; Labor, Agricultural; Marriage, Abroad; Owners; Plantation Mistresses; Pregnancy; Punishment; Resistance; Runaways; Slave Quarters, Life in; Violence, Sexual.

Suggested Reading

Elizabeth Fox-Genovese, *Within the Plantation Household: Black and White Women of the Old South* (Chapel Hill and London: University of North Carolina Press, 1988); William Kauffman Scarborough, *The Overseer: Plantation Management in the Old South* (Baton

Rouge: Louisiana State University Press, 1966); Leslie A. Schwalm, *A Hard Fight for We: Women's Transition from Slavery to Freedom in South Carolina* (Urbana and Chicago: University of Illinois Press, 1997); Brenda E. Stevenson, *Life in Black and White: Family and Community in the Slave South* (New York and Oxford: Oxford University Press, 1996); Marli F. Weiner, *Mistresses and Slaves: Plantation Women in South Carolina, 1830–1880* (Urbana and Chicago: University of Illinois Press, 1998); Deborah Gray White, *Ar'n't I a Woman? Female Slaves in the Plantation South* (New York: Norton, 1985).

Owners

Relationships between enslaved women and their owners—both male and female—capture the complex and complicated array of everyday experiences that they routinely faced. In many cases, their interactions included verbal, physical, and sexual abuse, coercive threats involving sale or punishment, and other limitations of basic human rights. Some bondwomen found opportunities to resist oppressive owners outright by running away or participating in truancy while for others, who could purchase their freedom or "choose" to have a sexual relationship with a male owner, manumission sometimes occurred. Many bondwomen, however, had few options other than to endure whatever degree of abuse or indignity their owners meted out to them. Regardless of how enslaved women navigated these interactions and however cruel, benign, or indifferent their owners might have been, these relationships were always profoundly unequal, exacerbated by gendered power dynamics, and shaped by widespread stereotypes about bondwomen.

Perhaps one of the most dramatic, chilling, and well-known accounts of an enslaved woman's interaction with her owner came from Harriet Jacobs, whose classic *Incidents in the Life of a Slave Girl* (1861) describes the violence, coercion, and humiliation she faced while she was enslaved in North Carolina as a young woman from 1813 to 1842. Writing under the pseudonym Linda Brent, Jacobs recounts acts of sexual assault she experienced at a young age and discusses secrets she would prefer to conceal as she describes her successful struggle to receive her freedom after several long years in hiding. Broken promises of freedom upon an owner's death are among the stories that she recalls since her own freedom was consistently denied. She also describes tensions with her mistress that resulted after her mistress' husband, Jacobs' owner, fondled and sexually abused her. As Jacobs makes clear, her mistress did nothing to intervene on her behalf or attempt to save her from this sexual exploitation, but only blamed and resented her for her husband's indiscretions. As is obvious in this case, although an enslaved woman may have lived or worked in the same dwelling as her mistress, the two women did not automatically share a bond of sisterhood because of their gender. Indeed, another formerly enslaved woman, Emma Knight, remembered that for her and her family, "De master of de house was better to us dan de mistress."

Despite the viciousness that sometimes characterized relationships between enslaved women and mistresses, male owners undoubtedly posed a considerable threat to bondwomen as well. The abuses they meted out to bondwomen spanned across a broad spectrum that ranged from outward sexual exploitation to more subtle but no less insidious practices. In some instances, male owners raped enslaved women for their own personal gratification and felt little or no remorse since stereotypes such as "Jezebel" cast bondwomen as always promiscuous and sexually insatiable, therefore "justifying" this behavior. Forced breeding is another topic that continues to engender controversy and is a compelling example that illustrates how enslaved women's bodies were certainly not their own. Under slavery, women were prized for their ability to bear numerous children which contributed to their owner's wealth. This economic fact drove an undisclosed number of owners to command enslaved women to engage in sexual intercourse with partners not of their choosing and whether they consented or not for the sole purpose of conceiving a child. Aside from these obvious cases of sexual exploitation and control, some male owners engaged in less outwardly cruel but no less exploitative practices. For example, those who purchased so-called fancy girls to serve as their concubines or, as in the case of Thomas Jefferson and Sally Hemings, simply engaged in a relationship with a bondwoman that—however consensual it may have been—occurred within a system of racial slavery in which she ultimately had no real choice in the matter.

Some owners, men and women, were reputed to be "kind" to those who they kept in bondage, but even in these cases the fact that they participated in slavery at all is telling. For instance, the practice of bestowing bondpeople on other slaveholders as "gifts" was likely perceived as an act of generosity among owners but certainly not to the enslaved women who were often given away as cooks or house servants to a recently married couple and separated from their own loved ones and friends. The relationships and interactions that existed between enslaved women and their owners, while falling across a continuum of experiences that ranged from violent to coercive to relatively benign, were in the end ultimately shaped by the oppressiveness of the system of chattel slavery within which they unfolded.

Sue Kozel

See also Breeding; Concubinage; Hemings, Sally; Jacobs, Harriet; Jezebel Stereotype; Miscegenation; Plantation Mistresses; Resistance; Violence, Sexual.

Suggested Reading

Thavolia Glymph, *Out of the House of Bondage: The Transformation of the Plantation Household* (New York: Cambridge University Press, 2008); Annette Gordon-Reed,

The Hemingses of Monticello: An American Family (New York: W.W. Norton & Company, 2008); Harriet Jacobs, *Incidents in the Life of a Slave Girl* (Boston, 1861. Reprint, New York: Signet Classic, 2000); Jessica Millward, " 'The Relics of Slavery' Interracial Sex and Manumission in the American South" in *Frontiers: A Journal of Women Studies* 31, 3 (2010), 22–30; Jessica Millward, "More History than Myth: African American Women's History since the Publication of Ar'n't I a Woman?" *Journal of Women's History* 19, 2 (Summer 2007), 161–67; Jennifer Morgan, *Laboring Women: Gender and Reproduction in New World Slavery* (Philadelphia: University of Pennsylvania Press, 2004); Deborah Gray White, *Ar'n't I a Woman?: Female Slaves in the Plantation South*, 2nd ed. (New York: W.W. Norton, 1999);

P

Plantation Mistresses

The role of the plantation mistress and her relationship to enslaved women was one of the most complex within the Old South. The domestic labor of black women on the plantation was allegedly intended to allow plantation mistresses

> *I would rather drudge out my life on a cotton plantation, till the grave opened to give me rest, than to live with an unprincipled master and a jealous mistress.* Harriet Jacobs, Incidents in the Life of a Slave Girl *(49)*

lives of leisure. Proslavery ideologues preached about the harmony and divine order of plantation life, but the reality was often quite different from these ideals. Domestic duties and household management in fact dominated white women's lives, but the majority of antebellum plantations functioned as southern factories for producing raw cotton. The planter's wife played a key role in this booming economy, especially during the half century after the founding of the nation when the Cotton Revolution began.

Planters in Louisiana raised cane, planters in Missouri grew hemp, planters in the Carolinas produced rice and indigo, and cotton cultivation expanded dramatically from the fertile Atlantic coast onto the southwestern frontier. Within this plantation world, a mistress was expected to supervise the care, feeding, and well-being of her own family as well as that of her husband's bondspeople—which included their ever-expanding families as the birth rate skyrocketed. Plantation mistresses, as Julia Cherry Spruill and Anne Firor Scott have outlined, played key roles within plantation culture from the colonial period onward. Their responsibilities covered five broad areas: food, clothing, shelter, medical care, and religious instruction. Women designated cabins for slave families and doled out weekly food rations. Also, they often undertook the seasonal role of providing shifts, trousers, and shirts—the most basic and minimal wardrobe—for all blacks on the plantation. All too often, enslaved mothers' ability to labor for their own families was usurped by their designation as field or house workers for the master. Mistresses were expected to tend to the health of their husband's workers, as evidenced in their household books, which could include concoctions to cure gonorrhea alongside a favorite cake recipe. Further, some white women on plantations took seriously their roles as advocates for their bondpeople's spiritual well-being—such as the plantation mistress who taught Frederick Douglass to read and write.

As Marli Weiner suggested, these actions were intended to humanize an inhuman institution. Even though many of the plantation mistresses of the Old South sensed slavery degraded women of both races, most failed to oppose the system or even attempt to modify it. The majority of plantation mistresses took advantage of their situations and many exploited enslaved women, as Elizabeth Fox-Genovese emphasized in her work, *Within the Plantation Household: Black and White Women of the Old South* (1988). And, Thavolia Glymph (2008) has argued, the violence produced by plantation slavery was not just limited to slaveholding men. Plantation mistresses might lash out at bondspeople, and deprivations and abuses at the hands of a mistress might increase enslaved miseries.

Bondpeople on plantations were very much affected by the attitudes and actions of plantation mistresses. Many struggled to manipulate these personal relationships in order to maximize their everyday comforts. The work of Deborah Gray White (1985), Jacqueline Jones, and Brenda Stevenson (1996), to name just a handful of the leading scholars on this topic, chronicle the contested relationships between mistresses and enslaved people.

White Southerners preached a party line of piety and purity for southern ladies, but denied ladyhood to African American women by virtue of their color and to enslaved women because of their inferior legal standing. Thus, plantation mistresses—asexual and alabaster—symbolically served as cultural counterpoints to bondwomen. Catherine Clinton suggests that the sexual dynamics of slavery were critical for those living on plantations. Hundreds of enslaved women were coerced into concubinage and thousands of mixed-race slaves were produced as a result of these liaisons. Antebellum patriarchs could emasculate enslaved men and desexualize their own wives, while at the same time despoiling and defiling enslaved women. The damage inflicted is impossible to measure, and its legacy casts a long shadow over modern American culture.

Illicit and interracial sexual activity was acknowledged behind closed doors even though polite society failed to hold masters accountable for these particular moral lapses. Fanny Kemble's journal (penned and circulated in the 1830s, though not published until 1863) provided eyewitness accounts of enslaved women's sexual exploitation through evidence gathered during her time as plantation mistress on her husband's antebellum estates in the Georgia Sea Islands. Northern abolitionists had, for decades, railed at the licentiousness stimulated by slavery, and Kemble, with an insider's view, verified this lamentable outcome. White northern women complained that such abuses—the physical and sexual violence perpetrated against enslaved women by masters—were slavery's vilest consequence. Kemble, like many plantation mistresses before her, struggled to improve the physical aspects of her bondswomen's lives by creating a slave hospital and bringing the pleas of pregnant women and nursing mothers to the attention of the slaveholder, her husband. But her demands for better treatment for enslaved women damaged her relationship with her husband. She schemed that she might sell her jewelry to buy one of her husband's workers and protect a couple from separation by slave sale. In this one instance, her wishes were granted, but for most of her time on the plantation she was reduced to handing out scraps of flannel, and bits of meat while her complaints about the overseer went unheeded.

Within the Old South if enslaved women resisted sexual predators and raised their voices (as raising a hand, even to protect their own bodies, was punishable by law), they might be dealt with harshly by being subjected to whippings, temporary exile, or even sale. Few found plantation mistresses able to protect them. Also, some suffered when they confessed to the mistress about the approaches or actions of errant males—especially lapses by those within the mistress's own family or the master himself. As a result, enslaved women found themselves constantly on guard against white women rather than seeking them as allies and the plantation mistress could and did cause even more misery when jealousy or anger erupted. This was certainly the case for Harriet Jacobs who wrote extensively in her autobiographical account *Incidents in the Life of a Slave Girl* about her own mistress's anger when her husband, Dr. Flint, pursued Jacobs sexually.

Plantation mistresses rarely challenged whatever harsh or unpleasant conditions they faced. Living within a very strenuous plantation environment meant that some might claim falling victim to "the vapors" and abandon their prescribed roles. By taking to their beds, they gained invalid status. Thus, a small number rejected caretaking roles in favor of being taken care of themselves. But many more drafted unmarried sisters or other extended kin into the family circle to share domestic and supervisory burdens. Almost all demanded the presence of female relatives during childbirth and with good reason, as death in childbirth was higher for white women in the South than white women in the North, and even higher than that of enslaved women. The physical toll and isolation of life on an antebellum plantation caused many plantation mistresses to seek relief in the highly addictive and widely prescribed drug laudanum.

A vanguard of white women in the North, educated women of wealth and privilege, sought an outlet for their energies in reform or other avenues. As respectable, notable Yankee housewives began to expand their horizons, southern antebellum communities discouraged women from stepping outside rigid boundaries and struggled to curb any signs of female autonomy. Evangelical activity outside the household was discouraged for elite antebellum southern women, lest it stir up sentiments of discontent. A former daughter of the slaveholding South, Angelina Grimke, launched her attack on slavery in 1836 by making her appeal to "the Christian women of the South," in hopes they might put faith into action and rise up against slavery. But the South closed ranks, and Grimke's pleas fell on deaf ears. George Fitzhugh claimed in his *Sociology for the South* (1854) that women were expected to keep in their proper places and obey their lords and masters, concluding, "There was no slave, after all, like a wife." Slavery and patriarchy were interlocking systems within plantation culture, intended to hold all women (black and white) and all those enslaved (women and men) circumscribed by the master's will.

But certainly by the time of secession and formation of a Confederate government in 1861, many white southern women proclaimed their patriotism and supported a separate slaveholders' republic. Through charity fairs, the founding of hospitals, and serving as nurses, plantation mistresses by the thousands invaded previously restricted male domains during wartime, in the name of "southern independence." Benevolence was an acceptable path, but active women were still a threat even when they were serving the war interests. The chief surgeon, a male doctor, at the Chimborazo Hospital in Richmond, feared a "petticoat government," but eventually elite white women mounted the barricades and served their Rebel government. Plantation mistresses defied doctrines of female submissiveness and women's dependence and contributed their talents to the cause of the Confederacy.

The home front, like the battlefront, became an important arena for confrontation and a particularly contested terrain when enslaved women exerted their hopes for emancipation and independence in the face of Confederate military defeat. The plantation mistress who had, like the poet suggested, folded away her dresses, braided her hair, and met the "stern needs of the hour," could not stem the tide of history, which engulfed the nation when slavery was defeated. She might bemoan the loss of so many lives, she might regret the liberation of her slaves, but she would become a symbol of an era past, a cause lost following the passage of the Thirteenth Amendment and the Confederate surrender in 1865.

Catherine Clinton

See also Concubinage; Emancipation; Family; Health; Jacobs, Harriet; Labor, Agricultural; Labor, Domestic; Motherhood; Pregnancy; Resistance; Violence, Racial; Violence, Sexual.

Suggested Reading

Catherine Clinton, *The Plantation Mistress: Woman's World in the Old South* (New York: Pantheon, 1982); Elizabeth Fox-Genovese, *Within the Plantation Household: Black and White Women of the Old South* (Chapel Hill: University of North Carolina Press, 1988); Thavolia Glymph, *Out of the House of Bondage: The Transformation of the Plantation Household* (New York: Cambridge University Press, 2008); Brenda Stevenson, *Life in Black and White: Family and Community in the Slave South* (New York: Oxford University Press, 1996); Marli Weiner, *Mistresses and Slaves: Plantation Women in South Carolina, 1830–1880* (Champaign: University of Illinois Press, 1997); Deborah Gray White, *Ar'n't I a Woman?: Female Slaves in the Plantation South* (New York: Norton, 1985).

Pregnancy

The experience of pregnancy among bondwomen in the United States is a difficult history to trace. Scholars have few testimonies from enslaved women about their pregnancies. Instead, historians must glean what they can from available records. Certainly, all women and girls of reproductive age and ability faced the added vulnerability of pregnancy and childbirth. For captured African women who were spared the intentional assaults to their bodies during the Middle Passage, it is safe to assume that many endured assaults to their dignity because they were not allowed to tend to their menstrual cycles. Recent scholarship suggests that pregnant women went through labor and childbirth while shackled in cramped spaces aboard New World slave ships. Therefore, because of the reality of sexual assault, bondwomen lived with the added threat of having to endure pregnancy and childbirth under such dire conditions.

My marster wanted his slaves to have plenty of chillum. He never would make you do much work when you had a lot of chillun, and had them fast. My ma had nineteen chillun, and it looked like she had one every ten months. My marster said he didn't care if she never worked if she kept havin' chillun like that for him. He put ma in the kitchen to cook for slaves who didn't have families.

—Unknown woman, former bondwoman (*Born in Slavery: Slave Narratives from the Federal Writers' Project, 1936–1938 Georgia Narratives, Volume IV, Part 4, 360–61*)

Generally speaking, enslaved women had multiple pregnancies and fewer live births due to high infant mortality rates. The average age at first menarche in the United States was 19 years old. Some women began their periods sooner, but most were able to reproduce by their late teens and early twenties. Hard labor and a poor diet served as the most obvious challenges to pregnancy among enslaved women. Fatigued and overworked, bondwomen continued to labor in the homes and fields of their enslavers. Depending on the plantation crop or the location of their work, bondpeople often labored from sunup to sundown. Nonagricultural women, also referred to as domestics, were "on call" 24 hours per day. Some slaveholders reduced bondwomen's workload toward the end of their pregnancies giving them lighter tasks. Others forced women to work until giving birth and then allocated three to six weeks of postpartum rest. All enslaved workers completed arduous fieldwork during harvest season. Bondwomen who were at the end of their pregnancies in the late fall and early winter often suffered miscarriages or delivered stillborn infants because of the seasonal rhythm of hard labor, poor nutritional diet, and physical weakness of the third trimester.

Frances Kemble, a British actress who married a southern slaveholder, visited her husbands' plantation in coastal Georgia and was astonished by the number of pregnant women on the estate. She recalled that enslaved women petitioned her on a regular basis, many seeking relief before, during and after pregnancy. [See box below "Enslaved Women and Pregnancy on a Georgia Plantation."] Women like Leah and Sophy lost nearly 50 percent of their children while six of the nine children Molly birthed survived. The idea that bondwomen gave birth and lost children, speaks volumes to the strength of enslaved women. Consider the emotional rollercoaster they experienced, perhaps cautiously celebrating life while at the same time, mourning the loss of their progeny, over and over again.

As if pregnancy was not challenging enough, enslaved women lived within a culture of reproductive slavery that had a distinct correlation to the number of sexual assaults they experienced. One factor that facilitated this correlation was the socially accepted view that bondwomen deserved sexual violation because of their allegedly heightened sexual appetites and lascivious natures. According to this view, conduct which would be considered abuse for a free woman was not abuse of an enslaved woman. Likewise, the lack of legal protection against sexual assault for slaves added to their sexual vulnerability. These realities validated a climate that based its needs for labor on unlimited sexual access to female slaves.

Reproduction during slavery impacted every segment of society, both public and private. An examination of legal cases as sites of public discourse illustrates the open nature and ease with which chattel slavery was discussed, but also the extent to which it impacted various areas of law. Slavery was not only made possible by virtue of a complex set of laws, it also contributed to the development of our legal culture. The legal discussion is particularly important because these selected civil court cases indicate the changes that took place in the judiciary in response to reproductive slavery. Judges were very familiar with allocating interests associated with reproduction and sex to parties other than enslaved women.

As early as 1809, one year after the act prohibiting involvement in the international slave trade became effective, nearly all slave states had enacted legislation that defined the status of the enslaved with the status of the mother. In fact, one South Carolina court noted that children "could be sold away from their mothers at any age because the young slaves stand on the same footing as other animals" (*M'Lain vs. Elder*, 2 Brevard 307, 1809). Being equal to animals in the eyes of the law, bondpeople lacked access to civil claims. They could not enter into legal contracts; therefore, they had no standing in court to protest the sale of a spouse by a slaveholder or the "rape" of a bondwoman by a member of the planter or enslaved class, among many others.

The overwhelming immersion of reproductive slavery into the fabric of the nation is reflected in the vast number of cases brought before courts in every slave state attempting to allocate interests in enslaved women's reproductive capacity. Court records during the era of the Domestic Slave Trade indicate that slaveholders and other interested parties brought cases to court seeking to enforce and protect the property interest in their slaves.

Cases that directly involved enslaved women and their reproductive capacities revolved around infertility, particularly if discovered soon after purchase. These cases arose in either tort claims for fraud or breach of contract claims. Occasionally, some cases applied a theory similar to product liability. When the purchaser of a slave discovered that there was some defect, historically, there was no remedy. During the nineteenth century this changed. Judges and juries routinely held for purchasers of women who did not reproduce to their satisfaction. For example, an Alabama slave owner received a refund for three slaves he bought specifically for breeding when he discovered that they had venereal diseases that rendered them infertile. In cases where the issue of fraud was raised, infertility became a question of fact. In one such case, the court stated that:

> if a buyer took possession of a woman who had been certified as fit to bear children by the seller, and it could be demonstrated that the seller knew the woman was incapable of having children, the sale was voided and the proceeds were refunded. (Quoted in White, 1985, 22)

In short, infertile women were treated like barren sows and passed from one unsuspecting buyer to the next. As one former slave pointed out:

> [i]f a woman weren't a good breeder, she had to do work with de men. But Master tried to get rid of a woman who didn't have chillun. He would sell her and tell de man who bought her dat she was all right to own. (Quoted in Mellon, 1988, p. 296)

Unless the deception was discovered, the bondwoman's new owner was likely to punish the enslaved. Similarly, the plaintiff bore the burden of establishing that the lack of reproductivity was due to a defect rather than the individual's willfulness. In meeting this burden, some plaintiffs relied on doctors to examine the enslaved for fertility. Since gynecology was in its early stages (often assisted by bondwomen), the exams associated with litigation may have included inserting fingers in the woman's vagina or palpitating her pelvic region. Although not accurate techniques for gauging fertility, doctors would then provide their expert opinion as to the veracity of the plaintiff's claim.

Other cases involved allegations of misrepresentation or fraud. The plaintiff/purchaser would argue that the buyer knowingly sold him an infertile slave. These cases indicate that the desire, indeed the right, to breed slaves was an enforceable expectation, and if the seller thwarted the legitimate expectations of the buyer, a remedy was due. Most of these cases indicate that the law tended to favor the unsuspecting or dissatisfied buyer. In what might be best understood as a slave breeder warranty rule, if a buyer took possession of a woman who had been certified as fit to bear children and it could be demonstrated that the seller knew the

Enslaved Women and Pregnancy on a Georgia Plantation

In her journal from the years 1838–1839, Frances Kemble, a distinguished English actress who had married a Georgia plantation owner in 1834, made these sad observations about the enslaved women on the plantation from the 1838–1839. Kemble, an abolitionist, was later divorced by her slave-owning husband.

Fanny has had six children; all dead but one. She came to beg to have her work in the field lightened.

Nanny has had three children; two of them are dead. She came to implore that the rule of sending them into the field three weeks after their confinement might be altered.

Leah, Caesar's wife, has had six children; three are dead.

Sophy, Lewis's wife, came to beg for some old linen. She is suffering fearfully; has had ten children; five of them are dead. The principal favor she asked was a piece of meat, which I gave her.

Sally, Scipio's wife, has had two miscarriages and three children born, one of whom is dead. She came complaining of incessant pain and weakness in her back. This woman was a mulatto daughter of a slave called Sophy, by a white man of the name of Walker, who visited the plantation.

Charlotte, Renty's wife, had two miscarriages, and was with child again. She was almost crippled with rheumatism, and showed me a pair of poor swollen knees that made my heart ache. I have promised her a pair of flannel trousers, which I must forthwith set about making.

Sarah, Stephen's wife; this woman's case and history were alike deplorable. She had four miscarriages, had brought seven children into the world, five of whom were dead, and was again with child. She complained of dreadful pains in the back, and an internal tumor which swells with the exertion of working in the fields; probably, I think, she is ruptured. She told me she had once been mad and had run into the woods, where she contrived to elude discovery for some time, but was at last tracked and brought back, when she was tied up by the arms, and heavy logs fastened to her feet, and was severely flogged. After this she contrived to escape again, and lived for some time skulking in the woods, and she supposes mad, for when she was taken again she was entirely naked. She subsequently recovered from this derangement, and seems now just like all the other poor creatures who come to me for help and pity. I suppose her constant childbearing and hard labor in the fields at the same time may have produced the temporary insanity.

Sukey, Bush's wife, only came to pay her respects. She had had four miscarriages; had brought eleven children into the world, five of whom are dead.

Molly, Quambo's wife, also only came to see me. Hers was the best account I have yet received; she had had nine children, and six of them were still alive.

This is only the entry for today, in my diary, of the people's complaints and visits. Can you conceive a more wretched picture than that which it exhibits of the conditions under which these women live?

Source: Frances Anne Kemble, *Journal of a Residence on a Georgian Plantation in 1838–1839*. New York: Harper & Brothers Publishers, 1864, pp. 190–91.

woman was incapable of having children, the sale would be voided and proceeds refunded.

The next group of illustrative cases comes from the law of inheritance. In these cases, judges were asked to determine who owned the future interests in enslaved children not yet conceived or born. In a colonial Pennsylvania case, the child of a bondperson was willed away from his mother even before birth: "In 1727, Isaac Warner bequeathed to his wife, Ann, a Negro woman named Sarah. To his daughter Ann Warner, an unborn child of the above named Sarah" (Turner, 1911, p. 24). Such gifts indicate that widely institutionalized commodification of enslaved women's bodies, in the north as well as the south. In another case, a South Carolina slave owner, Mary Kincaid, bequeathed a slave woman named Sillar to her grandchild and Sillar's two children to other grandchildren. Kincaid's will provided that if Sillar should bear a third child, he or she would go to yet another grandchild. These cases reinforced the notion that since slaveholders owned the bodies of their bondpeople, their children and future children, they also owned the reproductive capacities of their bondwomen.

Pamela Bridgewater and Daina Ramey Berry

See also Breeding; Childbirth; Health, Disabilities, and Soundness; Midwives; Mortality and Life Expectancy; Motherhood; Sexuality; Violence, Sexual.

Suggested Reading

Sharla Fett, *Working Cures: Health, Healing, and Power on Southern Slave Plantations* (Chapel Hill: University of North Carolina Press, 2002); David Barry Gaspar and Darlene Clark Hine, *More than Chattel: Black Women and Slavery in the Americas* (Bloomington: Indiana University Press, 1996); Eugene D. Genovese (New York: Vintage Books, 1976); Herbert Gutman, *The Black Family in Slavery and Freedom, 1750–1925* (New York: Vintage Books, 1977); James Mellon, *Bullwhip Days: The Slaves Remember: An Oral History* (New York: Grove Press, 1988); Jennifer L. Morgan, *Laboring Women: Reproduction and Gender in New World Slavery* (Philadelphia: University of Pennsylvania Press, 2004); Sowande' Mustakeem, " 'I Never Have Such a Sickly Ship Before': Diet, Disease, and Mortality in 18th-Century Atlantic Slaving Voyages," *Journal of African American History* 93 (Fall 2008), 474–96; Marie Jenkins Schwartz, *Birthing a Slave: Motherhood and Medicine in the Antebellum South* (New York: Harvard University Press, 2010); Edward Raymond Turner, *The Negro in Pennsylvania: Slavery—Servitude—Freedom 1639–1861* (Washington, DC: American Historical Association, 1911); Deborah Gray White, *Ar'n't I a Woman?: Slave Women in the Plantation South* (New York: W.W. Norton and Company, 1985).

Prices

When Ishe Webb, a former bondman was interviewed in the 1930s about his experience with slavery, he had vivid recollections about their prices. "My father was sold to another man for seventeen hundred dollars," he recalled. However, his

This valuation of 15 bondpeople was included in records of a U.S. District Court case in 1825. (National Archives.)

"mother was sold for twenty hundred" and "I have heard them say that so much that I never will forget it" (Born in Slavery, WPA Narratives, Arkansas Narratives, Volume 2, Part 7).

The price of an enslaved person reflected the expected flow of net revenue that the individual would presumably generate over his or her lifetime. As troubling as it may sound, slaveholders viewed bondpeople as commodities or goods—similar to machines employed in agriculture or manufacturing—and devised elaborate methods for determining their monetary worth. The cost of their food, clothing, healthcare, and shelter were calculated into their prices and other issues, such as age and health, also played a role in the value assigned to them at different stages in their lives. For bondwomen, issues that related directly to their gender also came to bear on the dollar amounts slaveholders, traders, and others calculated for them. Women's ability to bear children and be prolific "breeders" was perhaps the most obvious, desirable trait to slaveholders who sought to increase the number of enslaved people they possessed through natural increase.

Enslaved women's specific skills and even, in some cases, their perceived physical attractiveness could also help determine their financial value in the eyes of slaveholders. In 1806, James Davis of Silver Springs, PA advertised the sale of "A NEGRO WENCH." He noted that she was "A SLAVE for life, about 38 years of age, [and] capable of doing any kind of house work" (*Pennsylvania Herald*, March 7, 1806). Although Davis saw some value in the labor capacity of this unnamed bondwoman, he made no mention of her monetary value. Enslaved men and women were commodified in northern and southern markets; they were bought and sold like most forms of movable property (chattel). Early in a bondperson's life, slaveholders considered the costs to care for them to be greater than the profits they might earn from their labor and the price of enslaved children tended to be depressed. By around age 15, however, bondpeople were sufficiently productive to generate revenue equal to maintenance costs. From this point, their productivity typically increased if they did not experience any disabilities, ill health, or other circumstances that would have a negative impact on their ability to work. Healthy slaves thus generated greater profits for the slaveholder and garnered higher prices. At some point in all enslaved people's life cycle, their productivity declined and the values enjoyed by slaveholders shrank, forcing members of the planter class to decrease the overall value of the bondperson.

In addition to their ability to labor, other factors also weighed heavily in slaveholders' determinations of bondpeople's prices such as the kinds of skills they possessed, their health, and gender. Available data indicate that enslaved women were usually valued at a lower price in comparison with enslaved men with similar characteristics. A large part of this differential was due to the fact that much of the work performed by bondpeople was manual labor and slaveholders viewed enslaved men as being more productive at these tasks. Looking at the surviving plantation records, however, scholars recently discovered that women were highly valued workers with a variety of agricultural and nonagricultural skills. In fact, some women were skilled seamstresses, cooks, ginners, laundresses, and brickmakers who commanded high market values. The most highly valued women, however, were considered "fancy girls." These women were usually young, light-skinned, and possessed physical characteristics that white men found attractive. Slaveholders purchased them as potential concubines and as symbols of wealth and status because "fancy girls" were quite expensive in comparison to enslaved people who were deemed "average." Many bondwomen considered "fancy girls" were groomed to conform to antebellum standards of white womanhood—they were taught to act as gentile and cultured ladies—even as their enslaved status paradoxically marked them as supposedly sexually available.

Looking at women's experience on the auction block highlights their commodification. Black women in early America filled the pages of newspapers in sale ads,

Enslaved women such as Jane were sold with and without their children. The above receipt indicates that Jane's future children are included in this transaction. (Library of Congress.)

were the subjects of legal proceedings in ownership disputes, served as collateral for loans among debtors and creditors, and commanded strong prices in an evolving domestic market for "sound" slaves. They received monetary values based on their age, skill, and reproductive status (Berry, 2004 and forthcoming). When placed upon the auction block, they experienced the most degrading inspection, which involved poking, squeezing, and fondling various parts of their bodies. Some traders greased them down with oil to make them appear younger and more valuable.

Most often, the prices of enslaved people revolved around their ability to physically labor. Slaveholders based the value associated with the output of an enslaved person on the market value of the product that would be produced by the enslaved individual. For example, the value of products such as rice, tobacco, sugar, and by the early part of the nineteenth century in the United States, cotton. All of these crops are very labor intensive, requiring many hours of backbreaking labor to bring the final product to market. Enslaved prices depended primarily on their productivity and the market prices for the crops they produced such as cotton, rice, tobacco, and sugar. As cotton production spread westward, the price of bondpeople depended more and more on the market price of cotton. Thus, as either the price of these crops increased or the productivity of bondpeople increased, the price of an enslaved person would increase as the net revenue they were expected to generate over their lifetime would increase.

The larger-scale plantation production process was particularly suited to rice, sugar, and cotton, whereas tobacco could be profitably grown in smaller-scale operations. Thus, the spread of cotton production increased the demand for bondpeople. Some of this increased demand was satisfied by transferring bondpeople from the eastern states (the Old South) to the western states (the New South). However, the growing total demand had to be met by natural growth processes after January 1, 1808. Although many states had prohibited the importation of bondpeople from outside the United States prior to 1808, importation was possible in some states and territories until January 1, 1808. The Domestic Slave Trade among the states that had not outlawed slavery continued to be legal until the Civil War legislation that prohibited slavery in all states and territories of the United States.

The growing demand and the prohibition of importation of bondpeople changed the value associated with enslaved women, as they became the only source of additional slaves. The restriction on the supply of additional bondpeople to those born in the United States increased the value of all existing bondpeople. However, the ability to bear children enhanced the value of enslaved women after the importation of bondpeople was prohibited. Bearing children became a larger part of the productivity measure for bondwomen beginning in 1808. Coleman and Hutchinson (2006) found that bondwomen's prices increased more for those of prime childbearing age, ages 15 to 25, and for those nearest to that age, ages 10 to 14. The potential productivity of enslaved children under the age of 10 was too uncertain for the effect of import prohibition to be important. The impact on the price of the younger group of women was larger than the impact of the import prohibition on the price of unskilled bondmen. The prices for women over the age of 25 were not affected by the prohibition of importing bondpeople. Thus, the price of an enslaved woman depended primarily on her ability to perform household tasks, work in the fields, and/or bear children.

William Hutchinson

See also Breeding; Civil War; Concubinage; Domestic Slave Trade; Economy; Health, Disabilities, and Soundness; Labor, Agricultural; Labor, Nonagricultural; Labor, Skilled.

Suggested Reading

Daina Ramey Berry, " 'We'm Fus' Rate Bargain': Value, Labor, and Price in a Georgia Slave Community," in *The Chattel Principle: Internal Slave Trades in the Americas, 1808–1888*, ed. Walter Johnson (New Haven: Yale University Press, 2004), 55–71; Berry, *The Price for Their Pound of Flesh: The Value of Human Chattels* (forthcoming); Ashley N. Coleman and William K. Hutchinson, "Determinants of Slave Prices: Louisiana, 1725 to 1820," Vanderbilt University, Department of Economics, Working Paper #06-W24, December 2006, http://www.vanderbilt.edu/econ/wparchive/working06.html; Robert W. Fogel, *Without Consent or Contract: The Rise and Fall of American Slavery*, vol. I (New York: W.W. Norton, 1989); Walter Johnson, *Soul by Soul: Life Inside the Antebellum Slave Market* (Cambridge: Harvard University Press, 1999); Jennifer Morgan, *Laboring Women: Reproduction and Gender in New World Slavery* (Philadelphia: University of Pennsylvania Press, 2004).

Prince, Lucy Terry

Birth Date: 1730
Death Date: 1821

Lucy Terry Prince, commonly called Luce, is noted for her famous 30-line poem the "Bars Fight." Lucy, a respected storyteller used prose to express her sentiments about the Deerfield Massacre—the last Native American (Abenaki peoples) rebellion near two slaveholding properties (the Amsden and Allen residences) in Deerfield, Massachusetts. Of important note, the "Bars Fight" was written during a time period in North America's history when women and men of African descent had little or no access to education. "Bars Fight" was considered a detailed record of the massacre that occurred on August 25, 1746 in the "The Bars," (a colonial term for meadow or field). Lucy was among those persons who witnessed firsthand the attack where five English colonists died, one severely wounded, and another taken captive. Two Native Americans also died in the attack. Her poem provided an accurate account of the event and was the first known published poem written by a black woman in the North America. It was a part of the American oral cannon until it was published in 1855; the poem is among those published works written by black women in America that offers readers a snapshot into early American history and literacy.

Lucy, a former enslaved African was stolen from Western Africa as a child and taken to Bristol, Rhode Island where she was purchased at age four by Ebenzer and Abigail Wells. At age five, Lucy was baptized into the Christian faith at the Wells' home during the first wave of the Great Awakenings. She was later "admitted to the fellowship" of the Wells' church, the "Church of Christ in Deerfield." Ebenezer names the church as his second inheritor in his will, leaving the church a "silver tankard." Ebenzer and Abigail were childless; the couple owned two enslaved persons, Lucy and another identified as Cesar. Lucy spent most of her life

Bars Fight

August, twas the twenty-fifth,
Seventeen hundred forty-six,
The Indians did in ambush lay,
Some very valiant men to slay
Twas nigh unto Sam Dickinsons mill,
The Indians there five men did kill.
The names of whom Ill not leave out,
Samuel Allen like a hero fout,
And though he was so brave and bold,
His face no more shall we behold.
Eleazer Hawks was killed outright,
Before he had time to fight,
Before he did the Indians see,
Was shot and killed immediately.
Oliver Amsden he was slain,
Which caused his friends much grief pain.
Simeon Amsden they found dead.
Not many rods from Olivers head.
Adonijah Gillett, we do hear,
Did lose his life which was so dear.
John Sadler fled across the water,
And thus escaped the dreadful slaughter.
Eunice Allen see the Indians coming
And hoped to save herself by running:
And had not her petticoats stopped her,
The awful creatures had not catched her,
Not tommy hawked her on the head,
And left her on the ground for dead.
Young Samuel Allen, Oh! lack-a-day!
Was taken and carried to Canada.

laboring involuntarily as a house servant on the Wells' property until 1756. Ebenzer died in 1757.

At age 26, Lucy met Abijah Prince, a former enslaved man who served in the Massachusetts Bay militia during the French and Indian War. Abijah, commonly known as Bijah, was a servant of Reverend Benjamin Doolittle of Northfield, Massachusetts, the first settled minister in Northfield. Before his death, Doolittle freed Abijah who subsequently purchased Lucy's freedom and the two later married on May 17, 1756. Abijah acquired a parcel of land in Northfield and later,

Guilford, Vermont where the two moved to raise their six children: Caesar (b. 1756), Duruza (b. 1758), Drusella (b. 1760), Festus (b. 1763), Tatnai (b. 1765), and Abijah (b. 1769). Years later, Abijah became one of the grantees and founders of Sunderland, Vermont, a small town northwest of Guilford.

While living in Guilford, Lucy became known for her great oratory skills. She was popular among young people who enjoyed the wisdom and wit of her story-telling. Lucy often defended her rights and the rights of others in public debates. In 1785, a neighboring white family threatened the Princes. Lucy and Abijah appealed to the governor and his council for protection; protection was granted. When Colonel Eli Bronson challenged the Princes' claim to their land in Sunderland, Lucy argued their case before the Supreme Court of Vermont. She argued her case against two respected white lawyers—one who later became chief justice in Vermont—and won, setting precedence in Vermont history. Samuel Chase, the presiding judge, impressed with Lucy's art of persuasion, commented that Lucy's passion and logic were superior to any lawyer that argued a case in his courtroom.

Lucy was equally an advocate for enslaved and free blacks' right to education. Disenchanted by the absence of black students at Williams College, Lucy applied for admissions for her eldest son, Caesar. The application was denied on the bases of race. Lucy argued her son's case for three hours before the board of trustees. She quoted both biblical scriptures and prior legal cases to support her arguments; she subsequently lost her case. This defeat, however, did not stop Lucy's pursuit.

Lucy Terry Prince died in 1821 at her home in Vermont. Lemuel Haynes, an influential religious leader and abolitionist, preached an antislavery sermon at her funeral arguing that "tyrants and oppressors" in time, would "sink beneath Terry's feet." Similar sentiments were expressed by Terry in her famous poem "Bar Fight." Her obituary read "Her volubility was exceeded by none, and in general the fluency of her speech captivated all around her, and was not destitute of instruction and edification. She was much respected . . ." (Kaplan 1989, 237–41).

Renee K. Harrison

See also African Women and African-Born Women; North, The; Wheatley, Phillis

Suggested Reading

Broad Brook Grange, ed., *Official History of Guilford, Vermont, 1678–1961: With Genealogies and Biographical Sketches* (Vermont: Town of Guilford and Broad Brook Grange No. 151, 1961); Sharon Harley, *The Timetables of American History: A Chronology of the Most Important People and Events in African-American History* (New York: Touchstone, 1996); Josiah Gilbert Holland, *History of Western Massachusetts: The Counties of Hampden, Hampshire, and Berkshire* (Springfield: Samuel Bowles and Company, 1855); Sidney Kaplan and Emma Nogrady Kaplan, *The Black Presence in the Era of the American Revolution* (Amherst: The University of Massachusetts Press, 1989).

Punishment

Slave punishments were a means to intimidate, incite fear, and maintain control of enslaved Africans on many slave-owning properties. Punishments were often unreasonable and unwarranted. One former enslaved man recalled an enslaved woman's senseless beating for a minor offense. He remarked how she was stretched out, face downwards on the ground with her hands and feet fastened to stakes. Her enslaver commenced to "striking her with a leather trace belonging to his carriage-harness." The former enslaved man was told that she deserved the severe beating for "burning the edges of the waffles that she had cooked for breakfast" (Blassingame 1977, 372).

Abolitionist print, captioned "a punishment, practiced in the United States, for the crime of loving liberty," depicts a man flogging a female slave tied to tree. (*The Anti-Slavery Record*, Vol. 1, March 1835.)

Punishments varied from region to region and plantation to plantation. Both state and local slave codes provided European American enslavers and planters the legal leverage to punish an enslaved person at their own discretion. Moderate fines were imposed on whites who injured or incapacitated an enslaved person without the enslaver's consent. This stipulation protected the property of the enslaver; it was not instituted to protect the rights of the enslaved. As one southern state's 1740 slave code reads "WHEREAS, some doubt... penalty for cruelly scalding or burning a slave, cutting out his tongue, putting out his eye, or depriving him of any limb, a fine of L100. For beating with a horse-whip, cow-skin, switch or small stick, or putting irons on, or imprisoning a slave, no penalty or prohibition" (Brevard's Digest, 241). Severe injuries, such as burning or dismemberment, resulted in monetary fines because such offenses hindered the work performance of the enslaved person being treated as property.

For the most part, enslavers and planters incurred limited or no fines for the mistreating of the people that they enslaved. All of this, in some way, meant that the North American judicial system—laws, courts, law enforcement, etc.—protected the rights of European Americans. Such a system, in early American history, reinforced the notion that enslaved women, men, and children were inferior, nonhuman, and chattel property and, therefore, possessed limited or no legal rights or protection in the New World. One former enslaved man makes this point in his description of standing by while his wife endured punishment: "Garrison got mad with my wife, and took her off in one of the rooms, with his paddle in hand, swearing that he would paddle her; and I could afford her no protection at all, while the strong arm of the law, public opinion and custom, were all against me. I have often heard Garrison say, that he had rather paddle a female, than eat when he was hungry—that it was music for him to hear them scream, and to see their blood run" (Gates 1999, 349).

Slave punishments were the harshest during the seventeenth to nineteenth centuries as the slave trade from West and West Central Africa to North America intensified and fluctuated. Enslavers and planters used all forms of harsh tactics—"whipping, kicking, beating, starving, branding, cat-hauling, loading with irons, imprisoning" or "some other cruel mode of torturing"—to punish enslaved women, men, and children. One European businessman recalled how enslavers and planters often boasted of having "invented some new mode of torture to tame" an enslaved person. He remarked, "What is called a moderate flogging . . . is horribly cruel. Should we whip our horses for any offence as they whip their slaves for small offences, we should expose ourselves to the penalty of the law. . . . Thirty-nine lashes on the bare back, which tear the skin at almost every stroke, is . . . a very *moderate punishment* . . . Sometimes, after being whipped, some have been shut up in a dark place and deprived of food, in order to increase their torments" (Moulton 1839, 19–21).

Showing how slavery improves the condition of the female sex.

This image of enslaved women receiving punishments appeared in the *Anti-Slavery Almanac* in 1840. The imagery and its satirical title, "Showing How Slavery Improves the Condition of the Female Sex," aimed to raise awareness of the ills of slavery. (Library of Congress.)

Punishments varied from starvation to iron collars to public floggings to public lynchings for offenses ranging from learning to read and stealing chickens to absconding and plotting rebellions. One former enslaved woman recalled how the maltreatment of the enslaved, especially women and girls was a common practice. She described some enslaved persons' days of famine, toil, and punishment as "a constant misery." "I never had no white folks that was good to me," she remarked, "We all worked jest like dogs, and had about half enough to eat, and got whupped for everything" (Mellon 1988, 242).

Most often, enslaved persons were punished for stealing food, absconding, plotting rebellions, or learning to read. Intentional withholding and deprivation of food to control enslaved persons and enforce labor was a common practice on many slave-owning properties. Frederick Douglass noted that he never remembered during slavery "enjoying sufficiency . . . The rule was, no matter how coarse the food, only let there be enough of it" (Douglass 1986, 95–96).

Although laws were enacted making it illegal for enslaved persons to steal, and biblical scriptures were read admonishing them, countless enslaved persons stole to combat starvation. Many, including pregnant women, lamented that "we were so hungry we were bound to steal or perish" (Mellon 1988, 46). Punishment for stealing food resulted in flogging, imprisonment, and severing of fingers, hands, or other limbs.

Enslaved persons were also punished frequently for absconding and plotting rebellions. Those caught were often beaten severely, domesticated with an iron collar, and placed on display. Body restraints such as iron collars, chains, and barrels were used to punish or prevent the enslaved from running away. One European businessman recalled seeing a "colored woman, of intelligent and dignified appearance, who appeared to be attending to the business of the house, with an iron collar around her neck, with horns or prongs extending out on either side, and up, until they met at something like a foot above her head, at which point there was a bell attached. This yoke, as they called it . . . was to prevent her from running away, or to punish her for having done so" (McDowell 1839, 74).

In addition to absconding, enslaved women and men were also known to gather secretly in the woods to organize small- and large-scale slave insurrections. State laws defined slave insurrections as the assemblage of three or more armed slaves with the intent to obtain their liberty by force. Historian Herbert Aptheker notes that insurrections of this nature were surmountable. Slaveholding and nonslaveholding whites fear of slave conspiracies and revolts was widespread throughout both the South and North.

Both enslaved and free women worked alongside men such as Gabriel Prosser, Denmark Vesey, and Nat Turner to plot and participate in slave insurrections to obtain freedom for themselves and others. Two women in particular, identified as Lucy and Charlotte, gathered and strategized with Nat Turner in a revolt held in Virginia August 21, 1831. Many women who participated in these revolts throughout the antebellum period and beyond were publicly humiliated, beaten, imprisoned, lynched, burned, or beheaded.

Dismemberment and public floggings for educating oneself or for free Africans educating the enslaved were also forms of punishment. Denying or limiting the enslaved access to education was a means used by European Americans to disempower them. One former enslaved woman remarked, "White folks didn't believe in slaves larnin' anything. Dey thought hit would made de them harder to keep slaves, an' to make dem wuk. All de slaves dat I knowed couldn't read nor write" (Mellon 1988, 197). One former enslaved man recalled his impending punishment for reading: "I spent a good deal of time trying to improve myself; secretly, of course. One day, my mistress happened to come into my room, when my materials were about; and she told her father (old Capt. Davis) that I was learning to write. He replied that if I belonged to him, he would cut my right hand off" (Blassingame 1977, 234). Another former enslaved woman recalled the public humiliation and punishment she and other enslaved persons experienced: "One day Old Mistus saw us with a book and she come outside with stick candy held out in her hand, and she say, "I give you all of this . . . if you tell me where you got the book and learned the letters. I spoke up . . . and told her . . . she took us in the house and she held our heads between her legs and she whipped our back ends with a big wooden paddle. Then she stuck us up the chimney . . . and kept us there forty minutes . . ." (Mellon 1988, 309).

During the seventeenth to nineteenth centuries, European Americans injured and killed enslaved women, men, and children for minor offenses. Many of these punishments have gone unrecorded. The injuries and loss of African lives was considered damage to and loss of property, and not loss and degradation of human lives.

Renee K. Harrison

See also Branding; Breeding; Domestic Slave Trade; Medical Experimentation and Surgery; Overseers; Owners; Violence, Racial; Violence, Sexual.

Suggested Reading

William L. Andrews and Henry Louis Gates, Jr. *Slave Narratives* (Washington, DC: Civitas/Counterpoint, 1999); Henry Bibb, *Narratives of the Life and Adventures of Henry Bibb, an American Slave Written by; Himself*, in *The Civitas Anthology of African American Slave Narratives*, ed. Joseph Brevard, *Reports of Judicial Decisions in the State of South Carolina* (Charleston: W. Riley, 1839–40); Frederick Douglass, *Narrative of the Life of Frederick Douglass, an American Slave: Written by Himself* (New York: Penguin Books, 1986); Narratives of Annie Hawkins, Sarah Wilson, Louisa Adams, and John Mellon, in *Bullwhip Days: The Slaves Remember, an Oral History*, ed. James Mellon (New York: Avon Books, Inc., 1988); Narratives of James Curry and James Fisher in *Slave Testimony: Two Centuries of Letters, Speeches, Interviews, and Autobiographies*, ed. John Blassingame (Louisiana: Louisiana State University, 1977); Testimonies of Mr. Robert McDowell and Horace Moulton, in *American Slavery As It Is: Testimony of a Thousand Witnesses* (New York: American Anti-Slavery Society, 1839).

Q

Quilting

Some scholars argue or believe that the form of quilting that emerged in the United States and was practiced by black women during slavery serves as material evidence of African cultural retentions and continuities. Many scholars argue that quilting preserved skills in textiles that can be traced to West Africa. Quilting is said to offer a powerful testimony to the existence of a viable enslaved community that also maintained some autonomy for itself and met some of its own household needs within the rigorous constraints of the slave system in which few comforts were available.

Despite the symbolic and practical value of enslaved women's quilting skills, this labor was overlooked and devalued in comparison to the work of mostly male artisans who labored in trades such as blacksmithing and carpentry. Black female quilters were an almost invisible class of domestic workers who were often forced to work late into the night sewing blankets or covers that could withstand cold nights in drafty enslaved cabins and quarters. Black women commonly employed a range of approaches, patterns, and design motifs like the Jacob's ladder, which have recently become associated with movements for abolition, literacy, freedom, and civil rights. The topic of slavery and quilting has also been renewed in recent years in light of interest in the signals that quilts may have provided on the Underground Railroad.

Very few quilts made by enslaved women during the antebellum era today because of the fragility of textiles and the deleterious effects of harsh washing materials such as lye soap. Harriet Powers is one of the most well known black female quilters of the nineteenth century. She is known for her narrative Bible quilts—one of which is exhibited at the Smithsonian Institution. Events such as the Freedom Quilting Bee near Gee's Bend, Alabama have been instrumental in further celebrating the African American quilting tradition and showing the historic practice's overlap with modern art.

Black women's quilts have been immortalized in film as well as in literature by writers such as Alice Walker. Quilting has been recognized as a distinctly southern and African American tradition with links back to Africa. Most importantly, quilting is celebrated for its ability to let black women symbolically and literally knit bonds among one another and to serve as reigning symbols of family, tradition, and community.

Riche' Richardson

See also Seamstress Work; Underground Railroad.

Suggested Reading

John Beardsley, William Arnett, Paul Arnett, and Jane Livingston, *Gee's Bend: The Women and Their Quilts* (Atlanta: Tinwood Books in association with the Museum of Fine Arts [Houston], 2002); Carolyn Mazloomi, *Spirits of the Cloth: Contemporary African American Quilts* (New York: Clarkson Potter/Publishers, 1998); Jacqueline L. Tobin and Raymond G. Dobard, PhD, *Hidden in Plain View: A Secret Story of Quilts and the Underground Railroad* (New York: Doubleday, 1999).

R

Religion

Enslaved women often used religion to cope with and navigate the harshness of racial slavery. Many women created spaces of safe existence and believed faith was more than a motivating force of strength—it was, in fact, life. Themes of healing and wholeness were connected to religious thought and practice to maintain soundness of body and spirit on farms and plantations. Enslaved women's religion was central in their language and cultural expression; it reflected their concerns about love, labor, gender, surrogacy, pain, dread, and faith. It also provided a means for black women to create safe spaces of existence where they could frame positive images of themselves.

Not solely a source of faith for things to come, enslaved woman made use of the divine for many reasons such as assistance with political protest, fighting against gender injustice, and the practice of "doctoring" of self and community. Enslaved doctoring women significantly impacted their own enslaved families as well as slaveholding families. Such considerations of wholeness gave space for a broadly defined religious experience among enslaved women. These women would doctor all but the most severe of physical ailments. Though their work did not necessarily exclude conjurational practices, their daily sick care bore a different relationship to slave cultural life than the often clandestine and negatively viewed practices of hoodoo. Ultimately, their practices of doctoring were connected to divine empowerment granted onto them to serve the needs of their community. These practices brought together folk healing practices drawn from African traditional religious practices with notions of wholeness taken for the Protestant tradition. Healing, then, was in part a religious task. Within this religious landscape, enslaved women would inhabit powerful spiritual roles that had been passed down for generations.

Through their religious self-care response, enslaved woman aided their community of sufferers in changing their personal outlook and seeing themselves as fully lovable human beings. The embedded theme of healing and wholeness as found in the words of the fictional character Baby Suggs Holy in Toni Morrison's book *Beloved* is illustrative. When Baby Suggs preaches, "Here in this here place, we flesh; flesh that weeps, laughs; flesh that dances on bare feet in grass. Love it. Love it hard," her aim is to encourage a newly realized, fully human, black identity and an aggressive love of their own often despised black flesh. Hers was a concern for the well-being of the "least of these" while on Earth, as opposed to the sole emphasis being on what they might gain in the *future* glory of heaven. For many enslaved women, religion gave them a language and way of thinking to strategically focus on the experiential, social, and cultural aspects of life. What resulted were unique concerns about the Bible and its themes of God's love, healing power through Jesus, and desire to liberate God's people. The resulting religious expression among enslaved women projected the idea of a God who, even when full liberation for enslaved women is not established, participates in their survival. God in this sense is also working as a sustainer of enslaved people while they yet experience oppression, allowing them to "make a way out of no way."

Religious exhortation in the form of preaching took up a significant space for both men and women in the enslaved community. Men often took on the leadership roles within any religious gathering, drawing upon what had been observed in the paternalistic South. Enslaved women, however, exhibited the necessary qualities for religious leadership and gifts of religious expression through preaching or forms of verbal protest. Expressions of encouragement for a broken people, as exhibited in Baby Suggs Holy's exhortation, were only part of the complex relationship between enslaved women and religion. Enslaved women often sought to express their spiritual gifts as official church leaders and faced gender bias as they attempted to use their gifts to preach to enslaved people. For example, Jarena Lee embraced the African Methodist church and felt a call to preach after hearing Bishop Richard Allen preach in 1804. Although Bishop Allen acknowledged and allowed her to preach at his church, Lee found that other pulpits would not be opened to her. After much fighting against God's call, she concluded that was to go forth in spite of certain rejection. She still claimed her forthright call to preach and took advantage of opportunities to sermonize as an itinerate revivalist.

The itinerant preaching circuit would eventually become the most visible space wherein enslaved women could have their voices heard. Rebecca Protten, is viewed as an important figure in advancing the spread of Christianity among enslaved and free blacks throughout the Atlantic during the mid- and late 1700s. While many slaveholders were concerned that blacks' conversions to Christianity would unite them in opposition to enslavement, Protten embarked on a mission to evangelize and preach to hundreds of enslaved Africans. She was also instrumental in the establishment of one of the earliest Protestant congregations in the Americas. Free black woman Zilpha Elaw used her experience of conversion and sanctification to speak out against slavery and gender oppression. She emphasized the sanctification experience over the conversion experience because conversion was considered too "easy." Sanctification, a lifelong and arduous path to holiness, entailed far more of a challenge. Using these concepts, she was strengthened to speak out against oppression and framed her ministry as a triumph of the weak over the mighty on two fronts: enslaver and enslaved as well as male and female. Some enslaved women directly personified the traits of biblical figures. Harriet Tubman was viewed as a type of biblical religious figure for her role in securing freedom for enslaved blacks and was called "General Moses" and "the Moses of her people."

Religion was a significant part of enslaved women's experiences. Through personal faith and public exhortation, enslaved women were able to simultaneously encourage themselves and others. They were also able to navigate the atrocities of the slave experience with a confident and even sometimes defiant posture. Whether responding to racial oppression or subjection because of their gender, religion gave enslaved women a language and many tools to create new identities for themselves and their fellow sufferers.

Derek S. Hicks

See also Conjurers; Islam; Tubman, Harriet; Voodoo.

Suggested Reading

William L. Andrews, ed., *Sisters of the Spirit: Three Black Women's Autobiographies of the Nineteenth Century* (Bloomington: Indiana University Press, 1986); Harriet Jacobs, *Incidents in the Life of a Slave Girl* (Boston, 1861. Reprint, Clayton, DE: Prestwick House, Inc., 2006); Albert J. Raboteau, *Slave Religion: "The Invisible Institution" in the Antebellum South* (New York: Oxford University Press, 1978); Jon F. Sensbach, *Rebecca's Revival: Creating Black Christianity in the Atlantic World* (Cambridge: Harvard University Press, 2005); Milton C. Sernett, ed., *African American Religious History: A Documentary Witness*, 2nd ed. (Durham: Duke University Press, 1999); Delores S. Williams, *Sisters in the Wilderness: The Challenge of Womanist God-Talk* (Maryknoll: Orbis Books, 1993).

Representations

Enslaved African Americans had few opportunities to represent themselves. Instead, the letters, diaries, plantation records, court documents, literature, and art in which they are represented were usually created by those who viewed the enslaved from the other side of power, freedom, and race. For the enslaved female, this objectification was compounded by traits presumed to be inherent to her race and sex. Representations of enslaved women therefore operate at the intersection of gender, race, and status. If black was inferior to white, female inferior to male, and slave inferior to free, then the enslaved black female was the lowest of the low. Although enslaved women rarely documented their own self-representations, their day-to-day lives were marked by contests over representation: If slaveholders justified their exploitation of enslaved females by representing them as libidinous sex objects, devoted family retainers, or insensible laborers, bondwomen represented themselves to each other, enslaved males, and slaveholders in ways that often ran counter to the meanings of such controlling images as Jezebel, Mammy, or Mule.

Over the history of American slaveholding, theories of race coalesced into a coherent body of thought that saw traits as diverse as intellect, sexuality, emotional sensibility, and physical beauty as biologically determined facts. African heritage defined an individual as the European's intellectual inferior, a natural follower as opposed to a natural leader, sexually promiscuous and emotionally excitable. Gender ideology similarly defined males and females in dichotomous terms. Men were intellectual and ruled by reason while women were emotional and ruled by passion; manhood implied exerting control and dominance over self and others and womanhood suggested self-denial and subservience; fatherhood meant discipline and motherhood meant sentimentality.

Proslavery representations of enslaved females embodied these twin ideologies. For instance, the Jezebel myth represented the bondwoman as a seductress—a construction that combined ideas of black sexuality and female passion, and contrasted these bodily desires with the chaste figure of the white plantation mistress. This sexualization of enslaved females' bodies served to justify slaveholders' exploitation of them as breeders of further generations of slaves, and to displace responsibility for rape from white male perpetrators to their black female victims. Mixed-race bondwomen were particular targets for such rapists who viewed their victims' lighter complexions as evidence of European refinement combined with a black libido that invited sexual exploitation.

Abolitionist art and literature appropriated these fetishized representations of the fair-skinned enslaved female body and repackaged it as the "Tragic Mullata," a figure whose mixed ancestry embodied slavery's depravity. Sexualized representations of bondwomen were central to antislavery propaganda. Abolitionists focused upon her not as a seductress, but rather as a woman whose enslaved status denied her the right to chastity or the ability to nurture her family. She was frequently portrayed as a victim, often stripped naked or semi-naked before being brutally punished by a white man or driven to despair and suicide by the loss of her children or husband to the slave trader. Such representations suggest that far from rejecting the idea of black hypersexuality, many abolitionists remained pruriently fascinated by the possibilities of the black female body.

The representation of the enslaved female as a Mammy offered an alternative fusing of gender and race in the idealized plump body of a dutiful caregiver and a surrogate mother who provided everything from milk to love. The Mammy's love for her white charges was always portrayed as childish and fawning in contrast to the deep, almost inexpressible love of a white mother for her own children. What is notable about the Mammy figure are the defining qualities inhered to both her race and gender. Intellectual inferiority, natural subservience to men, sentimentality, and the nurturing instinct were all considered female traits. Yet, intellectual inferiority and natural subservience were also seen as definitive racial traits. That they came together in the construction of the Mammy demonstrates how such qualities were effectively magnified by their combination in raced and gendered representations of bondwomen.

Historical, artistic, and literary representations of enslaved females remained trapped within these discourses for many years after emancipation and have significant currency to the present day. This is partially due to the paucity of examples of the ways enslaved females represented themselves. The most sympathetic commentators were forced to rely upon images, which objectified her in raced and gendered terms. At best, she might be portrayed in ways familiar to the abolitionist with the focus upon her identity as familial matriarch, exploited victim, or brutalized worker. At worst, representations of black women may continue to perpetuate bodily exploitation, sexual objectification, and disempowerment.

Today, the understandings of race and gender have been radically transformed by the successes of the civil rights and feminist movements, as well as the impact of postmodernism and gender theory. These have called for a general rejection of the kinds of racist and sexist worldviews that served to objectify the enslaved female. The result has been a thorough and ongoing revisionism, with writers, artists, and researchers emphasizing agency over disempowerment and individual subjectivity over objectification. Studies that explore how enslaved females exploited representations such as Jezebel and Mammy to gain advantages for themselves or their offspring are also an important aspect of this revisionist trend. While race and gender remain key categories of analysis, their reevaluation as ideological discourses rather than biological or genetic facts has allowed the development of far more nuanced and subtle representations of black women.

Perpetuating the Mammy stereotype, this African American woman is pictured with a white child in the late 1890s. (Library of Congress.)

Ben Schiller

See also Jezebel Stereotype; Mammy Stereotype.

Suggested Reading

Stephanie M. H. Camp, "The Pleasures of Resistance: Enslaved Women and Body Politics in the Plantation South, 1830–1861," *Journal of Southern History* 68, 3 (2002), 533–72;

Mille-Christine, "The Double-Headed Girl"

Millie-Christine McCoy were conjoined twins born in North Carolina in 1851. Enslaved to the McCoy family, they and their parents were eventually bought by James Pearson Smith, who exhibited them in various traveling shows. Smith's wife taught them to read, write, and sing. They died in 1912. Below is an excerpt from their perspective on their life experiences.

Millie and Christine McCoy, formerly enslaved conjoined twins from North Carolina. (State Archives of North Carolina.)

Our parents were named Jacob and Menemia and at the time of our birth were part of the family of a Mr. McCoy. Shortly afterwards we and our parents changed owners, and were taken to Anson county, North Carolina. There we became separated from our parents, and after a few more transfers in the way of ownership, became the property of Mr. James P. Smith, who gave for us, two strange lumps of humanity, the sum of $6,000.... When we were infants, not much more than fifteen months old, Mr. Smith yielding to the advice of a number of his friends and well wishers, made arrangements for starting upon an exhibition tour through the Gulf States, intending to show us at all the principal cities and towns. Our local fame was communicated to the press generally throughout the South, and soon the "South Carolina Twins," or "double headed girl," became a magnet of attraction to the lovers of the curious in nature (pp. 6–7, Millie-Christine McCoy).

Although we speak of ourselves in the plural we feel as but *one person*; in fact as such we have ever been regarded, although we bear the names Millie and Christina. One thing is certain, we would not wish to be severed, even if science could effect a separation. We are contented with our lot, and are happy as the day is long. We have but *one heart*, one feeling in common, one desire, one purpose.

The song we sing, we have so often been requested to give copies of that we have concluded to insert it in our book. We must admit that, as a literary production, it has not much merit, but it conveys a good idea of our feelings.

Its not modest of one's self to speak,
But daily scanned from head to feet
I freely talk of everything
Sometimes to persons wondering.

Some persons say I must be two,
The doctors say this is not true;
Some cry out humbug, till they see,
When they say, great mystery!

Two heads, four arms, four feet,
All in one perfect body meet;
I am most wonderfully made,
All scientific men have said.

None like me, since days of Eve,
None such perhaps will ever live,
A marvel to myself am I,
As well to all who passes by.

Im happy, quite, because Im good;
I love my Savior and my God.
I love all things that God has done,
Whether Im created two or one.
by Millie-Christine McCoy

Excerpts from: *The History of the Carolina Twins: "Told in Their Own Peculiar Way" by "One of Them,"* pp. 6–7, 20–21. (Buffalo: Buffalo Courier Printing House, Date, 18–?.)

Patricia Morton (ed.) *Discovering the Women in Slavery: Emancipating Perspectives on the American Past* (University of Georgia Press, 1996); Rupe Simms, "Controlling Images and the Gender Construction of Enslaved African Women," *Gender and Society* 15, 6 (2001), 879–97; Deborah G. White, *Ar'n't I a Woman?: Female Slaves in the Plantation South* (rev. ed., W.W. Norton, 1999).

Resistance

Enslaved women refused to accept their assigned status as brute laborers and breeders, and they resisted bondage whenever possible. While discussions of slave resistance often focus on armed rebellion, resistance to slavery manifested itself in myriad forms that ran the gamut from violent uprisings to sheer survival. While women did not employ violent means to the same extent that men did, they sometimes openly attacked slaveholders and committed acts like murder and arson.

I had reasoned dis out in my mind; there was one of two things I had a right to, liberty, or death; if I could not have one, I would have de oder; for no man should take me alive; I should fight for my liberty as long as my strength lasted, and when de time came for me to go, de Lord would let dem take me.

—Harriet Tubman, runaway slave and "conductor" on the Underground Railroad (quoted in Sarah Bradford, *Harriet Tubman, The Moses of Her People* [1886])

More often women challenged their enslavement with more subtle acts of everyday resistance, including truancy, feigned illness, birth control, and abortion.

While discussions of slave revolts commonly focus on men, some women sacrificed their lives to support violent uprisings. A woman was executed along with three men, for the murder of seven whites during a rebellion in New York in 1708. While the men were hanged, the woman was burned alive. In 1712, women also participated in another rebellion in New York during which enslaved rebels armed with guns, knives, and clubs killed several slaveholders and wounded others. Among the captured rebels was a pregnant woman; other insurgents—including one woman—killed themselves rather than surrender. In 1732, Louisiana condemned a woman and four men as the leaders of a slave conspiracy. The group was executed and their heads were publicly displayed on pikes as examples to other would-be rebels.

Realizing that open assault on the slave system was tantamount to suicide, enslaved women found more covert means by which to attack their owners. A black woman in Charleston was condemned to death for arson in 1740 and in 1776, an enslaved woman was executed in Maryland for burning her owner's house, outhouses, and tobacco barn. Poison was a particularly effective weapon for women since they worked as cooks and maids. It is impossible to determine the extent of these surreptitious acts, however, court records reveal slaveholders' fears of women's potential to poison them. As early as the mid-eighteenth century, women in South Carolina and Georgia were burned alive after being convicted of poisoning their owners and both states passed laws forbidding the sale of poisonous drugs to blacks. In 1803, the conviction of Margaret Bradley on charges of attempting to poison two white people in York, Pennsylvania incited the local black community to revolt. They attempted to set fire to the town and managed to burn down 11 buildings before the militia quelled the uprising.

Rather than politically conscious, organized violent rebellion, resistance in the United States was generally individualistic and aimed at striking a compromise between enslaved laborers and their owners on acceptable levels of work, punishment, food, and shelter. Women engaged in subtle, everyday resistance that challenged their owners' exploitation of their labor. Field hands broke tools, neglected livestock, and participated in organized work slowdowns. House servants sabotaged their owners' meals and pilfered food to nourish their families. While their owners judged such actions as laziness or theft, enslaved women did not view them as wrong. Rejecting their assigned roles as chattel property working solely for the master's gain, women asserted their humanity by negotiating the nature of their labor and claiming its rewards whenever possible.

One effective means by which enslaved women denied their owners of their labor was by running away. Women's ability to abscond, however, was shaped by motherhood and gender-based labor assignments, which greatly limited their mobility. Childcare responsibilities prevented women from running away to the same extent as men. Children would slow their movements and lead more easily to their capture, and most women would not think of leaving their children behind. Additionally, skilled labor assignments that would legitimately bring laborers off plantations and allow them to learn the lay of the land were largely reserved for men. Despite these limitations, however, women constantly challenged their owner's efforts to confine them to plantations. They ran away to enjoy a taste of freedom, lied out in the woods for short periods of time, or traveled at night to visit family members on nearby plantations.

The most successful women runaways were often those who worked in skilled positions which granted them greater mobility and confidence in their ability to support themselves on the run. Some women escaped to nearby cities where they could find refuge and employment and blend into the free black community. Due to their more limited mobility, women were more likely than men to engage in truancy, where they left plantations for short periods of time, often visiting family members or hiding in nearby woods or swamps before returning on their own accord. Truancy enabled women to remain close to their families while satisfying their personal desires for freedom, if only for a short while. Refusing to be beaten by the overseer, a Louisiana woman named Celeste escaped to a nearby swamp and built a hut out of dead branches, camouflaged with palmetto leaves. For most of the summer she lived in the swamp, returning to the plantation each night for food.

Celeste's experience demonstrates that seemingly individual acts of resistance were often group affairs that depended on the collaborative efforts of enslaved women and men. Women often supported the resistance efforts of others in the community, risking punishment to provide runaways with food, clothing, and refuge. Mothers sometimes encouraged grown children to escape and take their freedom. During the Civil War, a house servant named Mary remained on the plantation, using her trusted position in her enslaver's house to support the escapes of her brother and her three adult children. Recognizing runaways' actions as personal protests against wrongs, which they too suffered, women who possibly would never have openly challenged slavery on their own sustained the resistance efforts of others in the enslaved community.

One of the main gendered differences in slave resistance was the greater likelihood of women to feign illness. Women were better positioned than men to feign illness, particularly because slaveholders depended on women's reproductive capacity to perpetuate the institution of slavery. With limited understanding of menstruation, pregnancy, and childbirth, slaveholders were concerned about getting the most labor out of women without damaging their reproductive organs. Women could enjoy lighter work assignments or sick days by pretending to be suffering from female complaints. In addition to offering women a break from strenuous labor, feigning illness cut into planters' productivity and profits. Slaveholders and overseers often complained of women "playing the lady" to avoid labor, however, it is difficult to determine whether women who claimed illness were indeed sick or engaging in passive resistance. While women were better able than men to feign illness because of maternity and reproduction, these very aspects of their lives adversely affected their health and made them more likely to be sick.

Another threat to women's well-being was the constant threat of sexual assault. Women sometimes violently resisted rape. When a woman named Sylvia failed to complete her assigned field labor, the overseer told her to remove her clothing. Anticipating physical and possible sexual assault as punishment, Sylvia defended herself, breaking a fence railing across the overseer's arms. A young woman named Celia was repeatedly raped by her owner, Robert Newsome, who purchased her in 1850 to be his concubine when she was merely 14. She bore two children by him. After five years of sexual assault, she killed him in self-defense and was hung for his murder. In resisting the sexual advances of enslavers and overseers, women challenged white men's ownership of their bodies. Slaveholders and overseers viewed sexual access to black women as their right and women often faced grave punishment for attempting to resist. The details of the sexually sadistic punishment a woman named Rose received after refusing the advances of her slaveholder's son were too revolting for one witness to relate. Resistance to sexual assault was most often futile, not to mention dangerous. A woman named Sophy explained that there was no use in risking a beating in an effort to fight off the driver's sexual advances when he had the strength to overpower her. Women's submission to these coerced sexual encounters did not constitute consent, but rather a desperate means of survival.

Victims of both sexual and reproductive exploitation, women challenged their owners' claims to their bodies and those of their offspring by practicing abstinence and using birth control methods. In order to increase their slaveholdings, enslavers often coerced enslaved women and men into sexual encounters they believed would result in the healthiest children. Women used covert means of reproductive resistance to challenge these forced unions and deny their owners human capital. Sarah Shaw Graves explained that she and her mother were separated from her father when they were sold from Kentucky to Missouri. Sarah's mother refused to have children by another man, so she intentionally married a man whom she knew could not father children. When Mary Gaffney's enslaver forced her to marry a man she did not like, she refused to have sexual relations with him. She relented only after the slaveholder found out and whipped her. Gaffney still refused to breed, however, and chewed cotton roots to prevent herself from getting pregnant. She gave birth to several healthy children after slavery ended. The cotton plant, which was a staple crop on most antebellum Southern plantations, contained the chemical gossypol, which reduced both female and male fertility. In addition to cotton root, women used indigo, turpentine, and gunpowder as contraceptives and abortifacts.

It is difficult to ascertain the extent to which women employed these forms of reproductive resistance, since women intended to keep these practices secret. Throughout the South, planters and doctors complained about enslaved women's use of birth control and abortion methods. One South Carolina planter punished a woman named Sibby because he believed she had deliberately miscarried, and he attributed the death of a woman named Willoughby to her having eaten gunshot prior to going into labor. If women did practice birth control and abortion, they certainly had good reason. Many would rather not bear children who would be counted among their owner's chattel property and could be sold away from them. Some doubtlessly wanted to avoid childbirth, which was dangerous for all women in the antebellum era, particularly for enslaved women who received little medical care. By refusing to acquiesce to their owners' demands, women resisted bringing forth children whose destinies they would not control and denied their owners of additional chattel property.

While slaveholders often accused enslaved women of neglecting and sometimes killing their children, infanticide was rare. Recent studies in medical history have demonstrated that many of the infant deaths that slaveholders attributed to smothering were actually cases of Sudden Infant Death Syndrome (or crib death), which were the fault of planters who overworked and underfed pregnant women, rather than the failure of enslaved mothers on whom these deaths were blamed. At times, women murdered their children out of love for their offspring, as a way to free them from bondage. In January 1856, Margaret Garner escaped from slavery in Kentucky with her husband, Robert, and her four children by crossing the frozen Ohio River into Cincinnati. The fugitives were quickly surrounded by slave catchers. Determined to kill herself and her children before she would allow them to be re-enslaved, Garner killed her infant daughter with a butcher knife before their pursuers overpowered them.

Garner's actions demonstrate the lengths to which enslaved women would go to shelter their children from the evils of slavery. Enslaved women loved their children dearly and struggled to protect them. One of the strongest forms of women's resistance was the development of family and community, which served to buffer Africans and their descendants against the abuses of slavery. Women served as the central figures in the slave family and were instrumental to its survival.

As mothers, women were the primary agents of cultural transmission, passing beliefs and practices down to the next generation. In perpetuating an independent African American culture, they raised their children to reject notions of black inferiority and assert their humanity. Aware of the dangers they would face, mothers imparted necessary survival skills to their children. In particular, they taught them dissembling tactics such as masking and protecting their true selves by feigning loyalty and obedience to slaveholders—how to show one face to their owners in order to mask and protect their true selves. By raising their children not simply to survive, but to struggle against slavery, women nurtured and sustained a culture of resistance.

Far from passive victims of exploitation, enslaved women risked their safety to resist slavery whenever possible. They attacked their enslavers, ran away, feigned illness, and engaged in reproductive resistance. Rather than simply support the actions of men, women led by their own example, raising future generations of rebels and encouraging a culture of resistance. Though their actions could not threaten the slave regime, they were far from insignificant. Women refused to accept their slaveholders' absolute power over their lives and constantly resisted on whatever level possible in a powerful attempt to preserve their dignity and assert their humanity.

Amani Marshall

See also Abortion; Celia; Contraception; Garner, Margaret; Infanticide; Runaways; Truancy.

Suggested Reading

Stephanie Camp, *Closer to Freedom: Enslaved Woman and Everyday Resistance in the Plantation South* (Chapel Hill: University of North Carolina Press, 2004); Angela Davis, "Reflections on the Black Woman's Role in the Community of Slaves," *Black Scholar* 3 (December 1971), 2–15; Darlene Clark Hine and Kathleen Thompson, *A Shining Thread of Hope: The History of Black Women in America* (New York: Broadway Books, 1998); Frances Kemble, *Journal of a Residence on a Georgia Plantation in 1838–1839* (New York: Knopf, 1961. Reprint, Athens: University of Georgia Press, 1984); Wilma King, " 'Suffer with Them Till Death': Slave Women and Their Children in Nineteenth-Century America," in *More Than Chattel: Black Women and Slavery in the Americas*, eds. David Barry Gaspar and Darlene Clark Hine (Bloomington: Indiana University Press, 1996); Melton A. McLaurin, *Celia, a Slave: A True Story* (New York: Avon, 1993); S. Mintz, "Margaret Garner," *Digital History*, http://www.digitalhistory.uh.edu/black _voices/voices_display.cfm?id=76 (accessed January 15, 2008); Liese M. Perrin, "Resisting Reproduction: Reconsidering Slave Contraception in the Old South," *Journal of American Studies* 35, 2 (2001), 255–74; Deborah Gray White, *Ar'n't I a Woman?: Female Slaves in the Plantation South*, 2nd ed. (New York: W.W. Norton, 1999); Betty Wood, "Some Aspects of Female Resistance to Chattel Slavery in Low Country Georgia, 1763–1815," *The Historical Journal* 30, 3 (1987), 603–22.

Runaways

Countless numbers of women resisted their enslavement by running away. They ran to escape physical abuse and sexual assault, to protest labor assignments, to challenge the transfer to a new slaveholder to reunite with loved ones from whom they had been separated, or simply to enjoy a taste of freedom. Runaways headed to free territory, enjoyed anonymity in southern cities, or sought temporary refuge in the vicinity of the plantation. While the vast majority of runaways did not permanently escape bondage, by running away they boldly challenged their enslaved status and asserted their humanity.

Running away was a perilous endeavor. Shortly after escaping, runaways would be pursued by the plantation overseer or by paid slave catchers with their vicious hunting dogs. They also had to avoid slave patrols, organized groups of men who controlled black movement in the countryside. Runaways had to contend with inadequate food and clothing, harsh weather, and their limited knowledge of geography. Upon capture they risked brutal punishment, sale to distant places, and death.

The challenge was even more daunting for women, whose mobility was much more limited than that of men. Women were bound more tightly to plantations than men, who were allowed to travel to visit wives on other plantations or sent throughout the countryside as messengers and skilled laborers. Lacking positions that would bring them legitimately off the plantation, most women did not have the opportunity to learn the local geography and would attract attention traveling alone through the countryside. Women were further bound to plantations by motherhood and childcare responsibilities. Mothers had to consider the care of their children while on the run. Small children would have to be carried, slowing women's movement, and infants crying from hunger would lead more easily to their capture. Most women did not consider leaving children behind. Women were less likely than men to attempt to escape because of the added risks. During the antebellum period, women made up 24 percent of the advertised runaway population in South Carolina and 29 percent of the runaways in Louisiana. In the Upper South, women ran away in smaller numbers, representing between 9 and 14 percent of the runaways in Virginia, North Carolina, and Tennessee. These numbers do not reflect women's lesser desire to resist slavery, but rather their more limited options for resistance.

Motherhood factored heavily into women's decisions to run away. In the narrative of her escape, Harriet Jacobs said, "I could have made my escape alone; but it was more for my helpless children than for myself that I longed for freedom" (Jacobs 1861/2006, 136–37). Desirous of escaping the sexual advances of her enslaver but unwilling to leave her children behind, Jacobs left her owner and hid for seven years in a cramped garret above the home of her free grandmother

Charity Still, who twice escaped from slavery. (Still, William, *The Underground Railroad*, Philadelphia: Porter & Coates, 1872.)

where she could see her children. In 1842, she escaped by boat to Philadelphia, and then made her way to New York, where she arranged to have her daughter meet her. The fear of being separated from their children often motivated women to escape with little ones in tow. While awaiting auction in Charleston, a woman named Nancy escaped with her five-year-old son in an effort to avoid being separated from him during their impending sale. In an attempt to protect their unborn children from harm, some women ran away while pregnant. After receiving a brutal beating from her owner, an expectant mother named Sylvia Heard crawled to the woods, where she remained for two weeks, during which time she gave birth to twins.

Due to the limitations motherhood placed on women's mobility, most women runaways were those who did not have small children living with them. They were either barren women who could not bear children, women whose children had died, or those who had been separated from their children through sale. The loss of children often served to motivate women's escapes, as women who could not produce healthy offspring were more likely to be sold and often resisted the transfer to a new slaveholder by running away. Additionally, women absconded to visit children who had been separated from them through sale. In advertising for female runaways, slaveholders acknowledged women's desires to reunite with their children and generally listed the places where their children lived as possible destinations.

Despite the prominence of the Underground Railroad in the historical memory of slavery, escape to permanent freedom was rare. The most famous American runaway, Harriet Tubman escaped from slavery in Maryland in 1849 and made her way to the North. She returned to the South on several occasions to rescue family members and lead runaways to the North. Between 1850 and 1860, she rescued hundreds of people from slavery, earning the title "Moses." For runaways in the Lower South, however, traveling thousands of miles to northern territory was not an option, particularly for women whose knowledge of geography and mobility were further limited by gender-based labor assignments and motherhood.

Instead, women were more likely than men to engage in absenteeism or truancy, where they resisted punishment and labor assignments by leaving their enslavers temporarily. Truants stayed out anywhere from one night to several weeks, finding refuge in the woods, swamps, or slave quarters on nearby plantations. Truancy could prove just as dangerous as attempting to escape to distant points. Fleeing the plantation to avoid a brutal flogging, a young woman named Louisa spent days in a swamp inhabited by snakes and alligators. The threat of starvation eventually forced her to return.

Women seeking longer tastes of freedom were more likely than men to head to nearby cities where they could seek refuge, blend into the free black population, and find employment. Skilled women could find positions working in private residences or businesses because of the constant demand

Harriet Tubman, hailed as "the Moses of her people" because she helped hundreds of bondpeople escape from slavery. Tubman is one of the most well-known female fugitives in U.S. history. (Library of Congress.)

for domestic help among urban residents. They found employment as maids, cooks, laundresses, seamstresses, market women, and prostitutes. Although the positions available to women were less numerous and lower-paying than those available to men, they provided female runaways with a means by which to support themselves. Many of these positions offered wages as well as refuge since women could live in the backrooms or slave quarters of their employers. Relying on their network of acquaintances and marketable skills, some women were able to create free spaces for themselves in the city and avoid capture for years at a time. A seamstress named Celia left her owner in 1851 and remained out in Charleston for over two years. Disguising herself in men's clothing, she was able to move freely throughout the city, supporting herself by plying her needlework skills and finding refuge with her husband.

Many skilled runaways had closely studied the mannerisms of the free people for whom they labored and used a combination of language skills, fine clothing, and employment skills to pass as free. Using the dress, speech, and deportment of free people, they created free identities for themselves that enabled them to blend into the city's free black population or travel to distant places. Ellen Craft was fair enough to pass as a white woman, but she had to devise an ingenious performance in order to successfully escape with her brown-skinned husband, William. The social mores of the time prevented a white woman from traveling with a black man, so Ellen passed as a white male slaveholder with William passing as "his" servant. Ellen sported men's clothing and a short haircut, covered her beardless chin with a bandage and tied her arm in a sling to excuse herself from signing papers during her journey. Ellen's elaborate performance enabled the couple to travel undetected by stage, steamer, and railroad from Georgia to Philadelphia.

Although the vast majority of runaways never reached permanent freedom, their actions are significant forms of resistance as they demonstrate women's desires for freedom and determination to challenge their enslaved status despite the consequences.

Amani Marshall

See also Craft, Ellen; Female Slave Network; Jacobs, Harriet; Resistance; Tubman, Harriet.

Suggested Reading

Stephanie Camp, *Closer to Freedom: Enslaved Woman and Everyday Resistance in the Plantation South* (Chapel Hill: University of North Carolina Press, 2004); William Craft, *Running a Thousand Miles for Freedom: The Escape of William and Ellen Craft from Slavery* (London: William Tweedie, 1860. Reprint, Baton Rouge: Louisiana State University Press, 1999); John Hope Franklin and Loren Schweninger, *Runaway Slaves: Rebels on the Plantation* (New York: Oxford University Press, 1999); Harriet Jacobs, *Incidents in the Life of a Slave Girl* (Boston, 1861. Reprint, Clayton, DE: Prestwick House, Inc., 2006); Frances Kemble, *Journal of a Residence on a Georgia Plantation in 1838–1839* (New York: Knopf, 1961. Reprint, Athens: University of Georgia Press, 1984); Wilma King, " 'Suffer with Them Till Death': Slave Women and Their Children in Nineteenth-Century America," in *More Than Chattel: Black Women and Slavery in the Americas*, eds. David Barry Gaspar and Darlene Clark Hine (Bloomington: Indiana University Press, 1996); Deborah Gray White, *Ar'n't I a Woman?: Female Slaves in the Plantation South*, 2nd ed. (New York: W.W. Norton, 1999)

S

Sale and Separation of Enslaved People

See Domestic Slave Trade

Scott, Harriet Robinson

Birth Date: 1815
Death Date: 1876

As the wife of Dred Scott, both Harriet Robinson Scott and her husband filed suit for their freedom in St. Louis in 1846. According to the established precedent of the time, the Scott family, consisting of husband, wife, and two young daughters, should have been declared free because they had resided and worked for their respective slave masters, even before marrying, in free territory. This was the national and state law according to the Northwest Ordinance and the Missouri Compromise.

For eleven years the family held on in a lawsuit that pitted them against the influence of the Chouteau family, one of the wealthiest and most influential families in America. Over time, Harriet's case was subsumed in Dred's case because it was easier for the courts to litigate one rather than two cases, and under the rule of coverture, a wife's case was subordinated to that of a husband, even if the husband was enslaved.

Although the Scotts were declared free at one point in the proceedings, through appeals, both the Missouri

Engraving of Harriet Scott, wife of Dred Scott, from *Frank Leslie's Illustrated Newspaper*, June 27, 1857. (Library of Congress.)

Supreme Court and later, the U.S. Supreme court reversed the rules for litigating for freedom. The ultimate declaration that black men have no rights that white men are deemed to respect and that two acts of Congress, both the Northwest Ordinance and the Missouri Compromise were unconstitutional in providing freedom for slaves, lead to heightened North-South tensions and eventually the Civil War. The ruling also created a three-tiered system of citizenship for black Americans, Native Americans, and white Americans.

Harriet Robinson Scott is now regarded as the principal force behind the law suit, because even at the time of filing suit, Dred Scott was elderly, suffering from tuberculosis, and unable to be of value for work, while Harriet was fit and 20 years younger then her husband. Moreover, the fate of their two daughters depended upon Harriet, their mother's designation as free or slave, rather than upon their fathers. Hence, the value of the "human capital" as the term has been coined, was in owning Harriet and the girls. To continue to control them, Dred's masters continued to litigate over the value of Dred who was thought to be hardly worth his keep. In all likelihood, without Harriet, who kept the family together, sent her daughters into hiding in the final stages of litigations, and supported the family by taking in laundry, the lawsuit would probably not have been sustained for 11 years.

Born a slave in Virginia, her master Lawrence Taliaferro brought Harriet to the headwaters of the free Northwest Territory about 1835. The area, now present-day St. Paul, was at the time only a fur trade base, a stone military fort, and the wooden house in which Taliaferro carried out the duties as Indian agent to the Dakota tribe. In 1836, Etheldred "Dred" Scott arrived with his master, Dr. John Emerson. Etheldred and Harriet married within the year. Dred was 40 and Harriet was 17. Taliaferro relinquished control of Harriet upon her marriage.

Harriet and Dred were present for the monumental treaty of 1837 during which the Dakota ceded thousands of acres of land in the North Woods to the U.S. government. The Scotts traveled by steamboat between Fort Snelling and St. Louis, Missouri at Dr. Emerson's direction. Harriet was pregnant with Dred's child, and somewhere north of Missouri, Harriet gave birth to Eliza on a steamboat called the *Gypsey*. In 1840, as the Army soldiers were burning down the cabins of squatters in the area to discourage advance land claims, the Scott family left the wilderness area to return to the nearest city, St. Louis, in a slave state, Missouri, with the Emersons.

When Dr. Emerson died in 1843 making no mention of the Scotts, it was legally unclear whether they were free or enslaved. His widow, Mrs. Emerson, and her brother, John F.A. Sanford who was tightly connected by marriage and business with the fur trading house of Chouteau, continued to assert a claim to them, however. The Scotts were hired out to a series of Emerson's and Sanford's relatives and acquaintances. Harriet gave birth to Lizzie, the Scott's second daughter, in 1844 at

Jefferson Barracks where the Scotts had been sent to work for the Bainbridges. Soon after, Dred was sent further south to help Captain Bainbridge as the army prepared to invade Texas and Mexico. Harriet remained in St. Louis working for a local merchant family as a laundress.

Two years later in March 1846, Dred returned and tried to purchase his own freedom. The widow Emerson refused to sign the formal papers, likely because releasing Dred would further attenuate her already weak connection to Harriet, the moneymaking laundress, and the potentially lucrative Scott children.

After years of litigation, multiple lawsuits, numerous attorneys, a new defendant, and a stay in jail, the freedom suit rose to the U.S. Supreme Court. In 1857, the Court decided *Dred Scott vs. Sanford*. The Scotts gained considerable national fame through their freedom suit. Harriet continued to protect her family by shielding her husband and children from public attention. As luck would have it, by the time that the Supreme Court decided the matter, Mrs. Emerson had moved to abolitionist Massachusetts and had married a free labor Congressman who was greatly embarrassed to discover that he owned the most famous slave in America. He quickly arranged for someone in Missouri to manumit the Scotts. Thus, ironically, after more than a decade of suing, Harriet and her family were freed as a result of the embarrassment of her master, rather than as a result of an adjudicated right. Dred died within a year, but Harriet continued to live with older daughter, Eliza in St. Louis as a laundress through the Civil War. She died in St. Louis on June 17, 1876.

Lea VanderVelde

See also Laws; Manumission.

Suggested Reading

Lea VanderVelde, *Mrs. Dred Scott* (New York: Oxford University Press, 2009).

Seamstress Work

Seamstress work entails the production of fabric in the form of clothing and household furnishings such as curtains, bedclothes, table linens, and upholstery. During the era of American slavery, seamstress work was a fundamental component of the lives of enslaved women. Whether sewing in the privacy of their cabins, with their mistresses, or in the company of other bondswomen engaged in making quilts, enslaved seamstresses were responsible for clothing themselves, their families, and the slaveholder's household.

Enslaved seamstresses were part of a small group of skilled laborers or artisans within the slave community. In addition to their sewing responsibilities, many worked as manual laborers by day, cultivating and harvesting the fields, while devoting their nights to their sewing chores. Describing the sewing duties of Vina, an enslaved woman, Kate Pickard states in *The Kidnapped and the Ransomed* (1856), that Vina "made all [her family's] clothes herself, and washed and mended them by night. Their stockings, too, she knit[ted], though she was obliged first to card the wool and spin it" (177).

Although many enslaved women divided their labors between the fields and sewing, an exceptional few were able to work almost exclusively as seamstresses. Former bondwoman Elizabeth Hobbs Keckley, for example, became an expert dressmaker and used her skills as a means to eventual manumission. Taught to sew by her mother, Keckley supported the impoverished family who owned her by hiring herself out to sew for affluent white women in St. Louis, Missouri. With a $1,200 loan from the "best ladies" of St. Louis, she purchased her son's freedom and her own in 1855. In 1860, she established a thriving dressmaking business in Washington, D.C., where she eventually became friend and dressmaker to First Lady Mary Todd Lincoln. Keckley's autobiography, *Behind the Scenes* (1868), recounts her early years as a bondwoman and her personal relationship with Mrs. Lincoln.

Seamstress work was not only a means to freedom, as in the life of Elizabeth Keckley; it also provided a livelihood for many formerly enslaved women. *Running a Thousand Miles for Freedom* (1860), for example, is a narrative of the 1848 escape of Ellen and William Craft from slavery in Macon, Georgia to freedom in Philadelphia. The Crafts later moved to England and, while there, supported themselves in trades they both learned as bondpeople—William worked as a cabinetmaker and Ellen worked as a seamstress.

For enslaved women, seamstress work served a variety of purposes. In addition to clothing the enslaved population and the households of slaveholders, seamstress work, in some instances, provided a path to freedom and economic sustenance.

Carol J. Gibson

See also Clothing; Craft, Ellen; Hiring Out; Keckley, Elizabeth; Labor, Skilled; Manumission; Quilting.

Suggested Reading

Elizabeth Keckley, *Behind the Scenes, or, Thirty Years a Slave and Four Years in the White House* (New York: Penguin Books, 1868, rpt, 2005); Sally G. McMillen, *Southern Women: Black and White in the Old South* (Arlington Heights: IL: Harlan Davidson, Inc, 2002); Kate E. R. Pickard, *The Kidnapped and the Ransomed: Being the Personal Recollections of Peter Still and His Wife "Vina," after Forty Years of Slavery* (Syracuse: W. T. Hamilton, 1856); William Tweedie, *Running a Thousand Miles for Freedom; or, the Escape of William and Ellen Craft from Slavery* (London: William Tweedie, 1860).

Sexuality

Examining the nature of enslaved female sexuality is a challenging historical endeavor because African American women enshrouded themselves in a "culture of dissemblance" in an effort to protect aspects of their sex lives from public view. Despite this intentional secrecy as well as other omissions in the historical record, there are several critical trends about female sexuality under slavery. According to most historians, the average enslaved female reached the age of menarche at 15 and generally, as it takes a few years after the start of menstruation to reach full fecundity, gave birth to their first children at approximately 19.

The issue of enslaved girls' and women's sexuality was heavily contested by the enslaved because they sought to control their own bodies even as those who legally owned them also did. Enslaved parents often attempted to shield their daughters from becoming sexually informed, sometimes to such an extent that they withheld basic knowledge about menstruation, conception, and childbirth in an effort to maintain their innocence for as long as possible. However, as most mothers and fathers were aware the natural biological process of sexual activity could be externally manipulated. Every enslaved girl and woman was subject to constant pressures to capitulate to sexual attention from all men, white and African American. In some cases, there is strong evidence that enslaved females were coerced into "forced breeding" arrangements in which their owners pressured them to have sex or marry enslaved men who they deemed appropriate or desirable mates for the sole purpose of producing children to increase the enslaved population. In other cases, slaveholders discouraged girls and women from pursuing intimate relationships with free black men or enslaved men who were considered undesirable for not exhibiting favorable physical traits like robust size or strength.

Enslaved girls and women were also susceptible to rape. The presence of any African heritage whatsoever justified to white men their right to dominate those that were considered at this time period to be inferior and promiscuous, and who were unprotected under the law. Not only did lawmakers consider the rape of an enslaved woman unpunishable, but they deemed it virtually impossible because of perceptions that enslaved women were naturally lewd and lascivious and therefore, undeserving of legal protection against sexual crimes. Personal recollections of sexual exploitation are sorely lacking due to the fact that there are few narratives written from the perspective of enslaved women. Those that do exist do not provide numerous, explicit details about the mechanics behind sexuality. One that does, however, is Harriet Jacobs's classic memoir, *Incidents in the Life of a Slave Girl*. As shared in her narrative, when she "entered on [her] fifteenth year—a sad epoch in the life of a slave girl," her master's true intentions became known and he "began to whisper foul words in [her] ear."

Enslaved females ultimately had a choice: to accommodate themselves to sexualized terrorism or to resist. There were powerful negative inducements to succumb to sexual overtures, including the threat of physical violence, or the possibility of sale of oneself or one's children as punishment for spurning sexual invitations. Positive motivations for women to participate in coerced sexual relationships were improved housing, better food rations, and other material benefits, and the hope for manumission. For those who chose to resist, there were a number of methods available to them including absconding, violence, and "gynecological resistance" which consisted of abstinence, abortion, and infanticide.

Notwithstanding outside interference, many enslaved females were able to successfully negotiate the terms of their own sexuality. Some enjoyed long-lasting partnerships and marriages with men of their choosing. Also, while it is a subject that begs further scholarship, there is evidence suggesting that some enslaved women had deep, meaningful sexual relationships with other women.

Nicole Ribianszky

See also Abortion; Breeding; Celia; Childbirth; Concubinage; Contraception; Courtship; Hemings, Sally; Infanticide; Jacobs, Harriet; Jezebel Stereotype; Marriage and Cohabitation; Midwives; Pregnancy; Violence, Sexual.

Suggested Reading

Edward E. Baptist, " 'Cuffy,' 'Fancy Maids,' and 'One-Eyed Men': Rape, Commodification, and the Domestic Slave Trade in the United States," *American Historical Review* 106, 5 (December 2001), 1619–50; Daina Ramey Berry, *Swing the Sickle for the Harvest is Ripe: Gender and Slavery in Antebellum Georgia* (Champaign: University of Illinois Press, 2007); Sharon Block, *Rape and Sexual Power in Early America* (Chapel Hill: The University of North Carolina Press, 2006); Susan Brownmiller, *Against Our Will: Men, Women, and Rape* (New York: Simon & Schuster, 1975); Thavolia Glymph, *Out of the House of Bondage: The Transformation of the Plantation Household* (New York: Cambridge University Press, 2008); Darlene Clark Hine, "Rape and the Inner Lives of Black Women in the Middle West: Preliminary Thoughts on the Culture of Dissemblance," in *Unequal Sisters: A Multicultural Reader in U.S. History*, eds. Ellen Dubois and Vicki Ruiz (New York: Routledge, 1990), 342–47; James Hugo Johnston, *Race Relations in Virginia and Miscegenation in the United States, 1776–1860* (PhD dissertation, University of Chicago, 1937; Amherst: University of Massachusetts Press, 1970); Helene Lecaudy, "Behind the Mask: Ex-Slave Women and Interracial Sexual Relations," in *Discovering the Women in Slavery: Emancipating Perspectives on the American Past*, ed. Patricia Morton (Athens: The University of Georgia Press, 1996); Michele Mitchell, "Silences Broken, Silences Kept: Gender and Sexuality in African American History," *Gender & History* 11, 3 (November 1999), 433–44; Jennifer L. Morgan, *Laboring Women: Reproduction and Gender in New World Slavery* (Philadelphia: University of Pennsylvania Press, 2004); Nell Irvin Painter, *Soul Murder and Slavery* (Waco, TX: Markham Press,

1995); Deborah Gray White, *Ar'n't I a Woman?: Female Slaves in the Plantation South* (New York: W.W. Norton & Company, 1985), 27–46.

Slave Quarters, Life in

Slave quarters refer to structures or clusters of structures inhabited by the enslaved. Quarters for field slaves were generally located at a distance from the plantation owner's house, while quarters for most house servants were often located close to it. The exact distances between the main plantation house and slave quarters changed over time and according to region, however, slave quarters were typically in view of the main house. The slave quarters were the center of life for all enslaved people, especially women. They were the locus of family life, domestic production, and re-creation. Within the quarters, children were born and raised, family values shared, traditions maintained, networks created, and hardships endured.

> People who had families lived by theyselves, but they didn't have but one room to their houses. They had to cook and sleep in this one room, and as their children got old enough, they was sent over to the big house. Everybody called it that. The house you lived in with your family was small. It had a fireplace and was only big enough to hold two beds and a bench and maybe a chair. Sometimes if you had chillun fast enough, five and six had to sleep in that other bed together.
>
> —Unknown woman, former bondwoman (*Born in Slavery: Slave Narratives from the Federal Writers' Project, 1936–1938 Georgia Narratives, Volume IV, Part 4,* 361–62)

Slave houses varied by time period and region but typically were one or two room cabins with rooms generally between 12- and 18-feet square. Cabins were built directly on the ground or set on piers. These cabins typically had a chimney, a hearth, a door, and a window. The windows were frequently unglazed. Most often the floors were dirt floors. Enslaved women transformed these rudimentary houses into homes.

Several sources of information provide insight into the lives of enslaved women within slave quarters. Slave narratives, court cases, family letters, traveler's accounts, and archaeological evidence all contribute to our understandings of women's daily activities. Women had many roles in the quarter, including mother, sister, daughter, friend, spouse, head of household, midwife, caregiver, cook, seamstress, nurse, culture bearer, and laborer.

Although frequently interrupted by slaveholders, family life and social networks were the core of life in the quarters. Women relied on each other, by choice and by force, for help with significant events and concerns in their lives such as birth control, childbirth, childcare, health, and well-being. Enslaved women were

Slave quarters on a plantation, possibly in Beaufort, South Carolina. Photographed by Mathew Brady, ca. 1862. (Library of Congress.)

denied many of the rights of motherhood and some attempted to avoid becoming mothers at all. Women shared knowledge of birth control methods with each other. Women learned whom they could trust for this kind of sensitive information based on social networks they established in the slave quarters. When women did become pregnant, enslaved midwives typically facilitated childbirth and children were born at home, within the slave quarters. Most pregnant women worked until they went into labor, then they were typically allowed one month to recover from childbirth before returning to the house or fields.

When women left the quarters for work at dawn, they usually left their young children in the care of older children or elderly women. At some plantations, women with infants were allowed to go to the quarters or nursery one to three times during the workday to nurse their infants. Aside from this, most activities of women within the quarter took place from sundown to sunup, on Saturday or Sunday, and on holidays, because this is when they were not working for the slaveholder. During the six-day workweek, women had little time or energy to invest in activities once they returned to the quarters every evening. However, they still managed to cook, sew, take care of children, garden, and engage in economic activities to obtain things they needed and desired.

Although plantation owners or overseers typically dictated the location and sizes of slave houses, people had more freedom to organize the space around and within their homes. Archaeological evidence reveals that yard space was an important activity space in the quarters. The preferred yard space was on the side of the slave house that was out of the view of the main house. This removed the activities of the enslaved from the view of the slaveholder. Most of the things bondpeople owned, such as animals and garden plots were kept in the yard and many household activities, such as cooking, took place in the yard as well.

In addition to yard space, many enslaved women had gardens or "provisioning grounds," which were intended to provide subsistence. Several former bondpeople recalled personal and family garden plots: "All the slave families had a garden spot for they own self, take out what they need whenever they need it" (Baker and Baker 1996, 53). A former enslaved individual recalled: "Every slave had a patch of his own . . . What he made on that patch belonged to him" (Ibid., 226). Gardens provided a sense of ownership and private property and offered a degree of personal empowerment to those who cultivated them.

Gardens played a critical role in enslaved women's ability to participate in the domestic economy. Enslaved women and men grew crops to supplement their diet and as a means of creating surplus to sell to the enslaver, others, or at market. The ability to generate surplus crops seems to have been contingent upon life cycle. Married women with young children were less likely to engage in marketing activities than single women, women with older children, and older women (Heath 2004, 26). In addition to gardening, many women also raised poultry in their yards to earn money. Basket, mat, and broom production within the home was another means of earning money. Enslaved women performed all of these activities on their own time, after long workdays.

Evidence of women's work in slave quarters, for themselves and slaveholders, is found in slave narratives and by archaeologists. Archaeologists have been excavating slave quarters to learn about the lives of the enslaved since the 1960s. Sewing tools, such as needles, thimbles, scissors, lacing rods, and straight pins demonstrate women's work within the quarters. These types of artifacts have been recovered at many slave quarters, including the quarters at Utopia, Andrew Jackson's Hermitage, and Thomas Jefferson's Poplar Forest. Many of these artifacts were recovered in subfloor pits within slave cabins. Enslaved women and men dug these pits in dirt floors to store root crops and personal belongings.

Aside from working in the quarters, women also engaged in leisure activities with their families and friends. Sometimes, this meant simply gathering together in small or large groups to talk and share stories. On other occasions, it meant sharing music and dancing. Marriah Hines, a former bondwomen from Virginia, recalled that evenings in the quarters were spent quilting, making clothes, spinning, telling jokes, talking, pulling candy, and singing accompanied by banjo (Perdue et al. 1976, 141).

Women could also expect occasional evening visits from husbands, family, or friends who lived on neighboring plantations if they received passes from their owners.

Although some plantations had hospitals where slaves went to convalesce, women might also spend time in the quarters if they were ill. Health and well-being practices, however, were generated in the quarters. In addition to growing crops for subsistence and economic means, enslaved women also planted herbs and plants with medicinal properties. In interviews with Works Progress Administration (WPA) officials in the 1930s, several former bondpeople recalled the natural medicines they used, and sometimes the women who administered them. Spiritual practices were also important for curing and prevention of illness.

Scholars have demonstrated that African and African American peoples wore glass beads in the past and present for medicinal and spiritual purposes. Particular types of beads were and are used to cure and prevent illness. Archaeologists have found similar types of beads in burials of enslaved African and African American infants in Virginia and New York. Their mothers probably placed these charms on them. Enslaved women also used personal charms of many types. Spiritual practitioners, women and men, known as conjurers, created charms.

Conjuring involves intervening with spiritual forces through ritual practices to elicit healing, protection, success, or to invoke or prevent harm. African American conjuring had its roots in West and Central African spiritual practices and supernatural beliefs. African conjuring practices and charm use were creolized in the Americas over time through the influence of European and Native American spiritual traditions. The continuity of charm use over generations indicates its significance. Charms offered women a means of empowerment when facing the unpredictable and a method of resistance to the harsh realities of daily life. These harsh realities included oppression, sickness, death, violence, and separation from their families and friends.

Slave quarters were a place where enslaved women planned, plotted, loved, hoped, and dreamed. They were also a place where they suffered, and sometimes perpetrated, violence. Rape, murder, incest, infanticide, domestic and interpersonal violence all occurred in slave quarters. Women endured these extreme hardships through reliance on friends, family, and through spiritual and religious practices.

Lori Lee

See also Community; Conjurers; Female Slave Network; Gardening.

Suggested Reading

T. Lindsay Baker and Julie Baker, eds. *The W.P.A. Oklahoma Slave Narratives* (Norman: University of Oklahoma Press, 1996); Elizabeth Fox-Genovese, *Within the Plantation Household: Black and White Women of the South* (Chapel Hill: University of North Carolina Press, 1988); Barbara Heath, "Engendering Choice: Slavery and Consumerism in Central Virginia," in *Engendering African American Archaeology*, eds. Jillian Galle and Amy Young (Knoxville: University of Tennessee Press, 2004); Dylan Penningroth, *The Claims of Kinfolk* (Chapel Hill: University of North Carolina Press, 2003); Charles Perdue Jr., Thomas Barden, and Robert Phillips, *Weevils in the Wheat* (Charlottesville: University Press of Virginia, 1976); Deborah Gray White, *Ar'n't I a Woman: Female Slaves in the Plantation South* (New York: W.W. Norton & Company, 1985).

Slaveholders, Free Black Women

One of the unexpected anomalies of slavery in the U.S. South has been the ownership of bondmen and women by free blacks. There has long been some controversy concerning its explanation (see Woodson 1924, v–viii; Woodson 1925, xxiv–xxv). Some argue that this was principally due to attempts to maintain family ties when it might otherwise not been possible given the southern slave law. Others claim that the primary reason was the drive for profits and incomes by free blacks, in a manner similar to the goals of other Southerners, with possibly no dramatic difference in the treatment of bondpeople by white and by black slaveholders. While larger slaveholdings no doubt reflect an attempt to be wealthy members of the planter class, the large number of relatively smallholdings might be attributed either to family connections or else to the financial constraints of individuals with low incomes. To date, there seems no fully satisfactory resolution of this debate, but it is clear that some small percentage of free blacks enslaved other black men and women before the Civil War, and there was some ownership of bondpeople in each state of the South where slavery was permitted.

Carter G. Woodson compiled the most complete listing of free black slaveholders from the manuscript schedule of the 1830 U.S. Census (1924). Woodson lists the names of each slaveholder, their geographic location, and the number of enslaved individuals owned by each. His estimates indicate that the free black slaveholders equaled about 2.5 percent of all southern free blacks, and that the four states of Louisiana, Virginia, Maryland, and South Carolina accounted for about eighty percent of all free black enslavers. Most holdings were quite small, with about 42 percent of all slaveholders having only one bondperson, and about 95 percent enslaving fewer than ten individuals in 1830. The average size of a slave holding was about 3.4. The number of slaveholders fluctuated over time, and declined sharply with the approach of the Civil War.

As a disproportionate number of the free blacks lived in cities, cities were the locale of the larger number of free black slaveholders of bondpeople. As there was a large population of mixed-race individuals among the free blacks, they tended to be the largest number of holders of enslaved blacks. In urban areas, there tended to be an unbalanced sex ratio, with more females among the free blacks. There was frequently a larger share of free black women among the slaveholders.

The bondpeople owned by free black women generally pursued the occupations of their holders, often performing occupations such as seamstress, washerwomen, pastry cooks, and other service industries. During the period 1823–1828 in the city of Savannah, there were 42 free black slaveholders of bondpeople, 31 of them women. The largest holding, of nine enslaved individuals, was by a free woman of color, Hannah Leion (Wood 2000, 16). In Charleston, about 42 percent of free blacks owned bondpeople in 1850, and about 64 percent of the slaveholders were women. By 1860, the share of female owners had fallen to 52 percent (Koger 1995, 23–24). Rural holdings, however, were predominately owned by male, and these were often the largest units. The largest black slaveholder in 1860 was the woman owner of a sugarcane plantation in Louisiana, Madame Cyprien Ricard and her son, with 152 enslaved people. Outside Louisiana, the largest slaveholder was cotton-planter William Ellison in South Carolina, who enslaved about 63 individuals in 1860 (Johnson and Roark 1984, 126–29).

The acquisition of bondpeople by free blacks was accomplished by several different means. The role of inheritance from enslaved men or, at times, from white slaveholders played a larger role, particularly for women, but the role of purchases made from earnings was also important, especially in urban areas. It is believed that most black slaveholders had previously been free and that some were manumitted by their former enslavers and provided with a gift of assets.

Stanley Engerman

See also Free Women.

Suggested Reading

R. Halliburton, Jr. "Free Black Owners of Slaves: A Reappraisal of the Woodson Thesis," *South Carolina Historical Magazine* 76 (July 1970), 129–42; Michael P. Johnson and James L. Roark, *Black Masters: A Free Family of Color in the Old South* (New York: Norton, 1984); Larry Koger, *Black Slaveowners: Free Black Slave Masters in South Carolina, 1790–1860* (Columbia: University of South Carolina Press, 1995); Loren Schweninger, *Black Property Owners in the South, 1790–1915* (Urbana: University of Illinois Press, 1990); Betty Wood, *Gender, Race, and Rank in a Revolutionary Age: The Georgia Low Country, 1750–1820* (Athens: University of Georgia Press, 2000); Carter G. Woodson, *Free Negro Owners of Slaves in the United States in 1830* (Washington, DC: The Association for the Study of Negro Life and History, 1924); Carter G. Woodson, *Free Negro Heads of Families in the United States in 1830* (Washington, DC: The Association for the Study of Negro Life and History, 1925).

South, The

Enslaved women were ubiquitous throughout the region that became known as the American South. Gradually increasing in numbers from the early seventeenth century, bondwomen eventually constituted a sizeable fraction of the nearly four million bondpeople in that region on the eve of the Civil War. Most of these women and their families remained there after the war and the subsequent abolition of slavery by the Thirteenth Amendment in 1865.

The term "the South" is generally used to describe the region located below the Mason-Dixon line, a surveyed 233-mile boundary line that extended from southern Pennsylvania to the Ohio River in the west. Over time though, especially after the 1820 Missouri Compromise, which attempted to balance the number of slave and free states in the new nation, the Mason-Dixon line only grew in symbolism as the young republic struggled over the slavery question in the years leading up to the Civil War. For some "the South" is often used to categorize the 11 slave states that seceded from the Union to form the Confederate States of America in 1861. Yet, the South extended well beyond the political borders of the Confederacy. In fact, the region also contained several states not in active rebellion against the federal government; these four states (Delaware, Kentucky, Maryland, and Missouri) did not secede and were termed "border states" by the Lincoln Administration since they did not strongly believe in the use of military force to settle the nation's problems.

As it was then, the South remains further divided, and usually into two distinct subregions: the Lower (Deep South) and the Upper South. States typically included in the Lower South are Georgia, South Carolina, and the Gulf States of Alabama, Mississippi, Louisiana and Texas. Sometimes, Florida and Arkansas are also grouped with the other Lower South states. Meanwhile, the Upper South includes Virginia, Maryland, Delaware, North Carolina, West Virginia (which only became a state two years before the end of slavery), and Tennessee, Kentucky, and Missouri. Although both areas form the South, they also differ in significant ways, mainly in terms of geography, climate, histories, patterns of settlement, demographics, and economics. In the case of enslaved women, these intraregional dynamics and variations certainly shaped the nature and quality of their enslavement experiences. As one historian has pointed out, there were *many* Souths; and the bondwomen scattered throughout the region certainly recognized that slavery was not the same in every southern slave state.

North American slavery traces its origins to the South. Well before racial slavery grew into a deeply entrenched national institution, the first people of African descent to settle in British North America arrived in the southern colony of Virginia on a Dutch man-of-war vessel in 1619. Though not initially marked as race slaves, these Africans most likely toiled alongside European indentured servants in the colony. Presumably, a few African women were also part of the human cargo that helped populate and settle this first permanent British colony on the continent. Over time, tobacco replaced indigo (a plant used to make purple dye) production and emerged as a highly valued cash crop in Virginia. Shortly thereafter, both Virginia and its neighbor to the north, Maryland, recognized race slavery as an acceptable means of extracting cheap and plentiful labor and ordering their inhabitants along racial lines. In 1662, Virginia enacted a law that made racial slavery hereditary. For enslaved women, particularly, this law maintained that slavery was not only a condition defined primarily by race, but also one that a mother could pass along to her children. Thus, the mother's slave status was transferred to her offspring, consequently marking generations mothered by bondwomen as unfree laborers throughout the British colonies and especially in the American South. In 1705, the earlier Virginia law on slavery was further expanded and hardened. Now, all non-Christian servants entering the colony would also become bound labor though the intended targets were clearly peoples of African descent. And according to this very law, bondpeople could also suffer the indignities and brutality at the hands of slaveholders without legal consequence. Therefore, slaveholders gained unchecked power over their enslaved workers, which sometimes meant violence and sexual exploitation of bondwomen.

Shortly after Virginia became the first British colony to codify race slavery, other southern colonies also began to invest heavily in African slave labor. Hence, the once fluid line between indentured servitude and slavery was now replaced by an evolving racial caste system that facilitated a thriving Transatlantic Slave Trade, which enriched both the North and South. After many successful slaveholders from Barbados settled in South Carolina, they ultimately realized that the coastal, swampy climate and easy port access made the colony ideal for rice cultivation. Around 1700, South Carolina planters introduced plantation labor to the colony, which other southern colonies gradually adopted. Within 15 to 20 years of settlement, or around 1720, bondpeople in South Carolina noticeably outnumbered the European population. Bondwomen, especially, constituted a sizeable portion of the population and proved invaluable to South Carolina's booming rice industry. Planters exploited enslaved women for their longstanding knowledge of rice cultivation, a skill many Africans brought to South Carolina and the rice low country that also later included parts of coastal Georgia. Many rice planters, therefore, were willing to pay top dollar for enslaved Africans from the "Rice Coast" of western Africa, as they provided valuable reproductive and physical labor.

Once brought to the rice plantations and assigned field duties, bondwomen performed many of the same tasks as men, though they usually worked in gender-segregated groups and completed much of their labor under the task system. The task system, unlike gang labor, afforded bondpeople small moments of "free time for themselves during which many women cared for their households and maintained small garden plots to support their families' nutritional intake. By dividing field work into highly specialized and timed tasks, most rice planters reinforced gendered, African divisions of labor among their bondpeople. Still, working separately from men in the fields did not mean easier or lighter work for women. In fact, their sex rarely shielded them from the notorious physical demands and potential health risks associated with rice cultivation. They worked the fields, pregnant or not, and with their hair tied in headwraps and skirts hiked above their knees, from sunup to sundown. They hoed, dug, and harvested rice just as the men, yet they suffered the additional burden of reproducing for the slaveholder's benefit.

In colonial Georgia, planters there also realized the potential profits rice could bring to the newly established colony (1733), but a ban on slavery slowed full-scale production until the 1760s. By then, bondwomen performed tasks and lived in conditions similar to those living in neighboring South Carolina. Over time, the enslaved population in Georgia increased by means of natural increase and slave importation. In fact, from 1760 to 1775, Georgia's enslaved population dramatically climbed. Initially, there were nearly 500 bondpeople living in Georgia and that number grew to approximately 18,000 by the 1760s. By 1860, however, the federal census counted more than 230,000 enslaved women living in Georgia compared to the 205,000 bondwomen in South Carolina. Most of these bondwomen worked on large rice plantations or on cotton plantations in the red clay hills of the Georgia Piedmont or in the lower Piedmont, or Black Belt counties. By 1860, however, most of Georgia's enslaved population lived and worked in the Black Belt, and their numbers were sometimes ten times greater than the enslaved populations found in the coastal rice counties.

One advantage to living in the rice low country was the relative degree of autonomy bondpeople enjoyed. Since many planters and their families refused to live in the unhealthy and harsh swampy conditions, their enslaved workers were able to live in an environment with little white interaction, and in the process, these coastal slave communities were able to retain some aspects of their African linguistic, agricultural, and religious traditions. In coastal Georgia, the Geechee culture flourished, and in South Carolina, similarly, the Gullah culture connected many bondpeople to their West African roots. Thus, mothers and fathers were able to pass down particular and prized aspects of African culture (the language, the spiritual traditions like the ring shout, or even special recipes and cooking techniques) to their progeny.

Moreover, some bondwomen even toiled in urban areas like Savannah, Charleston, and Richmond, where they often worked in street markets or in the homes of the wealthy and professional classes in the city. In Charleston, for example, urban slaves constituted nearly one-third of the city's population in 1860. Other southern cities also experienced sizeable urban enslaved populations. Life as an urban slave did provide a few advantages such as less arduous work, increased geographic mobility, and sometimes the opportunity to live away from the slaveholder's close scrutiny. Some bondwomen and their families lived in slave communities within these urban areas, which provided ample opportunities to socialize with other bondpeople and form some semblance of community. Still, most urban slaves in the South dwelled in the attics or back rooms of the slaveholder's home. If the slaveholder was wealthy enough, then his enslaved laborers sometimes lived in separate buildings near the main house. For many bondwomen, these close, intimate living arrangements sometimes put them at greater risk of sexual exploitation by profligate slaveholders and made them easy targets of jealous rage by the slaveholders' wives. Thus, urban bondwomen more often had to contend with additional risks of slightly more autonomy and lighter work than their sisters who toiled as field hands.

Following the American Revolution and the invention of the cotton gin in 1793, southern slavery took on a new dimension. Though the Revolution was fought in the name of liberty, it did little to secure the freedom of the enslaved in the South. Enslaved families endured dislocation, death, and wholesale disappointment as the war wreaked havoc on their homes and tore many bondmen away from loved ones. Unlike many of the bondpeople in the North, the war did little to change to legal status of those living in the South. Nonetheless, the American Revolution did provide the rhetoric of freedom that many would embrace to make their own cases for freedom. Once the war ended, slavery began to spread further southwest, especially as the lure of cotton wealth attracted many planters to the Deep South where cotton could grow in abundance.

Thus, the westward expansion of slavery following the Louisiana Purchase of 1803 not only enabled the growth of the South, it also further entrenched slave labor as a vital engine of the American economy. And as such, enslaved families living in the Upper South constantly feared the threat of separation and sale as the Chesapeake plantation economies began to stagnate. While many slaveholders recognized the large profits that accompanied the selling of slaves down South in the Domestic Slave Trade, it was not uncommon for bondwomen to realize that the nation's growing fixation on the cotton trade also meant the inevitability of losing their husbands or children to the Domestic Slave Trade, especially since Congress banned the African Slave Trade in 1808. Hence, bondwomen in the Upper South more frequently made attempts to escape the grip of slavery by running North or by taking advantage of the anonymity of urban living. In cities like Baltimore, Richmond, and Washington D.C., some enslaved women assumed free status and worked under oppressive conditions as domestics and nurses simply to earn enough money to buy family members out of slavery. Still, a majority of bondwomen labored on farms and plantations in the Upper South until the end of slavery.

From the 1800s onward, the quality of life for bondwomen throughout the South changed very little. With the addition of new southern states like Mississippi (1817), Alabama (1819), Arkansas (1836), and Texas (1845), bondwomen and their reproductive and physical labor were employed to both populate and work the quickly growing region. They were certainly pushed to work harder, to reproduce more and faster, and suffer many daily injustices that white women did not have to endure. They labored as field hands, spinners, nurses, cooks, and domestics on plantations in the Cotton Belt. They chopped sugar cane, cultivated rice and cotton on plantations in Louisiana. They grew hemp and tobacco in Kentucky. Bondwomen labored in the homes of elites in New Orleans, Galveston, Mobile, and Natchez and for some, in factories or on the battlefields during the heat of Civil War. Perhaps their most prized work, however, took place in their private homes where they reared children and taught them invaluable skills and lessons for coping with slavery and other aspects of life. It would be these life lessons that younger generations would then recollect as they attempted to navigate life in the South after the fall of the slavery regime in 1865. Since the Civil War had taken away many bondmen from their families, women became the backbones of black families and used their wisdom, strength, and faith to guide generations from slavery to freedom in the American South.

Jermaine Thibodeaux

See also American Revolution; Civil War; Labor, Nonagricultural; North, The; Wet Nursing.

Suggested Reading

Daina Ramey Berry, *Swing the Sickle for the Harvest Is Ripe: Gender and Slavery in Antebellum Georgia* (Urbana-Champaign: University of Illinois Press, 2007); John Boles, *Black Southerners, 1619–1869* (Lexington: University of Kentucky Press, 1984); Judith A. Carney, *Black Rice: The African Origins in Rice Cultivation* (Cambridge: Harvard University Press, 2001); Deborah Gray White, *Ar'n't I a Woman?: Females Slaves in the Plantation South* (New York: W.W. Norton, 1985); Peter Wood, *Black Majority: Negros in Colonial South Carolina from 1670 to the Stono Rebellion* (New York: Knopf, 1973).

T

Taboos and Superstitions

Taboos are social prohibitions that include restricted actions, foods, relationships, people, words, places, or other ideas or things. Breaking a taboo may result in social ostracizing, emotional guilt, and in cases when cultural taboos are codified laws, criminal offences and legal penalties. Taboos may be national, regional, and generational. In some cases, they are based on family or individual factors such as spirituality or religious beliefs. Anthropologists, historians, and sociologists have found that taboos exist in all cultures throughout history.

Superstitions are irrational beliefs based on fear and on ignorance of the laws of nature. The status of a superstition relies on a person's perspective. Often, outside observers consider beliefs foreign to their own cosmological understanding as superstitious. Additionally, people often consider beliefs that differ from the mainstream religion of society superstitious. In general, they are beliefs that are connected to a person's or a society's cosmological belief system. They are often components of a people's religious experience, but may also include some secular beliefs. Superstitions often relate to magic and the belief that a person can influence the natural world by tapping into a spiritual reality, thereby manipulating nature and natural outcomes. In this way, what some people or one society considers a superstition, another society might consider a valid and important piece of information relevant to their cosmological understanding of the universe. Like various faith-based beliefs of organized religions, superstitions overwhelmingly pertain to the unknown and the mysterious. They function to assuage fear by suggesting that a person has some power over the unknown if only they follow the prescribed action for which the superstition calls.

In slave communities in the United States, taboos and superstitions were integral parts of people's personal and social lives, dictating social interactions and providing the context for day-to-day life. They were often derived from beliefs and practices rooted in African traditions and influenced by Native American and European folk culture. Superstitions gave slaves ways to deal with each other, with their slave masters, and the daily trauma of slave life. Some of the major taboos and superstitions among slave women revolved around childbirth and midwifery, folk remedies, love and family, harmful magic, and the evil eye. For example, taboos around the family included whom not to marry. Superstitions warned people about what would happen to children from those illegal unions. The interpretation of dreams and ways to be rid of bothersome people were also important components of taboos and superstitious beliefs. To dream of a dying man warned a person to expect the death of a woman or girl. To dream of a dying woman warned of the death of a man or boy. To be rid of a bothersome foe, a person might bury chicken feet in a place where their foe would walk; soon the person would decide to leave or somehow be forced to leave the area.

Slaves passed on taboos and superstitions of the antebellum period to subsequent generations. They maintained those traditions and carried them to the North during the Great Migrations. Today, there are people who subscribe in part or in full to the spiritual practices of the slave ancestors and respect the so-called superstitions as strong components of their personal or communal spirituality. Women, mothers, deaconesses, teachers, and midwives in the African American community today, as in the antebellum period, serve as the major keepers and creators of evolving taboos and superstitions in their communities.

Sakina Mariam Hughes

See also Conjurers; Folk Medicine and Healing; Folklore and Folktales; Religion; Voodoo

Suggested Reading

Georgia Writer's Project, Drums and Shadows (Athens: University of Georgia Press, 1986); Newbell Niles Puckett, *Folk Beliefs of the Southern Negro* (Chapel Hill: University of North Carolina Press, 1926); Albert J. Raboteau, *Slave Religion: The "Invisible Institution" in the Antebellum South* (New York: Oxford University Press, 1980).

Taylor, Susie King

Birth Date: 1848
Death Date: 1912

My dear friends! Do we understand the meaning of war? Do we know or think of that war of '61? No, we do not, only those brave soldiers, and those who had occasion to be in it, can realize what it was. I can and shall never forget that terrible war until my eyes close in death. The scenes are just as fresh in my mind today as in '61.

—Susie King Taylor, former bondwoman and Civil War nurse (*Reminiscences of My Life in Camp with the 33rd US Colored Troops, Late 1st South Carolina Volunteers,* 50.)

Susie King Taylor, a Civil War chronicler, nurse, and teacher, was born on August 6, 1848 in Isle of Wight, Georgia, about 35 miles from Savannah. She was the first of nine children born to Hagar Ann Reed and Raymond Baker, and she was enslaved on the Grest Farm, which was owned by Valentine and Mary Grest. She grew up surrounded by her family and could trace her ancestry back to her great-grandparents. Baker was particularly close to, and lived with her grandmother, Dolly Reed for much of her childhood.

The Grests freed Reed, who lived in Savannah afterward. At age seven, Baker and two siblings went to Savannah to live with their grandmother. Like other southern states, Georgia had strict laws prohibiting slaves from learning to read and write. Despite the dangers, Baker's grandmother sent her and a grandson to a clandestine school run by a free woman of color. After studying in a second secret school, Baker convinced a white playmate and later, her landlord's son to serve as her informal teachers. In this unconventional manner, Baker obtained an education and wrote travel passes for family and community members. After Union forces secured Port Royal off the coast of South Carolina in late 1861, enslaved blacks in this region began flooding Union lines. Baker's family became a part of this migration in 1862 after the capture of Fort Pulaski. Soon after her arrival on St. Simon's Island, Baker was teaching 40 children

Susie King Taylor, pictured in her 1902 book *Reminiscences of My Life in Camp*. (Library of Congress.)

during the day and adults at night. Once the Union Army began accepting black men as soldiers and forming regiments, she was enrolled as a laundress. During that period with the regiment, she married Edward King, a soldier with the First South Carolina Volunteers. She traveled with the troops for the entire war, serving as a laundress, nurse, and teacher to the black soldiers. After the Civil War, King and her husband returned to Savannah where she operated a school. King's husband died shortly thereafter on September 16, 1866. Unable to compete with Beach Institute, a new missionary school operated for free blacks by the American Missionary Association, King began working as a domestic for wealthy whites.

King's domestic work took her to Boston in 1874. She stayed in Boston for the remainder of her life, working as a cook and laundress until she married Russell L. Taylor in 1879. While living in Boston, Taylor continuously worked to help Union veterans and to maintain the memory of black sacrifice and bravery during the Civil War. In 1886, she helped to organize the Women's Relief Corps, which aided Union veterans. In 1902, she published her memoirs, which focused primarily on the battles fought by black soldiers. Her book, *Reminiscences of My Life: A Black Woman's Civil War Memoirs*, remains the only one of its kind written by a black woman. It is informative for its insights into slavery, black soldiers' Civil War experiences, and the views of blacks about the North and race relations in the South after Reconstruction. Taylor died in Boston, Massachusetts on October 6, 1912.

Stephanie Wright

See also Civil War; Community; Education; Family; Free Women; Laws; Labor, Nonagricultural; North, The.

Suggested Reading

Susie King Taylor, *Reminiscences of My Life in Camp: A Black Woman's Civil War Memories*, eds. Patricia Romero and Willie Lee Rose (New York: Marcus Wiener, 1988); Heather Williams, *Self-Taught: African American Education in Slavery and Freedom* (Chapel Hill: University of North Carolina, 2005).

Thomas, Sally

Birth Date: 1787
Death Date: 1850

Born in 1787, enslaved Sally Thomas grew up on the 1,596-acre tobacco plantation of Charles Thomas in Albemarle County, Virginia. As a young woman, she drew the attention of one of the Thomas men (probably John L. Thomas, her enslaver's brother), and had to acquiesce to his sexual advances. In 1808, when she was 21, she gave birth to a mixed-race son, John, and the next year, in October 1809, to a second boy, whom she named Henry. Both were born in slavery. Following the death of her owner in 1814, and his widow in 1816, Thomas became part of the Thomas estate and, as such, was taken with her boys by a member of the family to the fast-growing town of Nashville.

Shortly after her arrival, Thomas obtained permission from the family member to hire herself out as a laundress, a practice common among urban slaves. She also secured an agreement to retain a portion of her earnings. Sometime later, she rented a frame house on the corner of Deaderick and Cherry Streets in the central business district. There she established her business, which specialized in washing and cleaning men and women's fine apparel. She converted the front room of her home into a laundry where she manufactured her own soap, blending fats, oils, alkali, and salt in a small vat.

As the city grew and expanded during the 1820s and 1830s, Thomas built up a loyal clientele. During the morning hours, she made her rounds to homes and businesses, collecting sheets, towels, dresses, shirts, trousers, coats, hats, jackets, and undergarments. She then returned to begin the arduous process of sorting and cleaning. Despite a recession during the early 1820s, the wealth of white residents rose dramatically during the decade. Consequently, the demand for Thomas' services increased. As her reputation for high-quality work spread, Thomas had more business than she could handle.

Even during these early years it was apparent that she was not enslaved in the usual sense. As time passed, she became what contemporaries term quasi- or virtually-free: she came and went as she pleased, rented her own house, ran her own business, and negotiated her own contracts. She bought and sold various items, and she possessed her own property. It was against the law for bond-people to act in such a manner, but residents of Nashville valued her services to such an extent that they either did not care or did not know that she was in fact enslaved.

Thomas dreamed of someday saving enough money to purchase her children's and her own freedom, but even with her drive and ambition this seemed unlikely. Her income varied, but it was rarely more than $15 or $20 a month. Young enslaved children were selling for as much as $300, and handsome, intelligent, "likely" women like Sally Thomas—despite being older—might bring $400 or $500. Her plan for her eldest son, however, did not involve buying him out of slavery. Instead, she made arrangements for him to work as a personal waiter and poll boy for Richard Rapier, a barge captain who navigated the western rivers. A short time after she made this arrangement Rapier shifted his operations to Florence, Alabama, located below Muscle Shoals on the Tennessee River. In 1824, she learned that Rapier had set aside one thousand dollars to purchase "the freedom of the mulatto boy, John, who now waits on me, and belongs to the Estate of Thomas" (Schweninger, 1975). In 1830, he was freed and took the name John H. Rapier. In the midst of this same period, in October 1827, at the age of 40, Thomas gave birth to her third son, James, who was also born enslaved. His father was John Catron, chief justice of the Tennessee Supreme Court and later a justice of the United States Supreme Court, who never admitted his paternity. Thomas sensed that it would be nearly impossible to save enough money to purchase her sons Henry—now a young man and worth a substantial amount—and James, who was worth $200 even as an infant.

By the early 1830s, Thomas' stringent economy bore fruit; she had saved several hundred dollars, mostly in Mexican gold coins, which she hid in the loft of their home. In 1834, however, she received devastating news. The Thomas estate was about to be broken up and distributed among various heirs. She initially returned to Virginia with James, but good fortune came her way when one of the family members took them back to Nashville, even though Thomas now had a new enslaver, John M. Martin, who was guardian of one of the minors involved. Through her long-time friendship with Ephraim Foster, a lawyer, Thomas negotiated to buy James with her savings and later purchased herself with the help of another lawyer, George Fogg. However, after both purchases she and her son remained enslaved in the eyes of the law. At the same time, to save Henry from possible sale, she urged him to run away. He eventually made it to Buffalo, New York and gained his freedom.

Despite her legal status, Thomas went about her business with energy and enthusiasm. She taught James the laundry business and arranged for him and her two grandchildren, John Rapier Jr. and James Rapier, to attend the same school following the death of their mother in Alabama. Thomas was so well known in Nashville by the 1840s that many residents thought she was free and owned her own home. In fact, she was so much a fixture in the city that when the U.S. census marshal arrived at 10 Deaderick Street in the summer of 1840, he listed her by name as the head of the household, which was an extremely rare status for bond-people. In summer of 1850, at age 63, she remained vibrant, energetic, and ebullient. But in early September, in the midst of a cholera epidemic in the city, Thomas contracted the dreaded disease and died within a few days. Although her death came quickly, her legacy would remain for generations.

Loren Schweninger

See also Concubinage; Domestic Slave Trade; Emancipation; Hiring Out; Laws; Urban Slavery.

Suggested Reading

John Hope Franklin and Loren Schweninger, *In Search of the Promised Land: A Slave Family in the Old South* (Oxford: Oxford University Press, 2005); Phyllis M. Hemphill, *Sally Thomas: Servant Girl* (Nashville: Winston-Derek Publishers, 1989); Loren Schweninger, "A Slave Family in the Ante-Bellum South," *Journal of Negro History* 60 (January 1975): 29–44.

Tituba

Birth Date: ~1676
Death Date: unknown

In 1692, over 150 persons were arrested in a span of less than eight months on charges of witchcraft in the largely Puritan community of Salem Village, Massachusetts. At the forefront of the flurry of accusations remained the confession of an enslaved woman known as Tituba. While there is little evidence of Tituba's life before her arrival in Massachusetts, it is likely that she spent her early life enslaved on a sugar plantation in Barbados. Purchased by Samuel Parris, Tituba moved with her owner's family to New England where Parris became the minister of Salem Village in 1689. Based on the accusations of her enslaver's daughter and niece, authorities arrested Tituba on February 29, 1692 for witchcraft after the girls claimed that she had cast a spell on them. After several days of questioning, Tituba succumbed to the pressure to confess. Not only did she implicate herself and two other women charged, but her confession ignited a widespread belief in the existence of a broader demonic conspiracy that threatened many of the values and traditions that defined Puritan life in colonial New England. Thus, Tituba's confession provided a license for the Puritan community to put its own members on trial in an effort to root out all suspected practitioners of witchcraft and any other encroachment on the social, economic, political, and religious status quo.

Scholarly debate about Tituba's life has focused on her racial and ethnic identity and its role in shaping her relationship to Puritan society. Although most of the available records documenting her existence in New England refer to her as an enslaved Indian woman, because her owner acquired her in Barbados—where there would have been a large enslaved African population—both scholarly and popular representations of Tituba's racial and ethnic identity have fluctuated over time. What is clear is that her gender, enslaved status, and non-European origins made her an outsider within Puritan society. Ironically, it was precisely because of her marginal social position that her coerced confession garnered legitimacy as a framework which the Salem Village community used to exorcise "evil" in the form of occult practices, nonconformity, and any other perceived threats to Puritan religious and social life.

Twenty-four people died during the Salem witch trials before the governor ordered a stay of execution. Although Salem authorities never indicted Tituba, she remained imprisoned until April of 1693 even though she eventually recanted her confession. Beyond her release from prison, the historical record is silent regarding Tituba's life after the Salem tragedy. What it is certain, however is that her initial confession unearthed many of the underlying tensions related to religious ideals, social values, and political reform that would transform colonial New England during the eighteenth century.

Kennetta Hammond Perry

See also Conjurers; Religion.

Suggested Reading

Elaine Breslaw, *Tituba, Reluctant Witch of Salem* (New York: New York University Press, 1996); Mary Beth Norton, *In the Devil's Snare* (New York: Alfred A. Knopf, 2002); Veta Tucker, "Purloined Identity: The Racial Metamorphosis of Tituba of Salem Village," *Journal of Black Studies* 30 (2000), 624–34.

Truancy

Truancy is the practice of leaving without permission and was one of many ways enslaved people resisted the brutal conditions of their lives. Unlike fugitives, who ran away to free territories to escape slavery, truants "stole away" from their enslavers for short periods of time before returning to work. Truants ran away for a variety of reasons, including avoiding punishment or being sold, visiting family or friends on neighboring properties, hunting or fishing in order to supplement meager rations, or simply getting away from the culture of the plantation. Truancy or absenteeism disrupted labor, particularly if an enslaved person left during a crucial time in the season, and because of the truant's outsider status, it often eroded the authority of whites. Truancy figured largely in enslaved women's resistance and its inclusion in the spectrum of slave resistance sheds new light on gendered definitions of resistance.

Slaveholders enacted various laws and statutes in response to widespread truancy. Enslaved people who traveled from one place to another were forced to carry passes signed by their owner. These passes stated where they were going, whom they were going to see, and at what time they were expected to arrive. Those without a pass could be arrested, jailed, and detained. In addition to requiring passes, laws against literacy ensured that both bondpeople and free blacks could not forge passes. Slaveholders employed patrollers to scour the roads for bondpeople who were out without passes. In Virginia, truancy was deemed a capital offense. While no one liked truancy, slaveholders were often divided on whether or not to devote resources to capturing truants. Some records suggest that bondpeople who were frequently absent were allowed to return to the plantation and receive their punishment and were not hunted by patrollers and overseers. Some slaveholders understood the need for blacks to "let off steam" and did not go after truants. It provided opportunities for them to carve a modicum of freedom for enslaved peoples in the geographical interstices of slavery and freedom.

Courtney D. Marshall

See also Community; Female Slave Network; Laws; Literacy; Maroon Communities; Mobility; Resistance; Runaways.

Suggested Reading

Stephanie Camp, *Closer to Freedom: Enslaved Women and Everyday Resistance in the Plantation South* (Chapel Hill and London: The University of North Carolina Press, 2004).

Truth, Sojourner

Birth Date: ~1797
Death Date: 1883

At the close of the eighteenth century, Isabella Baumfree was born into slavery in Ulster County, New York. She endured nearly 30 years of bondage, at the mercy of four different enslavers. However, she would go on to emancipate herself and refashion a self-made persona as Sojourner Truth—abolitionist, feminist, preacher for the oppressed, and a symbol of black womanhood.

Though presently considered a product of the South, her experience in slavery was rather distinct from her southern counterparts. Isolated in rural New York among a Dutch population, Isabella did not have the support of a large enslaved community and was most often the sole servant within the household. This isolation also made her vulnerable to constant scrutiny and sexual abuse by her enslavers, and burdened with a tremendous workload. From 1809 to 1826, she resided with the Dumont family. Despite the physical and mental abuse of these formative years, Isabella managed to marry and give birth to five children.

In 1827, New York law liberated bondpeople born before 1799; how-

I Sell the Shadow to Support the Substance: One of Sojourner Truth's well-known cartes-de-viste, which she sold, along with her biography, to raise funds. (Library of Congress.)

ever, those born after that date remained in bondage for an additional term. Isabella was discontented with waiting for freedom and bargained with her owner, John Dumont, to be freed a year early. Shortly afterward her hand was injured and Dumont reneged on his promise. Reluctant to wait any longer, she decided to strike out with only a meager supply of food and her youngest child in tow. Unlike most, Isabella left in broad daylight and walked 12 miles to the home of Quakers. When Dumont demanded her return and threatened to take her child, she firmly objected and her white cohorts purchased her for the remaining year.

Isabella remade herself as an itinerant preacher against slavery, renaming herself Sojourner Truth—someone never quite at home and always a proponent of truth. She joined the lecture circuit and quickly became a mainstay of abolitionism poised with contemporaries like William Lloyd Garrison and Harriet Beecher Stowe, but she held unique influence as a former bondwoman. As much as Truth was a preacher of abolition, she was also an orator of the gospel and helped to found the Kingston Methodist Church in 1827. She actively crafted an image dictating her narrative in 1850 to Olive Gilbert. Additionally, Truth sold photos with the inscription "I Sell the Shadow to Support the Substance" to finance the abolitionist cause, where she projected a respectable image of black womanhood, free from enslavement and sexualization.

Truth has become a symbol of the abolitionist and suffragist movements, but often focus is placed more on her physical presence and peculiar dialect, hence minimizing her to the infamous "Ar'nt I Woman" speech. Truth occupied several political and social spaces, transcending race and gender. She addressed white audiences with radical condemnation and preached a message of self-sufficiency to fellow black Americans. Early on Truth spoke out against slavery by using biblical scripture and personal experiences, taking a more political stance advocating for the Union at the outbreak of the Civil War. Through her sharp wit, moral conviction, and honesty Truth made a lasting impact for the antislavery cause.

Chyna Bowen

See also Abolition; Free Women; Religion; Resistance.

Suggested Reading

Nell Irvin Painter, *Sojourner Truth: a Life, A Symbol* (New York: W.W. Norton & Company, 1996); Margaret Washington, *Sojourner Truth's America* (Urbana: University of Illinois Press, 2009).

Tubman, Harriet

Birth Date: ~1822
Death Date: 1913

Sometime between 1819 and 1825, Araminta Ross was born in Dorchester County, Maryland—the fifth child of Harriet Green and Benjamin Ross. Araminta's parents were enslaved, and the law mandated that Araminta inherit this same status from her mother. Araminta's parents grieved when the slaveholder sold "Minty" at the age of six or seven to neighboring farmers. Little Minty's new owners used harsh physical punishment to teach her how to weave cloth, trap muskrats, care for their baby, and clean their house. The beatings Minty received as a child left permanent scars on her body and mind.

By the age of 14, Minty stopped closely supervised household work and began outdoor work usually performed by men. In 1844, Minty assumed a new role and a new name. She "married" a free man, John Tubman, and renamed herself Harriet. For the next five years Harriet earned wages—most of which she delivered to her owner, Edward Brodess. In early 1849, Brodess died and his wife sold Tubman's niece, Harriet, and her child. Fearing that they would also be sold, Tubman and her brothers ran away. However, they returned to Dorchester County because they did not know how to reach the North. Before the end of 1849, however, Harriet escaped alone to freedom in Philadelphia.

The joy of freedom in Philadelphia could not erase the loneliness Tubman felt being separated from her husband and family. When she learned that other family members were going to be sold, she returned to Baltimore to rescue them. With family and friends as co-conspirators, Tubman successfully removed her niece, Kessiah, and her child from the custody of an auctioneer. Tubman escorted Kessiah and her family back to Philadelphia. Next, Tubman extracted another family member and two friends from Maryland. Tubman's third mission was the most daring because she returned to Dorchester County to remove her husband with whom she had not been in contact and who had no desire to leave.

Harriet Tubman, probably at her home in Auburn, New York, ca. 1911. (Library of Congress.)

Tubman's initial rescue missions owed their success to her network of friends along the route from Maryland to Philadelphia and to her communication via letters and messengers with friends and family in Dorchester County on whom she could depend to follow her directions. On her third mission, she wanted to reunite with her husband, John. However, in her absence, he had taken another wife and refused to leave. Faced with returning to Philadelphia empty-handed and unmarried, Tubman abandoned her original intention to resume married life. With the experience of three successful round-trips into Maryland and the assistance of a network of friends and family along the way, Tubman created a system that enabled her to free hundreds of bondpeople.

Tubman had great confidence in herself and her accomplices, but she claimed to be a mere vessel used by God for His purposes. Although she framed her rescue work as a religious calling, the focus on her religious allusions by scholars has often eclipsed her abilities as a master strategist. The timing of her trips, for example, illustrates Tubman's strategic genius. Tubman operated on a seasonal cycle, which consisted of infiltrating a slave community in late fall, broadcasting her presence and departure plans via the slave grapevine, escaping with a large party in early winter, remaining in Canada during colder months, working as a domestic in the spring and summer, then setting out on a new mission again in late fall.

This seasonal regularity enabled those who desired to escape to make preparations for departure throughout the year and stay alert for Tubman's return—all by relying on the season and the slave grapevine with no need for dates or calendars.

In spite of Tubman's meticulous planning, some biographers have constructed a "miracle-worker" myth, embellished with supernatural allusions. The mythic qualities Tubman's contemporaries and subsequent biographers projected onto her erased her exceptional ability to strategize and ignored the economic hardships she faced. She was in fact a near destitute, former enslaved woman struggling to provide for herself, her liberated family, and her freedom-seeking travelers as a cook, laundress, and domestic servant in the North. Invoking God's intervention in her missions also served Tubman's own purpose. It preserved her feminine identity, which was diminished by her public image as a supernatural "Moses" and masculinized "General."

Always in need of funds, Tubman often solicited donations for herself and her missions at public appearances. Her talks reveal that she relished uniquely female devices and disguises. In one talk, Tubman recounted the successful raid she led on plantations along the Combahee River in South Carolina during the Civil War. Tubman quipped that she would never again wear a skirt on a military expedition. Alice Stone Blackwell recounted that Tubman used spirituals to signal to fugitives hidden along the roads since no one would notice an old colored woman singing as she trudged along. Tubman's approximate age at the time of these legendary rescues illuminates the intentionality of her operations and her preference for female disguises. Though often disguised as an elderly woman, Tubman was in her early forties at the time of these exploits. Her spectacular exploits reveal that she was a master strategist, a role so unusual for a woman of her times that she was revered as a marvel.

Veta Smith Tucker

See also Community; Domestic Slave Trade; Family; North, The; Punishment; Runaways.

Suggested Reading

Sarah H. Bradford, *Harriet Tubman: The Moses of Her People* (Mineola, NY: Dover Publications, 2004); Catherine Clinton, *Harriet Tubman: The Road to Freedom* (New York: Little, Brown, 2004); Beverly Lowry, *Harriet Tubman: Imagining a Life* (New York: Doubleday, 2007); Milton C. Sernett, *Harriet Tubman: Myth, Memory, and History* (Durham: Duke University Press, 2007).

U

Underground Railroad

The Underground Railroad is a term used to describe the covert network of people and places that assisted runaway bondpeople as they escaped the "peculiar institution" in the American South. Of course, this activity did not literally take place underground or via a railroad, nor was it an official organization with a defined structure. At its essence, the Underground Railroad was a loose network of people who attempted to move enslaved fugitives to and from safe places in a quick and largely secretive manner. The term "Underground Railroad" came into use in the 1830s, due to an increase in runaway activity to destinations to and near Philadelphia, Washington D.C., and Ripley, Ohio. The Underground Railroad took place predominately during the decades just prior to the Civil War. Its movement occurred primarily in the region of states bordering slave states, with the Ohio River serving as the locus of much of the activity. It was not uncommon however, for enslaved fugitives in the Deep South to travel further south to Mexico and Mexican territories. Despite its secrecy, the efforts of those involved in the Underground Railroad aided nearly 100,000 enslaved fugitives to escape the South and gain freedom over the course of a half-century.

Those who were active on the Underground Railroad developed their own language to describe participants, safe places, and other clandestine codes. For example, people who guided fugitives from place to place were called "conductors." The locations where bondpeople could safely find protection, food, or a place to sleep were similarly called "safe houses" or "stations." Those people who hid fugitives in their homes, barns, or churches were called "station masters." Those enslaved fugitives being led by a "conductor" or

Maria Weems escaped in male attire. (Still, William, *The Underground Railroad*, Philadelphia: Porter & Coates, 1872.)

"station master" were aptly called "cargo." Code words also enabled runaways to find their way to the North. William Still was one of the most famous conductors known for his published collection of essays detailing the escape stories of hundreds of fugitives. Lear Green and Anna Maria Weems are two bondwomen who benefited from Still's work on the Underground Railroad.

On Thanksgiving of 1855, Anna Maria Weems made it to freedom disguised as an enslaved male named "Joe Wright." This 15-year-old woman had been planning her escape for two years and she waited patiently for the day she reached freedom. The three- or four-day journey began in front of the White House and ended at William Still's home in Philadelphia. Weems, who cross-dressed as a male carriage driver actually navigated part of the journey, which included an over night stop in Maryland at the home of a slaveholder. Similar, to Weems, Lear Green took extreme measures to end her enslavement. She too ended her journey in Philadelphia and later settled in Elmira, New York, but she shipped herself in a chest. The run away advertisement of her escape read as follows: "$150 REWARD. Ran away from the subscriber, on Sunday night, 27th inst., my NEGRO GIRL, Lear Green_about 18 years of age, black complexion, round-featured, good looking and ordinary size . . . I have reason to be confident that she was

At eighteen years old, Leer Green shipped herself to freedom in a small chest. (Still, William, *The Underground Railroad*, Philadelphia: Porter & Coates, 1872.)

persuaded by a negro man named Wm. Adams . . . he had been heard to say he was going to marry the above girl" (Still, 281–82). Green escaped in a box along with a "quilt, a pillow, and a few articles of raiment, with a small quantity of food and a bottle of water" (Ibid). After 18 hours in the chest, Green reached freedom and married William Adams as her former slaveholder suspected.

Some fugitives used constellations to trace their routes to freedom. The Big Dipper, a constellation of seven stars whose "handle" pointed towards the North Star, was referred to as the "drinking gourd." Moreover, the Ohio River was frequently referred to by the biblical reference, the River Jordan. And Canada, the final destination for many fugitive wishing to ensure their freedom, was thusly called the "Promised Land." This language allowed people to communicate about the Underground Railroad without being too overt about their true intentions and plans.

Driving the Underground Railroad were the strong impulses of the abolitionist movement. In the late seventeenth century, Quakers near Philadelphia initiated the abolitionist movement on the principle that slavery stood against their Christian beliefs. By the first decade of the 1800s, nearly every northern state had moved to legally abolish slavery. Consequently, abolitionism then spread throughout the West, taking root in places that would soon become Ohio and Indiana. Southerners, on the other hand, stood in firm opposition to the abolitionist movement and took steps to thwart the dissemination of abolitionist literature throughout the region. Despite differences in opinions, abolitionists across the country held firm the belief that slavery violated not only human rights, but also their unyielding Christian faith. The Underground Railroad therefore, served as a common place for abolitionists to channel their efforts.

It is important to note that while conductors and fugitives operated on the Underground Railroad, all of their actions were illegal. Almost every state in the United States contained legislation restricting the movements, employment, and civil liberties of African Americans, regardless of their free or slave status. These laws also frequently allowed southern slave catchers to come north and reclaim runaway property. By the 1830s and 1840s, legal statutes expanded due to increased Underground Railroad activity and fear of violent uprisings from the black population. The passage of the Fugitive Slave Act of 1850 mandated that assisting or harboring fugitives was a federal offense, subject to six months in prison and a $1,000 fine. Free blacks were also subject to kidnapping by enslavers and catchers for their participation in the Underground Railroad.

Fugitives who escaped the Underground Railroad faced a long journey, fraught with uncertainty, fear, and the prospect of not reaching their goal. Winter proved to be the best time of year to escape. The long nights provided ample cover for travel. A frozen Ohio River also made for an easier escape. However, the colder weather could often make traveling north difficult. Finding safe resting places and people to trust weighed heavily on the minds of those traveling the Underground

Railroad. Fugitives might spend several weeks between stations and even when they did, they risked being found by slave catchers or pro-slavery northerners. By the 1850s, emboldened by the Fugitive Slave Act, slave catchers travelled north, with guns, horses, and bloodhounds, certainly eager to take fugitives back by any means. Thus, getting all the way north and even as far away as Canada grew more perilous over time.

While traveling the Underground Railroad, bondwomen especially faced unique obstacles. Fugitives were strongly encouraged to travel alone, thus increasing the chance for a successful escape. Female fugitives, however, frequently were unable to travel alone, as to escape alone often meant leaving behind family members, especially children. Attempting to escape with young children was very conspicuous; the pace of travel slowed, the amount of food increased, and the risk of discovery eminent due to a crying child elevated the likelihood getting caught. Female fugitives needed to weigh the options of escaping with greater ease or leaving behind their family. Though faced with these difficult decisions, a considerable number of female fugitives such as Anna Weems and Lear Green successfully escaped north, alone and with their children.

Not every runaway was fortunate enough to succeed. Though current estimates place the number of bondpeople who successfully escaped at 100,000, there are countless more who made the attempt and never made it to freedom. The limitless reasons included being discovered by slave catchers, abandoning the attempt, illness, and even death. But even for those who did not succeed, their attempts were not done in vain. Every attempt made by an enslaved person to release the bonds of slavery made it that much easier for the person behind them. Knowledge of safe escape routes and trustworthy people made the potential journey a reality for some fugitives. Information about the Underground Railroad was often transmitted in code, through songs and stories, enabling the information to spread quickly and covertly.

The fundamental element of the Underground Railroad was the assistance of the conductors, those people who provided fugitive slaves with food, directions, shelter, and places to hide. Conductors risked their lives and that of their families to help in any way that they could. They were also vulnerable to fines and imprisonment if their unlawful actions were discovered. One of the most widespread myths of the Underground Railroad is that the people who participated as conductors were solely white. While it is true that the majority of people who aided fugitives were white, there were also countless African American conductors who provided vital information and guidance.

African Americans who worked on the Underground Railroad faced their own set of struggles if caught. For those who were free, the threat of physical violence, property destruction, and even re-enslavement were very real. Bondpeople aiding and abetting fugitives also faced physical violence and the threat of being sold. Despite the grave and present dangers involved with participation on the

Underground Railroad, thousands across the country risked their lives to ensure the freedom of fugitives.

Katherine M. Johnson

See also Abolitionism; Laws; North, The; South, The.

Suggested Reading

David W. Blight, *Passages to Freedom* (New York: Harper, 2006); Fergus M. Bordewich, *Bound for Caanan: The Epic Story of the Underground Railroad, America's First Civil Rights Movement* (New York: Harper Paperbacks, 2006); Catherine Clinton, *Harriet Tubman: The Road to Freedom* (Boston: Bay Back Books, 2005); Ann Hagedorn, *Beyond the River: Untold Stories of the Heroes of the Underground Railroad* (New York: Simon and Schuster, 2004); John P. Parker, *His Promised Land: The Autobiography of John P. Parker*. ed. Stuart Seely Sprague (New York: W.W. Norton & Company, 1998); William H. Siebert, *The Underground Railroad from Slavery to Freedom: A Comprehensive History* (Mineola, NY: Dover Publications, 2006); William Still, *The Underground Railroad: Authentic Narratives and First-Hand Accounts*, ed. Ian Finseth (Mineola, NY: Dover Publications, 2007).

Urban Slavery

Bondwomen in urban centers worked as market peddlers or street vendors, as cooks at local taverns, bakeries or in private residences, as seamstresses and laundresses in private homes, and sometimes as day laborers in brick factories or other industrial settings. Slavery in the cities has often been characterized as a milder form of bondage than that which existed on the plantation estates of the South. Urban slaveholders viewed everyday social control devices such as the lash, passes, patrols, and geographic isolation as incompatible with the management of highly mobile enslaved labor forces in these more readily accessible commercial centers. Scholars documenting the experiences of enslaved hires, persons whose labor was rented out to temporary employers, have advanced this position.

Enslaved hires exercised a greater degree of autonomy over their lives than most bondpeople residing on plantations. Examples of this autonomy included their tendency to travel long distances beyond their slaveholder's immediate supervision, their ability to secure their own lodgings, negotiate labor contracts, bargain for cash incentives paid for loyalty or overtime, and decide how they spent their time and extra money outside of the urban workplace. White urban authorities often expressed their desire to place greater restrictions on the lives of slave hires, but several reasons rendered this proposition untenable. First, the triangulated orientation of slave hire systems compelled temporary employers of hired out bondpeople to avoid using extreme forms of labor discipline due to the prospect of having to pay damages to their owners. Second, ill treatment of enslaved hires might have prompted them to seek friendlier employers at the end of a contract year in what was a highly competitive labor market. Third, the more volatile capitalist economies in cities, along with increasing slave prices, transformed the act of buying as opposed to renting large numbers of bondmen into a losing financial proposition. Lastly, grocers, tavern keepers, and other small business owners became dependent on the patronage of urban enslaved hires. Consequently, drastic attempts by local authorities to regulate the behavior of enslaved hires encountered resistance from this segment of the white population.

The conditions outlined above appeared to transform the master-slave relationship for urban bondpeople into one resembling something closer to an association between employers and tenants. A profoundly different picture however emerges when the issues of gender, space, and time are incorporated into this discussion. Enslaved women consigned to domestic labor within the households of urban slaveholders frequently outnumbered male hires who dominated or represented sizable proportions of the unskilled labor forces found hard at work in the streets, factories, or on the docks of many northern and southern cities. Because of their close proximity to white slaveholders, enslaved urban women were far more vulnerable to the kinds of close surveillance, punishments, and sexual abuse endured by their counterparts employed in plantation households. Bondwomen often slept in attics, cellars, kitchens, or small quarters in the rear of an urban dwelling. They performed a myriad of tasks such as raising their owner's children, cooking, cleaning, sewing, and laundry. The scope of opportunities to translate their labor into manumission for themselves or relatives was therefore far more limited than those that could be accessed by male slave hires before 1840, especially in the older slave states of the Upper South. The high demand for enslaved female domestics in the industrial city of Richmond enabled them to take in extra wash or perform services for employers outside of their immediate households to accomplish this end. Meanwhile, enslaved women in Charleston exercised their traditional West African skills as traders in local markets. Some bondwomen also used their bodies as sex workers or concubines to secure manumission and/or elevate their social status, although this practice was more common in the cotton export cities of the Lower South.

Maryland's staple crop economy, which became unstable between the late eighteenth and early nineteenth centuries, afforded bondpeople the greatest opportunity to access manumission under a system known as term-slavery. Term slaves entered into contracts with their owners where they agreed to labor several years in exchange for their manumission. This system, resembling others in Spanish and Portuguese slave colonies, gave rise to the largest free black population in the South at Baltimore (1860). Term contracts were, however, long enough to prevent enslaved men and women from securing their manumission before they gave birth to more enslaved children. Scores of Baltimore free blacks therefore remained wedded to slavery long after they had met their contractual obligations.

The predicament of bondpeople in Baltimore and other cities of the Upper South and West grew even more precarious in the 1840s. The expansion of cotton agriculture, continued urbanization, and European immigration radically changed the occupational trajectory of black urban workers (enslaved and free) during this moment. Enslaved workers had, since the eighteenth century, been major contributors to the artisanal trades. The aforementioned factors, especially the growth of the "Cotton Kingdom" in the Lower South powered by male enslaved labor, effectively reversed the rise of bondpeople within the ranks of the artisanal class. Free blacks and enslaved workers in the Upper South consequently experienced little or no occupational mobility in this region's cities. The higher echelon jobs for free blacks (listed mostly as free coloreds or mulattoes on census rolls) included butchers or barbers, while the overwhelming majority were employed as day laborers. Meanwhile, the few remaining higher-wage skilled jobs were awarded to enslaved laborers employed in Richmond's many factories or to the black slave "mechanics" in Charleston. Male enslaved populations in southern cities, those who were not relocated by the Domestic Slave Trade to the cotton producing zones of the Lower South, were primarily low-wage unskilled workers. As a result, enslaved males represented the majority of the marriage market for free women of color in cities of the Upper South. Marriage for these women therefore became a personal risk or a financial liability. Nuclear family formation within the free black population was thus arrested by the expansion of urban slavery.

John Grant

See also Childcare; Concubinage; Domestic Slave Trade; Free Women; Hiring Out; Labor, Nonagricultural; Manumission; Mobility; Prices; Punishment; South, The; Violence, Sexual; West, The.

Suggested Reading

Ira Berlin and Herbert Gutman, "Natives and Immigrants, Free Men and Slaves: Urban Workingmen in the Antebellum American South," *The American Historical Review* 88, no. 5 (December 1983): 1175–200; Thomas Buchanan, "Mississippi Levees of Hope: African American Steamboat Workers, Cities, and Slave Escapes on the Antebellum," *Journal of Urban History* 30, no. 3 (March 2004): 360–77; Claudia Gail Goldin, *Urban Slavery in the American South, 1820–1860: A Quantitative History* (Chicago: University of Chicago Press, 1976); Gregg Kimball, *American City, Southern Place: A Cultural History of Antebellum Richmond* (Athens: University of Georgia Press, 2000); Suzanne Lebsock, "Free Black Women and the Question of Matriarchy: Petersburg, Virginia, 1784–1820," *Feminist Studies* 8, no. 2 (Summer 1982): 270–92; Suzanne Lebsock, *The Free Women of Petersburg: Status and Culture in a Southern Town, 1784–1860* (New York: Norton, 1984); Jonathan D. Martin, *Divided Mastery: Slave Hiring in the American South* (Cambridge: Harvard University Press, 2004); Richard Wade, *Slavery in the Cities: The South, 1820–1860* (New York: Oxford University Press, 1964).

V

Violence, Domestic

See Conflict, Intraracial

Violence, Racial

Many enslaved women experienced a lifetime of racial violence. Due to the social and historical constructions of race, black women often endured physical violence, sexual assault (including rape, forced breeding, and the manipulation of their reproductive lives), and even race-based medical experimentation.

Racial violence against enslaved women began during the Middle Passage. From 1518 to the mid-nineteenth century, between ten and eleven million Africans, not including those who died in transit, were forcibly transported across the Atlantic Ocean to plantations in the Caribbean and Americas. Captives were tightly packed onto ships, chained together in spoon fashion, and forced to lie in their bodily waste during a transatlantic journey that lasted from 1 to 3 months or longer. Enslaved women who survived the journey were stripped naked, examined to determine their reproductive capacities, and then sold on the auction block to the highest bidder. Once sold, slaveholders and overseers immediately began a behavior modification process, referred to as "seasoning," which was designed to break the spirits and obliterate the cultural identities of their newly acquired bondpeople. For example, Africans were forced to adopt new names, denounce their former religious practices, learn a new language, and accept their status as chattel property in a new land. Consequently, any action that enslaved women made to assert their independence was criminalized.

"Misconduct," including failure to complete assigned tasks or perceived disrespect toward white authority figures, resulted in brutal punishment. Slaveholders, slave traders, and overseers administered severe whippings, which were often public spectacles used to reinforce white racial domination and male patriarchy. For example, enslaved women were tied down or faced against a tree or wall, stripped of their tattered clothing, and given 50 to 100 lashes with a leather whip. Sometimes salt or pepper was rubbed into their open wounds (called "pickling") to prolong the pain. Moreover, punishment was meted out regardless of infirmity or pregnancy. According to eyewitness accounts, slaveholders dug holes to accommodate pregnant bondwomen's swollen abdomens and then proceeded with the whippings. If convicted of a capital crime, such as murder, in some states, pregnant bondwomen had their executions delayed until after giving birth to preserve the health of the enslaved offspring. Yet for the longest time, slaveholders could maim or kill their slave property without consequence in many jurisdictions.

Moreover, plantation mistresses also subjected domestic enslaved girls and women to severe abuse. Even though many of them knew of their husband's infidelities, the sexually victimized enslaved women became targets of the mistresses' wrath. As a result, some irate mistresses whipped or disfigured enslaved women or sold away their mixed-race children, who were fathered by the mistresses' adulterous husbands. The threat of selling a bondperson away from loved ones and family members was perhaps one of the most powerful weapons available to slaveholders.

Throughout the South, some able-bodied white males acted as slave patrollers, who were formal and informal officials charged with reinforcing white domination over a black underclass. They broke up large gatherings of bondpeople, suppressed slave revolts, inflicted impromptu punishments, and randomly searched slave quarters, often at night. In addition, they apprehended runaways—both male and female. Escape attempts often resulted in brutal punishment, including cutting off of one's ears, branding on the cheek, and hamstringing or cutting the tendons in the back of the legs to prevent the victim from walking.

The purpose of this frequent and horrific violence was to entrench white power, ensure obedience, and to dehumanize the victim and the entire enslaved community. Some slaveholders found sadistic pleasure in the violence that they inflicted. In his 1850 autobiography, *Narrative of the Life and Adventures of Henry Bibb, An American Slave, Written by Himself*, the author recalled statements made by the man who whipped his wife: "He had rather paddle a female than eat when he was hungry" (Bibb, p. 105).

Virtually every known nineteenth-century female slave narrative contained a reference to the ever-present threat and reality of sexual exploitation and coercion. For instance, in her narrative, *Incidence in the Life of a Slave Girl*, Harriet Jacobs (2001), who spent years eluding the unwanted sexual advances of her North Carolina master, wrote: "Slavery is terrible for men; but it is far more terrible for women" (66). Embedded in her bold pronouncement was the recognition that enslaved women faced a unique threat and danger—primarily the threat of sexual assault. More specifically, enslaved women were often coerced, bribed, ordered, and, of course, violently forced to have sexual relations with white slaveholders, his male family members, and by extension, his friends, and other male employees. Historian Darlene Hine estimated that at least 58 percent of all enslaved women between the ages of 15 and 30 had been sexually assaulted by white men.

In fact, bondwomen's reproductive lives were highly regulated by slaveholders, who had an economic stake in producing more a stable cadre of workers. On the auction block, enslaved women endured crude gynecological examinations, believed to help determine her capacity for childbearing. Once they were purchased, various strategies, ranging from manipulation to overt coercion, were used to encourage frequent childbearing. For example, women who did not produce were whipped or sold off to unsuspecting buyers as "damaged" goods. Other planters offered a reduction in arduous field labor, additional rations of food and clothing, and even monetary rewards. Although there is considerable debate about the extent of slave breeding, there are indeed documented cases of slaveholders who paired healthy bondpeople with the goal of producing more enslaved property. Mixed-race enslaved women, sometimes referred to as "fancy girls," were bred and sold, often for staggering prices, to wealthy slaveholders as concubines.

Regardless of the method—incentives, threats, rape, or forced breeding—on average enslaved women began childbearing about two years earlier than their white southern counterparts. More specifically, the average bondwoman became sexually active in her mid- to late teens, conceived her first child around age 19, and had a total of eight or nine pregnancies over the course of her reproductive life, resulting in an average of four or five miscarriages and four live births. The collective toll of this racial and reproductive violence on enslaved women was evident. Bondwomen's fertility decreased, miscarriage rates rose, and slave infant mortality averaged twice that of white infants. Surviving children, similar to farm animals, could be sold, which then separated families and created unimaginable grief.

During slavery, bondwomen were forced participants in medical experiments. For example, Dr. J. Marion Sims, hailed as the "Father of Modern Gynecology," performed surgery on 30 unanaesthetized enslaved women on the assumption that black women did not feel pain to the same degree as white women. Some women endured multiple operations before he successfully perfected a method to repair vesio-vaginal fistulas, which are tears in the vaginal walls that allow a continuous leakage of urine to flow into the vagina. Other surgeons performed risky and painful medical procedures, such as cesarean sections, on enslaved women before attempting them on white women.

Some slave jurisdictions developed elaborate systems of laws, which condoned and promoted violence against enslaved blacks. These were generally known as "slave codes." For example a 1705 Virginia law stated: "If any slave resist his master correcting such slave, and shall happen to be killed in such correction the master shall be free of all punishment as if such accident never happened." In addition, it was a criminal offense, punishable by 30 lashes, for an enslaved person to strike a white person, even in self-defense. Furthermore, these slave codes applied equally to bondmen and bondwomen.

Ultimately, enslaved women used many techniques to resist racial violence. During the Middle Passage, they participated in shipboard revolts. In the antebellum South, they poisoned their masters and their masters' families, ran away, shirked work, and simply fought back. For example, in 1835, Harriet Jacobs hid in her grandmother's attic crawlspace for seven years to escape her master's sexual advances. After she endured five years of brutal sexual assaults, Celia, a Missouri bondwoman, killed her master in self-defense and burned his body in a fireplace. Similarly, black women resisted control of their reproductive lives as well. They used medicinal herbs or chewed roots of the cotton plant to prevent or terminate pregnancies and, in extreme cases, committed infanticide. When faced with recapture and the return to slavery, Margaret Garner, the mother of four, made a fateful decision. She killed her two-year-old daughter and attempted to kill her other three children in a barn. Although she loved her children, in a single, tragic act of defiance, she decided to destroy her master's "property" rather than see her children suffer a life of slavery and servitude.

Historian Nell Irvin Painter argued that "soul murder" resulted from the habitual abuse and harassment of enslaved women and manifested itself as depression, low self-esteem, and anger. Despite the occurrences of ceaseless racial violence, black women actively resisted their victimization and became resilient survivors.

Carolyn West

See also Concubinage; Contraception; Domestic Slave Trade; Fancy Girls; Breeding; Garner, Margaret; Health, Disabilities, and Soundness; Infanticide; Jezebel Stereotype; Laws; Medical Experimentation and Surgery; Middle Passage; Overseers; Owners; Plantation Mistresses; Punishment; Representations; Resistance; Violence, Sexual; "Wench Betty," Murder of.

Suggested Reading

Ira Berlin, S. F. Miller, and M. Favreau, *Remembering Slavery: African Americans Talk about Their Personal Experiences of Slavery and Freedom* (New York: New Press, 1998); Henry Bibb, *Narrative of the Life and Adventures of Henry Bibb, An American Slave, Written by Himself* (New York: Published by the Author, 1850); Harriet Jacobs, *Incidents in the Life of a Slave Girl* (Mineola, New York: Dover Publications, Inc., 2001); Marie Jenkins Schwartz, *Birthing a Slave: Motherhood and Medicine in the Antebellum South* (Cambridge: Harvard University Press, 2006); Deborah Gray White, *Ar'n't I a Woman? Female Slaves in the Plantation South* (New York: Norton, 1985).

Violence, Sexual

Sexual violence is a general term for sexually aggressive behaviors, including rape, incest, harassment, coercion, and exploitation—all of which represent the most prominent aspect of black women's gendered experience under slavery. While both bondwomen and bondmen were vulnerable to day-to-day racial violence, bondwomen were especially subjected to more torment from the physical and psychological abuse of sexual violence. Recollecting years of her struggle against her master's sexual harassment in *Incidents in the Life of a Slave Girl* (1861), North Carolina former bondwoman Harriet A. Jacobs wrote that "Slavery is terrible for men; but it is far more terrible for women." The issue of sexual violence against bondwomen, however, was not considered as such among scholars of slavery for a long time. Until 1970s, historians saw sex between slaveholders and enslaved women as somewhat consensual by deeming it "sexual relations" or "miscegenation." But in the 1980s, black women scholars such as Deborah Gray White reconceptualized it as sexual exploitation, stating that the master-slave sexual relationship was not mutual, *but* forced and manipulated by the slaveholder's authority against the will of bondwomen. Black women scholars claimed that sexual violence against enslaved women was not accidental or random incidents; it was calculated and comprised of institutionalized assaults that were performed daily to the benefit of the slaveholder.

> *I never seed my father in my life ... Dey would not talk to me 'bout who my father wus nor where he wus at. Mother would laf sometime when I axed her 'bout him.*
>
> —Patsy Mitchner, former bondwoman
> (Born in Slavery: Slave Narratives from the Federal Writers' Project, 1936–1938 North Carolina Narratives, Volume XI, Part 2, 119)

There were several factors motivating the ubiquitous sexual violence against bondwomen, with the most important being the economic value of bondwomen both as producers and reproducers of labor. Because bondpeople were indispensable labor for the plantation economy in the South, slave owners endeavored to maintain and increase their property by purchasing, breeding, and fathering more slaves. After abolition of the Transatlantic Slave Trade in 1808 made the further purchase of slaves unfeasible except through the Domestic Slave Trade, slave breeding, and slave owners' sexual exploitation of bondwomen became more common practices in the slaveholding society.

Slave owners' sexual assaults upon bondwomen were particularly rampant because masters recognized reproduction of enslaved women as a profit-making function. Several factors worked to the slaveholders' advantage in their reproductive exploitation of bondwomen. First, following a 1662 Virginia statute, all colonial laws eventually stated that the conditions of children—slave or free—followed that of their mothers, thus defining all children born of bondwomen as slaves. With these laws, slaveholders were able to freely impregnate bondwomen without worrying about the status of their half-white children. Second, due to bondpeople's status as property, sexual abuse of black women was never considered rape. There were few legal rape cases of bondwomen on record because bondpeople were not allowed to testify against whites in court.

Finally, southern whites, and particularly white women, believed that no unwanted sex could exist with bondwomen, because they internalized the idea that black women were sexually promiscuous by nature. This image of the immoral, sexually unrestrained, and licentious black women is referred to as the Jezebel stereotype. In the minds of many southerners, contemporary notions of virtuous womanhood were reserved exclusively for white women. Furthermore, enslaved women sometimes made enemies of their jealous mistresses who just like slave husbands, accused bondwomen of having willful sexual relations with their husbands. Instead of blaming their own husbands for infidelity, plantation mistresses irrationally mistreated enslaved women in various ways. They often reproached bondwomen and even physically attacked them and their mixed-race children born of such infidelity. The wives also occasionally requested their husbands to sell off those children, thus forcing enslaved mothers into the family separation.

But slaveholders were not alone in their use and abuse of bondwomen as sexual outlets. Their sons, overseers, drivers and other men, who all understood the sexual privileges attached to their positions, frequently exploited bondwomen for sex. Thus, the sexual abuse of bondwomen was legally and socially sanctioned to serve slaveholders' economic and sexual demands. Like slavery itself, sexual abuse of bondwomen was also institutionalized.

Slave breeding can also be considered as another institutionalized form of sexual violence. To produce "good" slaves, slaveholders often actively intervened in mating bondwomen with strong, healthy bondmen. For example, Rose Williams, a Texas bondwoman, struggled against unwanted sexual advances by partners chosen by her enslaver. And if she and other bondwomen refused, they had to face punishments such as whipping and/or being sold. Thus, bondwomen and bondmen, both married and single, were sometimes forced engage in sexual practices and sexual relationships against their will. As unwilling breeders, bondmen as well as bondwomen can be considered victims of sexual violence. Historian Daina Ramey Berry uses the term "forced breeding" to highlight the violent - characteristics of breeding in the slave quarters, and considers it as an indirect form of rape.

By legal definition, rape is an unlawful sexual act inflicted upon a woman without her consent. Some scholars are reluctant to use the term "rape" to describe sexual violence of bondwomen because enslaved female rape victims were excluded from legal protection, and hence, they were legally impossible to rape. However, recent studies maintain "rape" as an appropriate term by drawing on a handful of extant evidence like the testimony of the aforementioned Harriet A. Jacobs and Celia, which underscore the frequent occurrence of rape incidents during the period of slavery. In the case of Celia, she was purchased in 1850 at age 14 by a 60-year-old, widowed slave owner in Missouri to serve as his concubine. He raped her en route to his home, and his sexual abuse continued for five years during which Celia bore two children and decided to take action.

It is no doubt that sexual violence scarred bondwomen and left enormous signs of physical and psychological trauma. Similarly, this violence also had a significant impact on the slave family. For enslaved married couples, it was extremely difficult to maintain monogamous relationships, given that they had to constantly endure forced extramarital sexual relations such as breeding with other partners, concubinage, and coerced sex with masters and others. Emasculated enslaved husbands, who were deprived of the right to protect their wives from sexual transgressions, often expressed their irate frustration on their wives rather than their masters or other offenders. In such cases, bondwomen who were already victims of sexual violence also became the targets of domestic violence.

Although bondwomen were very vulnerable to the devastating reality and aftershocks of sexual violence, they were not totally powerless in some of these situations. Many historical sources shed light on the wide range of day-to-day resistance conducted by enslaved women. Harriet A. Jacobs and Rose Williams, for example, refused the life of a concubine and slave breeder, respectively. Celia, on the other hand, took an extraordinary method of resistance by killing her master after years of sexual abuse. Also abortion and infanticide, which were more psychologically driven means of resistance for enslaved mothers, yet significant acts to protest the reproductive exploitation and the plantation economy, proved less uncommon during slavery. While sexual violence against enslaved women persistently deprived them of control over their own bodies, some women within their limited degree of personal autonomy struggled to defend their sexuality through these various forms of resistance.

Fumiko Sakashita

See also: Abortion; Breeding; Celia; Concubinage; Conflict, Intraracial; Fancy Girls; Girlhood; Jacobs, Harriet; Jezebel Stereotype; Life Cycle; Owners; Sexuality.

Suggested Reading

Daina Ramey Berry, *"Swing the Sickle for the Harvest Is Ripe": Gender and Slavery in Antebellum Georgia* (Urbana: University of Illinois Press, 2007), particularly 77–84; Harriet A. Jacobs, *Incidents in the Life of a Slave Girl: Written by Herself*, ed. Jean Fagan Yellin (Cambridge: Harvard University Press, 1987); Thelma Jennings, " 'Us Colored Women Had to Go Through a Plenty': Sexual Exploitation of African American Slave Women," *Journal of Women's History* 1, 3 (Winter 1990), 45–74; Melton A. McLaurin, *Celia, A Slave* (New York: Avon Books, 1991).

Voodoo

Voodoo is a religious tradition rooted in West African spirituality and developed in the Americas during the slavery. When enslaved Africans came to the Americas, they combined their traditions with Roman Catholic concepts to create distinctly American versions of voodoo. It may be spelled *voodoo, voudou, voudoun,* or

The voodoo meeting in the old brickyard. (Library of Congress.)

vodun. The word *vodun* may refer to the religion itself or to the spirit beings that make up its pantheon. Some related expressions of voodoo include Louisiana voodoo, Haitian voodoo, Candomblé in Brazil, Santeria in Cuba, and Obeah in Jamaica. It was practiced primarily in areas colonized by Catholics such as Louisiana, the Mississippi Delta region, the Georgia Sea Islands, and throughout the southeastern states, the Caribbean, and Latin America.

Voodoo in American slave communities had two major contributing ideologies: religious traditions of the Dahomey and religious traditions of Roman Catholicism. The Dahomey nations including the Yoruba, Fon, and Ewe were the foremost influences. The cosmology is based on the vodun, or spirits, that inhabit and govern the Earth. The creator is at the head of the hierarchical pantheon. Other spirits have a range of roles, powers, and influences on the world. Because of the open nature of voodoo and acceptance of unknown spirits, believers often incorporated gods and spirit beings from other religions. When practitioners came into contact with Roman Catholicism, their religion was flexible enough to easily incorporate Christian cosmology into its structure.

Many Catholic slave owners required their slaves to convert to Christianity. Slaves interested in maintaining their beliefs converted to Catholicism, but cloaked African traditions with outward expressions of Christianity. Catholic sacraments became code for voodoo concepts that only voodoo insiders recognized. Additionally, Catholic saints were simultaneously voodoo deities. For instance, the gods Shango, Oya, and Yemeya double as the Catholic saints Barbara, Catherine, and Mother Mary, respectively. In this way, the voodoo faithful simultaneously inhabited two worlds: the sanctioned Roman Catholicism and the forbidden religion of their ancestors. The reconciliation and union of differing religious traditions in this sense is also known as syncretism. American voodoo incorporated a rich amalgamation of beliefs due to the meetings of African, European, and Native American cultures in America.

Crucial to voodoo cosmology, women were the carriers of voodoo traditions and responsible for much of its continuity and livelihood throughout the slavery period and beyond. Women were mothers and teachers who had access to the social arenas within which voodoo had most relevance. Unrecognized by slaveholders, priestesses and conjurers gained status on plantations by attaining knowledge of African traditions and of the supernatural. Women used voodoo to aid in physical and spiritual healing, peacemaking, and protection of their families. They inspired fear, respect, and admiration as powerful and wise interlocutors between the spirit world and the physical world and were often the most significant figures on the plantation. Susan Snow, a former bondwoman in Alabama, spoke of how her mother could not be whipped by her enslaver due to the power of her conjure, or voodoo. Snow said that her mother was feared on the plantation for having such a reputation.

Because of its syncretistic nature, voodoo has been able to survive in the Americas for many generations through many forms. Voodoo's inclusive worldview enabled not only other religions and traditions to influence it, but also allowed generations to put their marks on the religion of their ancestors as well. Voodoo was also a basis of resistance in the spiritual and material world. It provided a spiritual foundation of daily resistance against the horrors of slavery. Furthermore, practitioners often commenced slave rebellions with voodoo rituals. Although American popular culture gave voodoo negative attention, it has recently been seen in a more positive light as a valid and enduring African religious tradition.

Sakina Mariam Hughes

See also Conjurers; Religion.

Suggested Reading

Donald J. Cosentino, ed., *Sacred Arts of Haitian Vodou*, (Los Angeles: UCLA Fowler Museum of Cultural History, 1995); Gary A. Donaldson, "A Window on Slave Culture: Dances at Congo Square in New Orleans, 1800–1862," *The Journal of Negro History* 69, 2 (Spring 1984), 63–72; Walter Rucker, "Conjure, Magic, and Power: The Influence of Afro-Atlantic Religious Practices on Slave Resistance and Rebellion," *Journal of Black Studies* 32, 1 (September 2001), 84–103.

W

"Wench Betty," Murder of

An enslaved woman known as "Wench Betty" appears in the court proceedings for Monmouth County, New Jersey in 1784. Laboring as a domestic servant, she worked in the home of Arthur Barcalow, who lived in the village of Allentown, part of the Township of Upper Freehold, New Jersey. Throughout court documents, she is referred to as "his Negro Wench" or "Wench of Arthur Barcalow." Betty's case is unusual because the details of her death are not clearly gleaned from the surviving historical record. As a result, we know little about her life except how she died, which was possibly at the hand of her slaveholder.

According to a series of court records on file at the New Jersey State Archives, Barcalow was indicted by several local slaveholders for murdering Betty. Ironically, the jury selected for the proceedings were also slaveholding whites from the same region. James Cox, the Monmouth County Coroner reported that Barcalow told Betty to "go home," but she did not immediately respond to his request. This order could have meant that Betty should return to the kitchen, a place where domestics had their living quarters, or she might have been expected to go to another place. Barcalow said she refused to go to the kitchen, and so he then proceeded to beat her first with a whip and later with a broomstick. The report dated April 17, 1784, noted that "a certain Black Woman named Betty [Lathan ?] and there lying dead" was certified by one dozen "honest and lawful Men of the County." One witness, Lewis Garrison recalled that on Friday, April 9, 1784, he saw a deceased Betty with an "arm bloody and appeared to have been cut with a whip but [he] did not examine the body." Further court records suggest that Mr. Barcalow:

> Not having the fear of God before his eyes, but being moved by the instigation of the Devil, with a broomstick did Arthur strike and beat the aforesaid Betty and on the head of the said Betty a Mortal Bruise did give of which said mortal Bruise the said Betty on the said day did languish and [illegible] on the said day died. And so the said jurors aforesaid on their oaths aforesaid say that aforesaid Arthur Barcalow the aforesaid Betty did kill and murder in manner and form aforesaid against the People of the State the Honor and Dignity of the Same.

Others such as Barcalow's son Derick signed an affidavit and attested that "Betty the Wench of Arthur Barcalow" was whipped with a "small whip" because "she would not go home when he bid her" and that "he would not have any quarreling at his house, on which she went." Derick then went into the house and saw "the said wench sitting in the kitchen, after sitting some time he went into the kitchen and found her dead." James Cox, the Coroner, signed these court documents. The appointed jurors were: Peter Imlay, Michael Mount, Jacob Hendrickson, Wm. Montgomery, Ales. Montgomery, Wm. Hutchinson, William [illegible], John Imlay, Jun., William Walton, Josiah Vanschoik, Timothy Hamburt, and Andrew Smith. In the same report, Daniel Barcalow said he "knows nothing of the said Negro," while Parthenia Lawrence said she was in Barcalow's house around the time of Betty's death. Lawrence admitted to seeing Barcalow "take down a whip and go with the same, but saw no violence offered to the Negro Wench." However, John Warrick testified the following:

> That Arthur Barcalow was at said place his Negro Wench Betty came there and he bid her go home which she refused, whereupon he gave her some stripes, and she went home, and he immediately followed, this Deponent in company with Joseph Brown, persued to see whether he would beat her any more, when they arrived at the said Arthur Barcalows they found him, the said Barcalow, beating her with a raw hide whip, and further he saw said Barcalow strike said wench one blow (with a broom stick) on the head as she was sitting in a chair, after which they went into the house, some short time after Derick Barcalow came into the house saying the wench was dead, on which this Deponent in company with other went where she was and found her where they left her actually dead . . .

Despite the hearing, Barcalow secured bail for 500 pounds with the help of his son and a friend.

A little more than a decade later, Monmouth County residents, including those from Upper Freehold, submitted a petition to the New Jersey legislature supporting the abolition of slavery. The signature of William Montgomery, the same name listed as a juror on the Barcalow case, is included on the 1796 petition. It is possible that Betty's death made an impact on him by encouraging him to support the end of slavery in New Jersey. One might also suspect that Montgomery always held antislavery sentiments. What is even more unclear are the slaveholding patterns and sentiments of Barcalow. In the available tax records that included the numbers of slaves owned per landowner, he is not listed as a slaveholder. In fact, according to reviewed tax records, none of the men named Derick, Arthur, or David Barcalow owned any bondpeople in 1778, 1779, 1780, 1781, 1782, 1784, 1785, and 1786. Derick Barcalow owned slaves in 1792, 1794, and 1797, and he was involved in a habeas corpus dispute over the enslavement a young man named Samuel Bone in 1796. The full and final outcome of Betty's case is unknown. As for Arthur Barcalow, the Grand Jury found that "no bill against the Prisoner is ordered [and] that he be discharged upon giving security." The ruling language indicates that Barcalow was not indicted for Betty's murder even though he was required to report back to court in the next session. Nonetheless, Betty's memory lives on, and her story reminds readers of the many unknown or unnamed enslaved women whose stories have not yet been told.

Sue Kozel

See also Owners; Resistance; Violence, Racial

Suggested Reading

File 34201. *(The) State v. Barcalow*, Monmouth Murder. *Inquisitions & Arthur Barcalow with Testimony*. New Jersey State Archives, Trenton, New Jersey; File 34095. *State v. Burkaloe*. Monmouth. Habeas Corpus. September 1, 1796. New Jersey State Archives, Trenton, New Jersey; *Petition of Inhabitants of Monmouth County to the General Assembly Opposing Slave Manumission*, Feb. 2, 1774. BAH 1-16, 1788–1796. New Jersey State Archives, Trenton, New Jersey; Minutes of the Monmouth County Court of Oyer and Terminer, July 27–August 2, 1784 Nisi Prius, July 27–30, 1784. Minutes July 27, 1984. New Jersey State Archives, Trenton, New Jersey; Moss, Jr., George H. Moss, Jr., ed. *Manumission Book of Monmouth County, New Jersey—1791—1844* (Freehold, New Jersey: Office of the Monmouth County Clerk, 1992); Tax Records Boxes 55 and 78, 1 Monmouth County: Upper Freehold Twp., 1779–1780 and 1792, 1794, and 1797, New Jersey State Archives, Trenton, New Jersey; U.S. Bureau of the Census, "Return of the Whole Number of Persons Within the Several Districts of the United States, According to 'An Act Providing for the enumeration of the Inhabitants of the United States'; Passed March the First, One Thousand Seven Hundred and Ninety-One." http://www.census.gov/prod/www/abs/decennial/1790.htm (accessed February 2, 2008); Giles R. Wright, *Afro-Americans in New Jersey*: *A Short History* (Trenton: New Jersey Historical Commission, 1988); Giles R. Wright, "Afro-Americans in New Jersey," http://www.njstatelib.org/NJ_information/NJ_by_Topic/History_of_NJ.php (accessed February 13, 2008); Giles R. Wright, "Moving Toward Breaking the Chains: Black New Jerseyans and the American Revolution," in *New Jersey in the American Revolution*, ed. Barbara J. Mitnick (Piscataway: Rivergate Books, 2005), 113–37.

West, The

Before slavery was introduced to Jamestown, women of African ancestry began their slow migration into the American West. In fact, African men and women were some of the earliest newcomers to the region, traveling to New Spain's northern frontier with explorers in the fifteenth and sixteenth centuries. Three enslaved women were listed with the Don Juan de Oñate party in 1598 and mulatto wives and children were part of the Juan Guerra de Resa Expedition in 1600. Legal records from the period help document the presence of female servants and slaves. Isabel de Olvera, a free servant from Queretaro, asked the mayor to document her free status before traveling to Santa Fe. An enslaved woman named Maria Morazán made an official request to the colonial governor for intervention in her sale price.

In 1821, Mexico won its independence from Spain. The new government abolished slavery in its territories, including New Mexico, Texas, and California. To increase its population, thousands of new immigrants were welcomed from the United States. As Texas began raising cotton and sugar cane as cash crops, the recruitment of settlers with enslaved Africans increased. Alongside this migration west, from 1830 to 1860, runaway bondpeople and free blacks headed to Texas seeking new opportunities under Mexican sovereignty. Harriet Newell Sands arrived from Michigan in 1834. Zelina Husk traveled from Georgia in 1835. Husk and a woman named Diana Leonard became washerwomen near San Jacinto. Fanny McFarland of Harris County made her living through real estate transactions. Soon, the opportunities for former enslaved people and free black women would come to an end due to the growing numbers of slaveholders entering Texas from the United States.

Texas plantations were the largest in the West and mirrored the harsh routine labor systems found in the American South. Along with harvesting crops, bondwomen worked as cooks, washwomen, maids, and seamstresses. By 1835, the population in Texas had grown to more than 38,000. Of that number, 150 were free blacks and 5,000 were enslaved. Ellen Payne, a bondwoman near Marshall, worked for a local doctor. Lavinia Bell arrived in Texas by force. Kidnapped as a young girl, and forced to work naked as a form of punishment, Bell was confined to the cotton fields near Galveston. In 1836, Texas won its independence from Mexico. Shortly thereafter, the slaveholding community helped legalize slavery and set a deadline for the constitutional exclusion of free blacks. Those still in Texas after January 1, 1842 were to be sold into slavery. Fanny McFarland refused to leave and made a formal petition stay. Although turned down, she remained in Houston until her death in 1866. An enslaved woman named Sylvia Routh, who had received her freedom through her owner's will, was jailed by the executor of the estate in 1837. She petitioned the court and, although granted formal guardianship of her six children and title to her land, she relocated to California in the late 1850s.

In California, the first enslaved person in the territory is believed to have been a 14-year-old girl named Juana, arriving in San Francisco from Lima in 1825. Africans, on the other hand, arrived in California before that date, traveling with

Spanish military expeditions in 1760s. Twenty-six of the forty-six original Los Angeles settlers were of African decent and the 1790 census recorded African origins for 18 percent of the population. In 1846, an enslaved woman known as Mary was taken from Missouri to California. Born in Johnson City, Missouri, her travels to California included experiences with a cholera outbreak and encounters with hostile Indian groups. Once in California, she sued for her freedom and won her case in San José, California. Slavery was also a part of the California Gold Rush of 1849. Black and white gold miners worked the Spanish Flat and between 200 and 300 blacks were held as bondpeople in the gold mines. After gaining statehood in 1849, California entered the Union as a nonslave state, though settlers took bondpeople into the Pacific Northwest between 1840 and 1860.

In the rush for new opportunities on the American frontier, many settlers from the East brought enslaved women with them. For example, black women were taken west as the servants and as bondpeople for newly converted Mormons seeking religious freedom in the Church of Jesus Christ of Latter Day Saints. Bridget "Bibby" Mason Tableau was born into slavery in Mississippi. After her owner, Robert Smith, converted, she was taken to Utah during the Mormon Third Migration. In 1851, Mason relocated to a new Mormon settlement in California. Once there, a local official was informed that her owner was illegally holding bondpeople. The Los Angeles County sheriff placed Mason and her family in protective custody and Mason won her petition for freedom in 1856. Ten years later, she became one of the first black women in Los Angeles to own land.

Bondwomen also resided in small towns in other western territories. Clara Brown was born enslaved in Tennessee. Freed by her owner's will in 1856, she convinced a gold prospector to take her to Colorado during the Pike's Peak Gold Rush. Believed to be the first African American woman to arrive in the Colorado's gold rush region, Brown opened a laundry and earned enough to bring 26 former enslaved people to Colorado, providing jobs, homes, and an education. In 1881, members of the Society of Colorado Pioneers reversed their policy of allowing only white men into the organization and elected "Aunt" Clara Brown to membership.

Along with the migration to the American West, enslaved women were also part of the Trail of Tears (1838–1839). During the forced relocation of the Native Americans in the southeastern United States to the American West, a significant number runaway bondpeople and Native Americans intermarried and produced mixed-race offspring. In addition, some Native Americans were slaveholders. The census taken prior to the trek listed the population of the Creek Nation as 22,694 members with 902 bondpeople and the Cherokee Nation with 16,542 members with 1,592 bondpeople. Many of these enslaved individuals were taken on the trek to Oklahoma. More than 175 bondpeople are believed to have perished along the trail with the Cherokee. Enslaved women in the Indian Nation made tools and clothing, cleared land, and planted cotton. Some adopted native dress and diet. Bondwomen were often used as interpreters, such as when Charles Latrobe and Washington Irving traveled on the western frontier in the 1830s, a black woman translated their conversations with a Cherokee farmer.

Although little is known of bondwomen and their contributions to exploration and settlement, legacies of these early interactions between Africans, Europeans, and native populations are still found in religious traditions, languages, and food ways in the American West.

Karen Jean Hunt

See also Free Women; Laws; Mobility; Runaways.

Suggested Reading

Roger D. Hardaway and Monroe Lee Billington, *African Americans on the Western Frontier* (Niwot: University Press of Colorado, 1998); Oscar L. Sims, "Biddy Mason," in *Notable Black American Women*, ed. Jessie Carney Smith (Detroit: Gale Research Inc., 1992), 732–34; Quintard Taylor, *In Search of the Racial Frontier: African Americans in the American West, 1528–1990* (New York: W.W. Norton, 1998); Kathleen Thompson, "Frontier West Women, Antebellum," in *Black Women in America*, 2nd ed., ed. Darlene Clark Hine (New York: Oxford University Press, 2005).

Wet Nursing

My massa had 15 chillun and my mama suckled every one of dem, 'cause his wife was no good to give milk.

—Jeff Calhoun, former slave
(Howell, Donna, ed., *I Was a Slave: True Stories Told by Former Slaves in the 1930s*, 27)

We lib on a big farm and my mudder suckle her thirteen chilluns and ole mistus' seven.

—Josie Brown, former slave
(Howell, Donna, ed., *I Was a Slave: True Stories Told By Former Slaves in the 1930s*, 26)

Wet nursing is the act of breastfeeding a child that is not the offspring of the nursing mother. Forced wet nursing was one of the many ways that slaveholders exploited enslaved women and infringed upon their maternal lives by requiring them to breastfeed multiple children. Since 3000 BC, wet nursing was a common practice. Depending on the social, economic, and religious climate of a particular civilization, societies viewed wet nurses along a value spectrum ranging from menial workers to a professional or highly esteemed woman. In seventeenth-century England, for example, it was customary for wealthy families to hire white nonelite wet nurses. Before the establishment of slave societies in the Americas, Europeans observed and recorded African women's lactation and breastfeeding behaviors. According to seventeenth-century travelogues, European explorers focused on women's fecundity as well as their productive and reproductive value, which included their breast milk production. In doing so, Europeans justified women's "fitness" as enslaved laborers.

In the American South, since slaveholders coerced enslaved women to breastfeed, they were continually lactating and readily available to serve as wet nurses for enslaved children as well as infants of white slaveholders. Mistresses who chose wet nurses did so because they were physically unable to breastfeed or to avoid the drudgery associated with breastfeeding. In addition to serving as wet nurses for their own slaveholders, bondwomen worked as hired nurses on other plantations. Regardless of where women labored as wet nurses, the work involved frequent feedings. Newborns needed be fed multiple times throughout the day, and slaveholders would allow women to take breaks and nurse children in order to secure the babies' survival. Sometimes, slaveholders mandated that white babies be prioritized in the order and length of feeding, which led to the malnourishment and premature weaning of slave women's biological children. Therefore, wet nursing was not only physically arduous for slave women, but also perhaps psychologically taxing, as they were forced to neglect their own babies in order to feed other infants.

Whites' perspectives on wet nursing varied by geographical region. For example, some southern whites did not believe that race "tainting" could be passed onto white children through wet nursing, while northern visitors to the South remarked with surprise and revulsion in their journals about this practice in slave societies. Historians disagree about how customary wet nursing was in the slave-holding South, especially in the nineteenth century when the scientific and ideological beliefs about the benefits of maternal breastfeeding became more popular. However, ex-slave narratives, diaries, letters, and advertisements requesting slave wet nurses for hire suggest the conventional practice of wet-nursing, even in the nineteenth century.

Ava Purkiss

See also Labor, Nonagricultural; Mammy Stereotype; Violence, Racial; Violence, Sexual.

Suggested Reading

Valerie A. Fildes, *Wet Nursing: A History from Antiquity to Present* (New York: Basil Blackwell Inc., 1988); V. Lynn Kennedy, *Born Southern: Childbirth, Motherhood, and Social Networks in the Old South* (Baltimore: Johns Hopkins University Press, 2010).

Wheatley, Phillis

Birth Date: 1754
Death Date: 1784

Phillis Wheatley was born in West Africa, but taken into the Transatlantic Slave Trade and sold to John and Susana Wheatley of Boston in 1761, at the age of seven.

Poet Phillis Wheatley, engraving by Archibald Bell, London, 1773. (Library of Congress.)

Although they purchased her as a house servant, she proved at an early age to be particularly gifted and was taught to read and write English along with the Wheatley's children. In addition to English, Wheatley learned Greek and Latin. Her education was remarkable given that in colonial America, educating the enslaved—and particularly females—occurred rarely and if done, was usually in more practical subjects other than classical languages. Wheatley first garnered attention at the age of 13 when she published a poem in the *Mercury*, a newspaper published in Newport, Rhode Island. Her fame and renown grew as her poem on the death of George Whitfield, a prominent Methodist preacher, drew the attention of Boston residents.

By 1773, Wheatley became the first enslaved person to publish a book of poems, beginning a long tradition of letters produced by men and women of African decent in the Americas. Many whites in early America were unconvinced that she was the author of these poems, largely as the result of assumptions about black racial inferiority. Others argued that her works were simply mimicry of early poems produced by whites, again claiming racist notions about African biological, cultural, and intellectual inferiority. Her *Poems on Various Subjects Religious and Moral* included testimony that she did, in fact, write the works about various men of Boston, including Governor Thomas Hutchinson and Lieutenant-Governor Andrew Oliver. Wheatley's poem, "On Being Brought from Africa to America" (1773), underscored the notion common among whites both North and South and across the Atlantic, that the Transatlantic Slave Trade served a benevolent purpose by bringing "benightened souls" into Christianity.

Although the Wheatley family owned several bondpeople, it is often claimed that Phillis enjoyed a privileged position within the household. Still, it is important to note that she remained in bondage regardless of her treatment. Her freedom only became official with the death of John Wheatley in 1778. The same year, Wheatley married John Peters, a free man of color from Boston, and gave birth to three children over five years. Despite her poetic talent, her publications, and the recognition by leading figures of the era, including George Washington and

Voltaire, Wheatley and John Peters struggled financially after the American Revolution. Both she and her husband discovered that the liberty earned from England did not also lead to either universal liberty or equality for all in America. As a result of their color, the couple struggled to survive. Her attempt to publish a second volume of poetry failed, and over time, Wheatley faded into obscurity.

Phillis's poetry offers a complicated picture for historians and scholars of literature. On the one hand, her work testifies to the abilities of people forced into slavery, but on the other, her writing gift was not truly recognized by many whites, who, instead, focused only on her race. Although her talent was celebrated for a short moment in the colonial period and was influential for later generations of black writers, at the time, however, it could not support her or her family in the newly formed United States. Phillis spent her last years working as a maid in a boardinghouse and died in poverty in 1784.

Timothy R. Buckner

See also American Revolution; Education.

Suggested Reading

Henry Louis Gates, Jr., *The Trials of Phillis Wheatley: America's First Black Poet and Encounters with the Founding Fathers* (New York: Basic Civitas Books, 2003); Phillis Wheatley and Vincent Carreta, *Phillis Wheatley, Complete Writings* (New York: Penguin Books, 2001).

Appendix: Population of Enslaved Women, 1750–1860

TABLE A.1 Slaves as a Percentage of the Total Population in Selected Years, by Southern State

	1750	1790	1810	1860
State	**Black/total population**	**Slave/total population**	**Slave/total population**	**Slave/total population**
Alabama				45.12
Arkansas				25.52
Delaware	5.21	15.04	5.75	1.60
Florida				43.97
Georgia	19.23	35.45	41.68	43.72
Kentucky		16.87	19.82	19.51
Louisiana				46.85
Maryland	30.80	32.23	29.30	12.69
Mississippi				55.18
Missouri				9.72
North Carolina	27.13	25.51	30.39	33.35
South Carolina	60.94	43.00	47.30	57.18
Tennessee			17.02	24.84
Texas				30.22
Virginia	43.91	39.14	40.27	30.75
Overall	37.97	33.95	33.25	32.27

Sources: Historical Statistics of the United States (1970), Franklin (1988).

TABLE A.2   Total Number of Enslaved Persons Living in the United States, 1790–1860

Year	Total Number of Enslaved
1790	697,897
1800	893,041
1810	1,191,364
1820	1,538,038
1830	2,009,050
1840	2,487,455
1850	3,204,313
1860	3,953,760

Source: U.S. Census returns from 1790–1860.

TABLE A.3   Antebellum Enslaved Female Population by State, 1820–1860

State	1820	1830	1840	1850	1860
Alabama	22,732	58,379	126,172	171,040	217,314
Arkansas	N/A	2,283	9,816	23,442	54,941
Connecticut	60	17	12	N/A	N/A
Delaware	1,954	1,486	1,234	1,116	938
Florida	N/A	N/A	12,679	19,506	30,397
Georgia	73, 740	108,714	141,609	192,825	233,005
Illinois	369	400	163	N/A	N/A
Indiana	92	3	2	N/A	N/A
Kentucky	62,818	82,904	91,254	105,918	112,474
Louisiana	32,498	51,677	81,923	118,935	159,749
Maryland	51,025	49, 552	43,536	44,424	42,876
Mississippi	15,964	32,560	97,208	154,626	217,330
Missouri	4,881	12,657	29,498	43,938	57,571
New Jersey	3,569	1,195	371	140	12
New York	5,000	62	4	N/A	N/A
North Carolina	98,466	121, 288	122,271	143,967	164,590
Pennsylvania	126	231	29	N/A	N/A
Rhode Island	30	14	4	N/A	N/A
South Carolina	124,668	159,932	168,360	197,228	205,835
Tennessee	40,360	71,387	91,582	120,679	139,349
Texas	N/A	N/A	N/A	29,461	91,377
Virginia	206,879	230,680	220,426	231,966	241,382
Total	671,491	814,581	1,238,153	1,599,211	1,969,140

Source: U.S. Census returns from 1820 to 1860. Some states excluded from the chart due to their extraordinarily small slave populations.

Selected Bibliography

Books and Articles

Alexander, Adele Logan. *Ambiguous Lives: Free Women of Color in Rural Georgia, 1789–1879*. Fayetteville: University of Arkansas Press, 1991.

Andrews, William. *Six Women's Slave Narratives*. New York: Oxford University Press, 1989.

Andrews, William L., Jarena Lee, Zilpha Elaw, and Julia A. J. Foote. *Sisters of the Spirit: Three Black Women's Autobiographies of the Nineteenth Century*. Bloomington: Indiana University Press, 1986.

Antezana, Darlene. "'Active, Smart, and of a Smiling Countenance': Delaware's Enslaved Women 1760–1820." PhD dissertation, Morgan State University, 2009.

Appleton, Thomas. *Searching for Their Places: Women in the South across Four Centuries*. Columbia: University of Missouri Press, 2003.

Araujo, Ana Lucia. *Living History: Encountering the Memory and the History of the Heirs of Slavery*. Newcastle, UK: Cambridge Scholars Publishing, 2009.

Archer, Jermaine O. *Antebellum Slave Narratives: Cultural and Political Expressions of Africa*. New York: Routledge, 2009.

Asante, Molefi K. *The Book of African Names*. Trenton: Africa World Press, 1991.

Baker, T. Lindsay, Julie P. Baker, and United States Work Projects Administration. *The WPA Oklahoma Slave Narratives*. Norman: University of Oklahoma Press, 1996.

Banks, Taunya Lovell. "Dangerous Woman: Elizabeth Key's Freedom Suit—Subjecthood and Racialized Identity in Seventeenth Century Colonial Virginia." *Akron Law Review* 41 (2008): 799–837.

Baptist, Edward E. "'Cuffy,' 'Fancy Maids,' and 'One-Eyed Men': Rape, Commodification, and the Domestic Slave Trade in the United States." *American Historical Review* 106, no. 5 (December 2001): 1619–50.

Baptist, Edward E., and Stephanie M. H. Camp. *New Studies in the History of American Slavery*. Athens: University of Georgia Press, 2006.

Battle, Whitney L. "A Yard to Sweep: Race, Gender, and the Enslaved Landscape." PhD dissertation, University of Texas, 2004.

Beardsley, John. *Gee's Bend: The Women and Their Quilts*. Atlanta, GA: Tinwood Books; Houston: Museum of Fine Arts, 2002.

Benjamin, Shanna Greene. "Trickster in Transition: Nineteenth-Century Representations of Aunt Nancy." In *Loopholes and Retreats: African American Writers and the Nineteenth Century*, edited by John Cullen Gruesser and Hanna Wallinger, 43–57. Piscataway: Transaction Publishers, 2009.

Berlin, Ira. *Generations of Captivity: A History of African-American Slaves*. Cambridge: Belknap Press of Harvard University Press, 2003.

Berlin, Ira. *Many Thousands Gone: The First Two Centuries of Slavery in North America* Cambridge: Harvard University Press, 1998.

Berlin, Ira, and Leslie S. Rowland, eds. *Families and Freedom: A Documentary History of African-American Kinship in the Civil War Era*. New York: The New Press, 1997.

Berlin, Ira, Marc Favreau, and Steven F. Miller. *Remembering Slavery: African Americans Talk about Their Personal Experiences of Slavery and Emancipation*. New York: New Press; Washington, DC; Library of Congress, 1998.

Bernhard, Virginia A., Betty Brandon, Elizabeth Fox-Genovese, and Theda Perdue, eds. *Southern Women: Histories and Identities*. Columbia: University of Missouri Press, 1992.

Berry, Daina Ramey. "In Pressing Need of Cash: Gender, Skill, and Family Persistence in the Domestic Slave Trade." *Journal of African American History* 91, no. 1 (Winter 2007): 22–36.

Berry, Daina Ramey. *Swing the Sickle for the Harvest Is Ripe: Gender and Slavery in Antebellum Georgia*. Champaign: University of Illinois Press, 2007.

Billings, Warren M. *The Old Dominion in the Seventeenth Century: A Documentary History of Virginia, 1606–1689*. Chapel Hill: Published for the Institute of Early American History and Culture at Williamsburg, VA, by the University of North Carolina Press, 1975.

Billington, Monroe Lee, and Roger D. Hardaway. *African Americans on the Western Frontier*. Niwot: University Press of Colorado, 1998.

Bilsky, Dana, "Tangled Skeins: Identification and Fantasmatic Genealogies of Slavery in Narratives by Jacobs, Crafts, Wilson, and Keckley." PhD dissertation, Northwestern University, 2005.

Blackburn, George, and Sherman L. Ricards. "The Mother-Headed Family among Free Negroes in Charleston, South Carolina, 1850–1860." *Phylon* 42, no. 1 (1981): 11–25.

Blassingame, John W. *The Slave Community: Plantation Life in the Antebellum South*. New York: Oxford University Press, 1979.

Bleser, Carol, ed. *In Joy and In Sorrow: Women, Family, and Marriage in the Victorian South, 1830–1900*. New York: Oxford University Press, 1991.

Blight, David W. *Passages to Freedom: The Underground Railroad in History and Memory*. Washington, DC: Smithsonian Books in association with the National Underground Railroad Freedom Center, 2004.

Bordewich, Fergus M. *Bound for Canaan: The Underground Railroad and the War for the Soul of America*. New York: Amistad, 2005.

Bradford, Sarah. *Harriet Tubman: The Moses of Her People*. Secaucus: Citadel Press, 1989.

Breslaw, Elaine G. *Tituba, Reluctant Witch of Salem: Devilish Indians and Puritan Fantasies*. New York: New York University Press, 1996.

Bridgewater, Pamela D., "Ain't I a Slave: Slavery, Reproductive Abuse, and Reparations." *UCLA Women's Law Journal* 14 (Fall–Winter 2005): 89–161.

Bridgewater, Pamela D. *Breeding a Nation: Reproductive Slavery, the Thirteenth Amendment, and the Pursuit of Freedom.* London: South End Press, 2006.

Brooten, Bernadette J., and Jacqueline L. Hazelton, eds. *Beyond Slavery: Overcoming Its Religious and Sexual Legacies.* New York: Palgrave Macmillan, 2010.

Brown, Kathleen M. *Good Wives, Nasty Wenches, & Anxious Patriarchs: Gender, Race, and Power in Colonial Virginia.* Chapel Hill: University of North Carolina Press, 1996.

Buchanan, Thomas C. "Levees of Hope: African American Steamboat Workers, Cities, and Slave Escapes on the Antebellum Mississippi." *Journal of Urban History* 30, no. 3 (2004): 360–77.

Burnham, Dorothy. "The Life of the Afro-American Woman in Slavery." *International Journal of Women's Studies* 1, no. 4 (July/August 1978): 363–77.

Butler, Octavia E. *Kindred.* Boston: Beacon Press, 1988.

Bynum, Victoria. *Unruly Women: The Politics of Social and Sexual Control in the Old South.* Chapel Hill: University of North Carolina Press, 1992.

Bynum, Victoria. "On the Lowest Rung: Court Control Over Poor White and Free Black Women." *Southern Exposure* 6 (November/December 1984): 40–44.

Byrd, W. Michael, and Linda A. Clayton. *An American Health Dilemma.* New York: Routledge, 2000.

Cameron, Diane, "Circumstances of Their Lives: Enslaved and Free Women of Color Wethersfield, Connecticut, 1648–1832." *Connecticut History* 44 (Fall 2005): 248–61.

Camp, Stephanie. *Closer to Freedom: Enslaved Women and Everyday Resistance in the Plantation South.* Chapel Hill: University of North Carolina Press, 2004.

Camp, Stephanie. "'I Could Not Stay There': Enslaved Women, Truancy and the Geography of Everyday Forms of Resistance in the Antebellum Plantation South." *Slavery and Abolition* 23, no. 3 (2002): 1–20.

Camp, Stephanie. "The Pleasures of Resistance: Enslaved Women and Body Politics in the Plantation South, 1830–1861." *Journal of Southern History* 68, no. 3 August 2002.

Campbell, Gwyn. "Children and Slavery in the New World: A Review." *Slavery and Abolition* (Ilford) 27 (August 2006): 261–85.

Campbell, Gwyn, Suzanne Miers, and Joseph C. Miller, eds. *Children in Slavery through the Ages.* Athens: Ohio University Press, 2009.

Carney, Judith. *Black Rice: The African Origins of Rice Cultivation in the Americas.* Cambridge: Harvard University Press, 2001.

Carretta, Vincent. *Unchained Voices: An Anthology of Black Authors in the English-Speaking World of the Eighteenth Century.* Lexington: University Press of Kentucky, 1996.

Castronovo, Russ. "Incidents in the Life of a White Woman: Economies of Race and Gender in the Antebellum Nation." *American Literary History* 10, no. 2 (1998): 239.

Chambers, Douglas B. *Murder at Montpelier: Igbo Africans in Virginia.* Jackson: University Press of Mississippi, 2005.

Chase-Riboud, Barbara. "Slavery as a Problem in Public History; or Sally Hemings and the 'One Drop Rule' of Public History." *Callaloo* 32, no. 2 (2009): 826–31.

Child, Lydia Marie. *An Appeal in Favor of That Class of Americans Called Africans*. 1833. Reprint, New York: Arno Press, 1968.

Chilton, Katherine. "'City of Refuge': Urban Labor, Gender, and Family Formation During Slavery and the Transition to Freedom in the District of Columbia, 1829–1875." PhD dissertation, Carnegie Mellon University, 2009.

Chireau, Yvonne Patricia. *Black Magic: Religion and the African American Conjuring Tradition*. Berkeley: University of California Press, 2003.

Christopher, Emma. *Slave Ship Sailors and Their Captive Cargoes, 1730–1807*. New York: Cambridge University Press, 2006.

Clark, Emily. *Masterless Mistresses: The New Orleans Ursulines and the Development of a New World Society, 1727–1834*. Chapel Hill: University of North Carolina Press, 2007.

Clinton, Catherine. *Half Sisters of History: Southern Women and the American Past*. Durham: Duke University Press, 1994.

Clinton, Catherine. *Harriet Tubman: The Road to Freedom*. Boston: Little, Brown, 2004.

Clinton, Catherine. *The Other Civil War: American Women in the Nineteenth Century*. New York: Hill and Wang, 1984.

Clinton, Catherine. *Plantation Mistress: Women's World in the Old South*. New York: Pantheon Books, 1982.

Clinton, Catherine. "'With a Whip in His Hand': Rape, Memory and African-American Women." In *African American History and Memory* Genvieve Fabre and Robert O'Meally, edited by, New York: Oxford University Press, 1994.

Clinton, Catherine, and Michele Gillespie, eds. *The Devil's Lane: Sex and Race in the Early South*. New York: Oxford University Press, 1997.

Clinton, Catherine, and Nina Silber. *Battle Scars: Gender and Sexuality in the American Civil War*. New York: Oxford University Press, 2006.

Close, Stacey K. *Elderly Slaves of the Plantation South*. New York and London: Garland Publishing, Inc., 1997.

Cody, Cheryll Ann. "Naming, Kinship, and Estate Dispersal: Notes on Slave Family Life on a South Carolina Plantation, 1786–1854." *William and Mary Quarterly*, 3rd ser., 39 (January 1982): 192–211.

Cody, Cheryll Ann. "Sale and Separation: Four Crises for Enslaved Women on the Ball Plantations 1764–1854." In *Working Toward Freedom: Slave Society and Domestic Economy in the American South*, edited by Larry E. Hudson Jr., 119–42. Rochester: University of Rochester, 1994.

Cody, Cheryll Ann. "There Was No 'Absalom' on the Ball Plantations: Slave-Naming Practices in the South Carolina Low Country, 1720–1865." *The American Historical Review* 92, no. 3 (1987): 563–96.

Coleman, Will. *Tribal Talk: Black Theology, Hermeneutics, and African/American Ways of "Telling the Story."* University Park: Pennsylvania State University Press, 2000.

Condé, Maryse. *I, Tituba, Black Witch of Salem*. Translated by Richard Philcox. New York: Ballantine Books, 1992.

Cosentino, Donald. *Sacred Arts of Haitian Vodou*. Los Angeles: UCLA Fowler Museum of Cultural History, 1995.

Courlander, Harold. *A Treasury of Afro-American Folklore*. New York: Marlowe & Company, 1996.

Craft, William. *Running a Thousand Miles for Freedom, or the Escape of William and Ellen Craft from Slavery (by W. Craft)*. London: W. Tweedie, 1860.

Davis, Angela. "Reflections on the Black Woman's Role in the Community of Slaves." *The Massachusetts Review* 13, no. 2 (1972): 81–100.

Donaldson, Gary A. "A Window on Slave Culture: Dances at Congo Square in New Orleans, 1800–1862." *Journal of Negro History* 69, no. 2 (March 1984): 63–72.

Donoghue, Eddie. *Black Breeding Machines: The Breeding of Negro Slaves in the Diaspora*. Bloomington: Authorhouse, 2008.

Dorsey, Jennifer Hull. *Hirelings: African American Workers and Free Labor in Early Maryland*. Ithaca: Cornell University Press, 2011.

Downs, Jim. "The Other Side of Freedom: Destitution, Disease, and Dependency among Freedwomen and Their Children during and after the Civil War." In *Battle Scars: Gender and Sexuality in the American Civil War* Catherine Clinton and Nina Silber, edited by. New York: Oxford University Press, 2006.

DuBois, Ellen Carol, and Lynn Dumenil. *Through Women's Eyes: An American History*. New York: Bedford/St. Martin's, 2005.

Dusinberre, William. *Them Dark Days: Slavery in the American Rice Swamps*. Athens: University of Georgia Press, 2000.

Edwards Ingram, Yvonne. "Medicating Slavery: Motherhood, Health Care, and Cultural Practices in the African Diaspora." Dissertation Abstracts International. A 67/01 (2006): 229.

Ellison, Mary. "Resistance to Oppression: Black Women's Response to Slavery in the United States." *Slavery and Abolition* 4 (May 1983): 56–63.

Eltis, David. *The Rise of African Slavery in the Americas*. Cambridge: Cambridge University Press, 2000.

Engerman, Stanley L., Eugene D. Genovese, Alan H. Adamson, and Mathematical Social Science Board. History Advisory Committee. "Race and Slavery in the Western Hemisphere: Quantitative Studies." Princeton: Princeton University Press, 1975.

Escott, Paul D. *Slavery Remembered: A Record of Twentieth-Century Slave Narratives*. Chapel Hill: University of North Carolina Press, 1979.

Eslinger, Ellen, "Freedom without Independence: The Story of a Former Slave and Her Family." *Virginia Magazine of History and Biography* 114, no. 2, (2006): 262–91.

Fede, Andrew. "Legitimized Violent Slave Abuse in the American South, 1619–1865: A Case Study of Law and Social Change in Six Southern States." *The American Journal of Legal History* 29, no. 2 (1985): 93–150.

Fellman, Michael, Lesley J. Gordon, and Daniel E. Sutherland. *This Terrible War: The Civil War and Its Aftermath*, 2nd ed. New York: Pearson Longman, 2008.

Ferguson, Sally Ann H. "Christian Violence and the Slave Narrative." *American Literature* 68, no. 2 (1996): 297–320.

Fett, Sharla M. *Working Cures: Healing, Health, and Power on Southern Slave Plantations*. Chapel Hill: University of North Carolina Press, 2002.

Fildes, Valerie A. *Wet Nursing: A History from Antiquity to the Present*. New York: Basil Blackwell, 1988.

Fischer, Kirsten. *Suspect Relations: Sex, Race, and Resistance in Colonial North Carolina*. Ithaca: Cornell University Press, 2002.

Fleischner, Jennifer. *Mastering Slavery: Memory, Family, and Identity in Women's Slave Narratives*. New York: New York University Press, 1998.

Fogel, Robert William. *Without Consent or Contract: The Rise and Fall of American Slavery*. New York: Norton, 1989.

Follett, Richard J. *The Sugar Masters: Planters and Slaves in Louisiana's Cane World, 1820–1860*. Baton Rouge: Louisiana State University Press, 2005.

Foster, Helen Bradley. *New Raiments of Self: African American Clothing in the Antebellum South*. New York: Berg, 1997.

Fox-Genovese, Elizabeth. "Strategies and Forms of Resistance: Focus on Slave Women in The United States." In *In Resistance: Studies in African, Caribbean, and Afro-American History*, edited by Gary Okihiro, 143–65. Amherst: The University of Massachusetts Press, 1986.

Fox-Genovese, Elizabeth. *Within the Plantation Household: Black and White Women of the Old South*. Chapel Hill: The University of North Carolina Press, 1988.

Frankel, Noralee. *Freedom's Women: Black Women and Families in Civil War Era Mississippi*. Bloomington: Indiana University Press, 1999.

Franklin, John Hope, and Alfred A. Moss. *From Slavery to Freedom: A History of African Americans*. New York: A.A. Knopf, 2000.

Franklin, John Hope, and Loren Schweninger. *Runaway Slaves: Rebels on the Plantation*. New York: Oxford University Press, 1999.

Franklin, Maria. "A Black Feminist-Inspired Archaeology?" *Journal of Social Archaeology* 1, no. 1 (2001): 108–25.

Fraser, Gertrude Jacinta. *African American Midwifery in the South: Dialogues of Birth, Race, and Memory*. Cambridge: Harvard University Press, 1998.

Fraser, Rebecca. *Courtship and Love among the Enslaved in North Carolina*. Oxford: University Press of Mississippi, 2007.

Fraser, Rebecca. "Courtship Contests and the Meaning of Conflict in the Folklore of Slaves." *Journal of Southern History* 71, no. 4 (2005): 769–802.

Fraser, Rebecca. Goin' Back Over There to See That Girl: Competing Spaces in the Social World of the Enslaved in Antebellum North Carolina." *Slavery and Abolition* 25, no. 1 (2004): 94–113.

Gaines, Ernest J. *A Lesson before Dying*. New York: A.A. Knopf, 1993.

Galle, Jillian Elizabeth. "Strategic Consumption: Archaeological Evidence for Costly Signaling among Enslaved Men and Women in the Eighteenth-Century Chesapeake." PhD dissertation, University of Virginia, 2006.

Galle, Jillian, and Amy L. Young, eds. *Engendering African American Archaeology: A Southern Perspective*. Knoxville: University of Tennessee Press, 2004.

Garraway, Doris. *The Libertine Colony: Creolization in the Early French Caribbean*. Durham: Duke University Press, 2005.

Gaspar, David Barry, and Darlene Clark Hine, eds. *Beyond Bondage: Free Women of Color in the Americas*. Urbana: University of Illinois Press, 2004.

Gaspar, David Barry, and Darlene Clark Hine, eds. *More Than Chattel: Black Women and Slavery in the Americas*. Bloomington and Indianapolis: Indiana University Press, 1996.

Gates, Henry. *Reading Black, Reading Feminist: A Critical Anthology*. New York: Meridian Book, 1990.

Gates, Henry. *The Trials of Phillis Wheatley: America's First Black Poet and Her Encounters with the Founding Fathers*. New York: Basic Civitas Books, 2003.

Gates, Henry Louis, Jr., and Hollis Robbins, eds. *In Search of Hannah Crafts: Critical Essays on the Bondwoman's Narrative*. New York: Basic Civitas Books, 2004.

Genovese, Eugene D. *Roll, Jordan, Roll: The World the Slaves Made*. New York: Pantheon Books, 1974.

Glymph, Thavolia. *Out of the House of Bondage: The Transformation of the Plantation Household*. Cambridge: Cambridge University Press, 2008.

Goldin, Claudia Dale. *Urban Slavery in the American South, 1820–1860: A Quantitative History*. Chicago: University of Chicago Press, 1976.

Gomez, Michael Angelo. *Exchanging our Country Marks: The Transformation of African Identities in the Colonial and Antebellum South*. Chapel Hill: University of North Carolina Press, 1998.

Gordon, Ann D., Bettye Collier-Thomas et al., eds. *African American Women and the Vote, 1837–1965*. Amherst: University of Massachusetts Press, 1997.

Gordon-Reed, Annette. *The Hemingses of Monticello: An American Family*. 1st ed. New York: W.W. Norton & Co., 2008.

Gordon-Reed, Annette. *Thomas Jefferson and Sally Hemings: An American Controversy*. Charlottesville: University Press of Virginia, 1997.

Gould, Virginia Meacham. "In Full Enjoyment of Their Liberty: The Free Women of Color of the Gulf Ports of New Orleans, Mobile, and Pensacola, 1769–1860." PhD dissertation, Emory University, 1991.

Griffin, Rebecca. "Courtship Contests and the Meaning of Conflict in the Folklore of Slaves." *Journal of Southern History* 71 (November 2005): 769–802.

Hagedorn, Ann. *Beyond the River: The Untold Story of the Heroes of the Underground Railroad*. New York: Simon & Schuster, 2002.

Hall, Gwendolyn Midlo. *Africans in Colonial Louisiana: The Development of Afro-Creole Culture in the Eighteenth Century*. Baton Rouge: Louisiana State University Press, 1992.

Harley, Sharon. *The Timetables of African-American History: A Chronology of the Most Important People and Events in African-American History*. New York: Simon & Schuster, 1996.

Harris, Leslie J. "Motherhood, Race, and Gender: The Rhetoric of Women's Antislavery Activism in the Liberty Bell Giftbooks." *Women's Studies in Communication* 32, no. 3 (2009): 293–319.

Hartman, Saidiya V. *Scenes of Subjection: Terror, Slavery, and Self-making in Nineteenth-Century America*. New York: Oxford University Press, 1997.

Hilliard, Kathleen Mary. "Spending in Black and White: Race, Slavery, and Consumer Values in the Antebellum South." PhD dissertation, University of South Carolina, 2006.

Hine, Darlene Clark. "Female Slave Resistance: The Economics of Sex." In *Hine Sight: Black Women and the Re-Construction of American History* by Darlene Clark Hine. New York: Carlson Publishers, 1994, 27–36.

Hine, Darlene Clark. *Hine Sight: Black Women and the Re-Construction of American History.* New York: Carlson Publishers, 1994.

Hine, Darlene Clark. "Rape and the Inner Lives of Black Women in the Middle West." *Signs* 14, no. 4 (1989): 912–20.

Hine, Darlene Clark, and Kathleen Thompson. *A Shining Thread of Hope: The History of Black Women in America.* New York: Broadway Books, 1998.

Hine, Darlene Clark, Wilma King, and Linda Reed. *"We Specialize in the Wholly Impossible": A Reader in Black Women's History.* New York: Carlson Publishing, Inc., 1995.

Hodes, Martha Elizabeth. *White Women, Black Men: Illicit Sex in the Nineteenth-Century South.* New Haven: Yale University Press, 1997.

Hodgson, Lucia. "Nature, Nurture, Nation: Race and Childhood in Transatlantic American Discourses of Slavery." PhD dissertation, University of Southern California, 2009.

Isenberg, Nancy. *Sex and Citizenship in Antebellum America.* Chapel Hill: University of North Carolina Press, 1998.

Jacobs, Harriet A. *Incidents in the Life of a Slave Girl, Written by Herself,* edited by Jean Fagan Yellin. 1861; Cambridge, 1987.

Jefferson, Thomas. *Notes on the State of Virginia.* Edited with an introduction and notes by William Peden. Chapel Hill: University of North Carolina Press for the Institute of Early American History and Culture, 1955.

Jeffrey, Julie Roy. *The Great Silent Army of Abolitionism: Ordinary Women in the Antislavery Movement.* Chapel Hill: University of North Carolina Press, 1998.

Jennings, Judith. "Religion, Liberty, Violence, and Resistance in the Writings of Two Early Female Abolitionists." In *(Re)Figuring Human Enslavement: Images of Power, Violence and Resistance,* edited by Adrian Knapp Ulrich Pallua, Andreas Exenberger, 109–30. Innsbruck: University Press, 2009.

Jennings, Thelma. "'Us Colored Women Had to Go through a Plenty': Sexual Exploitation of African American Slave Women." *Journal of Women's History* 1 (Winter 1990): 45–74.

Johnson, Karen A., "Undaunted Courage and Faith: The Lives of Three Black Women in the West and Hawaii in the Early 19th Century." *Journal of African American History* 91 (Winter 2006): 4–22.

Johnson, Michael P., and James L. Roark. *Black Masters: A Free Family of Color in the Old South.* New York: Norton, 1984.

Johnson, Sherita, "'Truth Is stranger than Fiction': Black Women in American Literature of the South." PhD dissertation, University of Illinois, Urbana-Champaign, 2005.

Johnson, Walter. *The Chattel Principle: Internal Slave Trades in the Americas.* New Haven: Yale University Press, 2004.

Johnson, Walter. "The Slave Trader, the White Slave and the Politics of Racial Determination in the 1850s." *Journal of American History* 87 (June 2000): 13–38.

Johnson, Whittington B. "Free African-American Women in Savannah, 1800–1860: Affluence and Autonomy Amid Adversity." *The Georgia Historical Quarterly* 76, no. 2, (Summer 1992): 260–83.

Jones, Bernie D. *Fathers of Conscience: Mixed-Race Inheritance in the Antebellum South*. Athens: University of Georgia Press, 2009.

Jones, Jacqueline. *Labor of Love, Labor of Sorrow: Black Women, Work, and the Family, From Slavery to the Present*. 1985. Reprint, New York: Basic Books, 2009.

Jones, Jacqueline. "'My Mother Was Much of a Woman': Black Women, Work, and the Family under Slavery." *Feminist Studies* 8, no. 2 (1982): 235–69.

Jordan, Winthrop D., and Sheila L. Skemp, eds. *Race and Family in the Colonial South*. Jackson: University of Mississippi Press, 1987.

Jua, Roselyne M. "Circles of Freedom and Maturation in Hannah Crafts' the Bond-woman's Narrative." *Journal of Black Studies* 40, no. 2 (2009): 310–26.

Kaplan, Sidney. *The Black Presence in the Era of the American Revolution, 1770–1800*. Greenwich: New York Graphic Society, 1973.

Kapsalis, Terri. *Public Privates: Performing Gynecology from Both Ends of the Speculum*. Durham: Duke University Press, 1997.

Kaye, Anthony E. *Joining Places: Slave Neighborhoods in the Old South*. Chapel Hill: University of North Carolina Press, 2007.

Kemble, Fanny, and John Anthony Scott. *Journal of a Residence on a Georgian Plantation in 1838–1839*. New York: Knopf, 1961.

Kent, Holly M. *How Did Women's Antislavery Fiction Contribute to Debates about Gender, Slavery and Abolition, 1828–1856?* Alexandria: Alexandria Street Press, 2009.

Kimball, Gregg D. *American City, Southern Place: A Cultural History of Antebellum Richmond*. Athens: University of Georgia Press, 2000.

King, Wilma. *The Essence of Liberty: Free Black Women During the Slave Era*. Columbia: University of Missouri Press, 2006.

King, Wilma. "Out of Bounds: Emancipated and Enslaved Women in Antebellum America." In *Beyond Bondage: Free Women of Color in the Americas*, edited by David Barry Gaspar and Darlene Clark Hine. Urbana: University of Illinois Press, 2004, 127–44.

King, Wilma. *Stolen Childhood*. Bloomington: Indiana University Press, 1996.

Koger, Larry. *Black Slaveowners: Free Black Slave Masters in South Carolina, 1790–1860*. Jefferson: McFarland, 1985.

Larison, Cornelius Wilson, and Silvia Dubois. *Silvia Dubois, (now 116 years old): A Biografy of the Slav Who Whipt Her Mistres and Gand Her Fredom*. Ringos: C.W. Larison, Publisher, 1883.

Larson, Jennifer. "Renovating Domesticity in Ruth Hall, Incidents in the Life of a Slave Girl, and Our Nig." *Women's Studies* 38, no. 5 (2009): 538–58.

Lasser, Carol. "Slavery, Gender and the Meanings of Freedom." *Gender & History* 13, no. 1 (2001): 161–66.

Lebsock, Suzanne. *The Free Women of Petersburg: Status and Culture in a Southern Town, 1784–1860*. New York: W.W. Norton and Company, 1984.

Lerner, Gerda. *Black Women in White America*. New York: Pantheon Books, 1972.

Lerner, Gilda. "Women and Slavery." *Slavery & Abolition* 4, no. 3 (December 1983): 173–98.

Leslie, Kent Anderson. *Woman of Color, Daughter of Privilege: Amanda America Dickson*. Athens: University of Georgia Press, 1995.

Li, Stephanie. "Resistance through the Body: Power, Representation, and the Enslaved Woman." PhD dissertation, Cornell University, 2005.

Li, Stephanie. *Something Akin to Freedom: The Choice of Bondage in Narratives by African American Women*. Albany: State University of New York, 2010.

Lucas, Marion B. "Freedom Is Better Than Slavery: Black Families and Soldiers in Civil War Kentucky." In *Sister States, Enemy States: The Civil War in Kentucky and Tennessee*, edited by Larry H. Whiteaker, W. Calvin Dickinson, and Kent T. Dollar, 9–24. Lexington: University Press of Kentucky, 2009.

Malone, Ann Patton. *Sweet Chariot: Slave Family and Household Structure in Nineteenth-Century Louisiana*. Chapel Hill: University of North Carolina Press, 1992.

Manring, Maurice M. "Aunt Jemima Explained: The Old South, the Absent Mistress and the Slave in a Box." In *The Object Reader*, edited by Fiona Candlin and Raiford Guins. London; New York: Routledge, 2009.

Marshall, Kenneth E. "Powerful and Righteous: The Transatlantic Survival and Cultural Resistance of an Enslaved African Family in Eighteenth-Century New Jersey." *Journal of American Ethnic History* 23, no. 2 (Winter 2004): 23–49.

Marshall, Kenneth E. "Work, Family and Day-to-Day Survival on an Old Farm: Nance Melick, a Rural Late Eighteenth- and Early Nineteenth-Century New Jersey Slave Woman." *Slavery and Abolition: A Journal of Slave and Post-Slave Societies* 19, no. 3 (December 1998): 22–45.

Martin, Joan M. *More than Chains and Toil: A Christian Work Ethic of Enslaved Women*. Louisville: Westminster John Knox Press, 2000.

Martin, Jonathan D. *Divided Mastery: Slave Hiring in the American South*. Cambridge: Harvard University Press, 2004.

Mazloomi, Carolyn. *Spirits of the Cloth: Contemporary African-American Quilts*. New York: Clarkson Potter/Publishers, 1998.

Mbiti, John S. *African Religions & Philosophy*. New York: Praeger, 1969.

McGregor, Deborah. *From Midwives to Medicine: The Birth of American Gynecology*. New Brunswick: Rutgers University Press, 1998.

McGregor, Deborah. *Sexual Surgery and the Origins of Gynecology: J. Marion Sims, His Hospital, and His Patients*. New York: Garland Pub., 1990.

McKivigan, John R., ed. *Abolitionism and Issues of Race and Gender*. New York: Garland, 1999.

McLaurin, Melton. *Celia, a Slave: A True Story of Violence and Retribution in Antebellum America*. Athens: University of Georgia Press, 1991.

McMillen, Sally Gregory. *Southern Women: Black and White in the Old South*. Arlington Heights: Harlan Davidson, 1992.

Medford, Edna Greene, ed. *The New York African Burial Ground: History, Final Report*. Washington, DC: Howard University, 2004. http://www.africanburialground.gov/Final-Reports/ABG_HistoryReportFinal_Tables.pdf.

Mellon, James *Bullwhip Days: The Slaves Remember: An Oral History*. New York: Grove Press, 1988.

Miles, Tiya. *Ties That Bind: The Story of an Afro-Cherokee Family in Slavery and Freedom*. American Crossroads Series. Berkeley: University of California Press, 2005.

Millward, Jessica. *Charity's Folk: Enslaved Women and Gendered Visions of Freedom in Revolutionary America*. Athens: University of Georgia Press, forthcoming.

Millward, Jessica. "Finding Charity Folks: Ghosts, Slavery, and Black Women's History in Revolutionary Maryland." *Journal of African American History* 98 (Winter 2013).

Minor, DoVeanna Fulton, and Reginald H. Pitts, eds. *Speaking Lives, Authoring Texts: Three African American Women's Oral Slave Narratives*. Albany: State University of New York Press, 2010.

Mintz, Steven. *Huck's Raft: A History of American Childhood*. Cambridge: Belknap Press of Harvard University Press, 2004.

Mitchell, Angelyn. *The Freedom to Remember: Narrative, Slavery, and Gender in Contemporary Black Women's Fiction*. New Brunswick: Rutgers University Press, 2002.

Monteith, Sharon. "Sally Hemings in Visual Culture: A Radical Act of the Imagination." In *Public Art, Memorials and Atlantic Slavery*, edited by Celeste-Marie Bernier and Judie Newman. London; New York: Routledge, 2009.

Morgan, Jennifer L. *Laboring Women: Reproduction and Gender in New World Slavery*. Philadelphia: University of Pennsylvania Press, 2004.

Morgan, Jennifer L. " 'Some Could Suckle Over Their Shoulder': Male Travelers, Female Bodies, and the Gendering of Racial Ideology, 1500–1770." *William and Mary Quarterly*, 3d ser., 54 (January 1997).

Morgan, Philip D. *Slave Counterpoint: Black Culture in the Eighteenth-Century Chesapeake and Lowcountry*. Chapel Hill: Published for the Omohundro Institute of Early American History and Culture, Williamsburg, Virginia, by the University of North Carolina Press, 1998.

Morrison, Toni. *Beloved*. New York: Knopf, 1987.

Morton, Patricia. *Discovering the Women in Slavery: Emancipating Perspectives on the American Past*. Athens: The University of Georgia Press, 1996.

Morton, Patricia. "Toward Discovering Slave Women." In *Disfigured Images: The Historical Assault on Afro-American Women*. New York: Greenwood Press, 2001, 137–49.

Myers, Amrita Chakrabarti. "The Bettingall-Tunno Family and the Free Black Women of Antebellum Charleston: A Freedom Both Contigent and Constrained." In *South Carolina Women: Their Lives and Times*, edited by Marjorie Julian Spruill, Valinda W. Littlefield, and Joan Marie Johnson. Athens: University of Georgia Press, 2009.

Norton, Mary Beth. *In the Devil's Snare: The Salem Witchcraft Crisis of 1692*. New York: Alfred A. Knopf, 2002.

Nwokeji, G. Ugo, and David Eltis. "The Roots of the African Diaspora: Methodological Considerations in the Analysis of Names in the Liberated African Registers of Sierra Leone and Havana." *History in Africa* 29 (2002): 365–79.

O'Donovan, Susan Eva. "Traded Babies: Enslaved Children in America's Domestic Migration, 1820–1860." In *Children in Slavery through the Ages*, edited by Gwyn Campbell, Suzanne Miers, and Joseph C. Miller, 88–102. Athens: Ohio University Press, 2009.

Oertel, Kristen Tegtmeier. *Bleeding Borders: Race, Gender, and Violence in Pre-Civil War Kansas*. Baton Rouge: Louisiana State University Press, 2009.

Okihiro, Gary Y. *In Resistance: Studies in African, Caribbean, and Afro-American History*. Amherst: The University of Massachusetts Press, 1986.

Onukawa, M. C. "The Chi Concept in Igbo Gender Naming." *Africa-London-International African Institute* 70 (2000): 107–17.

Painter, Nell Irvin. *Creating Black Americans: African-American History and Its Meanings, 1619 to the Present*. New York: Oxford University Press, 2007.

Painter, Nell Irvin. *Sojourner Truth: A Life, a Symbol*. New York: Norton, 1996.

Painter, Nell Irvin. "Soul Murder and Slavery: Toward a Fully Loaded Cost Accounting." In *U.S. History as Women's History: New Feminist Essays*, edited by Linda Kerber, Alice Kessler-Harris, and Kathryn Kish Sklar, 125–46. Chapel Hill: University of North Carolina Press, 1995.

Pargas, Damian Alan. "Disposing of Human Property: American Slave Families and Forced Separation in Comparative Perspective." *Journal of Family History* 34, no. 3 (2009): 251–74.

Pargas, Damian Alan. *The Quarters and the Fields: Slave Families in the Non-Cotton South*. Gainesville: University Press of Florida, 2010.

Parker, John P., and Stuart Sprague. *His Promised Land: The Autobiography of John P. Parker, Former Slave and Conductor on the Underground Railroad*. New York: Norton, 1996.

Parkhurst, Jessie W. "The Role of the Black Mammy in the Plantation Household." *Journal of Negro History* 23, no. 3 (1938): 349–69.

Patton, Venetria K. *Women in Chains: The Legacy of Slavery in Black Women's Fiction*. Albany: State University of New York Press, 2000.

Penningroth, Dylan C. *The Claims of Kinfolk: African American Property and Community in the Nineteenth-Century South*. Chapel Hill: University of North Carolina Press, 2003.

Perdue, Charles L., Thomas E. Barden, Robert K. Phillips, and Virginia Writers' Project. *Weevils in the Wheat: Interviews with Virginia Ex-slaves*. Charlottesville: University Press of Virginia, 1976.

Perrin, Liese M. "Resisting Reproduction: Reconsidering Slave Contraception in the Old South." *Journal of American Studies* 35, no. 2 (2001): 255–74.

Pickard, Kate E. R. *The Kidnapped and the Ransomed Being the Personal Recollections of Peter Still and His wife "Vina" after Forty Years of Slavery*. Syracuse: William T. Hamilton, 1856.

Pope-Hennessy, James. *Sins of the Fathers: The Atlantic Slave Trade 1441–1807*. Edison, NJ: Castle Books, 2004.

Quarles, Benjamin. *The Negro in the Making of America*, 3rd ed. New York: Simon & Schuster, 1996.

Raboteau, Albert J. *Slave Religion: The "Invisible Institution" in the Antebellum South*. New York: Oxford University Press, 1978.

Reaoch, Benjamin Moorhead. "Slavery, Women and the Gender Debate." PhD dissertation, the Southern Baptist Theological Seminary, 2009.

Rediker, Marcus. *The Slave Ship: A Human History*. New York: Viking, 2007.

Reinhardt, Mark. *Who Speaks for Margaret Garner?* Minneapolis: University of Minnesota Press, 2010.

Roberts, Dorothy E. *Killing the Black Body: Race, Reproduction, and the Meaning of Liberty*. New York: Pantheon Books, 1997.

Roediger, David R. "And Die in Dixie: Funerals, Death, & Heaven in the Slave Community 1700–1865." *The Massachusetts Review* 22, no. 1 (1981): 163–83.

Ross, Loretta. "African American Women and Abortion: 1800–1970." In *Theorizing Black Feminisms*, edited by Stanlie James and Abena Busia, 141–59. New York: Routledge, 1993.

Roth, Sarah N. "The Blade Was in My Own Breast: Slave Infanticide in 1850s Fiction." *American Nineteenth Century History* 8, no. 2 (2007): 169–85.

Salerno. Dorothy, ed., *We Are Your Sisters: Black Women in the Nineteenth Century.* New York: W.W. Norton, 1984.

Samuels, Ellen. "'A Complication of Complaints': Untangling Disability, Race and the Gender in William and Ellen Craft's *Running a Thousand Miles for Freedom*." *MELUS*, 31 (Fall 2006): 15–47.

Samuels, Ellen. "Examining Millie and Christine McKoy: Where Enslavement and Enfreakment Meet." *Signs* 31 (Autumn 2011): 53–81.

Scarborough, William Kauffman. *The Overseer: Plantation Management in the Old South.* Baton Rouge: Louisiana State University Press, 1966.

Schwalm, Leslie A. "Between Slavery and Freedom: African American Women and Occupation in the Slave South." In *Occupied Women: Gender, Military Occupation, and the American Civil War*, edited by LeeAnn Whites and Alecia P. Long. Baton Rouge: Louisiana State University Press, 2009.

Schwalm, Leslie A. *Emancipation Diaspora: Race and Reconstruction in the Upper Midwest.* Chapel Hill: University of North Carolina Press, 2009.

Schwalm, Leslie A. *A Hard Fight for We: Women's Transition from Slavery to Freedom in South Carolina.* Chicago: University of Illinois Press, 1997.

Schwartz, Marie Jenkins. *Birthing a Slave: Motherhood and Medicine in the Antebellum South.* Cambridge: Harvard University Press, 2006.

Schwartz, Marie Jenkins. *Born in Bondage: Growing Up Enslaved in the Antebellum South.* Cambridge: Cambridge University Press, 2000.

Schweninger, Loren. *Black Property Owners in the South, 1790–1915.* Urbana: University of Illinois Press, 1990.

Schweninger, Loren. "'To the Honorable': Divorce, Alimony, Slavery, and the Law in Antebellum North Carolina." *North Carolina Historical Review* 86, no. 2 (2009): 127–79.

Schweninger, Loren. "Property Owning Free African-American Women in the South, 1800–1870." *Journal of Women's History* 1 (1990): 14–44.

Schweninger, Loren. "Slave Women, County Courts and the Law in the United States South: A Comparative Perspective." *European Review of History: Revue europeenne d'histoire* 16, no. 3 (2009): 383–99.

Sensbach, Jon F. *Rebecca's Revival: Creating Black Christianity in the Atlantic World.* Cambridge: Harvard University Press, 2005.

Sernett, Milton C. *African American Religious History: A Documentary Witness.* Durham: Duke University Press, 1999.

Sernett, Milton C. *Harriet Tubman: Myth, Memory, and History.* Durham: Duke University Press, 2007.

Shaw, Stephanie. "Mothering under Slavery in the Antebellum South." In *Mothering: Ideology, Experience, and Agency*, edited by, Evelyn Nakano Glenn, Grace Chang, and Linda Rennie Forcey, 237–58. New York; London: Routledge, 1994.

Siebert, Wilbur Henry, and Albert Bushnell Hart. *The Underground Railroad from Slavery to Freedom: A Comprehensive History*. Mineola: Dover Publications, 2006.

Simms, Rupe. "Controlling Images and the Gender Construction of Enslaved African Women." *Gender & Society* 15, no. 6 (2001): 879–97.

Sims, J. Marion, Harry Marion Sims, and M.D. Rare Book Collection of Rush University Medical Center at the University of Chicago Stanton A. Friedberg. *The Story of My Life*. New York: D. Appleton and Co., 1884.

Sinha, Manisha, and Penny Von Eschen, eds. *Contested Democracy: Freedom, Race and Power in American History*. New York: Columbia University Press, 2007.

Smallwood, Stephanie E. *Saltwater Slavery: A Middle Passage from Africa to American Diaspora*. Cambridge: Harvard University Press, 2007.

Smith, Jessie Carney, and Shirelle Phelps. *Notable Black American Women*. Detroit: Gale Research, 1992.

Sommerville, Diane Miller. *Rape and Race in the Nineteenth-Century South*. Chapel Hill: University of North Carolina Press, 2004.

Sorensen, Leni Ashmore. " 'So That I Get Her Again': African American Slave Women in Runaways Selected Richmond, Virginia, Newspapers, 1830–1860, and the Richmond, Virginia, Police Guard Daybook, 1834–1843." PhD dissertation, College of William and Mary, 2006.

Spear, Jennifer M. *Race, Sex, and Social Order in Early New Orleans*. Baltimore: John Hopkins University Press, 2009.

Spruill, Marjorie Julian, Valinda W. Littlefield, and Joan Marie Johnson, eds. *South Carolina Women: Their Lives and Times*. Athens: University of Georgia Press, 2009.

Steckel, Richard H. "A Dreadful Childhood: The Excess Mortality of American Slaves." *Social Science History* 10, no. 4 (1986): 427–65.

Sterling, Dorothy, ed. *We Are Your Sisters: Black Women in the Nineteenth Century*. New York: W.W. Norton & Company, 1984.

Stevenson, Brenda E. "Distress and Discord in Virginia Slave Families, 1830–1860." In *In Joy and in Sorrow: Women, Family, and Marriage in the Victorian South*, edited by Carol Bleser, 103–24. New York: Oxford University Press, 1992.

Stevenson, Brenda E. *Life in Black & White: Family and Community in the Slave South*. New York: Oxford University Press, 1996.

Stevenson, Brenda E. " 'Marsa Never Sot Aunt Rebecca Down': Enslaved Women, Religion, and Social Power in the Antebellum South." *The Journal of African American History* 90, no. 4 (Fall 2005): 345–67.

Stone, Andrea. "Interracial Sexual Abuse and Legal Subjectivity in Antebellum Law and Literature." *American Literature* 81, no. 1 (2009): 65–92.

Stuckey, Sterling. *Slave Culture: Nationalist Theory and the Foundations of Black America*. New York: Oxford University Press, 1987.

Sutch, Richard. *The Breeding of Slaves for Sale and the Westward Expansion of Slavery, 1850–1860*. Berkeley: Institute of Business and Economic Research, University of California, 1972.

Tate, Gayle T. *Unknown Tongues: Black Women's Political Activism in the Antebellum Era, 1830–1860*. East Lansing: Michigan State University Press, 2003.

Taylor, Eric Robert. *If We Must Die: Shipboard Insurrections in the Era of the Atlantic Slave Trade*. Baton Rouge: Louisiana State University Press, 2006.

Taylor, Kay Ann. "Mary S. Peake and Charlotte F. Forten: Black Teachers during the Civil War and Reconstruction." *Journal of Negro Education* 74 (Spring 2005), 124–37.

Taylor, Quintard. *In Search of the Racial Frontier: African Americans in the American West, 1528–1990*. New York: Norton, 1998.

Taylor, Susie King. *Reminiscences of My Life in Camp with the 33d United States Colored Troops Late 1st S.C. Volunteers*. Boston: S.K. Taylor, 1902.

Thompson, Robert Farris. *Flash of the Spirit: African and Afro-American Art and Philosophy*. New York: Random House, 1983.

Tobin, Jacqueline, and Raymond G. Dobard. *Hidden in Plain View: The Secret Story of Quilts and the Underground Railroad*. New York, NY: Doubleday, 1999.

Truth, Sojourner. *Narrative of Sojourner Truth*, edited by Margaret Washington. Reprint, New York: Vintage Books, 1993.

Tucker, Veta Smith. "Purloined Identity: The Racial Metamorphosis of Tituba of Salem Village." *Journal of Black Studies* 30, no. 4 (2000): 624–34.

VanderVelde, Lea. *Mrs. Dred Scott: A Life on Slavery's Frontier*. New York: Oxford University Press, 2009.

Wade, Richard C. *Slavery in the Cities: The South, 1820–1860*. New York: Oxford University Press, 1964.

Washington, Margaret. *Sojourner Truth's America*. Urbana and Chicago: University of Illinois Press, 2009.

Webber, Thomas L. *Deep Like the Rivers: Education in the Slave Quarter Community, 1831–1865*. New York: Norton, 1978.

Weiner, Marli F. *Mistresses and Slaves: Plantation Women in South Carolina, 1830–80*. Urbana: University of Chicago Press, 1998.

West, Emily. *Chains of Love: Slave Couples in Antebellum South Carolina*. Urbana: University of Illinois Press, 2004.

West, Emily. "The Debate on the Strength of Slave Families: South Carolina and the Importance of Cross-Plantation Marriages." *Journal of American Studies* 33 (August 1999), 221–41.

West, Emily. "Surviving Separation: Cross-Plantation Marriages and the Slave Trade in Antebellum South Carolina." *Journal of Family History* 24 (April 1999), 212–31.

Wheatley, Phillis, and Vincent Carretta. *Complete Writings*. New York: Penguin Books, 2001.

White, Deborah Gray. *Ar'n't I a Woman?: Female Slaves in the Plantation South*. New York: W.W. Norton & Company, 1985.

Wilkie, Laurie A. *The Archaeology of Mothering: An African-American Midwife's Tale*. New York: Routledge, 2003.

Wilkie, Laurie A. *Creating Freedom: Material Culture and African American Identity at Oakley Plantation, Louisiana, 1840–1950*. Baton Rouge: Louisiana State University Press, 2000.

Willard, Carla. "Wheatley's Turns of Praise: Heroic Entrapment and the Paradox of Revolution." *American Literature: A Journal of Literary History, Criticism and Bibliography* 67, no. 2 (1995): 233.

Williams, Delores S. *Sisters in the Wilderness: The Challenge of Womanist God-talk.* Maryknoll, NY: Orbis Books, 1993.

Williams, Heather Andrea. *Self-taught: African American Education in Slavery and Freedom.* Chapel Hill: University of North Carolina Press, 2005.

Williams-Myers, Albert James. *A Portrait of Eve: Towards a Social History of Black Women in the Hudson River Valley.* New Paltz: Center for the Study of the African Presence in the Hudson River Valley, 1987.

Williams-Myers, Albert James. *On the Morning Tide: African Americans, History, and Methodology in the Historical Ebb and Flow of Hudson River Society.* Trenton: Africa World Press, 2003.

Wood, Betty. *Gender, Race, and Rank in a Revolutionary Age: The Georgia Lowcountry, 1750–1820.* Athens: University of Georgia Press, 2000.

Wood, Betty. "Some Aspects of Female Resistance to Chattel Slavery in Low Country Georgia, 1763–1815." *Historical Journal* 30, no. 3 (1987).

Wood, Betty. *Women's Work, Men's Work: The Informal Slave Economies of Lowcountry Georgia.* Athens: University of Georgia Press, 1995.

Yee, Shirley J. *Black Women Abolitionists: A Study in Activism, 1828–1860.* Knoxville: University of Tennessee Press, 1992.

Yellin, Jean Fagan, *Women and Sisters: The Antislavery Feminists in American Culture.* New Haven: Yale University Press, 1989.

Yellin, Jean Fagan, and John C. Van Horne, eds. *The Abolitionist Sisterhood: Women's Political Culture in Antebellum America.* Ithaca: Cornell University Press, 1994.

Young, Melvina Johnson. "Exploring the WPA Narratives: Finding the Voices of Black Women and Men." In *Theorizing Black Feminisms*, edited by Stanlie James and Abena Busia, 55–74. New York: Routledge, 1993.

Websites

African Burial Ground National Monument. U.S. National Park Service. www.nps.gov/afbg/index.htm. http://www.africanburialground.gov/ABG_Main.htm

Afro-Louisiana History and Genealogy. The Center for the Public Domain and University of North Carolina at Chapel Hill. Ed. by Gwendolyn Hall. http://www.ibiblio.org/laslave/

The Banneker-Douglass Museum. [In the former Mount Moriah A.M.E. Church, on property once owned by Charity Folks, an enslaved woman who was manumitted]. 84 Franklin Street, Annapolis, MD 2140. http://www.bdmuseum.com/index.html

The Bibliography of Slavery and World Slaving. 2011. Joseph C. Miller and the University of Virginia. At www2.vcdh.virginia.edu/bib/index.php

"Born in Slavery: Slave Narratives from the Federal Writers' Project, 1936–1938." American Memory. Library of Congress. http://memory.loc.gov/ammem/snhtml/snhome.html

"Celia, a Slave, a Trial (1855)" http://law2.umkc.edu/faculty/projects/ftrials/celia/celiahome.html

Colonial Williamsburg. [Substantial website of living history museum offers many online resources, including resources on enslaved people.] Williamsburg, VA 23187-1776. http://www.history.org/

Creole History: Free People of Color of New Orleans. http://www.creolehistory.com/

Digital History: Digital Slavery. 2011. University of Houston. http://www.digitalhistory .uh.edu/do_history/slavery/index.cfm

First-Person Narratives of the American South. Documenting the American South Collection, University Library of the University of North Carolina at Chapel Hill. At http://docsouth.unc.edu/fpn/

"The Geography of Slavery: Virginia Runaways," http://www2.vcdh.virginia.edu/gos/

Handler, Jerome S., and Michael L. Tuite Jr. "The Atlantic Slave Trade and Slave Life in the Americas: A Visual Record," Virginia Foundation for the Humanities and University of Virginia. http://hitchcock.itc.virginia.edu/Slavery/index.php

Historic American Buildings Survey/Historic American Engineering Record/Historic American Landscapes Survey, 1933–Present. [Includes slave quarters and plantations.] American Memory, Library of Congress. http://memory.loc.gov/ammem/collections/habs_haer/

"The Making of African American Identity: Vol. I, 1500–1865," 2009. Primary Resources in U.S. History and Literature. Toolbox Library, National Humanities Center. http://nationalhumanitiescenter.org/pds/maai/index.htm

"Manuscript Collections Relating to Slavery." 2010. New York Historical Society. https://www.nyhistory.org/slaverycollections/

Margaret Garner (opera) [website]. 2008. Danielpour, Richard (music) and Morrison, Toni (libretto). http://www.margaretgarner.org/

National Underground Railroad: Network to Freedom. U.S. National Park Service. http://www.nps.gov/subjects/ugrr/index.htm

National Underground Railroad Freedom Center. 50 East Freedom Way, Cincinnati, Ohio 45202. http://www.freedomcenter.org/

"North American Slave Narratives," Documenting the American South. University Library of the University of North Carolina at Chapel Hill. 2004. http://docsouth.unc .edu/neh/

"Race and Slavery Petitions Project" Digital Library on American Slavery, University of North Carolina Greensboro, http://library.uncg.edu/slavery/.

"Slavery: The Peculiar Institution." (Exhibits from the African American Odyssey.) American Memory. Library of Congress. http://international.loc.gov/ammem/aaohtml/exhibit/aopart1.html

Slavery in America. Thirteen/WNET New York. www.slaveryinamerica.org. For the original Web site for the 2004 show, see also http://www.pbs.org/wnet/slavery/

"Unknown No Longer: A Database of Virginia Slave Names," http://unknownnolonger .vahistorical.org/

About the Editors and Contributors

Editors

DAINA RAMEY BERRY is an associate professor of history at the University of Texas at Austin. She received her BA, MA, and PhD from UCLA. Dr. Berry taught at Michigan State University and Arizona State University prior to joining the faculty at UT Austin in January 2010. She is the author of *Swing the Sickle for the Harvest Is Ripe: Gender and Slavery in Antebellum Georgia* (University of Illinois Press, 2007) and has published articles in the *Journal of African American History*, the *Journal of Women's History*, and the *Georgia Historical Quarterly*. She is currently an Organization of American Historians Distinguished Lecturer and the recipient of fellowships from the American Council of Learned Societies, the American Association of University Women, and the Ford Foundation.

DELESO A. ALFORD teaches in the areas of race and the law, bioethics and the law, and critical race theory and torts. She is an associate professor of law at Florida A & M University College of Law, Orlando, Florida, with a research focus on critical race feminist theory and bioethics. A former Fulbright Scholar, she earned a BS, *magna cum laude*, at Southern University A & M College, a JD at Southern University Law Center, Baton Rouge, Louisiana, and an LLM at Georgetown University Law Center, Washington, D.C. She has published articles, including in the *Albany Law Review*, *Hamline Journal of Public Law and Policy*, *Georgetown Journal of Gender and the Law*, *American University Journal of Gender, Social Policy and the Law*, and the *Nova Law Review*.

Editorial Advisors

SHARLA FETT is an associate professor and Chair of the History Department at Occidental College.

WILMA KING is the Arvarh E. Strickland Distinguished Professor of History and Chair of the Black Studies Program at the University of Missouri Columbia campus.

JESSICA MILLWARD is an assistant professor of history at the University of California Irvine.

Editorial Assistants

JENIFER L. BARCLAY is a postdoctoral fellow of African American history at Case Western Reserve University.

TERRY P. BROCK is a doctoral candidate in anthropology at Michigan State University.

NEDRA K. LEE is a doctoral candidate in anthropology at the University of Texas at Austin.

KATRICE PETERSON is a Juris Doctorate (J.D.) candidate at Florida A&M University College of Law.

NICOLE RIBIANSZKY is an assistant professor of history at Georgia Gwinnett College.

JERMAINE THIBODEAUX is a doctoral student in history at the University of Texas at Austin.

Contributors

RACHEL J. ANDERSON is an associate professor of law at the University of Las Vegas, William S. Boyd School of Law.

TAUNYA LOVELL BANKS is the Jacob A. France Professor of Equality Jurisprudence at the University of Maryland School of Law.

JENIFER L. BARCLAY is a postdoctoral fellow of African American history at Case Western Reserve University.

CHYNA BOWEN is a doctoral student in history at the University of Texas at Austin.

PAMELA BRIDGEWATER is a professor of law at American University, Washington College of Law.

BRANDI C. BRIMMER is the Ford Foundation fellow at the Freedmen and Southern Society Project at the University of Maryland, College Park.

TERRY P. BROCK is a doctoral candidate in anthropology at Michigan State University.

MIRIAM FORMAN-BRUNELL is professor of history at the University of Missouri-Kansas City.

TIMOTHY R. BUCKNER is an assistant professor of history at Troy State University.

NIKKI BERG BURIN is an instructor of history at the University of North Dakota.

DIANE MUTTI-BURKE is an associate professor of history at the University of Missouri-Kansas City.

BEATRICE BURTON is a doctoral candidate in history at the University of Georgia.

ORVILLE VERNON BURTON is a professor of history at Clemson University and Director of the Clemson University CyberInstitute.

ASHLEY CALLAHAN is curator, Henry D. Green Center for the Study of the Decorative Arts, Georgia Museum of Art.

CATHERINE CLINTON holds a chair in American History at Queen's University in Belfast, Northern Ireland.

DALE COUCH is a retired senior archivist at the Georgia State Archives.

NICHOLAS PATRICK COX is a doctoral student in history at the University of Houston.

ANGELA RUTH DANLEY is an independent scholar.

NATHALIE DESSENS is professor of American history and civilization at the University of Toulouse, France.

ALEXANDRA CORNELIUS-DIALLO is an assistant professor of history and African Diaspora studies at Florida International University.

STANLEY ENGERMAN is the John H. Munro Professor of Economics and professor of history at the University of Rochester.

CLAUDINE L. FERRELL is an associate professor of history and American studies at Mary Washington College.

MARISA J. FUENTES is an assistant professor in the Departments of Women and Gender Studies and History at Rutgers, The State University of New Jersey.

CAROL J. GIBSON is an instructor of history at the University of Phoenix.

TIFFANY M. GILL is an associate professor in the department of history at the University of Texas at Austin.

LINDSEY GISH is a doctoral candidate in history at Michigan State University.

JOHN GRANT is an assistant professor of Africana studies at the University of Arizona, Tucson.

HILARY N. GREEN is an assistant professor of history and political science at Elizabeth City State University in North Carolina.

LASHAWN D. HARRIS is a visiting assistant professor of history at Michigan State University.

RASHIDA L. HARRISON is a visiting instructor at James Madison College at Michigan State University.

RENEE K. HARRISON is an assistant professor of African American religious practices and culture in the School of Divinity at Howard University.

DEREK S. HICKS is an assistant professor and Luce Diversity Fellow in Theological Education at the Wake Forrest University Divinity School.

SAKINA MARIAM HUGHES is a doctoral candidate in history at Michigan State University.

KAREN JEAN HUNT is librarian for African Studies and African American Studies at the Duke University libraries.

PATRICIA HUNT-HURST is an associate professor of textiles, merchandising, and interiors in the College of Family and Consumer Sciences at the University of Georgia.

WILLIAM HUTCHINSON is professor emeritus of economics at Vanderbilt University.

YVONNE EDWARDS INGRAM is a staff archeologist and coordinator for African American Archaeology, Department of Archaeological Research, Colonial Williamsburg Foundation.

BAYYINAH S. JEFFRIES is an assistant professor of the Department of Pan-African Studies at California State University, Los Angeles.

KATHERINE M. JOHNSON is the public programs assistant at the National Underground Railroad Freedom Center in Cincinnati, Ohio.

ANTHONY E. KAYE is an associate professor of history at Pennsylvania State University, University Park.

JILL E. KELLY is a doctoral candidate in history at Michigan State University.

KELLY KENNINGTON is an assistant professor of history at Auburn University.

SUE KOZEL is an independent scholar who teaches at Kean University and New Jersey community colleges.

ANTHONY LEE is a visiting lecturer at the University of California, Los Angeles.

LORI LEE is a doctoral candidate in anthropology at Syracuse University.

KENT ANDERSON LESLIE is an assistant professor of women's studies at Oglethorpe University, Georgia.

MASON LOWANCE, JR., is professor of English at the University of Massachusetts, Amherst.

AMANI MARSHALL is a history instructor at the Cambridge School of Weston in Massachusetts and former postdoctoral fellow at the University of Delaware.

COURTNEY D. MARSHALL is an assistant professor of English at the University of New Hampshire.

BARBARA McCASKILL is an associate professor of English at the University of Georgia, Athens.

JESSICA MILLWARD is an assistant professor of history at the University of California Irvine.

SHARON ANN MURPHY is an associate professor of history at Providence College in Rhode Island.

SOWANDE' MUSTAKEEM is an assistant professor of history and African American studies at Washington University in St. Louis.

DEIDRE COOPER OWENS is an assistant professor of history at the University of Mississippi.

DAMIAN ALAN PARGAS is an assistant professor of history at the University of Utrecht in the Netherlands.

ROSALYN TERBORG-PENN is university professor emerita of history at Morgan State University in Baltimore.

KENNETTA HAMMOND PERRY is an assistant professor of history at East Carolina University.

AVA PURKISS is a doctoral student in history at the University of Texas at Austin.

NICOLE RIBIANSZKY is an assistant professor of history at Georgia Gwinnett College.

RICHE' RICHARDSON is an associate professor of Africana Studies at Cornell University.

LINDA L. RODRIGUEZ is a lecturer in the English Department at Xavier University of Louisiana.

FUMIKO SAKASHITA is a doctoral candidate in American studies at Michigan State University.

KIMBERLY SAMBOL-TOSCO is a doctorate candidate in history at the University of Pennsylvania.

ELLEN SAMUELS is an assistant professor of gender and women's studies and English at the University of Wisconsin at Madison.

CALVIN SCHERMERHORN is an assistant professor of history at Arizona State University.

BEN SCHILLER is a lecturer in history at the University of East Anglia, UK, and a teaching fellow at the University of York.

LOREN SCHWENINGER is the Elizabeth Rosenthal Excellence Professor of History at the University of North Carolina, Greensboro.

RICHARD H. STECKEL is a professor of economics at The Ohio State University.

COURTNEY MOORE TAYLOR is an adjunct lecturer at the University of Florida and Santa Fe College in Gainesville.

JERMAINE THIBODEAUX is a doctoral student in history at the University of Texas at Austin.

VETA SMITH TUCKER is an associate professor of English at Grand Valley State University in Michigan.

LEA VANDERVELDE is the Josephine R. Witte Chair at the University of Iowa College of Law.

CAROLYN WEST is an associate professor of psychology at the University of Washington, Tacoma.

STEPHANIE WRIGHT is an independent scholar residing in Seattle, Washington.

JOHN J. ZABORNEY is an associate professor of history at the University of Maine at Presque Isle.

ANGELA M. ZOMBEK is a doctoral student in history at the University of Florida.

Index

Page numbers in **bold** indicate main entries in the encyclopedia.